In memory of
Rose and David Estreicher

and

With gratitude to
Lois and Richard Lester

*

EMPLOYMENT LAW STORIES

FOUNDATION PRESS

EMPLOYMENT LAW STORIES

*

Introduction: Nine Employment Law Stories

Samuel Estreicher and Gillian Lester

This volume is a work of contemporary history. Many of the books in Foundation Press's *Law Stories* series are populated by cases from the distant past, cases that have shaped the trajectory of modern law but are not themselves contemporary. Employment law as a field—the law of work outside the statutory regimes of employment discrimination and collective bargaining—is young. Only one story in this volume is more than 25 years old.

The nine stories to follow capture a critical moment in the emergence of a new path for regulation of social and economic relations in America. This legal moment reflects a late–20th Century period of ferment in the organization of production and the nature of workplace relations.

How did we choose the cases we chose? The cases canvass (albeit imperfectly) the major doctrinal areas of employment law, excluding discrimination and collective bargaining (each the subject of their own *Stories* volume). Although we had some ideas of our own, we followed the selections of our authors, each expert in the area about which they wrote.

We begin with the stories behind a pair of foundational cases in the development of common law wrongful termination jurisprudence. The California Court of Appeal's 1981 decision in *Pugh v. See's Candies*[1] was among a cluster of early state court decisions that began to raise questions about the virtually irrebuttable presumption that employment is at will, terminable at the pure discretion of the employer. Professor Joseph Grodin, who as an intermediate appeals judge wrote the opinion in *Pugh*, explains the context in which that case arose, how the case came to his court, and how it came to be assigned to his chambers. He discusses his own early interest, while teaching contract law, in the disparate way courts seemed to treat employment contracts as compared to other contracts, refusing to enforce promises of job security absent

---

[1] 171 Cal. Rptr. 917 (Ct. App. 1981).

"mutuality of obligation" or "independent consideration". He reflects upon his own thought processes in analyzing Pugh's case as one involving an implied promise of a contractual term, and in characterizing the contents of the promise to be implied.

Woolley v. Hoffman–La Roche[2] represented another important challenge, just two years before *Pugh*, to the presumption of at-will employment. The New Jersey Supreme Court embraced the principle that employee handbook statements could create a right against discharge without good cause. In Chapter 2, Professor J. H. Verkerke identifies the significant doctrinal hurdles that courts had to overcome to find a basis in contract law for enforcing handbook provisions. Moreover, Professor Verkerke's discussion of the events leading up to Woolley's termination show how complex and difficult it can be to determine whether good cause for discharge exists. His investigation of the human side of a case that most lawyers and students read only for its legal analysis reveals that Richard Woolley, was, by all accounts, an admirable man and his employer, Hoffmann–La Roche, had a reputation both in the local community and in the pharmaceutical industry for treating its employees fairly and well.

Professor Verkerke develops the idea that the *Woolley* court's opinion relies on what he calls a "legal-information-forcing" argument. Under this approach, the court places the burden of clarifying the legal relationship between two contracting parties on the more legally sophisticated party. Professor Verkerke situates the *Woolley* decision as a crucial step along a path from the traditional at-will presumption to a new, and currently stable, contractual equilibrium in which the overwhelming majority of employers contract expressly for an at-will relationship using a prominent disclaimer.

Johnston v. Del Mar[3] is a classic case from the 1980s, when the tort of wrongful discharge in violation of public policy appeared on the national scene. As Dean Schwab documents in Chapter 3, only nine states recognized the tort in 1979. By 1992, it was accepted doctrine in all but seven states. Dean Schwab tells how Nancy Johnston's employer asked her to label a semi-automatic weapon as "fishing gear" and ship it across the state. Johnston wondered whether this was illegal and called the Bureau of Alcohol, Tobacco, and Firearms to find out. She was fired for doing so, and sued for wrongful discharge in violation of public policy. From Nancy Johnston's perspective, she had done nothing wrong; she was merely acting as she believed a good citizen should in the face of what she reasonably believed was illegal activity. From the employer's perspective, Johnston's behavior was a costly act of meddling in its

---

[2] 491 A.2d 1257 (N.J. 1985).

[3] 776 S.W.2d 768 (Tex. App.—Corpus Christi, 1989).

legitimate activities (the shipment was in fact probably legal). The Texas Court of Appeals allowed the cause of action, but whether a reasonable but wrong employee who refuses to obey an employer instruction is protected by the wrongful-discharge tort remains an issue on the cutting edge of employment law.

One of the fears state courts have had in adopting worker protections like this is that it might chill the business climate in the state. These arguments played out in the *Johnston* litigation itself. But Dean Schwab suggests these concerns are overstated, describing an empirical study he conducted with others finding no evidence that states recognizing the wrongful-discharge tort suffered appreciable employment loss relative to those who did not.

Beyond stories tracing the histories of seminal wrongful discharge cases, our volume explores several important cases dealing with employee privacy, dignity, mobility, and ownership of intellectual property.

In the mid–1980s, urinalysis drug testing of workers by government and private employers expanded rapidly, provoking a spate of lawsuits challenging their legality. The high-profile cases involved constitutional challenges based on the Fourth Amendment's prohibition of unreasonable searches and seizures. For the typical private sector employee, however, constitutional arguments were unavailable, and a worker who wished to challenge mandatory workplace drug testing had to rely primarily on existing common law doctrines. Chapter 4's story of *Luck v. Southern Pacific Transportation Co.*[4] tells of one such worker and how one California court of appeal attempted to fashion a framework for analyzing employee privacy claims under the common law. Professor Pauline Kim tells us how Barbara Luck, arriving at work on an ordinary day, was confronted with the unexpected request that she produce a urine sample for testing, even though her employer admitted that it had no basis for suspecting her of drug use and had no complaints about her job performance. When she objected, she was first suspended, then terminated from her job. Her subsequent lawsuit raised the issue of whether an employer could require an employee in a non-safety-sensitive job to submit to suspicionless urinalysis testing, or whether such testing infringed the privacy rights of the employee.

Barbara Luck ultimately prevailed, but Professor Kim's analysis of the California court of appeal opinion reveals a deeply ambivalent court, struggling with the basic tension between recognition of employee rights of privacy and the traditional rule of at-will employment.

Professors Alan Hyde and Catherine Fisk tell the tales of workers who ran up against attempts by their former employers to control their use of workplace information.

---

[4] 267 Cal. Rptr. 618 (Ct. App. 1990).

The doctrine of "inevitable disclosure" of trade secrets purportedly permits an employer to enjoin a departing employee from taking a job at a competitor, on the grounds that he or she will "inevitably disclose" the former employer's proprietary information in the new job. Although the phrase "inevitable disclosure" appears in some older cases enforcing covenants-not-to-compete, the modern doctrine, granting an injunction against an employee who signed no such covenant, dates from *PepsiCo v. Redmond*, a 1995 decision of the U.S. Court of Appeals for the Seventh Circuit.[5] Interviews with lawyers and participants in the litigation led Professor Hyde to the surprising finding that this doctrine, at its inception, had little to do with confidential information.

The PepsiCo executives who wanted to sue a departing manager were initially concerned about raiding by a rival, not about any information. A theory involving trade secrets was advanced by their outside counsel, who saw no other grounds for suit and thought the case weak even as a trade secrets case. The district court judge who ruled for the company appears to have focused more on the defendant's trustworthiness than the information he might reveal to the new employer. Small misstatements in early witness statements came to loom large as evidence of their untrustworthiness. This encouraged the judge to issue an injunction for which Professor Hyde finds there was little, if any, supporting precedent.

Professor Fisk tells the story in Chapter 6 of Armand Ciavatta, the son of a working-class Italian–American family from New England whose dream was to become an inventor. Many inventors work as employees for the better part of their careers and are often required as a condition of employment to sign a contract giving the firm exclusive control over as a wide range of economically valuable information. Variously known as "invention assignment agreements," "holdover clauses" or "trailer clauses," these contracts often claim as firm property any invention the employee might make that has any relationship to the firm's business or, less frequently, to the business of the firm's subsidiaries and affiliated companies. In *Ingersoll–Rand v. Ciavatta*,[6] the New Jersey Supreme Court adopted a new and influential approach to the enforceability of such contracts. By melding the law of holdover clauses with the law of restrictive covenants and trade secrets, the court attempted to create a unified rule of reasonableness to govern a wide range of disputes between employees and firms over the control of economically valuable workplace knowledge.

While working as an engineer for Ingersoll–Rand, Mr. Ciavatta's attempts to interest the company in his ideas for inventions were

---

[5] 54 F.3d 1262 (7th Cir. 1995) (applying Illinois law).

[6] 542 A.2d 879 (N.J. 1988).

rejected. Only after he was fired from the company, and struck out on his own with an invention that would prove to threaten Ingersoll–Rand's market share in mine roof stabilizers, did the company take an interest in one of his ideas. Ingersoll–Rand sued to force Ciavatta to relinquish his patent. Mr. Ciavatta's 1988 victory before the New Jersey Supreme Court leads many who study the opinion to cast Mr. Ciavatta as a peculiarly American kind of hero—the genius inventor whose persistence in the face of professional skepticism proves doubters wrong. Professor Fisk's conversations with Mr. Ciavatta himself, however, unveil a more poignant and complex narrative. Ingersoll–Rand sales representatives waged a successful campaign to persuade their clients not to switch to Mr. Ciavatta's product. The struggle to keep his business afloat consumed much of the rest of Ciavatta's career. Ingersoll–Rand, meanwhile, eventually disbanded its research and development arm.

The stories behind common law cases, of course, give only a glimpse into the patchwork canvas of employment law. Statutes play a pivotal role in the regulation of the workplace, and some of the most compelling developments in work law took place in the backrooms of the legislative arena. Three of our stories are about statutes, and in one, no case is involved at all—only the life and times of a controversial piece of legislation.

Professor Cynthia Estlund's story of *NLRB v. Washington Aluminum*[7] tells the tale of a group of non-union machine workers who came to work one very cold January morning in Baltimore to find ice covering their welding equipment. When their foreman told the shivering huddle of workers that if they "had any guts at all, they would go home," they decided to do just that, and were subsequently fired for walking off the job. To most lawyers and law students familiar with the doctrine of employment at will, the case looks like an easy win for the employer. But the National Labor Relations Board, backed by a unanimous U.S. Supreme Court decision, ruled for the employees and commanded their reinstatement. The discharges violated the employees' rights under the National Labor Relations Act (NLRA) to engage in "concerted activities for the purpose of collective bargaining or other mutual aid or protection."

Washington Aluminum is conventionally classified as a "labor law" case; it does not appear in most employment law casebooks. Yet Professor Estlund offers it in Chapter 7 as a dramatic illustration of how "labor law" reaches beyond the unionized workplace and beyond the process of union organizing to up-end traditional and powerful assumptions about employer discretion and employment at will within the non-union workplace. The NLRA is the first and arguably the most far-

---

[7] 370 U.S. 9 (1962).

reaching of wrongful discharge laws. It protects a good deal of workplace discourse, protest, and resistance that is unrelated to unions or collective bargaining—from conversations among co-workers about their salaries to the cessation of work in protest of unsatisfactory working conditions.

The explosion of pre-dispute agreements to resolve workplace conflicts through private arbitration has fundamentally altered the way employment laws are enforced. On May 13, 1991, the Supreme Court held in *Gilmer v. Interstate/Johnson Lane Corp.*[8] that employees could enter into binding pre-dispute arbitration agreements encompassing claims they have against employers under the Age Discrimination in Employment Act of 1967 (ADEA)[9] and by extension other federal and state employment laws. This was a paradigm-shifting decision, as the ADEA and other federal statutes, viewed on their own terms, were previously thought to contemplate actions in court and implicitly prohibit pre-dispute waivers of any of the rights guaranteed in those laws. *Gilmer* did not come out of the blue. It had been prefigured by a series of decisions in the 1980s broadening the reach of the Federal Arbitration Act of 1925, including the Court's 1987 *Perry v. Thomas*[10] holding that an employee's arbitration agreement with his securities-industry employer preempted a state statute requiring that wage payment claims be heard in court and not be subject to arbitration. The Court had made clear in these rulings that it had changed its view of the competence of arbitrators to decide statutory claims.

In the story of *Gilmer v. Interstate/Johnston Lane Corp.* Professor Samuel Estreicher highlights the critical role of counsel and the effects of path dependence in shaping public law. *Perry* seems to have slipped in under the radar screen, not then eliciting *amici* briefs from plaintiff groups or the kind of widespread attention that *Gilmer* evoked.

Gilmer itself also did not provide an ideal vehicle, from the standpoint of the plaintiff advocates' community. Professor Estreicher's discussion of court documents exposes the failure of plaintiff's counsel in that case to argue below or before the Court that his client's employment agreement came within the § 1 exclusion from FAA coverage for "contracts of employment of seamen, railroad employees or any other class of workers engaged in foreign or interstate commerce." Finding that Gilmer's arbitration agreement was part of a registration process with the stock exchanges, and not part of an employment agreement as such, the Court left open resolution of the § 1 issue. Although that precise issue was decided a decade later in *Circuit City Stores, Inc. v. Adams* in a

---

[8] 500 U.S. 20 (1991).

[9] 29 U.S.C. §§ 621–633(a) (2005).

[10] 482 U.S. 483 (1987).

manner that left most employment covered by the FAA, the path had been set in *Gilmer*'s willingness to enforce arbitration by predispute agreement of statutory discrimination claims.

In the final chapter of this volume, *The Story of the Montana Wrongful Discharge from Employment Act,*[11] Professor Andrew Morriss recounts the history of the innovative wrongful discharge statute that replaced the at-will rule in Montana. Beginning with the state's nineteenth century adoption of a statutory at-will rule, Morriss traces the connections between the Wrongful Discharge from Employment Act (WDEA) and Montana's tort liability crisis in the 1980s. At that time, the Montana legislature and Montana Supreme Court were engaged in a running battle over the legislature's authority to limit tort recoveries against government entities. As part of its efforts to rein in tort awards, the legislature enacted the WDEA in place of common law tort actions for wrongful discharge. After explaining this history, Morriss then uses statistical techniques to examine the impact of replacing a tort law approach with a statute that offered smaller but more certain damage awards.

Work may be joyful or treacherous, rewarding or punishing, but it is a central aspect of our lives. For this reason, the stories that follow speak to all of us.

---

[11] Mont. Code Ann. § 39–2–901 *et seq.*

*

1

The Story of *Pugh v. See's Candies, Inc.*: "Implied in Fact" Promises in Employment Contracts

Joseph R. Grodin*

When I was appointed to District One, Division One of the California Court of Appeal in 1979, virtually all of my career had been devoted to the practice, study and teaching of labor law. And that meant labor law in the traditional sense, the legal relationship between employers and unions and between unions and their members. For a union-side labor lawyer, what has come to be called employment law barely existed, except as unions might be involved on one side or the other in discrimination cases under Title VII of the 1964 Civil Rights Act. There were federal wage and hour laws, to be sure, and state laws which regulated some aspects of the employment relationship, but this legislation seldom had significance for union-represented workers, since their collective bargaining agreements were almost always more worker-protective than the statutes.

As a consequence, I had scarcely any exposure to what little law existed pertaining to job security, or to what we would now call "wrongful termination" law. Union-represented workers were typically covered by agreements that required just cause for discipline, subject to determination by an arbitrator. I recall reading, however, the excellent book by Philip Selznick and Philippe Nonet, two sociologists of the law at U.C. Berkeley, "Law, Society, and Industrial Justice".[1] The authors traced the development of the law of the employment relationship: from a pre-industrial view that the relationship was one of status in which it was understood, on the basis of custom and policy, that employers had certain obligations toward their employees, including some guarantee of

* I would like to acknowledge the essential contributions of my colleagues on the California Court of Appeals who joined in my opinion in *Pugh v. See's Candies*: Justices John Racanelli and William Newsom.

[1] Philip Selznick & Philippe Nonet, *Law, Society & Industrial Justice* (1980).

job security, through the more modern *laissez-faire* view that the employment relationship is contractual in nature and terminable at will.

As the Selznick book observed, due to the generally superior bargaining power of the employer, "the employment contract became [by the end of the nineteenth century] a very special sort of contract—in large part a device for guaranteeing to management the unilateral power to make rules and exercise discretion". Still, it was a contract, and the at-will default position could in theory be modified by contrary agreement. The problem was that ordinary contract principles seemed not always to apply to contracts of employment.

In 1971, while still in practice, I taught a course in contract law at U.C. Hastings, and through the reading I did for that course I ran across a case called *Ferreyra v. E. & J. Gallo,*[2] decided six years earlier. Fernando Ferreyra was the foreman at a grape vineyard in Argentina when he met Ernesto Gallo, president of E & J Gallo Wineries, who was in Argentina on a visit. According to Ferreyra's evidence at trial, Gallo told him that he might have a job for him in California. Subsequently, Ferreyra wrote Gallo to remind him of the conversation, and Gallo replied by letter stating:

> I can offer you a job as foreman, at a salary of $450.00 per month. I can also provide you with very small house, but no furniture. What you would be worth to my organization would be determined quickly after you started working. I cannot make a commitment as to the length of time I would keep you, as that would depend entirely upon what we think of your production.

Ferreyra responded affirmatively, stating he would be in California as soon as he could obtain the necessary documents.

Ferreyra quit his job in Argentina, sold his family home, went to California with his wife and six children, and began working at Gallo's Livingston ranch on October 15, 1960, serving as crew boss or field foreman on one of several pruning and irrigation crews, and living in a house supplied by Gallo. He was paid $450 per month, but on January 1, 1961 his pay was reduced to $350 per month, at which time he was told he was too young and too "green" for the job. On April 10, 1961 he was terminated, but nevertheless given a letter stating that his work was found to be "satisfactory".

Ferreyra sued Gallo, contending that the exchange of letters created a contract of permanent employment such that he could be dismissed only for cause. At trial, however, after Ferreyra presented the evidence summarized above, the trial court granted Gallo's motion for nonsuit on the basis of authority which held that a promise of "permanent"

---

[2] 41 Cal. Rptr. 819 (Ct. App. 1964).

employment is to be treated as employment at will, unless the worker provides consideration "independent" of his work. Ferreyra contended that his actions in reliance upon Gallo's promise provided the requisite independent consideration, but the trial court disagreed, and the Court of Appeal affirmed on that ground.

I found the doctrine puzzling, and discussed it with my class. The exchange of correspondence was arguably ambiguous, and perhaps did not support Ferreyra's interpretation of the nature of Gallo's commitment, but that was not the basis for the trial court's ruling or the decision of the Court of Appeal. The Court of Appeal was certainly correct that under then-prevailing authority "independent" consideration seemed to be required in order to support a promise of "permanent" employment, but why? Was it because the courts did not believe that an employer would make such a promise unless the employer received something more than the employee's labor? Or because the courts did not trust juries to evaluate the evidence in such a case? Whatever the reason, the requirement was certainly contrary to generally applicable contract law principles. It constituted, in effect, a special rule applicable to the employment relationship, and one which operated to the detriment of employment security. The case stuck in my mind.

Following my appointment to the Court of Appeal, I soon found myself confronted with torrents of cases, most of which had nothing to do with either labor or employment law. The court clerk assigned cases to divisions of the court in rotation, and within each division cases were assigned by the Presiding Justice, usually in rotation and without regard to personal preference or prior expertise. Nor were my colleagues particularly deferential to the expertise I thought I had. In the first labor law case to come my way, I wrote an opinion which neither of my colleagues agreed with, and I ended up in dissent.[3] But one day, after I had been on the court about eighteen months, my colleague Justice William Newsom came to my chambers and asked my opinion about a case he had been assigned. I took one look at the briefs, and offered to take the case off his hands. He agreed, and so did the Presiding Justice, John Racanelli. The case was *Pugh v. See's Candies, Inc.*[4]

Prior Proceedings

From the briefs it appeared that Wayne Pugh, the plaintiff, had sued his employer, See's Candies, in San Mateo County Superior Court for

---

[3] The case was *Service Employees International v. County of Napa*, 160 Cal. Rptr. 810 (Ct. App. 1979), involving the arbitrability of a dispute under a collective bargaining agreement. Many years later I was gratified to see that the Court of Appeal had rejected the reasoning of the majority in that case in favor of my dissent. *United Transportation Union v. Southern California Rapid Transit District*, 9 Cal. Rptr.2d 702 (1992).

[4] 171 Cal. Rptr. 917 (Ct. App. 1981).

wrongful termination in violation of express and implied promises of continued employment, and in violation of public policy. Plaintiff also named as a defendant Bakers' Local No. 125, a labor union which represented See's workers, it being part of Pugh's theory that the union had conspired to have him terminated. Pugh was represented by a San Francisco sole practitioner, Joseph P. Stretch, and See's by Donald F. Farbstein of the San Mateo firm Farbstein, Brown & Pillsbury. Farbstein was an insurance defense lawyer, with no background in employment. The union was represented by Phillip J. Smith of the Oakland firm Smith, Clancy, Wright & Laws.

The case was tried before a jury in the courtroom of Judge Robert D. Miller. At the conclusion of plaintiff's evidence, which spanned six court days, both defendants filed motions for nonsuit. The union's motion was based primarily on its contention that the evidence was insufficient to support plaintiff's contention that it had conspired to obtain Pugh's termination. See's motion argued, among other things, that there was no "independent consideration" that would support an implied promise of continued employment. Judge Miller granted both motions and entered judgment for defendants, from which Pugh appealed.

Since See's had not yet produced any evidence on the record, the only evidence was what Pugh had introduced before the motions for nonsuit were granted. The question that would later come before the Court of Appeal was not who was right or wrong, but whether that evidence, viewed in a light most favorable to Pugh, would be sufficient to support a jury verdict in Pugh's favor on any of theories he advanced—a most favorable procedural posture from the standpoint of a plaintiff. Pugh's public policy tort claim, as well as his claim against the union, rested mainly upon his contention that his termination resulted from his refusal to participate in negotiations with the union for a contract he regarded as a "sweetheart deal" meaning (according to Pugh) that it gave See's certain advantages over competitors. My later reading of the record[5] (I still had time to read records in those days) would lead me to the conclusion that this contention was without evidentiary support, and that the public policy tort action, as well as the action against the union, had been properly dismissed. My colleagues eventually agreed.

But that conclusion left open the question why Pugh was terminated. The record revealed no direct answer to that question, up to the time the nonsuit motions were granted. According to Pugh he asked for an explanation and was told in response to "look deep within yourself" to find the answer. Pugh claimed he looked, and found nothing. If Pugh was an "at-will" employee the question would be irrelevant; See's would be free to fire Pugh without giving him, or the jury, any explanation at

---

[5] The appellate record is no longer extant.

all, and that was obviously the trial court's view of the matter. The issue was whether there was evidence that would support Pugh's contention that he was legally entitled to an explanation, perhaps one that would meet some threshold standard of good cause.

Factual Background

With respect to Pugh's breach of contract claim, this is what the record showed. See's Candies was started as a family enterprise in 1921 in Los Angeles, manufacturing fresh candy, principally boxed chocolates, under the corporate name of See's Candy Shops, Inc. In 1936 the business expanded to Northern California, in the form of a wholly owned subsidiary called "See's Candies", and began to manufacture in a plant on Market Street in San Francisco. Shortly after World War II the plant was moved to York Street in San Francisco, and in 1957 to South San Francisco. Laurence See was the Chief Executive Officer of both corporations from 1949 until his death in 1969, when he was succeeded by his brother, Charles See. In 1972 the company was sold to Blue Chip Stamps Corporation.

Wayne Pugh graduated from high school in 1939, worked for two other candy companies, and in January 1941, began working for See's as a washer of pots and pans. He understood that See's had a policy of promoting from within. Ed Peck, then president and general manager, frequently told him "If you are loyal to [See's] and do a good job, your future is secure". He was soon promoted to candy maker, a position which he held until, soon after the outbreak of World War II, he enlisted in the Air Corps. Upon his discharge in 1946 he returned to See's, again as a candy maker, and after one year was promoted to Production Manager, in charge of personnel, ordering of raw materials and supervising the production of candy. At that time the company was still rather small, employing between 40 and 50 people at peak season.

When the plant moved to York Street, around 1950, the physical facility was expanded and so was the work force, up to 150 production workers. Pugh had responsibility for laying out the design of the plant, taking constructions bids, and supervising construction. When the plant was completed he continued as Production Manager, and attended night school to study plant layout, economics, and business law. When the plant moved to South San Francisco, Pugh again assisted in the physical layout and supervision of the construction.

By 1969, when Laurence See died, the staff at the South San Francisco plant had grown to 250 regular employees and as many as 1,000 employees during peak seasons, and dominated the San Francisco Bay Area boxed candy market. In 1971, Pugh was promoted, at the suggestion of Charles See, to Vice President in charge of production, with a seat on the company's board of directors, "in recognition of his accomplishments". In 1972 he received a gold watch from See's, "in appreciation of 31 years of loyal service." During the entire period of his employment Pugh had never received any formal or written criticism of his work, and he regularly received salary increases and bonuses. Laurence See's practice, which was continued by Charles See, was one of not terminating administrative personnel except for good cause.

In May 1973 Pugh traveled with Charles Huggins, who had become company president, accompanied by their respective families to Europe, where they visited candy manufacturers and inspected new equipment. Huggins returned in early June, while Pugh stayed with his family on a planned vacation until June 25. Upon his return he received a message directing him to fly to Los Angeles and meet with Huggins the following day.

The preceding Christmas season had been the most successful in See's history, the Valentine's Day holiday of 1973 had set a new sales record for See's, and the March 1973 edition of See's in-house newsletter contained two pictures of Pugh with congratulations on increased production. Pugh went to Los Angeles with the expectation of receiving another promotion.

Instead, Huggins told him, without explanation, that his services were "no longer required", and handed him a termination notice directing him to remove immediately all personal papers and possessions, as well as "all keys, credit cards, et cetera," and to refrain from visiting or contacting Production Department employees. It was at this point that Pugh asked Huggins for an explanation and was told to look deep within himself. Huggins also said that "things were said by people in the trade that have come back to us," but declined to elaborate.

The Court of Appeal Decision

Pugh's brief on appeal made three independent arguments in support of his contention that See's must show good cause for his termination: (1) that See's had an "express policy of not terminating administrative personnel except for good cause," based on the testimony by Charles See that this had been the company's policy; (2) that See's had an "implied policy of not terminating administrative personnel except for good cause," based on Peck's assurance to Pugh when Pugh first came to work; and (3) that Pugh's longevity of service constituted "independent consideration" sufficient in itself to (a) support or (b) establish an implied promise of continued employment.

See's brief argued that whatever See's policy was, Pugh had not shown that he relied upon it to his detriment, nor that he furnished any consideration to support either an express or implied promise of permanent employment because—citing to the *Gallo* line of cases—he furnished no consideration to the employer other than his work. While both briefs referred to the decision in *Drzewiecki v. H & R. Block*,[6] neither cited to the critical passage in which the court in that case characterized the rule requiring independent consideration as a "rule of construction, not of substance." I was persuaded that the *Drzewiecki* analysis was correct, and that independent consideration should not be regarded as a legal requirement.

See's brief also argued that since Pugh was free to resign his employment at any time, there was no "mutuality of obligation", and that any promise See's might have made to Pugh was not binding for that reason as well. But I recalled even from my law school days that the notion of "mutuality" as a condition to the enforcement of contracts had long since become archaic in contract law generally, and there seemed to be no persuasive reason to resurrect it for employment contracts.

Between the *Gallo* decision in 1965 and 1981, when I undertook the *Pugh* case, there had been several developments in wrongful termination law which I had not closely followed at the time, but which now helped to assure me that my instincts might be correct. The year before, the Michigan Supreme Court had found statements in an employer's personnel handbook to create a binding limitation on the employer's power of termination,[7] and in the process had adopted the view of the Restatement of Contracts that "mutuality of obligation" is not a requirement for the enforcement of any contract, once the requirement for consideration is met.[8] And, the "independent consideration" requirement which underlay the Court of Appeal's opinion in the *Gallo* case had been thoroughly rejected by a variety of courts, including courts in California, as contrary to the general contract principle that courts should not inquire into the adequacy of consideration.[9]

So far, so good. But Pugh's case rested upon the proposition that in his situation a jury could find that the at-will position had tacitly been modified by the company president's explicit assurance of job security 32 years earlier, and by the employer's confirmatory conduct over time. Such conduct, it seemed, was sufficient to support an implied promise of continued employment—in other words, to support a reasonable expectation on Pugh's part that his employment would not and could not be terminated arbitrarily, without good cause.

---

[6] 101 Cal. Rptr. 169 (Ct. App. 1972).

[7] *Toussaint v. Blue Cross & Blue Shield of Mich.*, 292 N.W.2d 880 (Mich. 1980).

[8] *Id.* at 885.

[9] See authorities and cases cited in *Pugh*, 171 Cal.Rptr. at 925.

Some California decisions were helpful to Pugh's cause. The California Supreme Court, in *Marvin v. Marvin*,[10] had recently held that a partner to a non-marital relationship could acquire equitable rights to share in her partner's property, as if they were married, in part on the basis of what the court characterized as an "implied contract." This implied contract could be grounded in "the acts and conduct of the parties, interpreted in the light of the subject matter and of the surrounding circumstances".[11] Pugh's case did not depend upon finding an "implied contract", since his employment relationship was deemed to be contractual *ab initio*, but rather upon ascertainment of the *terms* of his contract with See's. Nonetheless, since employment is, like cohabitation, an ongoing relationship, *Marvin*'s reasoning was pertinent: if a course of conduct in such a relationship could give rise to a *contract*, based upon reasonable expectations, it could certainly give rise to a *promise* with respect to the contract's duration. Two appellate districts, moreover, had embraced the proposition that in California "contracts of employment are terminable only for good cause if *either* of two conditions exist: (1) the contract was supported by consideration independent of the services to be performed by the employee for his prospective employer, or (2) the parties agreed, expressly *or impliedly*, that the employee could be terminated only for cause."[12]

One appellate district in California had gone further. In *Cleary v. American Airlines, Inc.*,[13] the court held that an employee stated a cause of action when he alleged that he was discharged after eighteen years of employment on false accusations of theft and that there existed an express employer policy with specific procedures for adjudicating employee disputes. "Termination of employment without legal cause after such a period of time offends the implied-in-law covenant of good faith and fair dealing contained in all contracts," the court said, and while the alleged employer policy was not before the court, "its existence compels the conclusion that this employer had recognized its responsibility to engage in good faith and fair dealing rather than in arbitrary conduct

---

[10] 557 P.2d 106 (Cal. 1976).

[11] *See id.* at 118 n. 16: ("Contracts may be express or implied. These terms however do not denote different kinds of contracts, but have reference to the evidence by which the agreement between the parties is shown. If the agreement is shown by the direct words of the parties, spoken or written, the contract is said to be an express one. But if such agreement can only be shown by the acts and conduct of the parties, interpreted in the light of the subject matter and of the surrounding circumstances, then the contract is an implied one.") (*Skelly v. Bristol Sav. Bank* (1893) 63 Conn. 83 [26 A. 474], quoted in 1 Corbin, Contracts 41 (1963)).

[12] *Drzewiecki v. H & R Block*, 101 Cal. Rptr. at 173–174; see *Rabago–Alvarez v. Dart Industries, Inc.*, 127 Cal. Rptr. 222, 225 (Ct. App. 1976).

[13] 168 Cal. Rptr. 722 (Ct. App. 1980).

with respect to all of its employees." These two factors together, the court held, "operate as a form of estoppel, precluding any discharge of such an employee by the employer without good cause."

The opinion in *Cleary*, while headed in an appropriate direction, seemed a bit problematic. Violation of the covenant of good faith and fair dealing in the insurance context gave rise to tort remedies, but only on the basis of some egregious conduct on the part of the carrier independent of the failure to pay benefits. The *Cleary* opinion assumed that similar tort remedies would be available if the plaintiff were found to have been dismissed without cause and therefore, on the court's analysis, in violation of the covenant. But why an employee should receive tort damages on the basis of an implied covenant under circumstances in which the same conduct, if in violation of an express contractual provision, would give rise to only contract damages seemed to me difficult to explain. In any event, a theory of implied-in-fact promise provided a rationale more defensible in terms of traditional contract doctrine, especially as there were factors in addition to longevity that a jury might rely upon in order to find such a promise in this case. I advised my colleagues that I thought we should reverse the trial court on that ground, and they agreed.

The conclusion that Pugh had produced sufficient evidence to create a triable issue as to whether there existed implied limitations on his employer's power of dismissal left open, for purposes of remand, the question as to what limitations might appropriately be implied. We could, of course, have left the trial court to grapple with that question, but that would likely have resulted in another appeal no matter what the trial court decided. In our view, some guidance on remand, though sometimes controversial, was unquestionably appropriate in the circumstances of this case. But that made it necessary for the court to be a bit creative.

Past cases had used the term "good cause", but that was open to a variety of interpretations. In theory the issue was one for the jury, to be determined on the basis of what the jury believed was the implicit agreement, but in the absence of some indicia of intent or past practice some guidance seemed appropriate if the legitimate interests of employers were to be respected. On the other hand, both principles of judicial constraint and practicality cautioned against attempting to determine all questions which might arise, or to write a detailed prescription for cases to come. Apart from referring to a case which had talked about "good cause" as being a "fair and honest cause or reason, regulated by good faith on the part of the party exercising the power," and observing that "[c]are must be taken not to interfere with the legitimate exercise of management discretion,"[14] we made three limiting suggestions.

First, we suggested that "good cause" in the context of an implied promise of continued employment was different from what an employer would have to show in order to terminate an employment contract with a fixed term. In the latter context, courts had required a showing of some substantial misconduct in the nature of a material breach on the part of the employee, and that (while we did not say so explicitly) seemed too high a standard.

Second, we suggested that while the standards generated by labor arbitrators might provide useful guidance, the special context of labor arbitration had to be considered. Labor arbitrators were often quite independent in reviewing managerial decisions as to what conduct merits discipline, or as to what discipline is appropriate. But labor arbitrators, unlike jurors, are chosen by the parties on the basis of their familiarity with industrial practices, and it might be unrealistic to assume that the employer implicitly agreed to that degree of intrusiveness on the part of a jury through an implied promise of continued employment. We ended up suggesting—not too helpfully, I admit, that "for courts to apply the same standards may prove overly intrusive in some cases."

Finally, we decided that some consideration had to be given to the responsibilities of the particular employee and his or her relationship to management. In the case of an employee, such as Pugh, who occupied a "sensitive managerial or confidential position," we observed, "the employer must of necessity be allowed scope for the exercise of subjective judgment."

In the process of writing the *Pugh* opinion I remember considering the possibility of rejecting the at-will presumption altogether, in favor of a neutral, presumption-free approach to determining the term of employment. After all, the so-called "Wood's Rule" which purported to restate the at-will presumption as an established part of American common law was itself based on questionable foundations,[15] and while the presumption is reflected in Section 2929 of the California Labor Code, that section stems from the old 1872 Field Code, which does not have the same binding authority as other legislative enactments. The Field Code also embodied the principle of contributory negligence, but the California Supreme Court had held that to be a non-binding restatement of

---

[14] *R.J. Cardinal Co. v. Ritchie*, 32 Cal. Rptr. 545 (Ct. App. 1963).

[15] The American doctrine of at-will employment derives from a treatise by Horace Gay Wood, *Master and Servant* (1877). Numerous commentators have observed that the cases Wood cited for the existence of that doctrine fail to support it, *e.g.*, Clyde Summers, *Individual Protection Against Unjust Dismissal: Time for a Statute*, 62 Va. L. Rev. 481, 485 (1976); *cf.* Mayer G. Freed & Daniel D. Polsby, *The Doubtful Provenance of Wood's Rule Revisited*, 22 Ariz. St. L. J. 551 (1990) (defending Wood and his rule).

common law principles subject to change in light of changing conditions and views, and found it not to be an obstacle to judicial adoption of comparative negligence principles.[16] A similar approach might be taken in relation to Section 2929.

In the end, I refrained from proposing that approach to my colleagues. The at-will presumption was deeply engrained in California law, it had not been subject to the same sort of extensive academic and judicial criticism as the contributory negligence principle, and for an intermediate appellate court to abolish it by fiat would be overly presumptuous. The approach we did adopt did not involve any departure from precedent, and the instructions we provided on remand established a very cautious framework for its application. Still, we were relieved when the California Supreme Court denied the See's petition for review.

The Trial

One of the ironies in the *Pugh* case, not entirely unexpected, was that when the case finally did go to trial Pugh lost. He presented essentially the same evidence that he had offered before the nonsuit in his first trial, but this time the company had an opportunity to present its evidence—something which, in retrospect, it would have been well advised to do in the first place.

The company did not attempt to argue against the implication of a good cause requirement. On the contrary, it conceded that such a requirement was already part of the company's policies. Instead, it presented evidence that, at least in the eyes of Charles Huggins, Pugh was hardly an exemplary employee—that he failed to train assistants as directed, that he failed to cooperate with other members of the administrative staff, that he accepted gifts from employees despite directives that he not do so, and that on the business trip to Europe which Pugh took with Huggins and others Pugh was rude, argumentative, belligerent and uncooperative. The trial court instructed the jury in the language of the *Pugh* opinion (which had been incorporated into standard jury instructions for "wrongful termination"); and the jury, in its verdict, implicitly found there was good cause of Pugh's dismissal. Pugh, relying on *Cleary*, argued that See's had violated the implied covenant of good faith and fair dealing as well, and the jury found against Pugh on that theory also. On appeal, in *Pugh II*, the judgment in favor of See's Candies was affirmed.[17] By then I was on the California Supreme Court, and participated in the denial of Pugh's petition for review.

---

[16] *Li v. Yellow Cab Co.*, 532 P.2d 1226 (Cal. 1975).

[17] *Pugh v. See's Candies, Inc.*, 250 Cal. Rptr. 195 (Ct. App. 1988).

The Immediate Impact of Pugh and its
Continuing Importance Today

The afternoon of the day the *Pugh* opinion was filed I left for
Yosemite National Park, where what was then called the Labor Law
Section of the San Francisco Bar Association holds an annual retreat to
discuss development in the field, and, not incidentally, to enjoy the
scenery and one another's company. I had been invited to talk to the
group and, naturally, I took the opportunity to tell them about the
opinion. The reaction was interesting. The management lawyers accepted the opinion with some degree of enthusiasm, perhaps less out of
appreciation for the quality of its reasoning than because of the prospects it presented for utilizing their services. The union lawyers, I would
have to say, were rather indifferent, except for one, who with some
agitation complained that, by providing a degree of job protection to
unrepresented employees, I had just driven a stake in the heart of the
labor movement.

For a number of reasons, I think the union lawyer was quite wrong.
The degree of protection for job security provided by *Pugh* is nowhere
near the sort of protection workers can obtain through a collective
bargaining agreement and its provisions for arbitration, and so is not
likely to be seen as an adequate substitute even by workers who have
access to a lawyer willing to take their case to court. And that, it turns
out, is a major qualification. Damages recoverable under *Pugh* are
contract damages only—back pay and perhaps "front pay", since common law courts lack the power that arbitrators have to order reinstatement. Consequently wrongful termination actions based on *Pugh* alone
are not likely to be undertaken except by relatively highly paid employees. Lower-paid workers cannot afford the legal fees required, and
cannot find lawyers willing to take their cases on contingency unless the
facts support additional claims, such as tort claims or statutory discrimination claims, that might provide broader recovery.

For some years *Pugh* existed side by side with *Cleary* as complemen-
tary approaches to wrongful termination claims, *Cleary* providing the
alternative, obviously preferable from the plaintiff's perspective, of tort
damages. During that period some parts of the employer community
displayed a willingness to accept legislation that would embody a "just
cause" requirement for termination, enforced through a statutorily
mandated arbitration procedure, in exchange for protection against tort
liability, but the trial lawyer lobby was firmly resistant, and in the end
the California Supreme Court, while confirming *Pugh*, rejected the tort
damage aspect of *Cleary*.[18] By that time I was no longer on the court.

---

[18] *Foley v. Interactive Data Corp.,* 765 P.2d 373 (Cal. 1988).

Because of the limited damages available, *Pugh* claims are not, independently, a significant part of current wrongful termination litigation; it is the potential for tort damages and attorney's fees, through public policy, privacy or discrimination claims, that drives the cases. Moreover, many employers—more than I would have predicted—have opted for protecting themselves against *Pugh* claims through express contract provisions or written disclaimers declaring the at-will status of the particular employment. Others, however, have accepted the implications of *Pugh* and incorporated express provisions protective of job security, sometimes combined with procedures for mediation and/or arbitration. Whether, in the end, the *Pugh* opinion will have contributed to the job security or dignity of American workers is for others to say. I am content with my own belief that the case was correctly decided.

*

2

The Story of *Woolley v. Hoffmann–La Roche*: Finding a Way to Enforce Employee Handbook Promises

J.H. Verkerke[*]

If you could travel back in time to the early 1970s, it would seem very odd, perhaps even preposterous, for an employment lawyer to believe that statements in a company's employee handbook or personnel policy manual concerning job security would be legally enforceable. The consensus among American jurisdictions was that handbook terms, at least those relating to discharge, had no contractual significance. Courts considered these commonly used provisions that established disciplinary procedures, listed offenses warranting involuntary termination, or required just cause for discharge to be mere statements of company policy rather than enforceable promises. The virtually irrebuttable presumption that an employment relationship was terminable at will made it surprisingly difficult to enforce even individually negotiated agreements for job security. No one seriously thought that handbook promises would fare any better.

Several leading cases, decided in the first half of the 1980s, utterly reversed this consensus. Beginning with the Michigan Supreme Court's decision in *Toussaint v. Blue Cross & Blue Shield of Michigan*,[1] gathering momentum with the New Jersey Supreme Court's ruling in *Woolley v. Hoffmann–La Roche*,[2] and culminating in dozens of similar decisions around the country, American employment law firmly embraced the principle that employee handbook statements could create an implied contract. Under this new case law, a number of plaintiffs sought and received contractual protection against discharge without cause.

[*] Thanks to Ben Doherty, Ryan Schaffer, Keith Thornburg, and Alison White for helpful research assistance with this chapter.

[1] 292 N.W.2d 880 (Mich. 1980).

[2] 491 A.2d 1257 (N.J. 1985).

Despite these early judicial victories, however, the decisions themselves contained the seeds of the doctrine's demise. At pains to explain that employers would not be forced to retain incompetent employees or provide just-cause protection against their will, courts routinely invited firms to include prominent disclaimers in their employee handbooks. By indicating clearly that the handbook was not intended to have contractual effect and that workers were subject to termination for any reason or no reason at all, employers could opt out of these newly discovered contractual obligations and thus restore the long-standing rule of employment at will.

The New Jersey Supreme Court's decision in *Woolley* played a significant role in these developments and exemplifies legal changes that took place in other states. A closer examination of the case reveals the significant doctrinal hurdles that courts had to overcome, the legal fictions that they commonly employed to make handbook provisions enforceable, and the practical consequences of their decisions. Moreover, some of the legal arguments that the parties raised in the trial court and on appeal foreshadowed disputes that would trouble courts in subsequent years. The story of Woolley's termination also shows how complex and difficult it can be to determine as a factual matter whether just cause for discharge exists. Finally, the case warrants attention because the plaintiff, Richard Woolley, was, by all accounts, an admirable man and his employer, Hoffmann–La Roche, had a reputation both in the local community and in the pharmaceutical industry for treating its employees fairly and well.

The story of *Woolley v. Hoffmann–La Roche* also illustrates several broader theoretical issues that arise when courts consider whether to enforce employee handbook statements as contractual commitments. Hoffmann–La Roche carefully limited distribution of the Personnel Policy Manual on which Woolley based his claim to supervisory employees only. This fact suggests that the company intended to control its agents in the exercise of their managerial discretion rather than to provide legally enforceable protection against termination without cause. More generally, Hoffmann–La Roche saw the manual as an important statement of its management "philosophy" and part of the company's broader effort to maintain its good reputation in employee relations. However, these informal efforts to create a corporate culture and to enforce norms of fair treatment inevitably create some tension with the overlapping regime of legal rules. Courts often struggle to disentangle merely aspirational statements from more serious, and thus legally enforceable, commitments concerning job security or other employment benefits.

Employees, too, can find it difficult to distinguish informal norms from contractual rights. Indeed, the modern law of employee handbooks arises largely from judicial concern that job security provisions might mislead employees. The *Woolley* court's opinion, like many other decisions in this area, thus relies on what I have elsewhere called a "legal-information-forcing" argument.[3] Under this approach, the court places the burden of clarifying the legal relationship between two contracting parties on the more legally sophisticated party. Since the employer both drafts the employee handbook and is far more likely to know the relevant contract default rules, a legal-information-forcing rule in this context requires employers to include language disclaiming any contractual intent and expressly confirming that employees may be terminated at will. One might reasonably question whether these disclaimers genuinely prevent employee misperceptions.[4] Nevertheless, the contours of existing doctrine are clear, and a prominent disclaimer ordinarily precludes contractual claims based on employee handbook terms. The *Woolley* court's decision thus should be seen as a crucial step along a path from the traditional and virtually irrebuttable at-will presumption to a new, and currently stable, contractual equilibrium in which the overwhelming majority of employers contract expressly for an at-will relationship.[5]

Social and Legal Background

At the time of Woolley's termination in 1978, the national scene was a turbulent one. Jimmy Carter had been elected President two years before, and he proved unable to maintain price stability or encourage economic expansion during his single term in office. Continued stagflation—a period of persistently high inflation and low growth—combined with the unresolved Iranian hostage crisis to help Ronald Reagan win the 1980 election running on an economic platform that came to be known as Reaganomics. The new administration's large tax cuts and deficit spending sparked an economic recovery that continued until more than a year after the New Jersey Supreme Court issued its final decision in the *Woolley* case. After reaching a peak of 9.0 percent in 1982, the unemployment rate in New Jersey fell precipitously to 7.8 percent, 6.2 percent, and 5.7 percent in 1983, 1984 and 1985, respectively. Thus, although the memory of bad economic times was still fresh, the *Woolley* court considered and decided this case during a time of rapidly improving employment conditions.

---

[3] *See* J. H. Verkerke, *Legal Ignorance and Information–Forcing Rules*, Univ. of Virginia Law & Econ Research Paper No. 03–4, *available at* http://papers.ssrn.com/abstract=405560.

[4] *See* Pauline T. Kim, *Bargaining with Imperfect Information: A Study of Worker Perceptions of Legal Protection in an At–Will World*, 83 Cornell L. Rev. 105 (1997); Verkerke, *Legal Ignorance*.

[5] *See* J. Hoult Verkerke, *An Empirical Perspective on Indefinite Term Employment Contracts: Resolving the Just Cause Debate*, 1995 Wis. L. Rev. 837.

A decade earlier, the country saw the rise of the consumer and environmental protection movements and increased public concern about workplace safety. Congress created the Environmental Protection Agency and the Occupational Safety and Health Administration in 1970 and the Consumer Product Safety Commission in 1972. Although the election of Ronald Reagan in 1980 signaled something of a backlash against ambitious federal regulatory efforts, these political movements were by that time well entrenched, and they continue to influence public policy debates today. We should understand the court's decision in *Woolley*—along with prior and subsequent decisions in other jurisdictions—as part of this broader reformist movement that was most influential during the period spanning the mid–1960s to the early 1980s.

While these contemporary social and economic forces undoubtedly exerted some influence, the legal historical roots of the *Woolley* decision reach back to the oft-told story of the American adoption of the employment-at-will rule during the late 1800s.[6] Both the plaintiff and the New Jersey Supreme Court embraced the canonical account that credits Horace Gay Wood with inventing the rule and using his 1877 treatise on the law of master and servant to popularize it among the somewhat credulous judges of the time. On this view, courts endorsed Wood's rule because it favored employers' interests. Judges sought to encourage industrial activity and enforced the at-will presumption with a vengeance in order to ensure that employers would have more flexibility in labor relations than either the English rate-of-pay rule or reasonable notice requirements would have afforded.[7] More recently, some scholars have questioned this traditional narrative. They have sought to defend Wood against the charge that the rule had no support in contemporary case law,[8] and they have cast considerable doubt on the hypothesis that the at-will rule arose in response to industrialization.[9] It is doubtful that either of these revisionist historical arguments would have changed the outcome in *Woolley*. We should at least bear in mind, however, that the court's story of inevitable progression from jurisprudential darkness to

---

[6] For the conventional account, see Annotation, *Duration of Contract of Hiring Which Specified No Term, but Fixes Compensation at a Certain Amount Per Day, Week, Month, or Year*, 11 A.L.R. 469, 475–76 (1921); J. Peter Shapiro & James F. Tune, Note, *Implied Contract Rights to Job Security*, 26 Stan. L. Rev. 335, 341 (1974).

[7] *See, e.g., Martin v. N.Y. Life Ins. Co.*, 42 N.E. 416, 417 (N.Y. 1895).

[8] Mayer G. Freed & Daniel D. Polsby, *The Doubtful Provenance of "Wood's Rule" Revisited*, 22 Ariz. St. L.J. 551 (1990).

[9] Andrew P. Morriss, *Exploding Myths: An Empirical and Economic Reassessment of the Rise of Employment At–Will*, 59 Mo. L. Rev. 679 (1994). See also his chapter in this volume, *The Story of the Montana Wrongful Discharge from Employment Act: A Drama in 5 Acts.*

light relied on what some have argued is an inaccurate description of the initial development of the at-will rule.

Despite these historical cavils, no one can seriously doubt that, during the heyday of the employment-at-will doctrine, courts routinely ignored or discounted evidence of employer statements that employees reasonably might have understood to guarantee job security. New Jersey case law conformed closely to this pattern. In *Bird v. J.L. Prescott Co.*,[10] for example, the plaintiff was injured at work and agreed not to sue his employer in exchange for a written promise of lifetime employment. A New Jersey appellate court held that the writing was "no more than a friendly assurance of employment and ... not sufficiently definite to make an enforceable contract." In *Savarese v. Pyrene Manufacturing Co.*,[11] the New Jersey Supreme Court rejected a similar claim. The plaintiff alleged that his employer had induced him to play for the company baseball team in the Industrial Twilight League by assuring him: "If you get hurt ... you will have a foreman's job for the rest of your life." Even though plaintiff's claim was based on an oral promise made many years earlier, the decision placed absolutely no weight on the informal character of the promise. Instead, the court affirmed summary judgment for the employer because the alleged agreement failed to specify a salary term or indicate how the parties intended to handle different types of disability and "other possible future contingencies." In these cases, courts consistently imposed special requirements for enforcing employer promises of job security and exhibited the broad hostility to such claims that pervaded employment contract case law throughout much of the 20th Century.

Prior to *Woolley*, there were no published New Jersey decisions specifically addressing the enforceability of employee handbook promises of job security. Cases from other jurisdictions, however, consistently held that handbook statements were too indefinite, not supported by consideration, or lacking in mutuality of obligation.[12] Typical of these cases was *Johnson v. National Beef Packing Co.*,[13] decided in 1976 by the Kansas Supreme Court. The company's policy manual specified that new hires would be "probationary employees" for ninety days before becoming regular full-time employees, and it provided that "[n]o employee shall be dismissed without just cause." The court rejected Johnson's claim, reasoning that:

---

[10] 99 A. 380 (N.J. 1916).

[11] *Savarese v. Pyrene Mfg. Co.*, 89 A.2d 237 (N.J. 1952).

[12] *See, e.g., Johnson v. National Beef Packing Co.*, 551 P.2d 779 (Kan. 1976); *Chin v. American Tel. & Tel. Co.*, 410 N.Y.S.2d 737 (Sup. Ct. 1978).

[13] 551 P.2d 779 (Kan. 1976).

We find nothing in the manual expressly providing for a fixed term of employment, nor is there language from which a contract to that effect could be inferred. . . . [T]he manual . . . was only a unilateral expression of company policies and procedures. Its terms were not bargained for by the parties and any benefits conferred by it were mere gratuities. Certainly, no meeting of the minds was evidenced by the defendant's unilateral act of publishing company policy. . . . [A]n agreement to give permanent employment simply means to give a steady job some permanence, as distinguished from a temporary job or temporary employment.

Most other courts were similarly unreceptive to contract claims based on termination provisions contained in employee handbooks.

Even though longstanding authority tended to undermine Woolley's claim, there were also significant harbingers of change in New Jersey and elsewhere. Beginning with the California appellate court decision in *Petermann v. International Brotherhood of Teamsters*,[14] and gathering force with the Indiana Supreme Court's ruling in *Frampton v. Central Indiana Gas Co.*,[15] many jurisdictions had endorsed a then-novel tort theory of wrongful discharge in violation of public policy.[16] The New Jersey Supreme Court joined this growing trend in 1980 with its decision in *Pierce v. Ortho Pharmaceutical Corp.*[17] The plaintiff in *Pierce* ultimately failed to prove a violation. However, the court unequivocally endorsed the principle that an employee terminated for refusing to engage in conduct that contravenes "a clear expression of public policy" would state a claim. The court observed that the "twentieth century has witnessed significant changes in socioeconomic values that have led to a reassessment of the [at-will rule]." Commentators have "questioned the compatibility of the traditional at will doctrine with the realities of modern economics and employment practices" and a growing number of decisions from other jurisdictions had extended protection to employees who were discharged for reasons that contravened a sufficiently weighty public policy. Although Dr. Pierce's own tort claim was unsuccessful, the *Pierce* decision undoubtedly signaled that the court had become significantly more receptive to employees' efforts to overcome the at-will presumption.

Contract cases from other jurisdictions also paved the way for change in New Jersey, and none was more important than *Toussaint v.*

---

[14] 344 P.2d 25 (Cal. Ct. App. 1959).

[15] 297 N.E.2d 425 (Ind. 1973).

[16] *See generally* Stewart J. Schwab, *The Story of* Johnston v. Del Mar: *Wrongful Discharge in Violation of Public Policy* (chapter 3 in this volume).

[17] 417 A.2d 505 (N.J. 1980).

Blue Cross & Blue Shield of Michigan.[18] The plaintiff in *Toussaint* testified that, at the time he was hired, he met with an officer of Blue Cross and asked "how secure a job it was." The officer told Toussaint that "he knew of no one ever being discharged" and said that "as long as [Toussaint] did [his] job ... [he] would be with the company" until mandatory retirement at age sixty-five. The officer also handed Toussaint a manual of Blue Cross personnel policies that reinforced these oral assurances by establishing detailed disciplinary procedures and providing: "It is the policy of the company ... to release employees for just cause only." In addition to upholding an express contract claim based on the officer's oral assurances, the court swept aside all formal doctrinal barriers and strongly endorsed the enforcement of employee handbook promises:

> While an employer need not establish personnel policies or practices, where an employer chooses to establish such policies and practices and makes them known to its employees, the employment relationship is presumably enhanced. The employer secures an orderly, cooperative and loyal workforce, and the employee the peace of mind associated with job security and the conviction that he will be treated fairly. No pre-employment negotiations need take place and the parties' minds need not meet on the subject; nor does it matter that the employee knows nothing of the particulars of the employer's policies and practices or that the employer may change them unilaterally. It is enough that the employer chooses, presumably in its own interest, to create an environment in which the employee believes that, whatever the personnel policies and practices, they are established and official at any given time, purport to be fair, and are applied consistently and uniformly to each employee. The employer has then created a situation "instinct with an obligation."

The *Toussaint* court thus invited employees to bring contract claims grounded in their "legitimate expectations based on an employer's statements of policy." As we will see, the *Woolley* court relied heavily on quite similar reasoning.

One final line of cases bears mentioning as a precursor to the *Woolley* decision. In *Toussaint*, the court drew support from prior cases that had enforced severance pay promises contained in company policy manuals. As early as 1956, the Michigan Supreme Court had held that a promise of severance pay benefits could be enforceable.[19] In that case, the employer objected that its handbook severance provisions were not a promise but rather a "mere gratuitous statement of policy or intention" for which the employees had not supplied any additional consideration.

---

[18] 292 N.W.2d 880 (Mich. 1980).

[19] *Cain v. Allen Electric & Equipment Co.*, 78 N.W.2d 296 (Mich. 1956).

In terms that foreshadowed the reasoning of both *Toussaint* and *Woolley*, the court announced that the company's severance pay policies constituted an offer that employees accepted by continuing employment. Employees would reasonably have understood the policy manual as a firm commitment to provide those specific benefits, and they were thus entitled to rely on the employer's promise. Moreover, the court reasoned that the company had reaped "substantial rewards" in the form of an increased "spirit of co-operation and friendliness" in the workplace.

Just two years later, in *Anthony v. Jersey Central Power & Light Co.*,[20] the New Jersey Appellate Division reached precisely the same result using substantially similar reasoning. *Anthony* held that an offer of severance pay "in plain terms under circumstances which were unambiguous" justified a presumption of reliance on the part of any employee who subsequently provided services under those terms. The *Woolley* court would later endorse *Anthony* and extend its presumption of reliance to handbook statements concerning job security.

Pierce, *Toussaint*, and *Anthony* thus set the stage for change in the New Jersey law of employee handbooks. But before we consider the legal issues addressed in *Woolley*, we should examine more closely the facts that gave rise to this important litigation.

Factual Background

THE PARTIES

Defendant Hoffmann–La Roche, known more commonly as Roche, was, and remains today, a major producer of pharmaceutical products.[21] Founded by Fritz Hoffman in 1896 as F. Hoffmann–La Roche & Company, the firm had its corporate headquarters in Basel, Switzerland, and was a pioneer in the production of medicines on an industrial scale. Roche began its U.S. operations in New York City but relocated in 1929 to a much larger facility in Nutley, New Jersey. By the late 1930s, Roche had become the world's leading supplier of vitamins. The company steadily expanded its operations during the post-war period, both in the U.S. and in Europe. At the start of this litigation, in 1978, the company employed about 10,000 people. Roche was, according to the New Jersey Supreme Court, "a substantial company with many employees in New Jersey," and it enjoyed a "good reputation in labor relations." The company is now known as Roche Holdings and, after a period of aggressive expansion and acquisitions, it has approximately 65,000 employees worldwide. Some of Roche's more widely known products include Librium, Valium, Lariam, and most recently, Tamiflu.

---

[20] 143 A.2d 762 (N.J. Super. Ct. App. Div. 1958).

[21] For a more detailed history of Roche's activities, see http://www.roche.com/home/company/com_hist.htm (visited on Nov. 20, 2005).

Plaintiff Richard M. Woolley was by all accounts an unusually admirable person. One of his attorneys, Gerald Wahl, described him as a special individual who maintained his dignity throughout the sometimes stressful litigation process.[22] Defense counsel Frederick Kentz similarly found Woolley remarkably composed and noted that he harbored no animosity towards his former employer.[23] He loved the company and wanted to continue working there. Indeed, during a break from his deposition testimony, Woolley told Kentz that he would forgive the company for everything if they would just take him back. Even after being out of work for two years and suffering the indignities of the litigation process, Woolley held no grudge and wanted to rejoin what he and other employees considered the "Roche family."

Woolley was born on February 3, 1925, in Newark, New Jersey.[24] After high school, he enrolled in Trinity College, where he received military training in the Navy's V–12 Program while also taking a standard college curriculum. He served on active duty as a gunnery officer in the Navy from September 1945 until July 1946. After he left the Navy, Woolley enrolled at Rutgers University and completed a bachelor's degree in civil engineering. He worked as a licensed civil engineer in Illinois, Pennsylvania and New Jersey, before returning to Rutgers and, in 1960, earning an MBA. During the 1950s and 1960s, he moved among several companies in New Jersey and New York, including the Refinery Division of Arthur McKee and Company where he worked under Chief Draftsman Edward Mayerchak. Several years later Mayerchak would be instrumental in recruiting Woolley to work with him at Roche. At the time of his deposition, Woolley was fifty-four years old. He was married, with a teenage stepdaughter and three adult children from a previous marriage.

Woolley's Hiring and Early Employment at Roche

In October 1969, Roche was expanding its in-house engineering department to handle the work associated with constructing new facilities in Belvidere, New Jersey. Ed Mayerchak, Woolley's former boss at McKee, had moved to Roche and contacted Woolley to ask if he would be interested in joining him in the Corporate Engineering Department at Roche. Mayerchak respected Woolley and vouched for the quality of his work. He introduced Woolley to other Roche managers and shortly

---

[22] Telephone interview with Gerald Wahl (July 21, 2005).

[23] Telephone interview with Frederick Kentz (Aug. 9, 2005).

[24] This information about Woolley and the events leading up to the litigation is based principally on his deposition testimony taken on December 17, 1979. It has been supplemented with additional biographical material obtained from alumni files at Rutgers University and from birth, death and property records available online.

afterwards, Woolley received an offer to become the head of Roche's civil engineering section. Worried that his current position with Airco Cryoplants, Inc. would soon be eliminated or relocated to Niagara Falls, New York, Woolley promptly accepted the company's employment offer. Roche's reputation for treating employees well played an important role in his decision. Woolley accepted the position "knowing the reputation that Hoffmann–La Roche had." He considered Roche "an excellent company with tremendous benefits.... that maintained the employment of their personnel and had an excellent reputation in all these ways." According to Woolley's deposition testimony, his wife shared his admiration for the company.

Woolley did not inquire about job security and received no oral assurances of continued employment from the Roche officials with whom he interviewed. His offer letter explained that the company paid an annual service bonus and had been doing so for many years, but it also cautioned him that there was no promise that the bonus would continue in the future. He understood that it was the right of management to change benefit programs. However, Woolley apparently believed that changes were permitted only to improve benefits. He testified that if "I went there under the terms of four weeks vacation ... I don't think that they would have the right after I was there for two years to say, 'Okay. Your vacation is now three weeks.'" Woolley considered these benefits a part of his compensation and thought that the company could not reduce either benefits or salary unless he was moving into a new position at a lower grade in order to stay with the company.

Woolley started work on November 15, 1969, and about two weeks later, he received a copy of the Hoffmann–La Roche Personnel Policy Manual on which he would later base his contract claim against the company. The record includes only the nine pages of the manual that Woolley submitted to the trial court.[25] The manual specified that it should be distributed only to "supervisory personnel whose duties are such that a knowledge of company personnel policies is required." According to Woolley, "the average employee did not receive a copy."

Woolley's initial position at Roche was Section Head for civil engineering. He was responsible for managing a small but growing staff of in-house engineers who worked on expansion projects. In January 1976, he was promoted and the following January, was again promoted to become Group Leader for the civil engineering, piping design, plant layout, and standards and systems sections. He had about 50 engineers and designers working under him at the time of his termination. During the eighteen months leading up to his discharge, Woolley reported to Ed

---

[25] These pages are available in an online Appendix to this chapter at http://www.verkerke.net/stories.

Mayerchak who had become the company's Manager of Project Design. Mayerchak in turn reported to David Seltzer, the Director of Project Engineering, and Seltzer reported to Dr. Gerhard Frohlich, the General Manager of the Corporate Engineering Department. As we will see, responsibility for engineering work was also shared among various project engineers, plant engineers and operations managers. It is apparent that Roche's corporate management was organized in a comparatively complex hierarchical structure.

Asked at his deposition who had the authority to terminate employees at Roche, Woolley described a system of corporate checks designed to ensure careful deliberation. He explained:

> [T]o terminate somebody at Roche is a very difficult thing to do, and I could tell you from firsthand that I've seen people try to terminate other individuals, people on my level, where they did not get cooperation from people within their groups, and they tried to terminate these people, some of these people who directly disobeyed them and so on, and they could not terminate them because the personnel department stepped in and protected that individual, so you could make recommendations, but, without the proper material and backup, as far as I could see, there was no way you could terminate someone.

Testifying about whether one of his former employers had the right to terminate him, Woolley said, "I never felt that McKee would terminate me unless they ran out of work.... Whether they had the right or not, I'm not a lawyer, so I can't really say."

THE VITAMIN E PLANT PROJECT

The sequence of events that ultimately led to Woolley's termination in 1978 began four years earlier when his civil engineering staff worked on the piping design for a new Vitamin E capsule production facility known as Building 55. The piping project was somewhat unusual. The engineers assigned to the project, including two of Woolley's subordinates, Anton Ierubino and Bela Balogh, worked with a "task force" that operated out of another building. In April 1975, the project administrator, George Scott, wrote to tell Woolley that he was running out of money and that he would have to end the civil engineering section's participation in the task force. Woolley responded to Scott, writing that: "We have ceased all design as per our verbal discussion and your letter. We remain available to lend assistance as specifically directed through project engineering request with your approval." Woolley understood that any remaining "cleanup work" on the project would be the responsibility of the four project engineers working for Scott. Furthermore,

Woolley provided Scott with "a complete detailed description of what we did to date and what . . . remained to be done."

Woolley heard nothing more about the Vitamin E plant project until two years later, in April 1977, when his office received a request to investigate problems with piping supports in the facility. The plant had been plagued with problems that interfered with production and required costly maintenance. A troubleshooting committee had been formed six months earlier to try to remedy these same issues, but Woolley's staff was not invited to participate. For this new effort, Woolley's immediate subordinate Bela Balogh again assumed responsibility for the work and prepared preliminary designs and recommendations for improvements to the piping supports. However, progress was soon stymied when Balogh was unable to get the plant engineer, Gun Parekh, to cooperate in arranging a meeting with the chemical production department (CPD) managers who operated the Vitamin E plant. According to Woolley, Parekh was "a very difficult man to deal with." Woolley testified that his office only provided technical support to project engineers and thus had no authority to work directly with the client department. Balogh eventually enlisted the aid of Parekh's superior George Scott and held a meeting with the CPD staff on September 15, 1977. At that meeting, Balogh explained that work done by CPD personnel over the past several years had caused misalignment, missing supports, and stress on the expansion joints of the pipes. He also outlined two alternative procedures for completing the necessary repairs. The CPD managers agreed to get back to Balogh to tell him which approach they wished to take. According to Woolley, "they never got back to us and the job was canceled . . . a month and a half later, and that was the end of our work." It was not unusual for projects to be canceled before completion, and thus the November 1977 cancellation of the April work request did not provoke any suspicion on Woolley's part.

For four more months, Woolley's office again heard nothing about the Vitamin E facility's maintenance problems. On March 14, 1978, however, Woolley was summoned to tour the building with Seltzer and Mayerchak. The day before, the plant's production manager had written a memo to Dr. Frohlich, Seltzer's immediate superior and head of the corporate engineering department, enumerating some fifty deficiencies. Although nearly all of these issues involved instrumentation and process defects for which Woolley's section was not responsible, one of the items referred to continued trouble with pipe supports. At about the same time, the company had hired an outside consultant, Paul Hirshman, to review the production problems in Building 55. Hirshman's comments about missing pipe supports and potentially hazardous conditions evidently alarmed Frohlich, who became quite anxious and directed Seltzer to have Woolley "write a summary of how we handled the pipe supports on the Vitamin E job in Building 55."

During Woolley's March 14th tour of the plant, Seltzer relayed Hirshman's comments about missing supports and other problems with the piping design. Although he acknowledged that some of these concerns were well founded, Woolley testified at his deposition that many of Hirshman's criticisms were "out of line because they far exaggerated any problems in the area." On the way back to his office, Seltzer asked Woolley "why didn't you tell us about the supports that were needed here?" Woolley explained that the April 1977 work request had been canceled. Seltzer then told Woolley that "Dr. Frohlich would like you to write a report on everything that happened on the Vitamin E job." Woolley was initially reluctant to write the report because he worried that it might be read as an effort to incriminate other engineers involved in the project. In response to Woolley's concerns, his immediate supervisor Mayerchak emphasized the seriousness of the situation by asking him "would you rather get fired or would you rather have somebody else get fired?" As Mayerchak later told Woolley, "I wanted to scare you into putting down the facts and not trying to protect someone else." Mayerchak's strategy appeared to have been successful because Woolley later testified quite earnestly about his report that "[t]his is the facts. From the beginning it was the facts."

While he was preparing the report for Dr. Frohlich, Woolley met once more with Seltzer to discuss Hirshman's approach to the piping design. At that meeting, Woolley went to the blackboard to show why he felt that Hirshman's suggestions would not fix the defects they had identified with the piping in the Vitamin E plant. During this same period, Woolley and his staff were working with Hirshman to agree on a design for the needed repairs. Woolley testified that he met several times with Hirshman, Balogh, and Ierubino. "We gave a little, he gave a little, and we tried to work out our difficulties, and I think that ... we had most of our problem resolved." The changes that Roche ultimately implemented were "a combination of his ideas and our ideas." The work was not completed until the beginning of July 1978, more than a month after Woolley's last day on the job. As we will see, however, the production problems at the Vitamin E plant continued even after the pipe supports were repaired.

Woolley's Termination

Woolley submitted his initial report to Mayerchak (with copies to Seltzer and Frohlich) on April 5, 1978, and a very slightly revised version on May 3rd. Also on May 3rd, he was again called to Seltzer's office. Seltzer told Woolley that Dr. Frohlich had lost confidence in him and requested his resignation. Woolley expressed shock and amazement at what was for him a completely unexpected development. Seltzer said, "I tried to talk him out of it and I couldn't, and I'm sorry, but that's the way it is." Later that same day, Woolley spoke to Dr. Frohlich. As Woolley described the meeting, Frohlich said that he had "lost confidence because we didn't do anything on this job." Woolley told him that "we did and we tried," but the April 1977 work order had been canceled. Frohlich responded that "even if the job was canceled, you still should have worked on it." Woolley tried to explain that his office had to "work through ... project engineering. This is the way the organization chart is set up. This is the way that Mr. Seltzer requires that we work." Frohlich responded, "Well, then maybe we should change the organization chart." As Woolley summed up the conversation in his deposition testimony, Frohlich "didn't seem to understand the way that the department functioned and.... I wasn't about to stay there and beg for my job, so I got up and left, and that's about it."

On Monday, May 22, 1978, Seltzer wrote Woolley a letter formally requesting his resignation to be effective on July 15th. The letter offered eleven weeks of severance pay, time off from work to seek other employment, and an opportunity to receive personnel counseling at Roche's expense. The following Thursday, Woolley wrote in reply that he refused to resign because he felt that the request was unjust. After being asked for his resignation, Woolley had "continued to try to cooperate to the best of my ability to get the job done ... trying to help and convey in every way possible, continue to show them my respect for the company and my job with the hopes that maybe they would reconsider." In a particularly poignant exchange during his deposition, defense counsel asked Woolley "You knew all along from May 3rd, did you not, that if you didn't resign that you would be terminated?" Woolley responded, "Yes, I knew in a way, but down deep in my heart I felt that if I could work hard and show them that they were making a mistake and through certain correspondence and so on that hopefully, wishfully thinking, deep down inside that this thing, this irrational act, would not take place." It is hard to imagine a more candid window into the anguished state of mind of someone who believes that he is being unjustly terminated.

The events surrounding Woolley's final day at work were dramatic and emotional. Woolley had become severely depressed and, on Tuesday, May 30, 1978, his doctor directed him to stay home from work. The following day, he returned to Roche and went to the company infirmary to get a slip excusing his absence. Sometime that same morning, Woolley's personal doctor learned that he was at work and that he had been relieved of his supervisory responsibilities. The doctor spoke to Woolley's wife and told her to get in touch with him immediately and make him return home. Meanwhile, Woolley was sitting in the waiting room of the company infirmary. He testified at his deposition that he had a "nervous breakdown of the type where you lose control of yourself and you cry." Woolley had become "completely depressed" and "couldn't function" anymore. Members of the infirmary nursing staff immediately took him to consult with a Roche doctor. The company doctor told Woolley to go home after first talking with Bruce Fischer in the personnel department. Woolley then tried to enlist Fischer's aid in challenging his termination. Woolley asked him "to step in and request that I get equal and fair treatment under [the] termination procedures as set forth in the Roche . . . personnel policy manual." Fischer told Woolley that he would look into the matter, but there is no evidence that reveals whether or not he intervened in the case.

Woolley then went to his car and prepared a handwritten letter to Mayerchak. At his deposition, Woolley testified that the letter was not about his termination but instead "trying to get across to him the importance of some of the work that I was doing on the Vitamin E job with Mr. Hirshman. . . . I wanted to try to get a few things across to him before leaving." Woolley again broke down emotionally when he gave this handwritten letter to Eddie Barger, a designer who worked for him, and asked Barger to deliver it to Mayerchak. His coworker Balogh was also present and witnessed Woolley's emotional breakdown outside of their office building.

Hoffmann–La Roche formally terminated Woolley's employment on July 15, 1978, while he was away from work on short-term disability leave. At the time of his termination he was fifty-three years old. Sometime during Woolley's disability leave, a friend from a local engineering firm called to ask if Woolley would like to work for them on an hourly basis when he felt able. Woolley agreed and he began work on July 19 as a "job shopper" for Vector Engineering Company in Springfield, New Jersey. Vector appears to have been something like a temporary agency for engineering work. Woolley was assigned to work on a project for one of his former full-time employers, Airco in Murray Hill. In this new role, he was paid on an hourly basis at a rate of fifteen dollars per hour.

Untangling the Reasons for Woolley's Termination

As in almost any litigation, we cannot be entirely certain where the truth about Woolley's termination lies. Parties inevitably see events from diametrically opposed points of view. Management often believes sincerely that an employee has engaged in misconduct or that his performance falls short of an acceptable standard. The discharged employee believes just as fervently that criticism is unjustified, that company managers have unfairly singled him out, or that ulterior motives explain the decision to discharge. At best, a disinterested observer can try to evaluate the internal and external consistency of each side's arguments and make some effort to assess witnesses' credibility. However, the task is complex. Termination cases frequently turn on a contested subjective evaluation of an employee's performance. As in *Woolley*, judges and jurors ultimately must arbitrate between two self-interested reconstructions of inherently ambiguous events. We can surely hope that they do so conscientiously, but we should harbor no illusions that, for all of its expense, employment litigation often uncovers the elusive truth of the matter.

Roche's answer to plaintiff's first set of interrogatories provided the clearest available evidence of the company's avowed reasons for terminating Woolley:

> Plaintiff was terminated for poor performance as group leader of the piping and structural design sections during the period from April 1977 through March 1978. Plaintiff took no corrective action during this period with regard to known deficiencies in the piping installation in Building 55.... In March 1978, Engineering Management retained an outside consultant to analyze the piping installation problems. This consultant recommended corrective action. It was through discussions with the consultant and with plaintiff in April 1978 that it became clear to Management that plaintiff lacked initiative and exercised poor judgment for a full year prior to that time in that he had not properly performed his duties in directing design analysis and revisions for piping installation in Building 55. Plaintiff was employed as a Group Leader at the time and Management lost complete confidence in plaintiff's abilities to perform his duties. As a result of this poor performance and Management's loss of confidence in plaintiff, plaintiff was requested to resign on May 3, 1978. In addition, the resignation of another supervisory employee in Engineering, Mr. G. Scott, was requested and received at this same time in connection with this matter. Mr. Scott took no action whatsoever against Roche.

The same document also described company management's decision process in some detail:

> The decision to terminate plaintiff was made by Dr. Frohlich and concurred in by Mr. Seltzer on May 2, 1978. On May 3, 1978 Mr. Seltzer and Mr. Mayerchak requested plaintiff's resignation.... Plaintiff was clearly aware of Roche's concern over plaintiff's lack of performance in March 1978 when an outside consultant was hired. During that period, Mr. Mayerchak requested plaintiff to submit a report explaining his previous actions and advised plaintiff that he was in jeopardy of losing his job.... Mr. Seltzer and Mr. Mayerchak had continuous communications with plaintiff concerning his per-

formance and Roche's concern. . . . While Roche management is not obligated to follow any particular procedure in the termination of any employee, the Roche [Manual] gives the company philosophy with respect to termination of permanent employees and provides suggested guidelines for carrying out this philosophy. . . . The termination procedure set forth in the Manual was followed in this particular case. . . . Management considered, among other alternatives, placing plaintiff on probation prior to making a determination that plaintiff should be terminated. After serious consideration of many alternatives, Management concluded that the most appropriate determination in light of plaintiff's poor performance and the lack of Management's confidence in plaintiff's ability to perform was to request the resignation of plaintiff in May 1978.

Defense counsel's deposition questioning also hinted at other concerns. Frohlich and Seltzer were dissatisfied with Woolley's explanation for why his staff took no further action to address the piping support problems after the April 1977 work request was canceled. Several deposition questions suggested that Woolley and his subordinate, Balogh, had failed to warn CPD that an inadequately supported overhead pipe might fail and cause a hazardous condition. Perhaps the consultant Hirshman called attention to this potential hazard and made Frohlich fear that Woolley's inattention to the problem could have caused a serious industrial accident. Other questions suggested that Woolley failed to follow instructions from Mayerchak to include in his report drawings of the original design work for piping supports. Roche management may have concluded that Woolley was trying to avoid responsibility for errors in the original design.

Although Woolley himself acknowledged that one of the original drawings failed to show a guide on a pipe support in sufficient detail, he also testified that "there was nothing in those drawings to hide." According to his counsel, Woolley's view of the situation was that he had been unfairly singled out as a scapegoat for the problems with the Vitamin E plant.[26] He contended that his report described both the actions his staff had taken to correct the problems and the obstacles that they encountered. Seltzer condemned his failure to take "corrective action from April 1977 when many of the current problems were recognized by the design department as part of the CPD/Engineering Problem–Solving Program."[27] Woolley pointed out, however, that his staff had not participated in the CPD/Engineering troubleshooting committee. His group's only involvement with repair efforts began with the April 1977 work request and ended in November 1977 when that request

---

[26] Telephone interview with Gerald Wahl (July 21, 2005).

[27] Letter from David Seltzer to Richard Woolley dated June 12, 1978.

was canceled. As Woolley later speculated "that is probably where all the problems [began] because once a client cancels a project, we ... cannot charge any time to it."[28] He believed that company policy precluded him from acting independently to call attention to problems with piping supports. While Seltzer's letter faulted him for not "sternly protesting to departmental management" about the need for immediate corrective action, Woolley understood that his role was simply to provide technical assistance to the plant engineers. The corporate organization chart may help explain the reactive approach that Woolley pursued. Primary responsibility rested with the project engineering group and with the plant engineer for Building 55. On this view, Frohlich's offhand suggestion that "maybe we should change the organization chart" looks very much like an implicit admission that the intricate structure of the Roche corporate hierarchy impeded the prompt resolution of the piping problems in the Vitamin E plant.

Perhaps the most likely explanation for Woolley's termination is that his staff was deeply involved in a project that became a significant headache for Roche management. Frohlich appears to have told Seltzer to find out who was responsible for the production problems and to hold that person accountable. Touring the plant with Hirshman undoubtedly alarmed Frohlich enough to undermine his confidence in Woolley's judgment. In contrast, Woolley's account was that he and his staff participated in the initial design effort and provided a thorough progress report when the project engineer George Scott terminated their involvement. In response to the April 1977 work request, they diagnosed the piping problems and provided CPD with several remedial options. The cancellation of the work request again brought their involvement with the Vitamin E plant to a halt. The admittedly limited evidence available to us suggests that Woolley and his subordinates worked conscientiously and competently within the constraints imposed by Roche's corporate structure.

The fact remains that Vitamin E production suffered frequent interruptions, and Roche experienced unusually high maintenance costs for Building 55. In the end, Woolley, along with George Scott, seems to have borne the brunt of management's frustration over these ongoing production and maintenance problems. However, one of the great ironies connected with Woolley's termination is that these very same problems appear to have continued even after piping repairs were completed. Woolley had warned that the pipe support work was "not going to be a cure all," and an August 15th inter-office memorandum from CPD to Dr. Frohlich confirmed that "they were still dissatisfied with the plant. It

---

[28] Deposition of Richard M. Woolley (Dec. 17, 1979).

was still not operating."[29] An earlier memo from the Vitamin E plant manager had identified some fifty problems, of which concern about missing piping supports was only one. It thus appears that other issues such as malfunctioning instruments and various process defects were at least equally responsible for the frequent disruptions of Vitamin E production.

Prior Proceedings

INITIAL PROCEEDINGS IN THE TRIAL COURT

Sometime after his formal termination in July 1978, Woolley contacted Haynes & Donnelly, a Detroit law firm that had developed a national reputation for plaintiff-side employment litigation.[30] One of the name partners, Paul Donnelly, focused especially on age discrimination claims and had created a successful practice in that area. Gerald Wahl, who had recently joined the firm, assumed responsibility for Woolley's case. By this time, the Michigan Supreme Court had heard oral argument in *Toussaint v. Blue Cross & Blue Shield*, and though a final decision would not be issued until June 1980, Wahl was familiar with the plaintiff's arguments in that case. He believed that the plaintiff's approach in *Toussaint* suited Woolley's circumstances equally well and that courts in New Jersey would be just as receptive to the implied contract theory as the Michigan Supreme Court ultimately proved to be. As we will soon see, the *Woolley* opinion cited and relied extensively on the reasoning of *Toussaint*. However, the involvement of a Michigan law firm and Wahl's prescient hunch about New Jersey's willingness to embrace these arguments show that the jurisdictional cross-pollination in this area of employment law goes much deeper than is apparent from the text of the court's opinion alone.

On June 12, 1979, Woolley filed a complaint in three counts, two of which he later dropped. The remaining count was an implied contract claim alleging that Roche had made representations in "various personnel policy handbooks and other employee information booklets [that] as long as his performance was satisfactory, [Woolley] would be employed by defendant corporation until he wished to retire." Attached to the complaint as Exhibit A were nine pages excerpted from the Roche Personnel Policy Manual.[31] Woolley's complaint called particular attention to several alleged assurances of job security. The manual provided: "It is the policy of Hoffmann–La Roche to retain to the extent consistent with company requirements, the services of all employees who perform

---

[29] Id.

[30] Telephone interview with Gerald Wahl (July 21, 2005).

[31] The policy manual excerpts are available in an online Appendix to this chapter at http://www.verkerke.net/stories.

their duties efficiently and effectively." And it assured employees that the company "would like to insure that every reasonable step has been taken to help the employee continue in a productive capacity." Finally, Woolley allegedly relied on provisions in the manual that established procedures to be followed before termination. Taken together, he claimed that the provisions of the manual were a "firm offer" that he accepted by continuing his employment with Roche. The complaint thus concluded that when Roche terminated him without good cause and failed to follow the procedures specified in the manual, the company breached an implied contract to treat Woolley "in a just and fair manner with continued employment until he chose to retire."

During the discovery phase of the litigation, the parties exchanged document requests and interrogatories. Roche attorneys also took Woolley's deposition. Although the record contains a complete transcript of the questioning, it unfortunately omits the seventeen documentary exhibits that the parties produced at the deposition. Similarly, the record on appeal includes only very limited excerpts from plaintiff's and defendant's responses to interrogatories. Woolley gave notice that he intended to depose five Roche managers. Once Roche filed a motion for summary judgment on Woolley's remaining implied contract claim, however, the parties agreed to postpone those depositions. They reasoned that the legal issue of whether Roche's policy manual provisions could form the basis for an enforceable contract did not depend on any evidence that questioning Roche officials might reveal. Presumably, plaintiff's counsel would have used those depositions to explore in greater detail the events leading up to Woolley's termination. The examination undoubtedly would have shed additional light on whether Roche had good cause for firing, how carefully Woolley's superiors investigated his performance, and whether they seriously considered alternatives to termination. As we will soon see, however, the case settled shortly after the New Jersey Supreme Court issued its ruling.

Roche's Motion for Summary Judgment

On February 6, 1981, Superior Court Judge Nicholas Scalera held a hearing on Roche's motion for summary judgment. This motion framed the issue that the *Woolley* decision would ultimately resolve—whether statements in the company's Personnel Policy Manual concerning job security were legally sufficient to give Woolley contractual protection against termination without good cause. Arguing the motion for Hoffmann–La Roche was Frederick C. Kentz, III, a partner with the Newark business law firm of Crummy, Del Deo, Dolan & Purcell. Kentz later joined Roche as in-house counsel and currently holds the title of Vice President and General Counsel for the company's U.S. operations. Gerald Wahl, who, as we have seen, was a partner in the Detroit firm of

Haynes & Donnelly, represented Woolley and argued the motion for the plaintiff. Attorneys for both sides respected Judge Scalera, and Kentz has described him as a "good judge."[32] Their respect appears to have been justified. The transcript of the oral argument reveals an active and intellectually engaged judge who consistently pushed counsel to grapple with difficult issues. He posed challenging questions, and though he treated Kentz and Wahl respectfully, both attorneys had uncomfortable moments during the argument.

Judge Scalera especially pressed Kentz to reconcile Roche's position with the line of cases, including *Anthony*, which had enforced handbook severance pay promises as unilateral contracts. Kentz gamely distinguished *Anthony* on the ground that severance pay obligations were a "peculiar right or ... benefit" and thus unlike the more general claim that an employer must have good cause for termination. Kentz also urged an aggressive reading of the decision in *Pierce*, suggesting that the court had impliedly endorsed the demanding standards for contractual enforcement imposed in older New Jersey cases such as *Savarese*, *Hindle*, and *Bird*.[33] Employers thus would be safe from liability unless they fired an employee for reasons that violated public policy. Judge Scalera countered that Justice Pollock's majority opinion seemed to signal a willingness to reexamine the traditional at-will presumption in light of "the realities of modern economics and employment practices."

Picking up on this theme, Wahl found Judge Scalera a receptive audience for his argument that both *Pierce* and *Toussaint* strongly supported plaintiff's position. The *Pierce* decision revealed, in the judge's words, "a philosophy of our Supreme Court," and suggested that the court would be more receptive in the future to arguments seeking to erode the at-will presumption. Borrowing a concept from *Toussaint*, Wahl characterized employment-at-will as a rule of construction rather than a fixed substantive doctrine. However, Judge Scalera was skeptical that New Jersey law would allow him to construe a policy manual statement as an enforceable contract. Prior cases, such as *Piechowski v. Matarese*,[34] tended to enforce only promises for which employees gave additional consideration and refused to enforce those supported solely by continued employment.

Wahl rose to the challenge of identifying additional consideration. He argued that Woolley "performed more, he gave extra effort to his job, he stayed in his employment and had a different attitude," and that the

---

[32] Telephone interview with Frederick Kentz (Aug. 9, 2005).

[33] *See Savarese v. Pyrene Mfg. Co.*, 89 A.2d 237 (N.J. 1952), *Hindle v. Morrison Steel Co.*, 223 A.2d 193 (N.J. Super. Ct. 1966), *Bird v. J. L. Prescott Co.*, 99 A. 380 (N.J. 1916).

[34] 54 N.J. Super. 333, 148 A.2d 872 (N.J. App. Div. 1959).

company benefited from enhanced employee morale. Judge Scalera then helpfully echoed an idea that Woolley had first advanced during his deposition testimony, suggesting that Roche included a "for cause" provision in its policy manual in order to forestall unionization and avoid the burden of collective bargaining. Wahl willingly embraced this suggestion, which the New Jersey Supreme Court later would discuss approvingly.[35] Judge Scalera also asked Wahl if it would be permissible for the company to announce on Monday that it was rescinding the manual and then, on Tuesday, to tell Woolley, or any other employee, that he was fired without cause. Adopting a surprisingly pro-employer position, Wahl eagerly conceded that Roche retained the unilateral right to modify any provision of its manual.

> MR. WAHL: They could say all the rules are over with, [Roche] could change its personnel policies.
>
> THE COURT: In other words, they could say on Monday to everybody forget the manual it is no longer effective?
>
> MR. WAHL: That's correct.
>
> THE COURT: Okay, and then Tuesday they could say to Mr. Woolley you are fired?
>
> MR. WAHL: That's correct. . . .

As we will see towards the end of this chapter, courts have divided sharply between those that require independent consideration to support modification of a handbook and those that permit modification with no more than reasonable notice to employees.

Judge Scalera prefaced his oral ruling from the bench by acknowledging that *Pierce* reflected a "changing philosophy" in New Jersey and musing that "from a moral point of view" Woolley's plight appeared "most unfair." As a lower court judge, however, he felt bound to follow prior decisions such as *Savarese*, *Hindle*, and *Piechowski*, which had required exceptionally convincing proof that an employer intended to make a "long-range commitment." Any such agreement "must be clearly, specifically and definitely expressed," and the court must also consider whether "the employee gave some consideration additional to the mere agreement on his part to render services." Despite his evident sympathy for Woolley's situation, Judge Scalera reiterated that "absent a specific and definite contract" the employer has "unbridled authority to discharge an employee with or without cause." In his view, cases such as *Toussaint* were simply inconsistent with prior New Jersey decisions, and he was not free to deviate from those binding precedents. Finding that Woolley had failed to allege sufficient evidence of an agreement not to discharge him for other than good cause, the court granted defen-

---

[35] *Woolley v. Hoffmann–La Roche Corp.*, 491 A.2d 1257, 1264 (N.J. 1985).

dant's summary judgment motion and subsequently issued an order dismissing Woolley's complaint with prejudice.[36]

Briefs Submitted to the Appellate Division

On June 2, 1981, Woolley filed a timely notice of appeal. Surprisingly, the brief that his attorneys later submitted to the Appellate Division of the Superior Court of New Jersey was rife with typographical errors, transposed numbers, misspellings and missing words. Although not quite stream of consciousness in style, the brief lacked a clear structure and drifted somewhat aimlessly from point to point. It included a number of powerful arguments, but the overall effect on a reader was considerably less forceful and persuasive than a more orderly presentation would have been.

Woolley's brief largely reiterated and further elaborated arguments that he had presented to the trial court. It sensibly portrayed *Pierce v. Ortho Pharmaceutical* as symbolic of a national trend towards greater legal protection for employees, and extracted from *Toussaint* the broader policy argument that a court should protect an employee's "reasonable expectations" of job security. As the Michigan court put the point:

> It is enough that the employer chooses, presumably in its own interest, to create an environment in which the employee believes that, whatever the personnel policies and practices, they are established and official at any given time, purport to be fair, and are applied consistently and uniformly to each employee. The employer has then created a situation "instinct with an obligation." . . . Having announced the policy, presumably with a view to obtain the benefit of improved employee attitudes and behavior and improved quality of the workforce, the employer may not treat its promise as illusory.[37]

Anticipating a theme that would later figure prominently in academic commentary,[38] Woolley's brief condemned mutuality of obligation as "an outmoded legal concept." The brief also invoked the interpretive maxim that contractual ambiguities "should be construed against the [drafter] of the agreement."

Roche's brief was considerably more polished. It was clear, forceful, and well organized with very few typographical errors. The statement of

---

[36] *See Woolley v. Hoffmann–La Roche Inc.* No. L–50173–78E (N.J. Sup. Ct. Essex Cty. Feb. 27, 1981) (order granting defendant's motion for summary judgment).

[37] *Toussaint*, 292 N.W.2d 880, 892, 895 (Mich. 1980).

[38] Clyde W. Summers, *The Contract of Employment and the Rights of Individual Employees: Fair Representation and Employment at Will*, 52 Fordham L. Rev. 1082, 1082–87 (1984).

facts particularly emphasized that Mayerchak told Woolley just how concerned Dr. Frohlich was about the maintenance problems in the Vitamin E plant. Mayerchak had even warned that Frohlich's concerns were so serious that Woolley might be fired. In short, the brief suggested that Woolley was well aware of the company's dissatisfaction with his performance. The brief also described how Roche management deliberated carefully before deciding to request Woolley's resignation. In addition, the company had offered him eleven weeks' severance pay, paid time off to seek new employment, and an opportunity to receive professional personnel counseling. The brief thus painted a picture of a thoughtful, measured, and humane corporate decision-making process.

According to Roche, *Pierce* confirmed a "continuous line of decisions in New Jersey holding that only after a demonstration of sufficient definiteness and specificity will a court 'grudgingly' find a permanent contract."[39] Companies in New Jersey had formed employment relationships in reliance on this strong at-will presumption, and it would upset their well-settled expectations to entertain Woolley's claim. Disgruntled employees throughout the state would use a ruling in Woolley's favor to spin contractually enforceable protection out of innocent strands of policy manual language. These "bits and pieces gathered by aggrieved employees" would force employers to go to trial to defend their reasons for dismissing employees and invite courts to interfere with legitimate managerial prerogatives. Roche cautioned that creating a new cause of action based on policy manual statements would open the "floodgates" and allow "every disgruntled terminated employee" a chance to obtain judicial review of dismissal decisions. As we will see, the *Woolley* opinion repeatedly invites employers to use disclaimers to ensure that the floodgates for handbook claims remain firmly closed.[40]

DECISION OF THE APPELLATE DIVISION

The Appellate Division issued a *per curiam* opinion on June 1, 1982, barely two weeks after the case had been submitted for decision.[41] The court's perfunctory nine-page opinion treated Woolley's claim as a routine matter that fell squarely within the prior New Jersey case law on contracts for lifetime employment. The court broadly endorsed the trial judge's reasoning but offered little analysis of its own to justify upholding the dismissal of Woolley's suit.

---

[39] See Brief for Defendant–Respondent at 13 (quoting *Savarese v. Pyrene Mfg. Co.*, 89 A.2d 237, 240 (N.J. 1952)).

[40] 491 A.2d at 1257, 1269–71 (N.J. 1985).

[41] *Woolley v. Hoffmann–La Roche, Inc.*, No. A–4101–80T1 (N.J. Sup. Ct. App. Div. June 1, 1982) (submitted May 17, 1982).

Remarkably, the Appellate Division opinion contained no mention whatsoever of the cases that figured most prominently in the parties' briefs. The court ignored both Roche's argument that the New Jersey Supreme Court's decision in *Pierce* had reaffirmed the traditional at-will presumption and Woolley's rejoinder that the case's reasoning signaled a new willingness to erode that same presumption. Even more surprisingly, the Appellate Division thought to distinguish the comparatively obscure *Carter v. Kaskaskia Community Action Agency*[42] case but said nothing at all about the Michigan Supreme Court's far more influential *Toussaint* decision. Woolley had relied heavily on *Toussaint*, and Roche devoted considerable effort to rebutting his arguments. In light of this glaring oversight, one might question whether the Appellate Division judges even bothered to read the admittedly long and involved opinions in *Toussaint*.[43]

Whatever the explanation for its cursory analysis, the appeals court clearly viewed affirmance as the only plausible decision on these facts. In contrast, the transcript of the oral argument before Judge Scalera reveals a far more subtle and probing investigation of the issues. He considered carefully the proper interpretation of *Pierce*, the potential relevance of *Toussaint*, the issue of reliance, and even whether employers should be permitted to modify existing policy manuals. While Judge Scalera appears to have sensed its potential importance, the Appellate Division panel apparently did not, and its opinion shed no new light on the case.

The New Jersey Supreme Court Decision
INITIAL BRIEFING IN THE NEW JERSEY SUPREME COURT

Woolley promptly petitioned the New Jersey Supreme Court to certify an appeal of the Appellate Division's affirmance of summary judgment for Roche. Although the parties largely relied on the briefs they had filed with the court below, the very first page of Woolley's petition for certification framed the issues more effectively than anything he had submitted thus far in the litigation. Woolley contended:

> The egregious effect of the Appellate Division affirmation is: To allow New Jersey employers to promulgate personnel policy manuals, which both entice employees to work for and remain in the employ of the Defendant and which provide benefits to both the employee and employer, and then allow the employer to choose which to be bound by, [sic] but not all of the employee safeguards

---

[42] 322 N.E.2d 574 (Ill. App. 1974).

[43] The case was decided along with a companion case, *Ebling v. Masco Corp.*, 292 N.W.2d 880 (Mich. 1980), and together the cases fill thirty-six pages of the regional reporter.

and benefits included in its manual; and to provide no sufficient standard on which this distinction is to be based, thereby leaving employees with no guidance on which provisions of the manual they may justifiably rely [sic] on.

This passage is hardly a model of clear and precise legal writing, but it encapsulated concisely two arguments that ultimately proved persuasive to the New Jersey Supreme Court. First, it pointed out that employers are responsible for issuing policy manuals and that they presumably derive benefits from doing so. Second, Woolley implicitly invited the court to apply what I have described as a legal-information-forcing theory. He cast Roche as a legally sophisticated party that should be held responsible for any misunderstanding the company's policy manual may have created. In contrast, comparatively unsophisticated employees need clear "guidance" about when they may rely on the provisions of a manual. As we will soon see, the court translated Woolley's call for guidance into a requirement that employers must clearly disclaim any intent to provide contractually enforceable job security.

Woolley's petition also shrewdly focused the court's attention on New Jersey severance pay cases such as *Anthony*. According to Woolley, the lower court's decision drew an unprincipled distinction between enforceable severance provisions and unenforceable statements concerning job security. He argued that severance pay promises contained in policy manuals generally were no more specific or definite than similar commitments not to terminate employees without just cause. Moreover, the Roche manual itself contained both types of provisions. Woolley's petition argued that neither the court below nor existing case law offered employees any intelligible standard for deciding which statements gave rise to binding commitments and which did not.

The balance of the petition for certification focused on prior case law that the Appellate Division had so surprisingly ignored. Its cursory opinion had utterly failed to "analyze or acknowledge similar cases from other courts"—most prominently *Toussaint*—and contained nary a mention of the New Jersey Supreme Court's own recent decision in *Pierce*. The parties also exchanged sharply pointed arguments concerning the relevance of a case in which the New Jersey Supreme Court had recently denied certification. According to Roche, "employers and employees in this State have known for the past century that unless a contract of employment specifically and definitely sets forth the critical and necessary terms for a permanent contract for life, our courts will hold that the employment relationship is one terminable at will." Roche maintained that the court had recently refused to certify an appeal in *Dickhaus v. Jersey Central Power and Light*,[44] a case that allegedly involved facts and

---

[44] 446 A.2d 156 (N.J. 1982).

arguments "identical" to those of Woolley's suit. Woolley, in turn, contended that *Dickhaus* was distinguishable on the ground that Roche's Personnel Policy Manual was "clearly more specific and definite as to the obligations and duties of the employer" than the "general rules" at issue in *Dickhaus*.

TRAGEDY INTERVENES IN THE LITIGATION

Apparently convinced that Woolley's case was distinguishable from *Dickhaus*, the New Jersey Supreme Court certified an appeal and set a date for oral argument. But before the court could hear his case, Woolley died tragically in an auto accident. On November 26, 1982, the day after Thanksgiving, Woolley and his wife Susan were returning from dropping off their daughter at school. According to a newspaper account of the accident, Susan was driving when she apparently lost control of the car on Route 206 in Frankfort Township, Sussex County, New Jersey. Another car hit their vehicle broadside, and both Richard and Susan died the same day at the nearby Newton Memorial Hospital. Richard Woolley was fifty-seven years old at the time of his death. Susan Woolley was forty-one.

Although Woolley's untimely death did not postpone the upcoming New Jersey Supreme Court argument, it surely cast a pall over the litigation and affected how several issues in the case were resolved. First, Woolley's death deprived his survivors of both his testimony and his assistance in preparing for an eventual trial. It thus would have been far more difficult for them to produce convincing evidence that his discharge was unjust. Concern about this problem led the Supreme Court to rule, at least initially, that Roche would be precluded from arguing at trial that the company had good cause to terminate Woolley. Second, as we will soon see, Woolley's death dramatically affected the calculation of damages.

SUPPLEMENTAL BRIEFING

In December 1982, shortly after Woolley's tragic accident, the New Jersey Supreme Court granted a motion from Woolley's attorneys to file a supplemental brief concerning "new" law and, somewhat surprisingly, received a submission that devoted a mere three and one-half out of fourteen pages to discussing a case decided after Woolley's initial brief was filed. Instead, Woolley's counsel took the opportunity to reiterate their legal and policy arguments for reversal.

Much more than halfway through his brief on "new" law, Woolley finally argued that the New York Court of Appeals' recent decision in *Weiner v. McGraw Hill*[45] "clearly overrule[d]" *Chin v. American Tel. &*

---

[45] 443 N.E.2d 441 (N.Y. 1982) (filed on Nov. 18, 1982).

Tel. Co.,[46] an earlier New York case on which the Appellate Division had relied.[47]

There was, however, considerable irony in Woolley's decision to rely on *Weiner*. The case is notable for its holding that plaintiffs must demonstrate actual reliance on an employee handbook in order to maintain an implied contract claim. Moreover, Weiner's proof of reliance was far more substantial than Woolley's. Weiner left a job with a competitor largely on the strength of the assurances of job security that he received from McGraw–Hill management. Those assurances included an oral representation that the company had a firm policy not to terminate employees without just cause and an employee handbook, which promised that "the company will resort to dismissal for just and sufficient cause only, and only after practical steps toward rehabilitation or salvage of the employee have been taken and failed." Challenging Woolley's contention that *Weiner* overruled *Chin*, Roche pointed out that the New York Court of Appeals had not mentioned *Chin*. Moreover, the company argued that the *Weiner* decision rested heavily on facts that "demonstrated a conscious effort to negotiate an agreement terminable only for cause."

At Long Last an Opinion

The New Jersey Supreme Court heard oral argument on March 21, 1983, a little less than two weeks after receiving the last of the supplemental briefs. Frederick Kentz, who had handled Roche's defense throughout the litigation, once again argued for the defendant. On the plaintiff's side, Gerald Wahl was unable to make the trip to New Jersey, and so Timothy G. Hagan, another attorney from the Donnelly law firm in Detroit, stepped in at the last possible minute to handle the oral argument. He received the case file on Thursday, spent a couple of days familiarizing himself with the record, flew out to New Jersey, and argued the case the following Monday morning.[48] Although no transcript of the oral argument is available, Hagan reports that it became clear very early in the argument that the court intended to reverse the dismissal of Woolley's contract claim. The justices particularly pressed Kentz to explain why *Savarese* was correctly decided. They appeared to be skeptical about the special requirements for contract formation that this and other older cases had imposed. The questions for Hagan were less challenging and focused mostly on the consequences of Woolley's death. Hagan particularly sought to convince the court that *Anthony*'s analysis

---

[46] 410 N.Y.S.2d 737 (Sup. Ct. N.Y. Cty. 1978).

[47] *See Woolley v. Hoffmann–La Roche, Inc.*, No. A–4101–80T1 at 7–8 (N.J. Sup. Ct. App. Div. June 1, 1982).

[48] Telephone interview with Timothy G. Hagan (Nov. 22, 2005).

of severance pay promises should govern job security provisions as well. Even so, he acknowledged in an interview that he felt fortunate to have won; he had argued similar cases elsewhere that were unsuccessful.

The court issued a unanimous opinion on May 9, 1985, more than two years after hearing oral argument. It is difficult to know precisely what caused this long delay between argument and decision, but the opinion's author, Chief Justice Wilentz, wrote less often and tended to take much longer to issue opinions than his colleagues. During the three-year period surrounding the *Woolley* decision, the court produced 213 opinions and averaged 5.7 months between argument and decision.[49] During the same period, Wilentz authored ten opinions, averaging 10.3 months between argument and decision. Two of these opinions, including *Woolley*, took over two years from argument to decision, and those were the only New Jersey Supreme Court cases during this period that took so long to decide.

The court began with the at-will presumption. Citing student notes from the Harvard, Hastings, and Stanford law reviews,[50] the opinion observed that the "at-will rule has come under severe criticism from commentators who argue that the economic justifications for the development of the rule have changed dramatically and no longer support its harshness." The court eagerly embraced Woolley's argument that its own prior decision in *Pierce* was a harbinger of change in New Jersey law. Quoting precisely the passages that Woolley identified in his brief, the court cautioned that "any application of the employee-at-will rule (not just its application in conflict with 'a clear mandate of public policy'—the precise issue in *Pierce*) must be tested by its legitimacy today and not by its acceptance yesterday." The court thus read *Pierce* to signal a new approach to the employment relationship, one that allowed judges to consider the "underlying interests involved" and determine that the employer must comply "with certain rudimentary agreements voluntarily extended to the employees."

After setting this reform-minded tone, the court distinguished *Savarese* and similar precedents on the ground that those cases involved *individual* contracts for lifetime employment rather than terms "put forth by the employer as applicable to all employees." The court acknowledged that the overwhelming majority of jurisdictions flatly re-

---

[49] My thanks to Ben Doherty of the University of Virginia Law Library for designing the necessary Westlaw searches and calculating these figures.

[50] Note, *Protecting At Will Employees Against Wrongful Discharge: The Duty to Terminate Only in Good Faith*, 93 Harv. L. Rev. 1816 (1980); Comment, *A Common Law Action for the Abusively Discharged Employee*, 26 Hastings L.J. 1435 (1975); J. Peter Shapiro & James F. Tune, Comment, *Implied Contract Rights To Job Security*, 26 Stan. L. Rev. 335 (1974).

fused to enforce employee handbook provisions. These out-of-state cases, however, confused policy manual provisions with individual long-term contracts and therefore applied doctrinal rules that were appropriate only, if at all, for individual agreements. Expressly invoking the Michigan Supreme Court's reasoning in *Toussaint*, the court rejected the special requirements of additional consideration and specificity of terms. The strong at-will presumption that those requirements produced was merely a rule of construction designed to help courts "discover and implement the intent of the parties." Liberated from the constraining influence of these precedents involving "individual long-term employment contracts," Chief Justice Wilentz announced that "if there is a contract, it is one for a group of employees—sometimes all of them—for an indefinite term, and here, fairly read, one that may not be terminated by the employer without good cause." The court found no reason "to treat such a document with hostility."

Turning to the question of the employer's motivation for including job security terms in the policy manual, the court echoed Judge Scalera's speculation that without those terms collective bargaining would be "more likely." Roche thus promulgated the manual in order to avoid unionization. Although somewhat more measured than the trial judge's assertion that "[t]here is no question in my mind that Hoffmann–La Roche offered these good benefits to their employees to steer them away from ... collective bargaining," both statements significantly exaggerate the importance of this motive for the company's actions. Roche's outside counsel at the time reports that the company had never faced a union organizing drive or even the hint of unrest or dissatisfaction among employees.[51] Moreover, contemporary news reports contain no suggestion that Roche was vulnerable to organizing efforts. Somewhat ironically, Woolley himself was quite clearly a supervisory employee who would have been excluded from any bargaining unit that might have been formed at Roche. There can be no doubt that treating employees well tends generally to deter union organizing efforts. Nevertheless, both the trial judge and the New Jersey Supreme Court appear to have overestimated significantly any threat of unionization that Roche may have faced.

There is, however, a far more plausible account of the company's motivation for issuing the Personnel Policy Manual—Roche sought to control its supervisors and prevent them from terminating productive employees. The fact that the company distributed the policy manual only to "supervisory employees" tends to support this interpretation. According to the court, "it would seem clear that it was intended by Hoffman–La Roche that all employees be advised of the benefits [the manual]

---

[51] Telephone interview with Frederick Kentz (Aug. 9, 2005).

confers." Contrary to the court's assertion that Roche wanted all employees to know about the terms of the manual, however, Woolley testified in his deposition that there was no systematic effort to disseminate the provisions of the manual to rank-and-file employees. If Roche was so concerned about the threat of unionization, why would the company restrict the distribution of its policy manual to only those employees who were statutorily ineligible for collective bargaining? This pattern of distribution suggests instead that the manual was intended to guide the exercise of supervisory authority. Managers might violate company policy and discharge good employees inadvertently or intentionally, but in either case the policy manual, coupled with what Woolley himself described as vigorous enforcement of its terms by the Roche personnel department, would tend primarily to protect the company's interest in retaining productive workers. Indeed, the court itself conceded that the company "almost invariably honored" the policy manual provisions despite the fact that it did not consider them legally enforceable. In short, Roche argued that it treated Woolley and other employees fairly even though "it had no legal obligation to do so."

The court next explained why it thought that the termination clauses of Roche's policy manual "could be found to be contractually enforceable." Summarizing its earlier rejection of restrictive prior precedents, the opinion asserted that:

> [if an employer] circulates a manual that, when fairly read, provides that certain benefits are an incident of employment (including, especially, job security provisions), the judiciary, instead of "grudgingly" conceding the enforceability of those provisions, should construe them in accordance with the reasonable expectations of the employees.

The importance of this move from "grudging enforcement" to "reasonable expectations" can hardly be overstated. It was the crux of the court's reasoning. The decision rested ultimately on shifting a presumption. Rather than assuming that employers needed to be protected against unwanted contractual commitments, the court embraced an approach designed to protect employees. If employee handbooks and policy manuals contained language giving rise to reasonable expectations of job security, they would be presumptively enforceable The court's approach to these terms reversed preexisting case law and required employers to overcome a new presumption of enforceability.

Interestingly, however, none of plaintiff's briefs explicitly advanced this reasonable-expectations basis for enforcement. Nor did they propose the distinction between individual lifetime employment contracts and policy manuals that the *Woolley* court used to distinguish adverse precedents. Instead, Woolley focused on showing that statements in

Roche's policy manual met the demanding standards that prior cases had enunciated. Nevertheless, his attorneys may have profoundly influenced the court's reasoning through a less direct route. First, they emphasized repeatedly the court's own prior expression of misgivings in *Pierce* about the strength of the at-will presumption. As we have seen, the court readily accepted the notion that *Pierce* should be understood as a harbinger of change. Second, plaintiff's briefs quoted extensively from the Michigan Supreme Court's opinion in *Toussaint*. The *Woolley* court appears to have taken the reasoning of *Toussaint* very much to heart. Chief Justice Wilentz quoted a passage from *Toussaint* to justify rejecting the applicability of older cases involving individual claims for "lifetime employment." As we will see, the court similarly relied on a lengthy quotation from *Toussaint* to explain why there should be no requirement that employees prove reliance on the handbook terms that they seek to enforce. It also seems likely that the court derived its "reasonable expectations" standard for the enforceability of policy manual statements from *Toussaint*'s very similar analysis of employees' "legitimate expectations" of job security. None of the prior New Jersey cases contained language suggesting a "reasonable expectations" standard, and we should not let the subtle change from "legitimate" to "reasonable" expectations obscure the influence of the earlier Michigan decision on this case. Indeed, it was the Donnelly firm's experience litigating cases under *Toussaint* that led Woolley to seek out counsel from Detroit. It appears that, in this respect at least, Woolley chose wisely.

The court also rejected the notion that Roche's policy manual merely expressed the company's "philosophy" concerning labor relations and thus should have no contractual consequences. Its analysis followed precisely the pattern of an information-forcing rationale for enforcement.[52] According to the court, the manual had "all of the appearances of corporate legitimacy that one could imagine." A statement of official company policy was authoritative, and thus employees were justified in regarding the policy manual as "the most reliable statement of the terms of their employment." Moreover, these attractive terms were offered as an inducement to the workforce, and they involved "the single most important objective of the workforce: job security." The court emphasized employees' lack of sophistication. They "undoubtedly know little about contracts, and many probably would be unable to analyze the language and terms of the manual." Whatever Roche may have intended, the court believed that employees could read the policy manual as a promise not to fire them except for good cause. Repeatedly, the court stressed that the more sophisticated party should bear the burden of any ambiguity in the policy manual. The employer—the more sophisticated party—thus bore the burden of informing the legally less sophisticated

---

[52] *See* J. H. Verkerke, *Legal Ignorance.*

parties—its employees—that they were employed at will and that the termination provisions of the policy manual were not legally enforceable.

Having announced its intention to protect employees' "reasonable expectations," the court next confronted a challenging technical problem. How would conventional contract doctrine permit it to enforce an employee handbook or policy manual? The court ultimately concluded that Roche's manual could be construed as an offer of a unilateral contract that Woolley and other employees accepted by showing up for work, but the doctrinal path to this result proved remarkably circuitous. The most formidable obstacle to enforcement was the need to establish that employees provided consideration for the policy manual terms. Even if we were to assume for the sake of argument that a company genuinely sought continued work in exchange for policy manual provisions concerning job security, unilateral contract doctrine requires that employees be aware of the terms of the offer and provide their efforts in exchange for these promises. We know that Woolley did not receive Roche's handbook until several weeks after he started work. He also testified rather vaguely at his deposition about when he first read the specific provisions on which he based his claim. Thus, Woolley would have faced an uphill battle attempting to prove that he had continued to work for Roche in exchange for the job security provisions of the manual.

Chief Justice Wilentz recognized this problem and offered a solution based entirely on the reasoning of *Toussaint*. In a passage quoted at length in the *Woolley* opinion,[53] the Michigan court had adopted a theory of enforcement that dispensed with most formal doctrinal requirements for contract formation. Employees need not have negotiated for job security or even have known anything at all about a company's policy manual, and it made no difference if an employer reserved the right to change its policies unilaterally. Instead, the court found that the employer created "a situation 'instinct with an obligation' " to abide by whatever policies it had promulgated. The *Woolley* court thus joined *Toussaint* and *Anthony* in concluding that it was unnecessary for a plaintiff to produce any evidence that he relied on the employer's promise. The court conclusively presumed consideration, using a legal fiction to eliminate the biggest obstacle to the success of plaintiffs such as Woolley.

Similarly, the court brushed aside Roche's objection that the terms of its policy manual were too indefinite to warrant contractual enforcement. Distinguishing again between "a lifetime contract with one employee" and an agreement with an employer's "entire workforce," the opinion suggested that judicial review of good cause would demand of employers no more than "[e]ven-handedness and equality of treatment." Far more interesting, however, was the extent to which the court's

---

[53] *Woolley*, 491 A.2d at 1268 (quoting *Toussaint v. Blue Cross & Blue Shield of Mich.*, 292 N.W.2d 880, 892 (Mich. 1980)).

reasoning relied on an information-forcing rationale for enforcement. The court opined that:

> If there is a problem of indefiniteness ... it is one caused by the employer. It was the employer who chose to make the termination provisions explicit and clear. If indefiniteness as to other provisions is a problem, it is one of the employer's own making from which it should gain no advantage.
>
> * * *
>
> If ... the at-will employment status of the workforce was so important, the employer should not have circulated a document so likely to lead employees into believing they had job security.
>
> * * *
>
> It would be unfair to allow an employer to distribute a policy manual that makes the workforce believe that certain promises have been made and then to allow the employer to renege on those promises.

These passages present a classic information-forcing argument. The court blamed the comparatively sophisticated party for any ambiguity and invoked the *contra proferentum* norm to support a liberal reading of the policy manual provisions. Its approach imposed on the employer the burden of making workers' at-will status clear to them.

As we have already seen, however, a fair reading of the Roche Personnel Policy Manual suggests that the company adopted it solely to ensure that its supervisory employees would follow company mandated personnel procedures. The language of the manual was replete with qualifying phrases and spoke of what Roche managers "should" do rather than what they "must" do. The manual described itself as a "practical operating tool" for the "administration" of the company's "employee relations program." It merely stated a "philosophy" concerning terminations and aimed to provide "uniform guidelines" for administering company policies.[54] The manual surely did not hint that Roche intended to grant a legally enforceable right to protection against termination without good cause. However, workers often appear to have trouble distinguishing informal expressions of company policy or corporate culture from legally enforceable rights.[55] An employee conceivably could have read the manual's statement of termination policies and

---

[54] For additional examples, see Guidelines for Discharge Due to Performance ("We would like to ensure ..."; "each manager and supervisor should consider ..."; "... joint evaluation between the employee and manager is recommended"; "the employee should be given time, if possible, to remedy the situation"; "manager should also be considering ..."; "supervisor should then proceed ...") available at http://www.verkerke.net/stories.

[55] *See* Pauline T. Kim, *Norms, Learning and the Law: Exploring the Influences on Workers' Legal Knowledge*, 1999 U. Ill. L. Rev. 447; Jesse Rudy, *What They Don't Know*

procedures as expressing a binding commitment on the part of the company. The court's rule thus sought to protect unsophisticated employees by forcing their legally sophisticated employer to clarify the situation.

This information-forcing rationale lent support to the legal fiction of presumed consideration and together these two arguments were sufficient to resolve Woolley's claim. Nevertheless, the court also appeared to hedge its doctrinal bets. A puzzling three-paragraph footnote referred first to third-party-beneficiary doctrine, suggesting that one worker might accept the employer's offer of a unilateral contract on behalf of all. However, third-party-beneficiary doctrine requires that the parties intend for the contract to confer enforceable benefits on others—an implausible account of the circumstances surrounding the issuance of an employee handbook.[56] The court next discussed briefly the possible applicability of promissory estoppel doctrine, declining to address the issue because the parties had not raised the theory and opining that it did "not seem appropriate to the facts presented." Although Woolley's counsel made an abortive attempt to adopt an estoppel argument during oral argument before Judge Scalera, the court was correct that the estoppel theory did not appear in the appellate briefs. As a formal matter, however, the doctrine was no more problematic than the unilateral contract theory on which the court ultimately relied. It is necessary under one theory to presume consideration and under the other to presume reliance on the termination provisions of the policy manual. Finally, the footnote suggested that "the doctrine of unconscionability of the Uniform Commercial Code ... is analogous to the employment-at-will rule." No one could doubt that unconscionability doctrine is intended to "protect the disadvantaged party in a one-sided bargain." However, the court inartfully seemed to suggest that the at-will doctrine serves the same purpose. A more careful reading of the source on which the court relied reveals that the author intended to draw an analogy between the use of unconscionability doctrine to protect the weaker party in a franchise relationship and the possibility of using the same doctrine to ameliorate the harsh effects of the at-will doctrine on employees.[57] The

---

Won't Hurt Them: Defending Employment–At–Will in Light of Findings that Employees Believe They Possess Just Cause Protection, 23 Berkeley J. Emp. & Lab. L. 307 (2002).

[56] *See Lawrence v. Fox*, 20 N.Y. 268 (1859); Restatement (Second) of Contracts § 302 (1981) ("Unless otherwise agreed between promisor and promisee, a beneficiary of a promise is an intended beneficiary if recognition of a right to performance in the beneficiary is appropriate to effectuate the intention of the parties and either (a) the performance of the promise will satisfy an obligation of the promisee to pay money to the beneficiary; or (b) the circumstances indicate that the promisee intends to give the beneficiary the benefit of the promised performance.").

[57] *See* Susan F. Marrinan, *Employment–At–Will: Pandora's Box May Have an Attractive Cover*, 7 Hamline L. Rev. 155, 193 (1984).

utter implausibility of the court's musings on these subjects perhaps explains why it relegated them to a footnote.

Recall that in a colloquy with Judge Scalera, Woolley's counsel conceded that Roche retained the unilateral right to change the manual's termination provisions by simply notifying employees of the new terms. In a brief and largely unilluminating paragraph, the New Jersey Supreme Court acknowledged that the company had expressly reserved the right to make changes and that "generally" such changes, even those affecting the terms and conditions of employment, were permissible. Without elaboration or further discussion, however, the court declined to say whether an employer's right to modify would extend to handbook statements requiring good cause for termination. The court's formal unilateral contract analysis could justify either a restrictive or a permissive rule governing modification. If issuing an employee handbook constitutes an offer of employment under the handbook terms for as long as the working relationship continues, then employers ordinarily must obtain employees' consent to modify contractually enforceable good cause provisions.[58] However, a court might just as easily construe a handbook as merely a promise to honor its terms until the employer notifies workers of a change. Prominent decisions in both Michigan and California have adopted this more permissive standard and allow employers to modify job security terms prospectively after providing reasonable notice.[59]

Finally, the court ended as it had begun—by inviting employers to use a clear and prominent disclaimer. Showing a remarkably prescient understanding of how most employers would respond to its ruling, the concluding sentence of the court's opinion offered a recipe for avoiding just cause protection:

> All that need be done is the inclusion in a very prominent position of an appropriate statement that there is no promise of any kind by the employer contained in the manual; that regardless of what the manual says or provides, the employer promises nothing and remains free to change wages and all other working conditions without having to consult anyone and without anyone's agreement; and that the employer continues to have the absolute power to fire anyone with or without good cause.

The court's explanation of this requirement essentially reprised the information-forcing rationale for enforcement. Fairness demanded that

---

[58] *See Demasse v. ITT Corp.*, 984 P.2d 1138 (Ariz. 1999).

[59] *See In re Bankey v. Storer Broadcasting Co.*, 443 N.W.2d 112 (Mich. 1989); *Asmus v. Pacific Bell*, 999 P.2d 71 (Cal. 2000). The issue of modifying employee handbook terms does not appear to have reached the New Jersey Supreme Court in the years after *Woolley* was decided.

employers abide by the terms of a policy manual that "ma[de] the workforce believe" that employees enjoyed protection against discharge without cause. But there were "simple ways" to avoid promulgating an enforceable handbook. Roche, as the more legally sophisticated party, should be responsible for preventing any confusion or misunderstanding about the enforceability of the company's policy manual. Thus, the court unanimously reversed the courts below and remanded Woolley's contract claim for trial. The decision also instructed the trial court that if Woolley succeeded in proving the manual contained an enforceable promise of job security, "the only issue remaining shall be Woolley's damages." However, Roche had carefully preserved for trial the issue of whether the company had good cause to terminate Woolley. Five months after its initial ruling, the court finally admitted that Roche was correct and issued an order modifying its prior judgment.[60]

The Immediate Impact of Woolley v. Hoffmann–La Roche

Richard Woolley tragically did not live to see the New Jersey Supreme Court ruling in his favor. However, his attorney Gerald Wahl has said that Woolley was confident that ultimately he would be vindicated in his dispute with Roche.[61] The court's ruling obviously revived his contract claim and gave his survivors reason to believe that they were likely to prevail at trial. After all, Roche would be precluded by the ruling from arguing either that Woolley had not provided consideration or that the terms of the policy manual were too indefinite for enforcement. The Supreme Court had instructed the lower court that "[t]he provisions of the manual concerning job security shall be considered binding unless the manual elsewhere prominently and unmistakably indicates that those provisions shall not be binding or unless there is some other similar proof of the employer's intent not to be bound." These instructions fell somewhat short of directing a verdict for the plaintiff, but they left Roche with no realistic chance of showing that the manual should be unenforceable. Even after prevailing on its motion to clarify the court's instructions concerning good cause, the company faced a daunting challenge. Roche needed to convince a jury that the company had fired the now-deceased Woolley for a good reason. Although it is surely possible to conjure up images of harder arguments or more sympathetic plaintiffs, the company found itself in an unenviable position.

In these circumstances, the prudent strategy for Roche was to settle the case, and that is exactly what the company did. Woolley's untimely

---

[60] See *Woolley v. Hoffmann–La Roche*, 499 A.2d 515 (N.J. 1985) (order on motion for clarification).

[61] Telephone interview with Gerald Wahl (July 21, 2005).

death diminished the amount of lost wages attributable to his termination. If Woolley had been employed by Roche on the date of his death,
however, then his survivors would have received in addition the proceeds
of a company-provided life insurance policy. Although we do not have
access to the precise terms of the settlement, attorneys for both sides
have acknowledged that these principles guided the parties in reaching
an agreement.[62] The settlement appears to have included lost wages up
until the date of Woolley's death plus an amount equal to the life
insurance proceeds that his survivors would have received. Following
customary practice in employment litigation, the parties included a
confidentiality clause in their settlement agreement.

The company also sought to eliminate any exposure to future
contract claims based on its Personnel Policy Manual. Roche's counsel
reports that the company promptly incorporated a clear and prominent
disclaimer into the manual,[63] and this practice continues today. The
current version of this disclaimer appears prominently on many pages of
the Roche USA corporate website. For example, a distinctive blue box
above the company's policy on acceptable business practices contains the
following language:

IMPORTANT NOTICE:

THIS MANUAL IS NOT A CONTRACT. NO PROMISE OF
ANY KIND IS MADE BY THE INFORMATION CONTAINED
IN THIS MANUAL. HOFFMANN–LA ROCHE INC. AND ITS
RESPECTIVE DIVISIONS AND SUBSIDIARIES ("ROCHE"),
AT THEIR DISCRETION, MAY CHANGE OR WITHDRAW
ANY POLICY, PRACTICE AND PROCEDURE, AS WELL AS
ANY OTHER CONDITION OF EMPLOYMENT (INCLUDING
WAGES AND BENEFITS) WITHOUT ANYONE'S AGREE-
MENT.

NOTHING IN THIS MANUAL SHOULD BE CONSTRUED AS
CHANGING THE AT WILL EMPLOYMENT RELATIONSHIP
BETWEEN ROCHE AND ITS EMPLOYEES. THIS MEANS
THAT THE EMPLOYMENT RELATIONSHIP MAY BE TER-
MINATED BY ROCHE AT ANY TIME, WITH OR WITHOUT
CAUSE AND WITH OR WITHOUT ADVANCE NOTICE. SIMI-
LARLY, ANY EMPLOYEE MAY TERMINATE HIS OR HER
EMPLOYMENT AT ANY TIME, FOR ANY REASON, WITH
OR WITHOUT ADVANCED NOTICE.[64]

---

[62] Telephone interview with Gerald Wahl (July 21, 2005); telephone interview with
Frederick Kentz (August 9, 2005).

[63] Telephone interview with Frederick Kentz (Aug. 9, 2005).

[64] *See* http://www.rocheusa.com/rochebusinesspractice.asp (last visited Feb. 28, 2006).

Of course, the New Jersey Supreme Court had invited precisely this sort of response to its decision, and like Roche, many other employers lost no time incorporating disclaimers into their employee handbooks. Contemporaneous news reports confirm that the case garnered immediate attention in the New Jersey business community. Several stories appeared the day after the court issued its ruling.[65] These stories particularly emphasized the court's concern about fairness to employees and its suggestion that employers could avoid contractual liability by including clear and prominent disclaimers in their policy manuals. One quoted Woolley's local counsel Thomas Tucker's prediction that the case would have a "very significant impact" and force employers to "clearly spell out what policies are binding."[66]

This is precisely what employers did. Two weeks after the decision, an article appearing on the front page of the business section chronicled employers' "swift and direct" reaction to the court's ruling.[67] A management attorney described the case as "one of the most significant decisions handed down by the N.J. Supreme Court in the area of employment in the last 20 years." Another attorney said that "hundreds of corporations are at this very minute updating their manuals and worrying about their liability." Although a few employment lawyers recommended that companies should simply remove handbook language that might imply job security, Marvin Goldstein and many others advised employers to use disclaimers instead. Immediately after the oral argument in Woolley, Goldstein began telling clients to review their policy manuals and to incorporate disclaimers as necessary. By the time the court finally issued its decision, about half of Goldstein's clients had already updated their employee handbooks. He said that among the other half, "[e]very substantial employer we represent is beside themselves [sic] trying to decide what they should do now."

In contrast, lower courts in New Jersey had little trouble applying the new approach to employee handbooks. They easily distinguished as unenforceable handbooks that contained clear disclaimers of contractual effect or situations in which employers had expressly confirmed the at-will status of all employees. In the absence of such exculpatory language, however, courts routinely denied summary judgment and permitted

[65] *See Workers' Writes N.J. Court: Promises in Handbook Are a Bar to Firing*, Phila. Daily News, Business Section, at 101 (May 10, 1985); Marianne Lavelle, *Court Rules Guarantees in Employee Handbooks Are Binding*, Phila. Inquirer, Local Section, at B07 (May 10, 1985); *High Court Narrows Companies Right to Fire At Will*, The Record (Bergen County, N.J.), at a17 (May 10, 1985).

[66] *Workers' Writes N.J. Court: Promises in Handbook Are a Bar to Firing*, Phila. Daily News, Business Section, at 101 (May 10, 1985).

[67] Sid Karpoff, *Firms React to Ruling on Implied Job Guarantees*, The Record (Bergen County, N.J.), Business Section, at c1 (May 23, 1985).

plaintiffs to proceed with implied contract claims.[68] During the period immediately following *Woolley*, the most controversial legal question was whether the decision should be given retroactive effect. New Jersey's six-year statute of limitations for contract claims potentially made a full six years' of employment terminations subject to challenge. Nearly five years after the *Woolley* decision, however, the New Jersey Supreme Court resolved this uncertainty. In *Grigoletti v. Ortho Pharmaceutical Corp.*,[69] the court held that *Woolley* involved a significant break from past precedent and "made fundamentally new law." Although the court had found ample support for its approach in *Pierce* and *Anthony*, those cases had not "clearly foreshadowed" the new rule for employee handbooks. Thus, the court concluded that the *Woolley* decision should apply only prospectively to conduct occurring after the date of the decision.

Woolley also influenced courts outside of New Jersey and attracted the attention of many commentators.[70] Fifteen out-of-state cases have discussed *Woolley* at some length, and nearly one hundred cases have cited the New Jersey decision. Moreover, roughly 350 published secondary sources have cited or discussed the case. The New Jersey Supreme Court's ruling contributed significantly to the rising tide of state decisions enforcing employee handbooks as contracts. Along with the Michigan Supreme Court's *Toussaint* decision, *Woolley* thus became one of the leading cases in this area of employment law.

The Continuing Importance of Woolley

The court's decision in *Woolley v. Hoffmann–La Roche* has become part of the fabric of contemporary employment law. The proposition for which it stands is now utterly unremarkable. This legal principle is so widely accepted that we note today only the few isolated jurisdictions that still refuse to enforce employee handbook promises.[71] Studying *Woolley* closely, however, has continuing value.

First, the case was part of a nationwide movement that reversed courts' longstanding hostility to implied contract claims. *Woolley* helped

---

[68] For a detailed discussion of the subsequent case law interpreting and applying *Woolley*, see *Sellitto v. Litton Systems, Inc.*, 881 F. Supp. 932, 936–37 (D.N.J. 1994). The New Jersey Supreme Court issued two decisions elaborating on *Woolley*'s holding that a manual's job security provisions could be binding. See *Witkowski v. Thomas J. Lipton, Inc.*, 643 A.2d 546 (N.J. 1994); *Nicosia v. Wakefern Food Corp.*, 643 A.2d 554 (N.J. 1994).

[69] 570 A.2d 903, 916–17 (N.J. 1990).

[70] The Westlaw KeyCite result for the case runs to forty-eight pages.

[71] *See, e.g., Linafelt v. Bev, Inc.*, 662 So.2d 986, 989 (Fla. Dist. Ct. App. 1995) ("In Florida, policy statements are not employment contracts unless there is an express reference in the statement to a period of employment and the benefits to accrue therefrom.").

to replace the "grudging" and reluctant approach of earlier case law with the more modern concept of protecting employees' "reasonable expectations"—a transition that produced our contemporary under-standing of employment contract law. Plaintiff's counsel often struggled to express this theme clearly. Whatever their failings, however, Woolley's attorneys earned their fee by relentlessly focusing the New Jersey Supreme Court's attention on *Toussaint* and on *Pierce*. Extensive quota-tions from both cases found their way directly from plaintiff's briefs into the court's opinion. Although those briefs were sometimes inartfully written, Woolley's counsel cleverly encouraged the sort of jurisdictional cross-pollination that we so often see in this and other areas of employ-ment law.

We also have much to learn from studying the facts of this case in greater detail. As a practical matter, for example, it is often difficult to know whether an employer had good cause to discharge an employee. The situation in *Woolley* is no exception. Roche management expressed grave concerns about how Woolley managed the piping design for Build-ing 55. As we have seen, however, shifting and widely dispersed responsi-bility for engineering work on the Vitamin E plant also appear to have contributed to the piping problems for which Woolley lost his job. Indeed, operational disruptions at the facility continued unabated even after Hirshman's corrective measures were completed. A close analysis of the available facts also sheds light on the question of why Roche drafted its personnel policy manual. We can be fairly certain the court was wrong to believe that Roche intended the termination provisions of the manual to discourage employees like Woolley from joining a union. His own deposition testimony confirmed what the terms of the manual explicitly provided—only supervisory employees received the manual. In any event, Woolley and most other Roche managers would have been ineligible to join any bargaining unit that formed at the company.[72] The court's explanation thus seems implausible on its face. The available evidence suggests instead that Roche sought to control its managers in the exercise of their discretion and to prevent them from firing produc-tive employees.

Doctrinal issues proved equally challenging. First, the case illus-trates how formal contract rules could have frustrated the public policy objectives that led the court to find Roche's policy manual enforceable. Traditional consideration doctrine would have required Woolley to show that he was aware of the manual's terms and that he proffered his services, at least in part, in exchange for those terms. Without the legal fiction of presumed consideration, Woolley's own claim surely would

---

[72] *See* David M. Rabban, *Distinguishing Excluded Managers from Covered Profession-als Under the NLRA*, 89 Colum. L. Rev. 1775 (1989).

have failed. More significantly, courts would have been unable to develop an expansive doctrine of handbook enforcement. Each claim would depend on its own peculiar facts. Unable to prove that they knew of and relied on a handbook's terms, many, or perhaps even most, employees would find it impossible to bring contract claims that current employee handbook law recognizes. Employers responded to decisions like *Toussaint* and *Woolley* by eliminating naked "for cause" provisions, inserting disclaimers into their handbooks, and requiring all employees to sign confirmations of at-will status. These efforts gave rise to a second wave of cases that considered whether employers may modify existing employee handbook terms. Although courts have divided sharply over whether employers must obtain consent from incumbent employees and provide independent consideration to implement such changes,[73] Woolley's counsel adopted a surprisingly pro-employer position at oral argument before Judge Scalera. We have seen, however, that formal contract doctrine offers little insight into these questions. Instead, courts should candidly acknowledge that they are adjusting contractual enforcement to serve policy goals such as trying to protect employees from misleading assurances of job security or allowing employers greater flexibility in structuring their labor relations.

By far the most important legacy of the *Woolley* decision, however, is the widespread use of handbook disclaimers and confirmations of at-will status.[74] The court's opinion begins and ends by inviting employers to contract expressly to maintain an at-will relationship. In between, the court relies heavily on what I have called the legal-information-forcing rationale for enforcement. The opinion repeatedly expresses concern that unsophisticated employees will misinterpret the terms of an employer's policy manual. They may mistakenly assume that its job security provisions are legally binding. Indeed, Woolley himself appears to have been somewhat confused about whether Roche had a right to reduce his salary or benefits once he had started working for the company. The court thus demands that the legally sophisticated party bear the burden of clarifying the prevailing legal rules. As we saw, employers throughout the country have responded to this and similar decisions by including prominent disclaimers and requiring workers to acknowledge in writing that they have no contractual protection against termination.[75] The question remains, however, whether these exculpatory terms function as

---

[73] Compare *Demasse v. ITT Corp.*, 984 P.2d 1138 (Ariz. 1999), with *In re Bankey v. Storer Broadcasting Co.*, 443 N.W.2d 112 (Mich. 1989); and *Asmus v. Pacific Bell*, 999 P.2d 71 (Cal. 2000).

[74] For further discussion of the use of disclaimers see Verkerke, *Empirical Perspective*; Verkerke, *Legal Ignorance*.

[75] *See* Verkerke, *Empirical Perspective*.

the information-forcing argument supposes that they will. Although disclaimers ostensibly serve the purpose of clarifying the parties' legal relationship, it seems doubtful that boilerplate clauses genuinely inform the majority of employees about prevailing legal rules. Like many similar documents, employees frequently sign them without reading. If this practice is truly widespread, then perhaps we need a new justification for these legal-information-forcing doctrines.[76] The *Woolley* decision thus leaves us with an important question about its reasoning, but we should have no doubt about the case's significant role in the development of modern employment contract law.

---

[76] For an exploration of several alternative justifications for legal-information-forcing rules, see Verkerke, *Legal Ignorance.*

*

3

The Story of *Johnston v. Del Mar*: Wrongful Discharge in Violation of Public Policy

Stewart J. Schwab*

Factual Background

Imagine yourself in Nancy Johnston's shoes. In the summer of 1987, she was a shipping clerk for Del Mar Distributing Company, a sporting-goods distributor in Corpus Christi, Texas. Del Mar is a family-run business with about 45 employees, doing about $8 million in business a year. The founder and manager, Bill Miller, Sr., got his start in the early 1950s by inventing the Mr. Champ line of fishing lures. He thought up their aerodynamic shape while making diagonal slices in a loaf of pumpernickel. For many years, Miller assembled lures out of his home, but later sold the rights to the lures and broadened his business into a full-fledge distribution company. Eventually his son, Bill Miller Jr., took over the business.[1]

One day, Nancy Johnston's boss handed her a semi-automatic weapon, asked her to wrap it up and label it "fishing gear," and ship it by United Parcel Service (UPS) across the state to a grocery store in Brownsville. Johnston was required to sign her name on the shipping documents. Would you do this? Is it even legal? What if this dangerous "fishing gear" got in the wrong hands? Isn't something fishy going on?

Here's what Nancy Johnston did. She first went to her boss to ask if UPS was supposed to know of the contents of packages it was handling. The boss didn't respond. Still troubled, Ms. Johnston then called the U.S. Department of Treasury's Bureau of Alcohol, Tobacco and Firearms to ask about mislabeling of weapons. Within a few days, the boss found out about her inquiry and fired her.

---

* I thank Professor Michael Heise and research assistants Casey Johnson and Joshua Mahoney for their help.

[1] David Sikes, *Spoon Feeding*, Corpus Christi Caller–Times (July 4, 2004), available at http://www.caller.com

Nancy Johnston was outraged. She had done nothing wrong, and was merely acting as she thought a good citizen should. Who knew what hands this rifle might fall into, when it was being shipped as "fishing gear"? Fortunately for Nancy Johnston, her predicament occurred at a time when a new consensus was emerging in state courts across the country. Employees fired for refusing to perform an illegal act could sue their employer for the tort of wrongful discharge in violation of public policy.

Before delving into Nancy Johnston's story, a brief history of this new tort will help set the context of her litigation.

Legal Background: The Creation of a New Tort

By the time of the *Johnston* case in 1987, the tort of wrongful discharge was becoming well recognized in American common law, although the contours varied considerably from jurisdiction to jurisdiction. Just three decades earlier, the tort did not exist. The creation of this tort is a story in itself.

The "employment at will" doctrine became firmly established in the United States in the latter part of the nineteenth century,[2] and held sway throughout the United States until at least the middle of the twentieth century. In the hey-day of the doctrine, the judiciary simply refused to get into the business of scrutinizing why an employer fired a worker. Unless there was a very clear contract specifying the criteria for discharge, backed by extra consideration, employers were free to fire at any time, just as employees were free to quit at any time.

Some firings hurt not just the worker, however, but also directly harm society above and beyond harm to the worker. In such cases, even where the employer and employee have expressly or impliedly agreed to an at-will relationship, courts are called on to remedy the termination to encourage the parties to consider this larger public interest. In the latter part of the twentieth century, American courts gradually created the Tort of Wrongful Discharge in Violation of Public Policy (WDVPP).

The earliest chink in employment at will came in 1959 from California, in *Petermann v. International Brotherhood of Teamsters*.[3] A legislative committee was investigating the Teamsters union. The union asked one of its employees, Peter Petermann, to give false testimony. When he refused to perjure himself, he was fired. This seemed not only unfair to

---

[2] For an analysis of the spread of the at-will doctrine, see Andrew P. Morriss, *Exploding Myths: An Empirical and Economic Reassessment of the Rise of Employment At-Will*, 59 Mo. L. Rev. 679 (1994), who shows that the doctrine was adopted earlier in the Midwest than in New England and the industrial powerhouses of New York and Pennsylvania.

[3] 344 P.2d 25 (Cal. Ct. App. 1959).

the worker, but it also directly hampered the government investigation. The California Court of Appeal held that the employer's right to discharge an at-will employee was limited by "considerations of public policy." But the employee only asked for accrued salary since his discharge. There was no clear indication that a new tort, complete with compensatory and punitive damages, was being born.

The *Petermann* case sat conspicuously alone for over a decade. The next judicial step was taken by the Indiana Supreme Court in 1973, where the court recognized tort damages in a wrongful-discharge case. In *Frampton v. Central Indiana Gas Co.*,[4] a worker was fired for filing a workers' compensation claim after being injured at work. The filing would increase the employer's rates. The court conceded it knew of no cases in Indiana or elsewhere that held such a discharge to be actionable, but analogized to a retaliatory eviction in landlord-tenant law. The court held that "[r]etaliatory discharge for filing a workmen's compensation claim is a wrongful, unconscionable act and should be actionable in a court of law."

The following year, Pennsylvania hinted in dicta that a dismissed employee might sue on public policy grounds,[5] but sustained the dismissal of the employee's complaint on the particular facts. The same year, New Hampshire came on board, but only with contract damages. In *Monge v. Beebe Rubber Co.*,[6] a worker was fired for refusing the sexual advances of her supervisor. In recognizing her cause of action, the court cited *Petermann*, *Frampton*, and also a groundbreaking article by Lawrence Blades in the *Columbia Law Review*.[7] With almost no direct judicial authority (and without citing the 1959 *Petermann* case), Professor Blades had argued for judicial recognition of a tort of "abusive discharge" to correct the power imbalance between employers and employees.

Oregon was next, in 1975. In *Nees v. Hocks*,[8] a secretary for a law firm had been called for jury duty. Her employer, fearing the trial might last over a month, wrote a letter requesting that the court clerk grant her an exemption. The secretary presented the employer's letter to the clerk, but also said she wanted to serve. Her employer fired her and she sued. She won a jury trial, and the case eventually got to the Oregon Supreme Court. The principal question, as the justices saw it, was

---

[4] 297 N.E.2d 425 (Ind. 1973).

[5] *Geary v. United States Steel Corp.*, 319 A.2d 174 (Pa. 1974).

[6] 316 A.2d 549 (N.H. 1974).

[7] Lawrence Blades, *Employment at Will v. Employer Freedom: On Limiting the Abusive Exercise of Employer Power*, 67 Columbia L. Rev. 1404 (1967).

[8] 536 P.2d 512 (Ore. 1975).

whether the employer's firing "amounts to a tort of some sort." They
had difficulty knowing what label to put on the tort. The employee's
lawyer suggested calling it a prima facie tort. This obscure tort had a
long pedigree, particularly in New York, and Professor Blades had
argued that his "abusive discharge" tort could be likened to prima facie
tort. The essence of a prima facie tort is that an injurer should compen-
sate the victims of intentional, culpable, non-justifiable wrongs.[9] Relying
on *Petermann, Monge*, and *Frampton*, the Oregon high court declared
that it had "not hesitated to create or recognize new torts when
confronted with conduct causing injuries which we feel should be compensable." Without naming the tort, the Oregon Supreme Court held
that the employer should pay damages when it fired a worker "for such
a socially undesirable motive" as retaliating for her jury service.

Display 1

**Percentage Growth of Judicial Recognition of Wrongful Dis-
charge in Violation of Public Policy Tort, By Year**

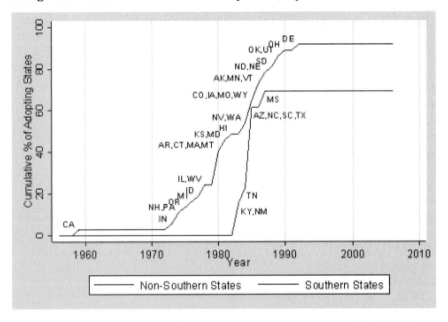

NOTE: 4 Southern states (AL, FL, GA, LA) and 3 non-Southern states (ME, NY, RI) have
not adopted the tort of wrongful discharge in violation of public policy.

SOURCE: Data from David H. Autor, John J. Donohue III, and Stewart J. Schwab, *The
Costs of Wrongful-Discharge Laws*, 88 Rev. Econ. & Stat. 211 (2006).

---

[9] *See generally* Restatement (Second) of Torts § 870 (Liability for Intended Consequences—General Principle); Morris. D. Forkosch, *An Analysis of the "Prima facie Tort"
Cause of Action*, 42 Cornell. L.Q. 465 (1957).

By the end of the 1970s, some nine states had recognized a cause of action for wrongful discharge in violation of public policy, using one label or another. The 1980s saw a deluge of judicial decisions. By 1985, Texas in *Sabine Pilot Service Inc. v. Hauck*[10] had joined some 32 states in recognizing the wrongful-discharge action. By 1992, all but seven states recognized the tort. The most prominent hold-out was New York, which declared that recognition of the tort action should come from the legislature, not the judiciary.[11] Display 1 on the previous page charts the growth.

As this tort became more common, courts resisted amorphous appeals to public policy but insisted that plaintiffs point to the violation of a specific statute or regulation. Successful WDVPP claims almost invariably fall in one of four categories. The first category is when an employee is fired for refusing to commit an illegal act. The 1959 *Petermann* case, where the employee was fired for refusing to perjure himself in a government investigation against the employer, is the classic example of category one. Category two occurs when an employee is fired for carrying out a public obligation. The classic example comes from *Nees v. Hocks*, where the employee was fired for serving on jury duty. Yet another category of cases arises from employees fired for claiming an employment benefit. The archetypical example here is the *Frampton* case, where the employee was fired for filing a worker's compensation claim when injured at work. The final grouping of cases involves employees fired for reporting illegal activities of the company. Whistleblowing is also related to the first category, that of an employee fired for refusing to do an illegal act. The distinction is that whistleblowing occurs when an employee reports on the wrongdoing of others in the company or the company itself. Category one occurs when the employee refuses to do an act where she herself might be doing something illegal. Obviously, the line between these two is a fine one.

Of course, public-policy tort claims were not the only area where courts were eroding the employment-at-will rule. Over this same period, courts were also recognizing implied-in-fact contract claims in situations where they had never done so before. An early example is *Pugh v. See's Candies, Inc.*[12] Pugh, a long-time employee, was fired after receiving assurances that he had a solid future with the company. The *Pugh* court recognized a potential claim of breach of contract and remanded the case for trial (where Pugh lost). Employment handbooks were another source of breach-of-contract claims. By the 1990s, over forty states had recog-

---

[10] 687 S.W.2d 733 (Tex. 1985).

[11] See *Murphy v. American Home Products Corp.*, 448 N.E.2d 86 (N.Y. 1983).

[12] 171 Cal. Rptr. 917 (Cal. Ct. App. 1981). See Justice Grodin's chapter in this volume.

nized causes of action based on employee handbooks and other implied contracts in appropriate situations.

In addition to the public-policy tort claims and the implied-in-fact contract claims, a third category of cases eroding at-will employment involved claims of violation of the implied covenant of good faith and fair dealing. The classic illustration is the *Fortune* case[13] from Massachusetts. There, a salesperson had done all the work for obtaining a large contract but was fired just before the deal was closed, thereby depriving him of a substantial commission. Even though the company had not violated the express terms of the contract, which declared that a commission was due only when the deal was finalized, the court found the firing violated an implied covenant of good faith and fair dealing. While general contract law routinely recognizes an implied covenant of good faith and fair dealing, only about ten states have recognized this claim in employment contracts.

The Johnston Litigation

After being fired, Nancy Johnston consulted a young lawyer, Ryan Stevens, a solo practitioner in Corpus Christi. Stevens had graduated from South Texas College of Law five years earlier, and had a varied civil practice. Stevens knew that Texas traditionally was a strong "employment at will" state, adhering to the rule that an employer could fire an employee at any time and for any reason, absent a specific statute restriction restricting the reasons for discharge. Nevertheless, two years before, the Texas Supreme Court in *Sabine Pilot* had recognized a wrongful discharge claim in similar circumstances. There, a boat deckhand was told to pump the bilges into the water, even though a placard on the boat stated this was illegal. The employee called the United States Coast Guard, who confirmed that pumping bilges was illegal. When the deckhand refused to pump the bilges, he was fired. The Supreme Court majority held that the at-will employee could bring a cause of action in these circumstances. The concurring opinion in *Sabine Pilot* suggested that the proper measure of damages would include past and future lost wages and benefits, and punitive damages.

Armed with the *Sabine Pilot* precedent, Ryan Stevens filed a complaint on behalf of Nancy Johnston. Even before discovery into the facts, Del Mar filed for summary judgment, asserting that Johnston failed to state a cause of action. The trial court granted the motion and dismissed the case. The court distinguished *Sabine Pilot*, because Johnston could not show that shipping a weapon as fishing gear was indeed illegal. It was one thing for an employee to be fired for refusing to do an illegal act.

---

[13] *Fortune v. National Cash Register Co.*, 364 N.E.2d 1251 (Mass. 1977).

Being fired for an act that might or might not be illegal was altogether different, reasoned the trial court. Johnston appealed.

THE COURT OF APPEALS DECISION

In her appeal, Johnston first complained that she had not been allowed any discovery. She particularly wanted communications between Del Mar and the Bureau of Alcohol, Tobacco and Firearms, and UPS as well as "copies of regulations of any nature regarding the shipment of firearms and ammunition."[14] Johnston needed this discovery, she argued, to determine whether the act she was requested to do was illegal.

Johnston's main argument in her eight-page brief, however, was that she had stated a viable cause of action based on *Sabine Pilot*. If an employee could be fired for simply inquiring if she were committing an illegal act, it would create an "obvious chilling effect" on the *Sabine Pilot* cause of action that protects employees fired for refusing to perform an illegal act.

In its responding brief, Del Mar complained that Johnston improperly wanted to expand the exceptions to the at-will rule to include whistleblowers. Texas had a statute protecting government employees from discharge for bringing to light illegal activities in state or local government.[15] But the Texas legislature specifically limited the whistleblower statute to public-sector employees. The judiciary should not expand the statute, argued Del Mar, to cover private-sector employers. With a concluding rhetorical flourish, Del Mar argued that if the Court "were to cause a small crack to appear in the dam called the at-will rule, numerous challenges to reasons for discharge would be brought before the Courts, sweeping away the 'at-will' rule which has served Texas so well in the past."[16]

The Court of Appeals sided with Johnston, agreeing with her "chilling effect" argument.[17] The court refused to put the employee to an unacceptable choice of (1) subjecting herself to discharge for trying to find out if an act was illegal; or (2) remaining ignorant about the law (which is no excuse), performing the act and, if it turns out to be illegal, facing possible criminal sanctions. The court therefore held that public policy prohibits the discharge of an employee who reasonably and in good faith attempts to find out if the act requested by the employer is illegal.

---

[14] Appellant Johnston's Brief at 6, *Johnston v. Del Mar Distributing Co., Inc.*, 776 S.W.2d 768 (Tex. App.—Corpus Christi, 1989).

[15] Tex. Rev. Civ. Stat. Ann. art. 6242–16A (Vernon 1988).

[16] Respondent Del Mar Distributing Co., Inc.'s Brief at 9.

[17] *Johnston*, 776 S.W.2d at 771.

The Court of Appeals expressly warned that it was not considering a broad whistleblower exception to employment at will. Rather, it limited its ruling to employees who inquired about their own potential criminal liability. We will return to the halting common-law protection of whistle-blowers later in this chapter.

SUBSEQUENT LITIGATION

Del Mar applied for a writ of error to the Texas Supreme Court. In its petition, Del Mar emphasized the cost to employers and harm to the Texas economy that the wrongful-discharge action would impose. As a specific point of error, Del Mar complained that the lower court's encroachment on the at-will employment doctrine "will damage the state's economy ... and impair the attraction of new business to the state." Del Mar warned that this new rule would give an employee the ability effectively to disrupt a business by merely inquiring about the legality of requested actions.[18]

Del Mar outlined several costs caused by encroachments on the at-will rule. First, exposure to litigation would make employers reluctant to fire employees, even for good reasons. Second, employers would face increased costs in documenting the reasons for terminations. Third, it would decrease morale of coworkers and employers when unreliable or incompetent employees are kept on for fear of lawsuits. Fourth, employers would be reluctant to "take a chance" on unproven job applicants if termination were made more difficult. Further, it would increase judicial case loads dealing with employment disputes. Finally, employers deciding where to relocate or expand businesses would avoid states in which the judicial system was seen as intruding unnecessarily on their employment decisions.

In support of its business-climate argument, Del Mar quoted *Whittaker v. Care–More, Inc.*,[19] where the Tennessee Court of Appeals refused to cut back the employment-at-will doctrine for fear of deterring business growth:

> [W]e are compelled to note that any substantial change in the "employment-at-will" rule should first be microscopically analyzed regarding its effect in the commerce of this state. There must be protection from substantial impairment of the very legitimate interests of an employer in hiring and retaining the most qualified personnel available or the very foundation of the free enterprise system could be jeopardized.

---

[18] Petitioner Del Mar Distributing Co., Inc.'s Application for Writ of Error, Supreme Court of Texas.

[19] 621 S.W.2d 395, 396–97 (Tenn. Ct. App. 1981).

... Tennessee has made enormous strides in recent years in its attraction of new industry of high quality designed to increase the average per capita income of its citizens and thus, better the quality of their lives. The impact on the continuation of such influx of new businesses should be carefully considered before any substantial modification is made in the employee-at-will rule.

We consider below the empirical evidence of the effect of inroads of employment at will on the economy of adopting states.

Del Mar hoped its business-climate argument would make the court hesitate to recognize an exception to employment at will. In her reply brief, Johnston took on the argument and in particular the quote from the Tennessee *Whittaker* case. That decision, wrote Johnston, "in no uncertain terms places economic gain over an individual's social justice.... The people of the state of Texas deserve a better quality of life, not simply an increase in the average per capita income."[20]

To bolster its petition for review to the Texas Supreme Court and demonstrate the concern of employers, Del Mar convinced the Texas Employment Law Council (TELC) to author an *amicus* brief. TELC is an association of large Texas employers in significant industries throughout the state. Its member companies range in size from several hundred to more than 50,000 employees. As the *amicus* brief explained, the Texas employer community is "keenly interested in and would be directly and significantly affected by restrictions—based on an individual employee's personal perceptions of what acts should or might be illegal—on the right of employers to choose and direct their at-will employees in the efficient furtherance of *lawful* business activities."[21]

Despite Delmar's petition, supported by the TELC, the Texas Supreme Court declined to consider the case, and the case returned to the trial court. The defendant deposed Johnston for 10 hours on a Saturday, and then, in the words of her lawyer, "paid her some money" and settled the case. Nancy Johnston used the money to go back to school, and eventually lost contact with her lawyer.[22] As so often happens, the actual litigant disappears from the story.

Harming the Business Climate: An Empirical Analysis

One of the key debates in the *Johnston* briefs was whether judicial erosion of at-will employment would harm the business climate in Texas. Will employers in Texas hesitate to hire workers if the state recognizes

---

[20] Petitioner Del Mar Distributing Co., Inc.'s Reply Brief at 6.

[21] Texas Employment Law Council's Brief as Amicus Curiae Supporting Petitioner Del Mar Distributing Co., Inc. at 3.

[22] Telephone Interview with Ryan Stevens (July 27, 2005).

claims of wrongful discharge in violation of public policy (or implied-in-fact contract claims or violations of good faith and fair dealing)?

Usually, lawyers simply resort to rhetoric in addressing the business-climate issue. However, a natural social-science experiment is provided by the fact that various states have adopted the public-policy tort at different times. This makes it possible to analyze whether employment levels have gone down, relative to other states, when a state has recognized the cause of action.

Display 2 provides an example. Recall that Texas first recognized the tort of wrongful discharge in violation of public policy in 1985 in the *Sabine Pilot* case. By contrast, the Florida courts refused to recognize this tort throughout the 1980s (and even today). Display 2 charts the employment levels of Florida and Texas two years before and two years after the *Sabine Pilot* decision. It shows that employment in Florida grew by over 942,000 workers, while employment in Texas grew by only 323,000 workers from a bigger base. The difference between 1983 and 1987 in the differences in employment was 619,400 workers. Arguably, Florida and Texas have otherwise similar employment conditions. Did the *Sabine Pilot* decision lead to a slowdown in employment growth in Texas relative to Florida?

Display 2
Number of Employees in Florida and Texas Two Years Before and After 1985 *Sabine Pilot* Decision

	1983	1987	Difference
Florida	3,905,400	4,848,100	942,700
Texas	6,193,600	6,516,900	323,300
Difference	−2,288,200	−1,668,800	619,400

Source: Bureau of Labor Statistics, available at http://data.bls.gov/PDQ/outside.jsp?survey=sm

One should not make too much of this single comparison, because the differences could be caused by many factors other than the *Sabine Pilot* decision. Over time, however, the 50 state laboratories provide repeated observations of the relative effect on employment when a state recognizes the tort of wrongful discharge in violation of public policy. If states adopting an exception to employment-at-will consistently have lower employment growth, one might infer a causal connection.

Display 3 shows the cumulative effects on employment (as a proportion of the state's population) when a state first recognizes the tort of wrongful discharge in violation of public policy. The display comes from a recent study by MIT economist David Autor with Yale law professor John Donohue and the present author.[23] It plots the employment-to-population ratios (separately for men and women) in states that adopted the public-policy tort relative to states that did not adopt the tort from the 48 months prior to adoption to the 96 months following adoption. Points above the x-axis would indicate in increase in employment for adopting states, while points below the x-axis indicate a decline in employment for adopting states. As Display 3 reveals, there is no clear pattern either above or below the line. Even after adding other controls, the authors find the public-policy doctrine is associated with a small (0.1 to 0.2 percent) reduction in employment, but the effect is never statistically significant. Thus, this study cannot reject the hypothesis that adoption of the public-policy tort has no impact on employment.

By contrast to the lack of effect of the public-policy tort, the authors do find that employee-handbook and other implied-contract exceptions lower employment. Display 4 plots the employment-to-population ratios before and after a state court announces implied-contract exceptions. It shows that the employment-to-population ratios dip when a state court first recognizes an implied-contract exception to employment at will, reaching a low point about 2 to 2.5 years after the court decision. When adding the full controls, the authors conclude that the adoption of an implied-contract exception causes a decline of 0.8% to 1.7% in the ratio of employment to population. Display 4 also suggests, however, that over time the employment reduction is less dramatic; by six or seven years after the court decision, the negative effect is statistically insignificant. One explanation for this lessening impact over time is that employers initially over-react to the new doctrine, but learn to adjust to it over time.

One puzzle from these results is why judicial recognition of an implied-contract exception to employment at will reduces employment when recognition of the public-policy tort action appears to have no effect. After all, in most states successful wrongful-discharge plaintiffs get complete tort damages, which can include punitive damages.

Perhaps the answer is that employer discharges in violation of public policy are fairly rare, particularly as limited by many courts to clear violations of express legislative commands, rather than violations of vaguer, merely judicially articulated norms of public policy. Successful cases, especially when accompanied by punitive damages, attract attention, but properly advised profit-maximizing employers would appropriately discount the danger. Often these cases are idiosyncratic, so there may be little systematic response by employers.

---

[23] David H. Autor, John J. Donohue III, and Stewart J. Schwab, *The Costs of Wrongful–Discharge Laws*, 88 Rev. Econ. & Stat. 211 (2006).

Display 3
**State Log Employment-to-Population Ratios Before and After
Adoption of Public–Policy Exception: Monthly Leads and Lags
From 4 Years Before to 8 Years After Adoption**

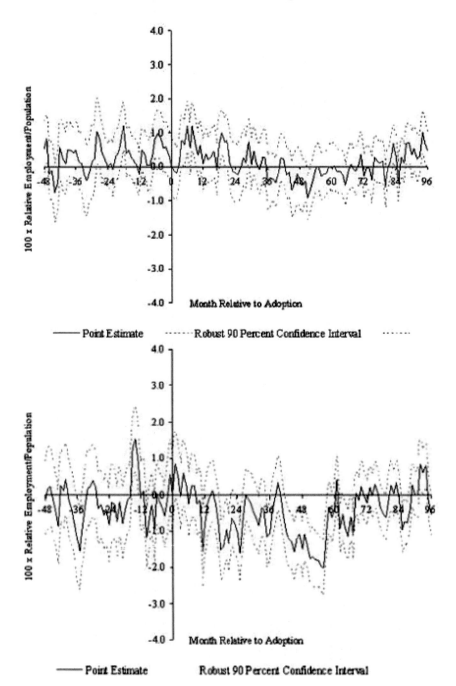

Display 4
State Log Employment-to-Population Rates Before and After Adoption of Implied–Contract Exception: Monthly Leads and Lags From 4 Years Prior to 8 Years After Adoption

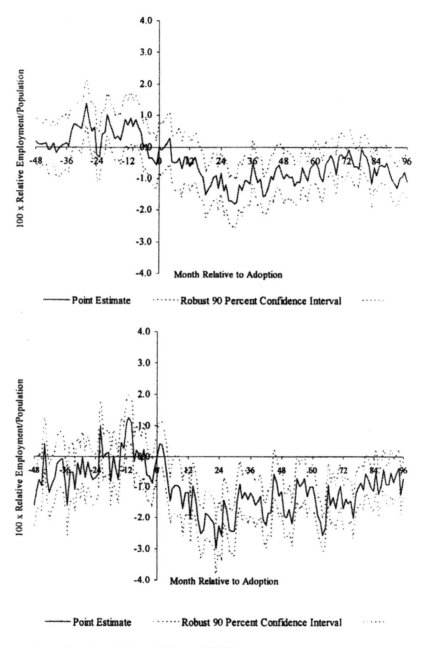

Source: Autor, Donohue & Schwab Figure 1 (2006).

By contrast, changes in employment contract law can alter employer behavior toward many more employees. The clearest example of wide impact occurs when handbooks given to an entire workforce are held to be legally enforceable. But even implied-contract claims based on individual, often oral, assurances can have widespread effects on the workforce. One corporate defense to these claims is to bureaucratize hiring, evaluation, and promotion decisions. Contracts will say things like "immediate supervisors cannot change the terms of employment; only statements in writing by the vice president for human relations can do so." Managers are told to operate more by the book. Under this reasoning, the implied-contract action imposes greater costs on employers, who respond by reducing the size of the workforce. Over time, however, employers adjust in various ways, such as including disclaimers against legal enforceability in employment manuals, and the disemployment effects are reduced.

Being Reasonable versus Being Right

One legal puzzle in the *Johnston* case is whether Nancy Johnston's boss indeed asked her to do an illegal act. Doesn't it violate some law to mislabel a semi-automatic rifle as "fishing gear" and ship it across the state? The answer is complicated and may depend on factual details. Firearm shipments are highly regulated by federal statute and regulations of the Treasury Department's Bureau of Alcohol, Tobacco and Firearms (ATF). It is generally illegal to use the Postal Service to mail concealable firearms,[24] and non-licensees cannot mail any firearm to a non-licensed resident of another state but can mail a shotgun or rifle to a resident of their own state.[25] In our case, the employer instructed Johnston to use UPS, a private shipping company, rather than the Postal Service. A nonlicensee may ship a firearm by common carrier to a resident within state or to a licensee interstate, but the carrier must be notified that the shipment contains a firearm (and the carrier cannot cause a label to be placed on the package indicating it is a firearm).[26] The statute separately sanctions false statements intended to mislead dealers,[27] so the mislabeling as "fishing gear" might be illegal, depending on

---

[24] 18 U.S.C. § 1715 ("Pistols, revolvers, and other firearms capable of being concealed on the person are nonmailable").

[25] See 18 U.S.C. § 922(a) and ATF regulations posted at http://www.atf.treas.gov/firearms/faq/faq2.htm#b7.

[26] Id.

[27] 18 U.S.C. § 922(a)(6) makes it unlawful "for any person in connection with the acquisition ... of any firearm from a licensed ... dealer knowingly to make any false or fictitious oral or written statement ... intended or likely to deceive such ... dealer ... with respect to any fact material to the lawfulness of the sale or other disposition of such firearm...."

whom the label "fishing gear" was intended to mislead. Critical facts are
not in the record, including whether Del Mar or the Brownsville grocery
store were firearm licensees for this purpose, and whether UPS was
given any notice that the package contained a firearm. Nancy Johnston
nearly conceded she could not show the shipment was illegal (at least
without more facts). Given it is an intrastate shipment by private
carrier, it probably slips through the regulatory cracks and is legal.

So, it appears that Del Mar's request to Nancy Johnston was lawful,
but also that Johnston was reasonable in thinking she was asked to do
something illegal (or at least in thinking it was worth an inquiry).
Whether a reasonably mistaken employee is barred from a public-policy
tort action remains an unsettled issue.

Many courts require only that an employee hold a reasonable, good
faith belief that the requested or reported action be illegal.[28] Most
whistleblower statutes,[29] including the whistleblower provisions of the
Sarbanes–Oxley Act,[30] similarly protect the reasonably mistaken whistleblower. Other courts and whistleblower statutes require the employee to
be correct.[31]

The argument against protecting erroneous workers is that they are
insubordinate, and insubordination is a grievous wrong in the American
workplace. It is one thing to protect insubordinate workers who are
correct that the employer's request is illegal; it is another to protect

[28] See, e.g., *Green v. Ralee Engineering Co.*, 960 P.2d 1046 (Cal. 1998) (upholding a
public-policy tort claim for an employee who was fired after he complained to management
about an aircraft-parts quality-control failure that the employee reasonably believed was
illegal); *Schriner v. Meginnis Ford Co.*, 421 N.W.2d 755 (Neb. 1988) (holding that public-
policy claim extends to an employee who acts in good faith and upon reasonable cause in
reporting his employer's suspected criminal act).

[29] See, e.g., Mich. Comp. Laws sec. 15.362 (protecting reports of violations "unless the
employee knows that the report is false"); Cal. Lab. Code sec. 1102.5 (protecting disclosure
where the employee "has reasonable cause to believe" a statute has been violated).

[30] 18 U.S.C. § 1514A; see *Collins v. Beazer Homes USA Inc.*, 334 F. Supp. 2d 1365
(N.D. Ga. 2004) (denying employer's motion for summary judgment, noting that the
standard of the Sarbanes–Oxley Act is one of a reasonable person, even if the employee
misunderstands the requirements of law).

[31] See, e.g., *Bordell v. General Elec. Co.*, 667 N.E.2d 922 (N.Y. 1996) (affirming
summary judgment for employer, noting that a cause of action predicated on a private-
sector whistleblower law requires proof of an actual violation of law, in contrast to a public
employee whistleblower statute that protects an employee who "reasonably believes" the
government has violated the law); *DeSoto v. Yellow Freight Systems, Inc.*, 957 F.2d 655
(9th Cir. 1992) (applying California law, rejecting retaliation claim of employee who refused
to drive a truck that he erroneously thought had illegally expired registration papers);
Callantine v. Staff Builders, Inc., 271 F.3d 1124 (8th Cir. 2001) (applying Missouri law,
dismissing employee nurse's wrongful-discharge action when she was dismissed for refusing to sign a legal backdated patient-visit form).

insubordinate workers who are wrong. The argument was forcefully put
by the TELC, as *amicus* in the *Johnston* case. TELC posed a hypothetical which pits the erroneous beliefs of a lay employee, sympathetic with
environmental claims but knowing nothing about environmental law,
against legal experts employed by the company:

> An employee operates cooling and recycling pumps at a chemical
> manufacturing plant on the Sabine River. He is instructed by his
> employer to discharge thousands of gallons of recycled water into
> the river below the plant. A staunch environmentalist, he harbors a
> good faith doubt that such discharges are legal, and certainly be-
> lieves they should not be; however, company management employs
> environmental and legal experts who are familiar with every rele-
> vant state and federal statute, regulation, impact statement and
> plant rule, and all deem the discharge in question lawful and proper
> under existing conditions. The employee responsible for executing
> the discharge obviously lacks their expert knowledge. He merely
> thinks the discharge may be unlawful, and believes that it should be.
> He therefore disregards his employer's instructions pending his own
> "investigation" into the issue, perhaps spending a few hours at-
> tempting to call EPA officials or perusing whatever pertinent litera-
> ture is available in his control room. In the meantime, additional
> fresh water is pumped into the plant to replace recycled water that
> was to be discharged, thereby producing a flood throughout the
> plant resulting in costly damage to company equipment, expensive
> lost production time, and perhaps even the risk of injury to other
> employees. Sooner or later, of course, the employee learns that the
> discharge was perfectly legal and proper, but he need not be con-
> cerned about losing his job since he had refused to perform his
> duties as requested while investigating the legal implications of so
> doing. Thus, for a brief period, his personal concerns and policy
> predilections effectively rendered his employer's business activities
> "illegal," something that untold volumes of *public* policy expres-
> sions—i.e., the applicable statutes and regulations—did not do.[32]

The counter-argument is that workers need some breathing space,
and should not be required to be lawyers in deciding whether to break
the law. If a worker reasonably believes the request is illegal, the
counter-argument runs, the employer should not be able to fire with
impunity. The position of Nancy Johnston is especially sympathetic. She
was reasonably unsure whether the request was lawful, and so asked the
appropriate government agency. She should not be fired for acting
reasonably.

---

[32] Brief for Texas Employment Law Council as Amicus Curiae Supporting Petitioner at
pp. 13–14, n. 4, Del Mar Distributing Co. v. Johnston, No. C–9282 (Jan. 25, 1990).

In an attempt to split the baby, some have suggested a distinction between insubordinate workers and whistleblowers. Insubordinate workers must be correct that the employer's command was illegal, even if a worker who merely reports the misconduct of others without disobeying an order need only have a reasonable belief that the conduct be illegal. In this latter case, the employee has not been insubordinate. This requires, of course, a sharp delineation between an employee who is being asked to do an (allegedly) illegal act from an employee who is merely observing the (allegedly) illegal conduct of others. In some cases, a worker can be in both categories at the same time by refusing an act and telling others about the request. In other situations, it is unclear whether the worker is in one category (refusing to do an illegal act) or another (blowing the whistle on the company or other employees). Indeed, Nancy Johnston's inquiry to ATF sounds like a whistleblower, even if she prefaced her inquiry by saying she wants to know whether shipping a rifle as "fishing gear" is illegal. The court treated her, however, as making an inquiry in preparation for refusing to do an illegal act. This is because Texas has not recognized a common-law whistleblower action, but only an action of wrongful discharge for refusing an illegal act.

Ultimately, the line is probably too fine to attempt a distinction. Indeed, there is something perverse about treating more harshly a worker who is reasonably trying to avoid acting from a worker merely tattling on others. Why give extra protection to tattlers? Exactly where the law will come down on this remains uncertain. If Nancy Johnston remains a role model, however, a reasonable belief that the requested action is illegal will be enough to sustain the cause of action.

*

4

The Story of *Luck v. Southern Pacific Transportation Co.*: The Struggle to Protect Employee Privacy

Pauline T. Kim[*]

In recent years, employers have increasingly made use of new technologies to test and monitor the condition, activities and location of individual employees. The introduction of these practices in the workplace has often been sharply contested, with employees claiming that the practices invade their personal privacy and employers justifying their use as legitimate business tools. Employers have always had an interest in gathering information about applicants and employees, but until relatively recently, the types of information available and the means for collecting it were quite limited. For the most part, employers had to rely on information provided by applicants, as well as reference checks, to evaluate prospective employees, and on direct observation to assess the performance of current employees. Then, in the 1980s, employers adopted urinalysis drug testing programs on a broad scale, provoking a spate of legal challenges claiming that the practices violated employee privacy rights.

Luck v. Southern Pacific Transportation Co.[1] is one such case. Brought in the mid–1980s, it was one of the earliest cases to litigate the issue of workplace drug testing, and therefore, was important in developing the law regarding drug testing—and the law of employee privacy more generally. It is not a "landmark case" in the traditional sense—it was not decided by the United States Supreme Court; nor did it establish binding national precedent. The Supreme Court's decisions in *Skinner v. Railway Labor Executives' Association*[2] and *National Treasury Employ-*

---

[*] I would like to thank Kay Lucas, Ellen Lake, John True, Edward Chen, and, especially, Barbara Luck, for taking the time to talk about the case with me. My thanks also to Jason Retter who provided able research assistance.

[1] 267 Cal. Rptr. 618 (Ct. App. 1990).

[2] 489 U.S. 602 (1989).

ees Union v. Von Raab[3] are the high-profile cases that addressed the constitutionality of employee drug testing. But those decisions turned on the Fourth Amendment to the United States Constitution, which applies only to public employers or private employers acting at the behest of the government. Most employees, like the plaintiff in *Luck*, are employed by private entities and the Fourth Amendment has no direct application. These employees must look for protection to state laws and in the mid–1980s it was quite unclear to what extent the existing patchwork of state constitutional, statutory and common law doctrines might protect employee privacy. *Luck* is the story of how one court in California, confronted with an employee challenge to workplace drug testing, attempted to build a framework for analyzing employee privacy claims.

Social and Legal Background

The *Luck* case arose in a period of dramatic growth in the use of drug testing in the workplace. The technology for testing urine and other bodily fluids for drugs and alcohol had existed in the early 1970s, but its use was mostly confined to the forensic and medical contexts. Then, in the 1980s, the use of urinalysis tests in the workplace exploded, one facet of a much larger national anti-drug campaign. The Reagan administration decided in the early 1980s to focus on the problem of illegal drug use in American society and made combating illegal drug trafficking a top priority. In addition to devoting greater resources to drug interdiction, the government sought to address the demand side of the equation as well, most famously with Nancy Reagan's "Just Say No" campaign. During this period, President Reagan appointed a federal "Drug Czar" and invoked the imagery of war. This rhetoric and extensive media coverage created a crisis atmosphere in which illegal drug use became widely perceived as one of the nation's top social problems.[4] Ironically, data collected by the National Institute on Drug Abuse suggested that illegal drug use had begun declining in the late 1970s, significantly before Reagan's announced War on Drugs.[5]

In this atmosphere of perceived crisis, the federal government embarked on a course that would lead, by mandate and by example, to the widespread adoption of drug testing policies by employers. In 1986, Reagan issued Executive Order No. 12564, declaring a "drug-free Federal workplace" and directing the head of each federal agency to "develop a plan for achieving the objective of a drug-free workplace" and "establish a program to test for the use of illegal drugs by employees in

---

[3] 489 U.S. 656 (1989).

[4] John Gilliom, *Surveillance, Privacy, and the Law* 17–34 (1996).

[5] *Id.* at 21; Michael R. Gottfredson & Carolyn Uihlein, *Drug Testing in the Workplace: A View from the Data*, 33 Wm. & Mary L. Rev. 127, 129–38 (1991).

sensitive positions."[6] Within a short period of time, drug testing became a standard feature of federal government employment. In addition, various federal agencies responsible for regulating private industries such as transportation issued regulations mandating the use of drug tests for specified types of employees in certain situations. Even among private firms not covered by such regulations, drug testing policies spread rapidly, such that by the end of the decade, an estimated 17 million, or 20% of workers in the private, non-agricultural workforce were subject to drug testing.[7]

The dramatic expansion of workplace drug testing did not occur without controversy, and both individual workers and unions filed lawsuits to challenge the new policies. In the mid–1980s, when these cases were first brought in significant numbers, the legal doctrines protecting employee privacy were somewhat inchoate. Many of the early challenges were based on the Fourth Amendment, which forbids unreasonable searches and seizures, although there was uncertainty about whether its restrictions applied in the workplace setting and whether drug testing constituted a "search." It was not until the late 1980s that the Supreme Court made clear that the Fourth Amendment did protect government employees from intrusions by their employer[8] and that urinalysis testing infringed "legitimate expectations of privacy," triggering Fourth Amendment scrutiny.[9] What was clear from the outset was that the Fourth Amendment's restrictions only applied to government action. Thus, unless their employer instituted drug testing at the direction of the government, employees working in the private sector could not rely on the federal constitution.

Private-sector employees, then, had to look to other sources of law for protection. Most states recognized a common law tort of invasion of privacy, and it had been applied in a handful of cases to impose liability on employers who had unreasonably intruded on their employees' privacy—for example, by searching their homes or personal effects. However, prevailing on such a claim was not easy, because the tort required proof of an "unreasonable intrusion upon the seclusion of another" that was "highly offensive to a reasonable person."[10] The case law made clear that trivial offenses would not suffice; rather, liability was reserved for those intrusions severe enough to satisfy the "highly offensive" standard. Nor

---

[6] Exec. Order No. 12,564, 3 C.F.R. 224 (1987), reprinted in 5 U.S.C. § 7301 (2006).

[7] *Workplace Drug Testing and the National Institute on Drug Abuse: An Interview with J. Michael Walsh*, 12 Geo. Mason U. L. Rev. 475, 477–78 (1990).

[8] *O'Connor v. Ortega*, 480 U.S. 709 (1987).

[9] *Skinner v. Railway Labor Executives' Ass'n*, 489 U.S. 602 (1989).

[10] *Restatement (Second) of Torts* § 652A(2) (1977).

was it easy to predict how this standard might be applied, for the level of "offensiveness" of a particular intrusion often depended upon who was deciding the issue.

In a handful of state constitutions, the right to privacy is explicitly mentioned, offering another possible source of protection. Like the federal constitution, these provisions often applied only to government actions. In California, however, where the *Luck* case was brought, it was an open question whether the state constitutional right to privacy restrained private actors as well as the government. Voters in California had amended the state constitution in 1972, approving a ballot initiative that added privacy to a list of "inalienable rights" of "all people" found in Article I, section 1 of the constitution. The California Supreme Court described "the moving force" behind the amendment as concern about "the accelerating encroachment on personal freedom and security caused by increased surveillance and data collection activity in contemporary society."[11] The election brochure supporting the initiative had argued for its passage by citing the "loss of control over the accuracy of government and business records of individuals" and warning that "[a]t present there are no effective restraints on the information activities of government and business."[12] This language at least suggested that the privacy provision might apply to both public and private actors, although when the *Luck* case was filed it was far from certain that the California courts would accept this interpretation.

Not only were their privacy rights ill-defined, but private-sector employees faced the additional challenge of asserting those rights against a legal backdrop that favored employer prerogatives over most personnel decisions. The traditional common law rule had long been that one hired for an indefinite term was presumed to be an at-will employee and could quit or be fired for any reason or no reason at all. Throughout the 1980s at-will employment remained the default presumption in virtually every American jurisdiction,[13] although a developing body of law made it possible for some employees to challenge their terminations.

One route available to discharged employees was to argue that they were not in fact at-will employees, because they had agreed to a different arrangement. These contract-based claims took several forms. Most straightforward were cases in which an employee could point to an express agreement—written or oral—that the employment would continue for a specified period of time, or that the employer's right to discharge

---

[11] *White v. Davis*, 533 P.2d 222, 233 (Cal. 1975).

[12] *Id.* at 774–75.

[13] The exception is Montana, which passed a law in 1987 requiring employers to have cause for firing non-probationary employees and limiting damages in wrongful discharge suits. See Professor Morriss's chapter in this volume.

was limited by a requirement of good cause. Somewhat more controversial were "implied-in-fact" contract claims, which found the existence of a good cause limitation based on the entire course of dealing between the parties. In 1981, a California Court of Appeal had recognized such a claim in *Pugh v. See's Candies, Inc.*,[14] holding that an implied promise to discharge only for good cause could be based on factors such as the duration of employment, consistent commendations and promotions, lack of direct criticism of the employee's work, assurances of job security, and the personnel policies and practices of the employer. Finally, discharged employees had begun to assert claims based on the implied covenant of good faith and fair dealing. The duty to act in good faith was implied as a matter of law in all contracts, and had been used by courts to protect the reasonable expectations of parties to commercial and insurance agreements. However, because the purpose of the implied covenant was to ensure good faith performance of a contract's *express* terms, it was unclear whether or how it applied to at-will employment contracts.

Even at-will employees could argue that they fell within an important exception to the at-will rule which imposed liability for discharges that violated public policy. In one of the earliest cases, *Petermann v. International Brotherhood of Teamsters*,[15] an employee alleged that he was fired after he refused to lie when subpoenaed to testify before a state legislative committee. The court permitted his wrongful discharge claim to proceed, holding that "in order to more fully effectuate the state's declared policy" the law should deny the employer "his generally unlimited right" of discharge. Later courts extended this principle to other situations in which an employee was fired for refusing to do something unlawful, or for fulfilling a public obligation. By the mid–1980s, the doctrine of wrongful discharge in violation of public policy was widely accepted throughout the United States, although the precise contours of the tort remained unclear. While generally accepting the principle that public policy placed limits on an employer's power to discharge, courts disagreed about how to define "public policy." In particular, no consensus existed as to whether the public policy exception would protect an employee fired for asserting a right of privacy.

Thus, at the time the *Luck* case was filed, the law applicable to employee drug testing was quite uncertain. The technology itself was new, and virtually no existing cases were on point. The very nature of the privacy right, and how it interacted with the law of the workplace more generally, were matters of controversy. Courts, like the *Luck* court, that confronted the earliest challenges to workplace drug testing neces-

---

[14] 171 Cal. Rptr. 917 (Ct. App. 1981).

[15] 344 P.2d 25 (Cal. Ct. App. 1959).

sarily shaped our current understanding of employee privacy rights in important ways.

Factual Background

On Thursday, July 11, 1985, Barbara Luck arrived at work and found a notice on her desk instructing her to report to another room in order to provide a urine sample for drug testing.[16] Luck, a computer programmer working in Southern Pacific Transportation Company (SP)'s downtown San Francisco office, was stunned. She had heard nothing about the possibility of drug testing by her employer, nothing even about a problem with drug use or abuse among its employees. When she asked her managers whether there was some suspicion that she was using drugs or some problem with her work, she was told "no." It was merely a random test that had been ordered by Robert Byrne, the vice president of the Engineering Department, and all Department employees were required to comply.

Luck knew little about the law of privacy, but felt in her gut that what the company was asking her to do was wrong. "It just seemed so commonsense," she later explained, "that you must have some reason to ask someone to pee in a cup and then search their body fluids." If the police had shown up at her house wanting to search her drawers, she would not let them do it without a warrant, even if she knew there was nothing bad in them. Similarly, she reasoned, her employer should not be able to demand that she produce a urine sample for testing without some reason. When her supervisors acknowledged that there was no basis for suspecting her of any wrongdoing, she refused to submit to the urine test and asked instead to speak with Byrne. The test seemed so unreasonable in her situation that Luck hoped to convince him not to insist on testing her.

But Byrne was out of town that day, and so Luck's immediate supervisors suspended her for refusing to submit to the urine test. They told her that she would be given a hearing within ten days to two weeks where she would have a chance to make her arguments. No hearing ever took place, however. Instead, she received a letter the following week

---

[16] All of the factual details reported in this chapter are based upon the briefs in the case and telephone interviews with Barbara Luck, with her attorneys Kathleen Lucas and Ellen Lake, and with Edward Chen and John True, who participated in the case as *amici* while they were staff attorneys at the American Civil Liberties Union of Northern California and the Employment Law Center of the Legal Aid Society of San Francisco, respectively. I am grateful to all of these individuals for taking the time to speak with me about the case. In the interests of full disclosure, I report that I was employed as a staff attorney at the Employment Law Center of the Legal Aid Society of San Francisco in the past, but did not participate in the *Luck* case in any manner.

discharging her for insubordination and terminating her health insurance benefits retroactive to the date she had refused to be tested.

Barbara Luck had worked for Southern Pacific since 1979, when she was hired as a draftsperson. She moved to a computer programming job several months later, then in 1981 she was promoted to the position of "engineering programmer"—essentially a computer programmer in the Engineering Department. Her job entailed programming computers and maintaining computer records for the company. She sometimes traveled to the company's regional offices to install computers and instruct office personnel on how to use various programs. For example, she developed and trained others to use programs describing the location of equipment and material used in track replacement. At the time she was asked to submit to the drug test, Luck had worked for Southern Pacific for six and half years and had consistently received excellent reviews of her work.

The testing program that led to Luck's termination had been instituted at Byrne's initiative. At the time, SP did not have any written policies regarding across-the-board urine testing of employees. Pursuant to a written policy, individual workers were subject to "for cause" testing if they were involved in accidents or had exhibited abnormal behavior. The collective bargaining agreement covering the company's union workers also addressed testing, limiting the circumstances under which it could occur. But no official SP policy governed suspicionless testing of non-union employees like Luck. Byrne's order to implement testing applied to every non-union employee in the Engineering Department, from the vice-president on down. He had no particular reason to suspect that any of them used illegal drugs or abused alcohol; however, he believed that an across-the-board testing program would have an important deterrent effect.

Out of the approximately 500 employees in SP's Engineering Department, all except Luck consented to the drug test. Although it is impossible to know how each of them felt about the test, at least a few shared Luck's objections. Several seemed to agree that the test was unnecessary and unwarranted, but suggested that taking the test was "not a big deal." Even if the testing was bad policy, it was not worth "rocking the boat." At least one of Luck's colleagues initially refused to submit to the test, but soon gave in and took it. He later called Luck at home and told her that he agreed with her that the testing was offensive and humiliating, but not offensive enough that he was willing to risk losing his job given that he was the sole provider for his wife and two pre-school age children.

When Luck learned she would likely be suspended for objecting to the drug test, she became panicked about the possibility of losing her health insurance. She was three months' pregnant and her husband had no health insurance because he had quit his job to start his own business six months earlier. Luck, who had previously had a miscarriage, was particularly concerned that she might face complications with her current pregnancy or extraordinary medical expenses for herself or her baby. She asked her supervisors if she could take an early maternity leave rather than risk losing her health benefits. She was told that had she made that request a day earlier, she would have been permitted to take a leave and retain her benefits, but once she had refused to submit to the drug testing, that option was no longer available to her. Several weeks later, after Luck had filed suit, SP reversed its earlier decision and offered her a leave that would preserve her health and life insurance. By then, however, she had already converted her SP group health insurance to an individual policy and she declined, fearing that if she re-enrolled in SP's health insurance, her pregnancy would be excluded as a preexisting condition.

After receiving her notice of termination, Luck immediately sought legal advice. When she initially contacted attorney Kathleen Lucas, her goal was simply to get health insurance coverage. She did not plan on suing the company—she simply wanted someone to intercede so that she could take a leave and retain her health benefits instead of being fired immediately. Lucas had left a large law firm in San Francisco several years earlier to start her own practice focusing on representing employees asserting wrongful discharge and discrimination claims. As a mother of young children, she was moved by Luck's predicament and agreed to help her out. Lucas expected that she would be able to negotiate some kind of resolution regarding the health insurance issue, but to her surprise, SP "dug in their heels." When the attempt at an informal resolution failed, Luck filed suit.

Prior Proceedings

TRIAL COURT PROCEEDINGS

In the trial court, Luck was represented by Lucas and Mark Rudy, another San Francisco lawyer who specialized in representing discharged employees in wrongful discharge cases. Because their initial goal was to get Luck reinstated in order to avoid the loss of her benefits, they filed suit quickly. From the lawyers' perspective, the case was straightforward factually. The termination letter spelled out clearly the company's reasons for terminating Luck—her refusal to submit to the drug test. There was little factual dispute about what had happened. More difficult was determining the legality of SP's reasons for the termination in view of the novelty of workplace drug testing at the time. Given the uncertainty of the law, Luck's complaint included a number of different legal theories, drawing on the developing body of wrongful discharge law and citing the California constitution's explicit protection of personal privacy.

In addition to identifying potential legal theories, the lawyers needed to decide what relief to ask for. One possibility would have been to seek an injunction prohibiting SP from engaging in across-the-board testing, thereby bringing a broad challenge to employer drug testing in the absence of individualized suspicion. Ultimately, her lawyers decided to seek only individual relief for Luck in the form of damages. Given the novelty of drug testing litigation, a broader challenge to the employer's policy seemed too risky. This decision proved to be a wise one, given subsequent events. The trial judge's rulings later in the case made clear that a broader challenge would not have succeeded. And, because San Francisco subsequently passed a law prohibiting suspicionless drug testing by employers in the City, the issue of across-the-board testing was moot by the time of trial—at least for employees in the San Francisco office in which Luck had worked.

The case was tried in October 1987 before San Francisco Superior Court Judge Maxine Chesney. Luck's attorneys focused on the lack of any justification for testing Barbara Luck. They established that there had been no problems with her job performance that might give rise to a suspicion of drug or alcohol abuse. Rather, she was an excellent employee with a "good future with the company." And they challenged the employer's safety rationale by eliciting testimony that Luck's job did not require her to be around moving rail stock and that none of her duties posed a safety risk. One of her former supervisors admitted that Luck "did not have any duties that affected the public safety." Her lawyers emphasized that she spent most of her days "at her computer, wearing high heels and a dress."

In presenting their defense, SP's lawyers emphasized the serious risk posed by alcohol and drug abuse by railway workers, and the company's responsibility for protecting the public safety. They pointed to evidence of past drug and alcohol abuse in the railroad industry and the serious harms that had resulted. The company also tried to portray Luck's duties as safety-related. The computer programs she was responsible for were used to maintain track, and the condition of the rails were important in preventing operational hazards. Moreover, *some* Engineering Department employees clearly had safety-related duties. Vice–President Byrne testified that it was too difficult to draw meaningful distinctions between those employees with safety-sensitive jobs and those without. Because the Engineering Department operated as an integrated unit, he believed that all employees needed to be tested.

The company also argued that urinalysis testing was a valid condition of employment to which Luck had agreed in accepting the job. It pointed out that Luck, along with all other SP employees, had consented to undergo a pre-employment physical exam, including a urine test. At that time she had signed a form permitting the company "to determine my physical fitness for employment" and conduct further examinations "from time to time as considered necessary by the Company." Asserting that Luck had consented to the testing, SP argued that her later refusal to comply constituted insubordination—a legitimate reason for termination.

The trial, which lasted nearly a month, was quite intense for Luck. She attended trial every day, listening to the testimony of former co-workers and supervisors, most of whom she had not seen since her termination. Unlike many employment cases, there was no dispute about the quality of Luck's work performance at SP, or the true reason for her termination. The employer's witnesses candidly admitted that she had been a good employee, and that there was no problem with her work performance. Perhaps the most awkward moments came when the employer's counsel called her gynecologist to testify. Luck had alleged emotional distress as one element of her damages, including a claim that the stress caused by her termination had contributed to a difficult pregnancy. Once such a claim is included, the defendant has the right to conduct discovery on the plaintiff's physical and emotional condition and to elicit trial testimony challenging the alleged connection between the termination and any symptoms.[17] In Luck's case, that meant that her gynecologist could be cross-examined about the details of her condition during pregnancy and delivery. Reflecting on this aspect of the case, Luck found it ironic that her efforts to assert her privacy rights had led to further intrusions on her medical privacy.[18]

In response to the parties' cross-motions for directed verdict, Judge Chesney ruled that SP's interest in ensuring public safety justified the random testing program in general; however, she found a jury issue as to whether testing Luck was necessary given the company's stated safety rationale. The case was submitted to the jury on three theories: that Luck's dismissal for refusing to submit to the urinalysis test was a wrongful termination in violation of public policy, that it violated the implied covenant of good faith and fair dealing, and that her employer's actions constituted the tort of intentional infliction of emotional distress. After deliberating less than a day, the jury found for Luck on all three theories. Specifically, it found that the employer's safety rationale did not justify including Luck in the drug testing program, and awarded her

---

[17] *See, e.g.*, Vinson v. Superior Court, 740 P.2d 404 (Cal. 1987).

[18] The trial was not without its lighter moments—for example, when SP's counsel arranged to have the urine collection container used in the drug testing program admitted as "Exhibit PP."

$180,092 in lost wages and benefits, $32,100 for emotional distress and
$272,850 in punitive damages.

As one of the first decisions involving a challenge to drug testing by
a private employer, the verdict garnered significant attention in the
media and the legal community. Although the lawyers for SP immediately made clear that they intended to appeal, the verdict itself was notable,
particularly given its size. While far from condemning the use of drug
testing generally, it signaled caution against random testing of current
workers without cause.

<h2 style="text-align:center">APPELLATE PROCEEDINGS</h2>

The same lawyers who had tried the case for the employer—Robert
Bogason of SP and Wayne Bolio of the law firm McLaughlin & Irvin—
represented it on appeal. Luck's attorneys, who primarily focused on
trial work, brought in Ellen Lake, an appellate lawyer, to handle the
appeal. A central challenge facing both sides was how to frame the
debate over privacy rights and drug testing in the employment context.

Appellant's Opening Brief. Southern Pacific filed its opening brief in
the California Court of Appeal on November 15, 1988. Although the
company raised numerous arguments for overturning the verdict below,
the brief was often conceptually unclear about how its arguments fit
together with one another and with the three causes of action on which
Luck had prevailed below. This lack of clarity ultimately provided the
court of appeal with an avenue for upholding Luck's damage award in its
entirety, even while ruling against her on several critical points of law.

Although the case had been submitted to the jury on three distinct
causes of action, the company's brief raised a number of general objections to the verdict, rather than specifically attacking each of the three
claims in turn. Only one section was directed at a specific cause of
action—the implied covenant of good faith and fair dealing. Luck's
wrongful discharge claim was mentioned in passing in a section on the
California constitutional right of privacy. The tort of intentional infliction of emotional distress was not specifically challenged in any of the
brief's arguments.

Much of SP's opening brief focused on whether its drug testing
program violated the California constitutional right of privacy. Although
the brief never makes clear the precise connection between the state
constitutional privacy right and the lawfulness of Luck's discharge, its
argument implicitly assumed that the verdict on the wrongful discharge
in violation of public policy claim turned on the constitutionality of SP's
actions. The company first contended that the constitutional right to
privacy did not apply to Luck's situation at all, because it only limited
government actions and SP was a private employer. It further asserted

that the constitutional provision was aimed only at limiting the *disclosure* of private information, a risk not raised by its urinalysis program. Citing the federal government's express promotion of "drug free working environments," it argued that public policy favored, rather than prohibited, the use of drug detection programs.

Even if the California constitutional right of privacy applied, SP argued that its across-the-board testing program was justified. Relying on cases evaluating public employer drug testing programs under the Fourth Amendment, the company contended that Luck had a diminished expectation of privacy because she chose to work for a railroad, in an industry that is traditionally heavily regulated. SP also asserted that the trial court erred in considering only safety as a legitimate interest justifying its urinalysis testing program. The railroad contended that it also had strong interests in deterring drug use, promoting efficiency, creating a drug-free workplace and ensuring public confidence in the integrity of the railroad industry.

Regarding Luck's claim for breach of the implied covenant of good faith and fair dealing, the company argued that the claim should not have gone to the jury. It asserted that the implied covenant does not apply in the absence of a contract between the parties. Pointing out that Luck had failed to establish the existence of any agreement with SP that guaranteed her job security, it contended that she was an at-will employee and the implied covenant simply did not apply.[19]

Respondent's Brief. In contrast to the company's submission, Luck's responsive brief was far clearer about the relationship between her wrongful discharge claim and her constitutional privacy rights. It declared: "Southern Pacific discharged Luck in violation of public policy for refusing to submit to a mass urine test that would have violated her right of privacy under the California constitution." This argument entailed several steps. First, Luck argued that urinalysis testing constitutes a "significant invasion" of the constitutional right to privacy. By compelling employees to urinate for testing purposes, it invades their bodily integrity. The subsequent testing of the urine sample further implicates privacy rights by revealing highly personal information including information about lawful medications taken by the employee. And because urine tests could not detect current impairment, Luck argued that urinalysis tests constituted a sort of "chemical surveillance" of its workers' home lives.

---

[19] The brief raised additional issues incidental to the core privacy and wrongful discharge claims, such as whether the federal Railway Labor Act, 45 U.S.C. §§ 151–188 (2006), preempted Luck's claims, and whether she had failed to mitigate her damages. The court of appeals ultimately rejected SP's arguments on these points.

Luck next argued that because the urinalysis testing program invaded employees' constitutional privacy rights, SP bore the burden of proving that it was justified by a compelling interest and was the least intrusive alternative for achieving that purpose. She argued that the company's safety rationale could not justify across-the-board testing in the absence of any evidence of drug or alcohol abuse in the Engineering Department. Luck further contended that mandatory urinalysis was not "the least intrusive alternative" to achieving its safety goal because the company could have trained supervisors to identify impaired workers and should have exempted employees, like Luck, whose jobs did not threaten public safety, rather than mandating tests across-the-board.

As the final step in her argument, Luck asserted that firing an employee for refusing to submit to an unconstitutional invasion of her privacy met the elements of the tort of wrongful discharge in violation of public policy. Unlike its discussion of the California constitutional right of privacy, respondent's brief spent little time developing this argument. The California Supreme Court had recently addressed the requirements of a public policy claim in *Foley v. Interactive Data Corp.*,[20] and Luck's appellate counsel was concerned that that opinion could be read in a way that might be harmful to her case. Uncertain whether or how SP might exploit *Foley*, she chose to keep her discussion on this point to a minimum rather than trying to respond to arguments that SP had not yet made, and simply asserted that Luck's privacy claim involved a "firmly established" public policy, because privacy was a fundamental interest guaranteed by the California constitution.

Luck's brief also contested the company's legal explanation of the implied covenant of good faith and fair dealing claim. Although it is true that the implied covenant claim rests on the existence of a contract of employment, Luck argued that it was not necessary for the employee to prove an agreement requiring good cause for termination. Rather, the covenant was implied in *all* contracts, even contracts for at-will employment. Rather than challenging her at-will status, Luck alleged that SP's express policies and the oral promises of her supervisors guaranteed her a hearing before she was terminated for refusing to submit to the drug test. In her view, it was the company's failure to provide her with such a hearing that constituted a bad faith violation of the implied covenant. Thus, Luck's implied covenant claim rested on her allegation that she had been deprived of *procedural* rights promised by her employer, not any substantive right requiring good cause for discharge or contractually guaranteeing her personal privacy.

In the very last section of her brief, Luck asserted that SP had not appealed the verdict on her intentional infliction of emotional distress

---

[20] 765 P.2d 373 (Cal. 1988).

claim. Because emotional distress damages and punitive damages are appropriately awarded for intentional infliction of emotional distress, she claimed that the damage awards should be upheld on the basis of the unappealed tort claim, regardless of any errors that may have affected her other two causes of action.

Appellant's Reply Brief. SP's reply brief, filed April 7, 1989, had a clarity and focus that was lacking in its opening brief. The lawyers' legal analysis had undoubtedly been sharpened by three important cases that had been decided in the months since their opening brief was filed. In December 1988, the California Supreme Court had decided *Foley v. Interactive Data Corporation*, a critical case defining the contours of wrongful discharge law in California. And in March 1989, the United States Supreme Court handed down *Skinner* and *Von Raab*—two decisions addressing the constitutionality of urinalysis drug testing under the Fourth Amendment to the U.S. Constitution.

In *Foley*, a discharged employee sued his former employer on several theories, including wrongful discharge in violation of public policy and breach of the implied covenant of good faith and fair dealing. The plaintiff, Daniel Foley, alleged that he was fired after reporting to a company officer that a recently hired manager was the subject of a criminal investigation for alleged embezzlement from a prior employer. By the time Foley brought his suit, a claim for wrongful discharge in violation of public policy was widely recognized, not only in California, but many other states as well, although its exact contours were not well defined. Foley argued that his discharge was forbidden by the public policy that "imposes a legal duty on employees to report relevant business information to management."

The California Supreme Court, while affirming the vitality of a tort claim for wrongful discharge in violation of public policy, refused to find a violation in Foley's situation. It stated that a wrongful discharge claim must be based on a public policy "about which reasonable persons can have little disagreement, and which was 'firmly established' at the time of discharge." The court also attempted to distinguish when a *public*, as opposed to a purely private, interest was at stake. It explained that even where an asserted public policy has a "statutory touchstone," courts should still inquire whether the discharge "affects a duty which inures to the benefit of the public at large rather than to a particular employer or employee." In Foley's case, the court concluded that no substantial public policy prohibited his discharge because any duty to disclose information only served the private interest of the employer. In a footnote, the court explained its reasoning: "The absence of a distinctly 'public' interest in this case is apparent when we consider that if an employer and employee were *expressly* to agree that the employee has no obligation to, and should not, inform the employer of any adverse information the employee learns about a fellow employee's background, nothing in the state's public policy would render such an agreement void."

SP's reply brief aggressively used the *Foley* decision to challenge Luck's public policy claim. According to the company, *Foley* had made it "crystal clear" that a wrongful discharge claim must be based on a public policy that is "so established that it is subject to no doubt." Then, it subtly recharacterized Luck's argument, recasting the relevant public policy as one about the legitimacy of drug testing policies rather than a public policy protecting employee privacy. This shift allowed the company to argue—underlining its words for emphasis—that "there is not now, and there certainly was not at the time of Respondent's discharge, a 'firmly established' public policy that drug testing violated the constitutional right of privacy." Pointing to numerous recent court challenges, SP asserted that drug testing was a matter of "nationwide debate," not an issue about which "reasonable persons can have little disagreement." Thus, the very novelty of the drug testing issue was used to argue that no firmly established public policy was at stake. SP also seized on the *Foley* court's efforts to distinguish public from purely private interests. Citing the language in the court's footnote, SP argued that Luck *could* have consented to the urinalysis test. Concluding that such an agreement would not be unlawful, it contended that no public policy was violated when Luck was terminated for refusing to be tested.

Foley also addressed a claim of breach of the implied covenant of good faith and fair dealing. That claim had increasingly been invoked by discharged employees in the California courts—its application easing the harshness of the traditional at-will rule where a worker's discharge appeared to be motivated by bad faith. Although the implied covenant was understood in the commercial context as a contract claim, the California courts had permitted plaintiffs bringing bad faith claims in the insurance context to sue in tort. In the years prior to *Foley*, a number of courts of appeal in California had extended the reasoning of the insurance cases to employee discharge cases. Addressing the issue for the first time in *Foley*, the California Supreme Court rejected the analogy between the employment relationship and that between insurer and insured, holding that tort damages are not available for breach of the implied covenant of good faith and fair dealing in the employment context. Citing this aspect of *Foley*, SP argued for striking the compensatory and punitive damages from the jury's award.

SP's reply brief also sought to capitalize on the United States Supreme Court's opinions in *Skinner* and *Von Raab*, decided weeks after Luck had submitted her brief to the appeals court. In *Skinner*,[21] the

---

[21] 489 U.S. 602 (1989).

Supreme Court upheld the constitutionality of regulations promulgated by the Federal Railroad Administration (FRA) which mandated drug and alcohol testing of railroad employees involved in a major train accident. The Court first held that urinalysis drug testing did implicate privacy rights protected by the Fourth Amendment, and proceeded to apply a balancing test to determine whether the testing required by the regulations was "unreasonable." In light of the safety-sensitive nature of the jobs subject to testing, the Court upheld the regulations, concluding that the Government's "compelling interests" outweighed any intrusion on employee privacy. *Von Raab*[22] involved a challenge to the United States Customs Service policy of requiring all employees transferred or promoted to certain positions to undergo urinalysis drug tests. The Court concluded that the testing was constitutional in regards to positions that were directly involved in drug interdiction or involved carrying firearms, based on the Government's compelling interests in safety and in ensuring that "front-line interdiction personnel are physically fit, and have unimpeachable integrity and judgment." However, it expressed skepticism about whether testing was justified for all of the covered positions and remanded to the Court of Appeals to determine whether the category of employees subject to testing because of their access to classified materials was too broad.

Although SP was a railroad, Luck was not a covered employee under the FRA regulations because of the nature of her job. And in the absence of direct government involvement in the decision to test her, *Skinner* and *Von Raab*, which turned on the Fourth Amendment to the United States Constitution, did not directly apply to her case. Nevertheless, SP argued that the significance of *Skinner* and *Von Raab* was that they had upheld mandatory drug testing in the absence of individualized suspicion, and had approved deterrence of drug use as a rationale for drug testing. Although these assertions were not inaccurate, the reasoning contained in the two Supreme Court cases cut both ways. On the one hand, as SP argued, the Court had upheld drug testing policies similar in many respects to its own: urine samples were not collected under the direct observation of a monitor; SP tested only for substances that might have an adverse effect on work performance; and there was no indication the company did not treat the information as confidential.

On the other hand, the testing approved in *Skinner* and *Von Raab* entailed advance notice to employees and was triggered only upon the occurrence of certain events. By contrast, SP had not announced the drug tests prior to the day of testing and had implemented across-the-board testing, a form of testing arguably more intrusive than post-accident or pre-promotion testing. Moreover, the Court in *Skinner* un-

---

[22] 489 U.S. 656 (1989).

equivocally affirmed that urinalysis drug testing infringed "expectations of privacy that society has long recognized as reasonable." It found that monitoring the act of urination as required by the regulations implicated privacy interests. And because testing bodily fluids "can reveal a host of private medical facts about an employee, including whether he or she is epileptic, pregnant, or diabetic," it held that the subsequent chemical analysis constituted a further invasion of privacy. Perhaps most significantly, the Court's decision in *Skinner* rested heavily on the safety-sensitive nature of the jobs at issue—highlighting precisely the lack of a safety rationale for testing Luck that had been emphasized by her lawyers at trial.

In its reply brief, SP also belatedly attempted to counter Luck's argument that her damage award could be upheld on the basis of her intentional infliction of emotional distress claim because the latter had not been challenged on appeal. Although it had not specifically attacked the jury's verdict on the emotional distress claim, the company argued that it had appealed "every fact underlying Respondent's claim for intentional infliction of emotional distress" in its opening brief, and that it was not required to repeat those arguments specifically in connection with the emotional distress claim, as it was "derivative of the other causes of action." Thus, it dismissed Luck's argument as one of "form over substance."

Brief of the Amici. In addition to the parties, the American Civil Liberties Union of Northern California (ACLU/NC) and The Employment Law Center of the Legal Aid Society of San Francisco (ELC/SF) filed a joint brief as amici curiae on behalf of Barbara Luck in the court of appeal. Edward Chen and John True, staff attorneys at the ACLU/NC and ELC/LAS, respectively, had for some time been concerned about intrusions on employee privacy and, in particular, the threat posed by the growing popularity of drug testing among employers. For a variety of reasons, they viewed the appeal in Luck's case as a good opportunity to try to establish the substantive privacy rights of current employees. Barbara Luck was an attractive litigant because it seemed clear that her refusal to submit to the testing was based purely on principle. Because she was an established employee, thirty-four years old, married and pregnant at the time of the test, there was no reason to suspect she would have tested positive, and the company's lawyers never tried to suggest otherwise. In addition, the lack of any safety-related job duties seemed fairly clearly. Sensing a chance to establish the privacy rights of private-sector employees, Chen and True, recruited Steven L. Mayer, Matthew G. Jacobs and Carl L. Blumenstein from the San Francisco firm of Howard, Rice, Nemerovski, Canady, Robertson & Falk to draft a brief on behalf of the two public interest organizations that would lay out the case for legal limits on workplace drug testing.

Although their brief paralleled the privacy arguments of Luck's briefs in many respects, the *amici* had greater latitude to raise broader policy arguments for protecting employee privacy and limiting employers' prerogative to mandate drug testing. They began with an exposition of the science underlying urinalysis drug tests, explaining that such tests do not measure whether a subject is currently under the influence of a drug. Rather, urinalysis tests for presence of drug metabolites, the inert by-products that are present in urine after the body metabolizes a particular drug. These metabolites can be detected long after any psychoactive effect has ceased, sometimes for weeks after. Because the levels of metabolites present in urine vary from one individual to another and are affected by factors such as a person's hydration, urinalysis does not provide information about the frequency, amount or timing of drug use. The brief also pointed out that reliable interpretation of the results required the tested individual to provide information about prescription and other legal medications recently taken, because such substances sometimes produced metabolites similar to those of illegal drugs, resulting in false positive results. Given these limitations of urinalysis tests, the *amici* argued that when drug tests are administered without any other indicia of abuse, they are not probative of on-the-job impairment. What they do detect, they contended, is private off-duty behavior, and employers have no legitimate interest in regulating such behavior unless there is a direct nexus between that conduct and an individual's job performance.

The *amici* also sought to advance a broad interpretation of the California constitutional right to privacy, arguing that its protections are "far more expansive than that afforded under the federal constitution"—and that it protected against both government and private action. They further contended that any invasion of the right to privacy must be justified by a compelling interest, a test "far more exacting" that the balancing test applied by federal courts under the Fourth Amendment. Rather than emphasize the nature of Luck's particular job, the brief advanced a broader challenge, asserting that SP's across-the-board testing policy was unconstitutional even apart from its specific application to Barbara Luck.

New Precedent. After all the briefing in *Luck* was completed, but before the court issued its decision, another division of the California court of appeal issued the first appellate decision dealing directly with workplace drug testing. That case, *Wilkinson v. Times Mirror Corp.*,[23] involved a challenge to a pre-employment drug testing policy. Applicants for positions such as legal writer or copy editor were required to undergo a urinalysis test for drugs and alcohol as a condition of employment, and

---

[23] 264 Cal. Rptr. 194 (Ct. App. 1989).

a positive result would disqualify the applicant from employment. Several attorneys who were denied employment after refusing to submit to the drug test sued on the grounds that it violated Article I, Section 1 of the California constitution and sought an injunction prohibiting future testing. The *Wilkinson* court decided that the constitutional right of privacy did protect against private conduct, but that a compelling interest was not always necessary to justify an intrusion. It concluded that the employer's testing policy did not violate the plaintiffs' constitutional right of privacy. Crucial to its decision was the fact that the plaintiffs were not employees, but *applicants*, who should reasonably expect that they would have to disclose personal information and undergo a pre-employment physical exam. Thus, by the time the *Luck* court issued its decision, it was no longer writing on a completely blank slate. At least one other court had addressed some of the same issues, although the two cases could be factually distinguished.

The Appellate Court Opinion

Although the appeal in *Luck* clearly called for the court to better define the scope of employee privacy rights, the legal posture of the case presented a bit of a puzzle. The briefs all focused on the California constitutional right of privacy, and yet none of the three causes of action on which Luck had prevailed was a constitutional one. The trial court had dismissed the claim of invasion of her constitutional right of privacy on the grounds that Luck had avoided any intrusion by refusing to submit to the testing. She might have used the constitutional right offensively, as in *Wilkinson*, by seeking to enjoin SP's across-the-board testing policy. However, as discussed above, her lawyers made a strategic choice to seek relief only in her individual case. Thus, her complaint against her employer stemmed not from any *actual* invasion of her privacy, but from her employer's *response* when she had resisted a *threatened* invasion. More precisely, her claims turned on whether SP was permitted to terminate her employment for asserting her state constitutional privacy rights, rather than on any direct violation of those rights.

The California Court of Appeal resolved this puzzle in an unexpected way.[24] Both parties and the amici had premised the arguments in their briefs on the assumption that the state constitutional right of privacy was the basis for Luck's wrongful discharge in violation of public policy claim. The implied covenant of good faith and fair dealing claim did not depend on the constitutional right, but rather on Luck's assertion that SP's explicit policies entitled her to a hearing prior to termination, and that it had failed to comply with those policies in bad faith.

---

[24] 267 Cal. Rptr. 618 (Ct. App. 1990).

Nevertheless, the court's opinion recast the argument, stating that "[t]he validity of the jury's finding of bad faith turns on whether Luck had a constitutional right to privacy allowing her to refuse to submit to urinalysis." By structuring the discussion in this way, the privacy interests protected by the California constitution were subordinated to the question of whether the employer had breached the implied covenant of good faith and fair dealing.

The purpose of the implied covenant is to make effective the express promises of the parties to a contract. It operates as a sort of gap filler, insuring that neither party acts in bad faith to deprive the other of the benefits of their agreement. Thus, what constitutes a breach of the implied covenant depends upon what was agreed to in the actual contract. Luck's brief had emphasized the procedural guarantees she was promised under SP's policies and by her supervisors. The court of appeal, however, assumed that Luck's claim depended on the existence of an agreement requiring good cause for her termination. Although Luck had not claimed that she was anything other than an at-will employee, the court considered whether the circumstances of Luck's employment gave rise to a *Pugh*-type implied-in-fact contract guaranteeing her job security. Noting that Luck had been employed for six and a half years, that she had been promoted and that she had received grade and salary increases, the court concluded that an implied contract existed, and that SP was required to have good cause to terminate Luck. Having found the existence of a good-cause contract, the court then framed the critical question as whether Luck's termination for objecting to the drug test was without good cause, and therefore, in bad faith.

Given this framing of the issue, the court's extensive discussion of the state constitutional privacy right took place in a subsection under the topic "Implied Covenant of Good Faith and Fair Dealing." That discussion conveyed the sense that the court understood the constitutional right of privacy to be a robust one. By including it among the rights guaranteed in Article I, Section 1, the court wrote, "California affords privacy the constitutional status of an inalienable right, on a par with defending life and possessing property." Citing the U.S. Supreme Court's decision in *Skinner*, the court found that both the collection and analysis of urine entailed in drug testing intrude upon protected privacy interests. It then held that the constitutional privacy provision was intended to restrain the activities of both government and business, and, therefore, applied to private employers like SP. Although the constitution does not provide absolute protection of personal privacy, the court held that intrusions must be justified by a "compelling interest," a burden it recognized as heavier than the balancing analysis required under the Fourth Amendment. The court distinguished the recent *Wilkinson* decision, noting that that case had involved job applicants.

Because Luck was an *employee*, not an applicant, her termination "was a sufficient burden on her right to privacy to merit application of the compelling interest test."

The court then turned to SP's asserted justifications for testing Luck. It found that although that the railroad had a clear interest in ensuring safety, the constitutionality of its actions turned on whether testing Luck was necessary to further that interest. After reviewing the evidence presented at trial, the court agreed with the determination in the trial court that Luck did not have any safety-sensitive duties. The court also considered, and rejected, the railroad's argument that its testing program was justified by non-safety interests such as deterrence, efficiency and public confidence, finding none of these interests to be compelling. In the absence of a "clear, direct nexus" between the employee's duties and the nature of the feared harm, the court concluded that none of the company's asserted rationales could justify the invasion of Luck's privacy.

SP's arguments based on *Skinner* and *Von Raab* had little traction with the California court of appeal. Although the company argued that those cases supported the constitutionality of its testing policies, the *Luck* court instead cited *Skinner* for the proposition that urine testing implicates important privacy interests, quoting it at length:

> [C]hemical analysis of urine ... can reveal a host of private medical facts about an employee, including whether she is epileptic, pregnant, or diabetic. Nor can it be disputed that the process of collecting the sample to be tested, which may in some cases involve visual or aural monitoring of the act of urination, itself implicates privacy interests. As the Court of Appeals for the Fifth Circuit has stated: "There are few activities in our society more personal or private than the passing of urine. Most people describe it by euphemisms if they talk about it at all. It is a function traditionally performed without public observation; indeed, its performance in public is generally prohibited by law as well as social custom."

As for SP's safety justification, the *Luck* court distinguished it from the policies approved in *Skinner* and *Von Raab*, pointing out a critical difference between "unsupervised employees who work in the field" and those, like Luck, who work in a traditional office environment where impairment is more easily detected. According to the court of appeal, the decisions in *Skinner* and *Von Raab* turned on "the immediacy of the threat" involved in operating a train or carrying a firearm. Those cases "provide no basis for finding that an office employee constitutes a safety risk when the chain of causation between misconduct and injury is greatly attenuated."

The company's efforts to use the California Supreme Court's recent decision in *Foley* to challenge the verdict were more successful. *Foley*'s conclusion that tort damages are not available for claims of breach of the implied covenant of good faith and fair dealing in the employment context had been quickly followed by another California Supreme Court decision making that holding retroactive.[25] Because the *Luck* court had framed the relevance of the constitutional right of privacy in terms of the implied covenant claim, its finding that urinalysis testing invaded her right to privacy gave rise only to contract damages. The jury's award of emotional distress and punitive damages could not be sustained on this basis.

In addition, the court of appeal relied on the *Foley* decision to reject Luck's wrongful discharge in violation of public policy claim. Luck's theory at trial had been that her discharge for objecting to an invasion of her privacy violated public policy. In sharp contrast to its earlier expansive discussion of the constitutional right of privacy, this section of the opinion minimized the significance of Luck's privacy interests. Purporting to apply the *Foley* standard, it argued that the right of privacy is "by its very name, a private right, not a public one." Next, it applied the "void-if-contracted-for" test suggested in a footnote in *Foley*. Reasoning that Luck and Southern Pacific could have lawfully agreed that she would undergo urinalysis testing, the court concluded that firing her for refusing to do so did not violate public policy. In evaluating whether the public policy asserted by Luck was "firmly established," as required by *Foley*, the court of appeal accepted SP's characterization of the public policy inquiry as whether there was a policy specifically opposed to drug testing rather than, more broadly, one of protecting fundamental privacy rights. According to the court, the "explosion of hotly contested" drug testing cases established that the issue of drug testing was one about which reasonable people disagreed. Because at the time SP attempted to test Luck no major drug testing case had yet been decided, the court concluded that "there was no firmly established public policy against urinalysis" and that therefore Luck failed to state a wrongful discharge claim.

After limiting Luck's implied covenant claim to contact damages and rejecting her public policy discharge claim altogether, the court of appeal appeared poised to strike down the tort damages she had been awarded by the jury. However, in a short section—unpublished pursuant to court order—it upheld the award of damages on the basis of Luck's third claim—intentional infliction of emotional distress.[26] Rejecting SP's argument that it had adequately challenged all of the underlying facts, the

---

[25] *Newman v. Emerson Radio Corp.*, 772 P.2d 1059 (Cal. 1989).

[26] 267 Cal.Rptr. 618 (Ct. App. 1990).

court held that intentional infliction of emotional distress is "an independent tort, not a mere element of damage" and concluded that SP's failure to specifically challenge that cause of action on appeal left the jury's verdict intact. Because a claim of intentional infliction of emotional distress supported an award of tort damages, including punitive damages, it upheld the jury's award in its entirety.

Judge Marcel Poché, one of the three appellate judges to hear the case, dissented from the majority's decision regarding Luck's public policy claim. Unlike the majority, he found the requirement that the public policy be "firmly established, fundamental and substantial" easily satisfied by the inclusion of privacy in Article I, section 1 of the California constitution. After all, he argued, the very nature of a constitution is "to enunciate high public policy." The void-if-contracted-for test suggested by the *Foley* court might be useful for determining whether a *statute* served a public policy or merely regulated conduct between private individuals. However, it made no sense to apply such a test to a constitutional right, and nothing in *Foley* required such an application. Judge Poché also contended that the majority had identified the wrong public policy. Contrary to SP's assertion, the relevant public policy was not one prohibiting urinalysis but the important policy of preserving personal privacy. That latter policy had been articulated by Californians in 1974 when it was added to the constitution's list of "inalienable rights," and therefore had been "firmly established" years before Luck was fired. He wrote that "unless we accept the perfectly logical and defensible position that inalienable personal rights inure by their very nature to the benefit of all Californians and thus to the public benefit, we accord no practical protection to the very rights given the greatest deference by our constitution."

The Impact of Luck

For Barbara Luck personally, the court of appeal decision represented a clear victory. She felt vindicated that the court of appeal had agreed that she had a right to stand up and say "no" to an invasion of her privacy and that SP should not have fired her for doing so. After both the California Supreme Court and the United States Supreme Court declined SP's petitions for further review, the company duly paid the full amount of damages awarded by the jury.

Media reports characterized the *Luck* decision as a "major setback" to employer drug testing programs[27] or, more dramatically, a "death blow" for random testing.[28] Although these descriptions were undoubted-

---

[27] Harriet Chiang, *Major Setback for Drug Tests by Employers*, S.F. Chron., June 1, 1990, at A1.

[28] Michael A. Verespej, *Death Blow for Random Testing*, Industry Week, July 2, 1990, at 47.

ly exaggerated, the case clearly had an impact. *Wilkinson* had upheld a pre-employment drug testing policy, and *Skinner* and *Von Raab* had approved of certain forms of post-accident and pre-promotion testing under the Fourth Amendment. In *Luck*, a court of appeal had clearly found a limit to employers' freedom to mandate urinalysis testing. The decision signaled caution in subjecting current employees who do not have safety-sensitive jobs to suspicionless testing. One of SP's attorney predicted that the decision would cause other companies to cut back on their drug testing programs.[29] Although the bottom line result of the case—affirming the $485,042 jury verdict in full—suggested a clear victory for employee privacy rights, the reasoning of the court of appeal presaged some of the difficulties of protecting employee privacy—difficulties which would become increasingly evident over time.

At the time it was issued, the *Luck* opinion contained one of the most thorough analyses applying the California constitutional right of privacy in the workplace context. The court of appeal clearly stated that urinalysis "intrudes upon reasonable expectations of privacy," thereby triggering the constitutional analysis, and that private employers as well as government actors are bound by the privacy provision. In addition, it held that the California constitution required intrusions on personal privacy to be justified by a "compelling interest." The court also made clear that any such intrusion "cannot be upheld absent a clear, direct nexus between the employee's duties and the nature of the feared harm." Until the California Supreme Court directly addressed these issues several years later—altering the analysis in significant ways—the *Luck* opinion was a leading case interpreting the state constitutional privacy right.

Although the court's interpretation of the constitutional right was quite expansive, its choice to frame the analysis as an element of a good faith claim seriously limited the force of the privacy right in the employment context. First, as noted above, tort damages are not available in the employment context for breach of the implied covenant of good faith and fair dealing in California. More importantly, many employees would not be able to establish the existence of an implied-in-fact contract protecting them from termination in the absence of good cause, either because they could not show the facts necessary to give rise to a *Pugh*-type claim or because their employment was explicitly at will. The implication of the court's implied contract analysis was that at-will employees could not argue that their constitutional privacy rights limited their employer's power to terminate them.

---

[29] Harriet Chiang, *Major Setback for Drug Tests by Employers*, S.F. Chron., June 1, 1990, at A1.

In contrast to the contract theories, the tort of wrongful discharge in violation of public policy is available even to at-will employees. The *Luck* court, however, took a step toward foreclosing this avenue by ruling that privacy rights could not be the basis for a public policy claim. This result was not ordained by the California Supreme Court's opinion in *Foley*. In fact, just weeks before the *Luck* decision, another California court of appeal had reached the opposite conclusion, permitting a wrongful discharge claim to proceed on the theory that firing an employee for refusing to take a suspicionless drug test violated public policy. That case, *Semore v. Pool*,[30] also sought to follow the guidance set out in *Foley* that a wrongful discharge claim must be based on a duty that inures to the benefit of the public at large rather than a particular employer or employee. The *Semore* court wrote that privacy is "a right [the plaintiff] shares with all other employees. In asserting the right, he gives it life . . . [T]he assertion of the right establishes it and benefits all Californians in the same way that an assertion of a free speech right benefits all of us." Rather than a purely personal right, the *Semore* court understood privacy as having an important social dimension. This understanding is consistent with Fourth Amendment doctrine which asks whether a "legitimate expectation of privacy" exists, an inquiry which turns on social norms and past practices.

The *Semore* court also reached a different conclusion when applying *Foley*'s "void-if-contracted-for" test. According to the court, an employee might agree not to assert a right to privacy; however, "if the intrusion violates the right to privacy, it is illegal whether or not it is pursuant to an agreement." Thus, the mere existence of an agreement would not answer the question whether that contract should be unenforceable because it was against public policy. The *Semore* court's analysis on this point highlighted a certain question-begging quality to the test suggested by the *Foley* court. To determine whether a public policy exists by asking whether an agreement circumventing the alleged policy would be void is merely to restate the question. In order to decide whether the parties' agreement would be void, one first needs some way of knowing what public policy requires or forbids.

Another crucial difference in the *Semore* court's analysis was its characterization of the public policy at issue. Stating the policy in terms of a right to privacy, it easily found it to be fundamental and clearly established by the California constitution. It acknowledged, however, that recognition of a public policy protecting privacy would not by itself resolve the controversy before it. Rather, the ultimate resolution of the case "depends upon balancing an employee's expectations of privacy against the employer's needs to regulate the conduct of its employees at

---

[30] 266 Cal. Rptr. 280 (Ct. App. 1990).

work." Permitting the public policy claim to proceed did not guarantee the plaintiff victory; it merely moved the case to the next step—an examination of the competing interests at stake to determine whether or not the intrusion was justified. By contrast, the *Luck* court's narrow characterization of the public policy at issue as a "policy prohibiting urinalysis" essentially cut off any examination of whether particular drug testing policies were warranted in light of their intrusiveness. By defining the relevant public policy in this way, the *Luck* court required evidence of a policy *specifically* addressing drug testing. However, urinalysis was a relatively new technology and had only very recently been used in the workplace. At the time Luck was fired, virtually no court or legislature had spoken to the issue because it was only just emerging. The differing approaches taken in *Semore* and *Luck* raise the question whether the regulation of new technologies should always await legislative action, or whether common law doctrines can and should act as a backstop, permitting scrutiny of new forms of privacy intrusions in egregious cases.

Although *Luck* was a California case, decided under state law, other states' courts have frequently looked to California precedent in the employment area. As one of the earliest cases challenging workplace drug testing policies, *Luck* had the potential to establish a framework for analyzing employee privacy claims, not only in California but also across the nation. The court of appeal ultimately upheld the jury verdict in Luck's favor in its entirety; however, it did so in a manner that offered little assistance to employees in other jurisdictions seeking to assert privacy rights. The *Luck* court's most comprehensive analysis of the plaintiff's privacy claim and the competing interests at stake in the debate over drug testing occurred in its discussion of the California constitutional right of privacy. Only a handful of other states similarly have constitutions that expressly protect privacy, and of those, most had clearly limited their application to government actors. In addition, the *Luck* court used implied contract theories, rather than the tort of wrongful discharge in violation of public policy, to protect her right to object to intrusive employer practices. Most jurisdictions at that time had adopted the public-policy tort but were less accepting of claims based on the implied covenant of good faith and fair dealing. With the *Luck* and *Semore* courts' resolutions of the public policy claim in conflict, courts in other jurisdictions found little clear guidance on whether employees discharged for asserting privacy rights should receive protection.

Subsequent Developments

In the years following *Luck*, the California Supreme Court directly addressed the scope and application of the state constitutional right to privacy. A 1994 case, *Hill v. National Collegiate Athletic Association*,[31] challenged the NCAA's policies for drug testing college athletes. The court confirmed that the constitutional privacy provision restrained private as well as governmental entities. However, it rejected the approach of *Luck* and other lower courts requiring that an invasion of privacy be justified by a "compelling interest." Rather, it explained, the constitutionality of a particular invasion should be evaluated in light of "the specific kind of privacy interest involved and the nature and seriousness of the invasion." Any privacy concerns should be "carefully compared" with the justifications for the intrusion in a balancing test. Using this less rigorous standard of review, the court upheld the NCAA's drug testing policies; however, because *Hill* did not involve employee testing, its impact on the rationale of *Luck* was somewhat unclear.

Several years later, the California Supreme Court decided its first privacy case involving workplace drug testing. That case, *Loder v. City of Glendale*,[32] challenged a city's use of mandatory pre-employment and pre-promotional drug tests. The court first considered the plaintiff's challenge under the Fourth Amendment to the United States Constitution and concluded that urinalysis testing of all *current* employees seeking promotion to any other position—even non-safety-sensitive jobs—violated the Fourth Amendment, but that such testing of *applicants* for city employment did not.[33] The opinion next considered the validity of the pre-employment tests under the California constitution. It recognized that while drug testing "unquestionably implicates privacy interests protected by the state Constitution," it was "much less of an intrusion" on applicants, who should reasonably anticipate a medical examination as part of the hiring process. At the same time, the court found that the employer had a greater interest in suspicionless testing of applicants than employees, because it had no alternative means of detecting performance problems prior to hire. Given the financial burdens and morale problems that might result from hiring someone who abuses drugs or alcohol, the court concluded that the balance favored the employer's interest and upheld the city's mandatory testing of job applicants. By so deciding, the *Loder* court endorsed treating the privacy claims of current employees differently from those of applicants, an outcome consistent with the different results in *Luck* and *Wilkinson*.

Because *Loder* involved a broad challenge to an employer's drug testing policies—not an individual claim of unlawful discharge as a result

---

[31] 865 P.2d 633 (Cal. 1994).

[32] 927 P.2d 1200 (Cal. 1997).

[33] Because the court concluded that the across-the-board testing of current employees seeking promotion violated the Fourth Amendment of the federal constitution, it declined to decide whether such testing also violated the California constitution. *Id.* at 1226.

of their application—the California Supreme Court had no opportunity to address the applicability of the public policy tort. Thus, the conflict between the approaches taken in *Luck* and *Semore* remains unresolved in California. One court of appeal in California sought to avoid the conflict altogether, arguing that the "attempt to shoehorn the privacy claims ... into the *Foley* model" was mistaken.[34] In that case, the plaintiff argued that he was wrongfully terminated for asserting his privacy rights when he refused to enroll in an in-patient alcohol treatment program at his employer's insistence. Rather than deciding whether protecting privacy can be a public policy, the court wrote:

> What is really at stake ... is a violation of a fundamental state constitutional right that is directly and independently enforceable against both private and governmental entities, where the threat of discharge is simply the means by which the employer applies economic coercion to the employee's decision whether to exercise (or waive) those rights, and/or where termination of employment is a form of punishment or retaliation for the employee's choice to exercise (or refusal to waive) those rights.

The court then permitted the plaintiff's claim to proceed directly under the state constitutional privacy provision, without trying to fit his claim in the framework of the public policy tort.

If the California Supreme Court endorses this approach, it would provide recourse even for at-will employees fired for asserting a right to privacy, while avoiding the conundrum of whether protecting privacy can be the basis of a public policy tort. Such an approach may also be available in states where a statute protecting privacy provides a right of action. For example, in Massachusetts a statute grants each person a right "against unreasonable, substantial or serious interference with his privacy," and gives courts jurisdiction to enforce the right.[35] Pursuant to that statute, the Supreme Judicial Court of Massachusetts permitted employees to challenge their dismissal for refusing to submit to a drug test, and, in the case of one employee whose job was not safety related, determined that the employer's interest in testing was outweighed by the employee's privacy rights.[36]

For most private employees in most states, however, their practical ability to raise privacy claims against their employer may depend on whether or not privacy rights are considered a source of public policy.[37] Some courts have permitted such wrongful discharge suits, finding

---

[34] *Pettus v. Cole*, 57 Cal. Rptr.2d 46 (Ct. App. 1996).

[35] Mass. Gen. Laws Ann. ch. 214, § 1B (2006).

[36] *Webster v. Motorola, Inc.*, 637 N.E.2d 203 (Mass. 1994).

[37] *See* Pauline T. Kim, *Privacy Rights, Public Policy and the Employment Relationship*, 57 Ohio St. L. J. 671 (1996).

evidence of a public policy protecting personal privacy in a variety of
sources, including state constitutional provisions and the common law
tort of invasion of privacy.[38] Although the state constitutional right of
privacy in these states does not apply to private actors, courts have
found that the values expressed in those constitutional provisions can
form the basis for a public policy protecting privacy. Those values are
reinforced by the state's recognition of the common law privacy tort, and
perhaps by miscellaneous state statutes protecting specific types of
personal privacy as well. Other courts have concluded that these sources
of law generally protecting privacy are inadequate to show a clear
mandate of public policy necessary to support a wrongful discharge
claim.[39]

Even where courts are willing to find that privacy rights are a
protected public policy, employees do not always prevail. As in *Semore*,
recognition that protecting employee privacy can be a public policy is
only the first step. Courts then consider whether the intrusion on
privacy in the particular case is justified by balancing the employer's
interest in the intrusion against the employee's privacy interest. In the
case of drug testing, how that balance is struck typically turns on the
nature of the employee's job and whether it poses a safety risk to
others.[40] Many of the early drug testing challenges were ultimately
unsuccessful because the employees tested held positions with acknowledged safety risks. Nevertheless, the *way* in which the courts reached
their conclusions had an important impact on later privacy challenges.
Where employees were permitted to bring privacy claims based on the
public policy tort, but lost because of the safety-sensitive nature of their
jobs, a framework remains in place by which later, unjustified intrusions
on employee privacy may be challenged. On the other hand, in jurisdictions in which courts rejected privacy rights as a source of public policy
out of hand, at-will employees often lack any legal protection against
discharge for resisting unwarranted intrusions on their privacy.

One might not view this latter situation as troubling, given that a
state legislature could enact specific protections for employee privacy if it
wanted.[41] Indeed, some have argued that such an approach is preferable,

---

[38] *See e.g., Luedtke v. Nabors Alaska Drilling, Inc.*, 768 P.2d 1123, 1132–33 (Alaska
1989); *Hennessey v. Coastal Eagle Point Oil Co.*, 609 A.2d 11, 19 (N.J. 1992); *Twigg v.
Hercules Corp.*, 406 S.E.2d 52, 55 (W. Va. 1990).

[39] *See, e.g., Gilmore v. Enogex, Inc.*, 878 P.2d 360, 368 (Okla. 1994); *Roe v. Quality
Transp. Serv.*, 838 P.2d 128, 130–32 (Wash.App. 1992).

[40] *See, e.g., Luedtke v. Nabors Alaska Drillings, Inc.*, 768 P.2d 1123, 1133–37 (Alaska
1989); *Webster v. Motorola, Inc.*, 637 N.E.2d 203, 207–08 (Mass. 1994); *Hennessey v. Coastal
Eagle Point Oil Co.*, 609 A.2d 11, 20–23 (N.J. 1992).

[41] Approximately half of the states have enacted statutes regulating drug testing in the
workplace. For a compilation of these statutes, see Matthew W. Finkin, *Privacy in*

because it should be the role of legislatures, not courts, to enunciate public policy. However, the doctrine of wrongful discharge in violation of public policy is itself a judge-made law, one that has been adopted in the overwhelming majority of American jurisdictions. Its widespread acceptance is premised on the understanding that the employment-at-will doctrine (another judicially created doctrine in most states) has limits, and that it is the appropriate role of the courts to identify those limits where the legislature has not clearly spoken.

The difficulty, of course, lies in determining when the public policy exception ought to apply. Most courts look for some independent source of law such as a constitutional, statutory or regulatory provision that expresses a policy disapproving the employer's motivation, even though that statement of policy may not specifically forbid discharging an employee for that reason. For example, *Petermann*,[42] in which an employee was fired for refusing to lie before a state legislative committee, found the relevant public policy clearly articulated in a state statute criminalizing perjury, even though it said nothing about retaliation against an employee who refused to commit perjury. Even where an independent source of policy exists, courts still must determine how specifically it must speak to the particular facts in a case. If an employee is fired for refusing to do something she believes is against public policy, must she establish that the acts she objected to are *actually* illegal or only that they violated the spirit and general purpose behind existing law?[43] Courts differ on this and related questions affecting how narrowly or broadly the public policy exception is defined.

Beliefs about the nature of the employment relationship greatly influence views about the appropriate scope of the public policy exception—and whether it should apply in situations like Barbara Luck's. For those who see employment primarily as a locus of exchange—labor for wages—the relationship between employer and employee is fundamentally a matter of contract.[44] Questions about the parties' respective rights

---

Employment Law 542–690 (2d ed. 2003). Some of these statutes attempt to protect employee privacy by limiting the circumstances in which drug testing can be required, or by mandating procedural safeguards. Others create incentives—such as immunity from liability—to encourage private employer drug testing.

[42] *Petermann v. International Bhd. of Teamsters*, 344 P.2d 25 (Cal. Ct. of App. 1959).

[43] *Compare Adler v. American Standard Corp.*, 432 A.2d 464 (Md. 1981) (rejecting wrongful discharge claim where allegations were too vague to show actual violation of statute relied upon for public policy), *with Strozinsky v. School District of Brown Deer*, 614 N.W.2d 443, 456 (Wis. 2000) (holding that public policy may be implicit and that court should examine "the spirit" as well as the letter of constitutional, statutory and administrative provisions for expressions of public policy).

[44] *See, e.g.*, Richard A. Epstein, *In Defense of the Contract at Will*, 51 U. Chi. L. Rev. 947 (1984).

can be answered by looking to their agreement. If an employee has consented to undergo urinalysis drug testing—or vehicle searches or video surveillance—as a condition of employment, she cannot later complain about these practices. If the employee refuses to consent, no agreement is reached and the at-will employment simply terminates. On this view, the law should not step in to interfere with the parties' agreement absent some fraud or coercion. And the public policy exception should be narrowly cabined to reach only those situations in which the employer's decision to discharge has some negative effect on third parties—an effect not taken into account by the employer and employee in reaching their bargain.[45] From this perspective, there is no reason for the law to protect privacy because employees themselves can decide how much they value their personal privacy and whether or not to consent to various intrusions.

An alternative perspective views the employment relationship quite differently, simultaneously seeing a risk of employer abuse of power and a potential for the workplace to function as a community. This view is deeply skeptical that agreement signifies voluntary consent, holding that individual workers often lack sufficient clout to assert even strongly held preferences in the face of employer demands. This inequality in bargaining power argues against deferring to the agreement between the parties if the substantive terms of the employment offend basic values. More affirmatively, as Cynthia Estlund has argued, work can be "a locus of associational life and of human connectedness."[46] Experiences at work importantly shape workers, both in terms of their individual development and their capacity to participate as citizens. The National Labor Relations Act, which gave workers the right to organize into unions and bargain collectively, embodied these ideas, seeing in organized labor both a counterweight to organized capital and a mechanism for facilitating individual voice and participation in workplace governance. Former California Justice Joseph Grodin has argued that with the waning of labor power, contemporary forms of regulation can and should be understood "as a bringing of constitutional values to the private sector workplace" such that "workers have rights that are analogous in some significant respects to the kinds of rights that citizens enjoy within the political community."[47] Although this view remains contested, it argues that employees' legitimate claims to privacy—and other basic dignitary

---

[45] See Stewart J. Schwab, *Wrongful Discharge Law and the Search for Third–Party Effects*, 74 Tex. L. Rev. 1943 (1996).

[46] Cynthia Estlund, *Working Together: How Workplace Bonds Strengthen a Diverse Democracy* (2003).

[47] Joseph R. Grodin, *Constitutional Values in the Private Sector Workplace*, 13 Ind. Rel. L. J. 1, 3 (1991).

rights—are as much a matter of public concern as ensuring the integrity of public proceedings, as in *Petermann*.

Conclusion

The widespread adoption of workplace drug testing programs in the 1980s was merely the first wave in a series of technological developments expanding the ability of employers to monitor, test and collect information about their employees. Today, employers have available tools enabling them to monitor employee email and computer usage, to conduct visual and audio surveillance through the workplace, to track employees' exact location through global position monitoring systems and sensor technologies and to test bodily tissues for genetic susceptibility to disease. How employers choose to deploy these and other technologies and whether the law will constrain their use will be influenced by the experience with workplace drug testing and the legal challenges it provoked.

Luck is an important part of that experience, highlighting the struggle to articulate when and how private employees have protectible interests in privacy. In many ways, the *Luck* opinion was a deeply ambivalent decision. On the one hand, it recognized the fundamental nature of privacy and acknowledged that urinalysis testing infringed that right in significant ways. On the other hand, it exhibited a reluctance to permit employees to fully vindicate that right vis à vis their employers. It confined its approval of the jury's verdict to a narrow contract analysis, rejecting the potentially more expansive public policy claim. This latter issue—whether employee privacy rights should limit an employer's unfettered authority to discharge an at-will employee—is part of a much larger debate over the nature of the employment relationship and the appropriate scope of the public policy exception. As technological advances make possible new forms of intrusions, workplace privacy will continue to be one of the fields on with that debate is played out.

5

The Story of *PepsiCo, Inc. v. Redmond*: How the Doctrine of Inevitable Disclosure of the Trade Secrets of Marketing Sports Beverages Was Brewed

Alan Hyde[*]

When a brash young marketing executive for PepsiCo named Bill Redmond accepted in 1994 a job with Quaker Oats, marketing its product Gatorade, he had no idea that anyone would think that there was anything wrong with that. One of the most-commented developments in corporate management in the 1990s was the increasing tendency to recruit top executives from outside the firm. Large U.S. corporations that had traditionally filled top executive positions from within their own ranks, such as IBM and Chrysler—or Quaker Oats—turned increasingly to outsiders.[1] Even more unusual patterns appeared, such as hiring senior corporate executives as temporary employees or consul-

---

[*] The author thanks student research assistants Helen Walters (Rutgers) and Pedro Toledo (Cornell), Julie Jones of the Cornell Law School Library, and those who agreed to be interviewed.

[1] *See generally* Charles C. Heckscher, *White Collar Blues: Management Loyalties in an Age of Corporate Restructuring* (1995); *Broken Ladders: Management Careers in the New Economy* (Paul Osterman ed. 1996); Edward P. Lazear & Paul Oyer, *Internal and External Labor Markets: a Personnel Economics Approach*, 11 Labour Economics 527 (2004). On general trends toward shorter job tenures and greater personnel mobility, see Peter Cappelli, *The New Deal at Work: Managing the Market–Driven Workplace* (1999); Peter Cappelli et al., *Change at Work* (1997); David T. Ellwood et al., *A Working Nation: Workers, Work, and Government in the New Economy* (2000); Stephen A. Herzenberg et al., *New Rules for a New Economy: Employment and Opportunity in Postindustrial America* (1998); Paul Osterman et al., *Working in America: A Blueprint for the New Labor Market* (2001); Paul Osterman, *Securing Prosperity: The American Labor Market—How It Has Changed and What to Do About It* (1999).

tants.[2] Food and beverages were no different.

By and large, employment law accommodated this development. Firms may negotiate a wide range of employment contracts. The law imposes very few implied obligations to supplement those actually negotiated. For example, state courts retreated from earlier suggestions that an executive who had been around for a long time thereby acquired implied contractual rights to job security.[3]

Redmond's job change, however, marked a curious legal development going the other way—resulting in a decision impeding executive mobility despite the absence of an express no-competition clause. A federal judge in Chicago enjoined him from taking the Gatorade job for six months, on the fairly novel ground that he would "inevitably disclose" some unidentified PepsiCo secret at Gatorade. The Seventh Circuit affirmed this injunction.[4] Though not the first "inevitable disclosure" of trade secrets case, it is often described as the "seminal"[5] ruling on the doctrine.

Everything about the doctrine of "inevitable disclosure" of trade secrets is controversial, including whether or not it is a doctrine. Some think that, for all the discussion, actual adoptions are few.[6] Some think that it has been widely accepted, and a good thing.[7] Some have criticized it harshly.[8] These questions largely lie outside this chapter, though our

---

[2] Jeffrey L. Bradach, *Flexibility: The New Social Contract Between Individuals and Firms?*, Harvard Bus. Sch., Working Paper No. 97–088 (May 1997).

[3] *See, e.g., Guz v. Bechtel Nat., Inc.*, 8 P.3d 1089 (Cal. 2000).

[4] *PepsiCo, Inc. v. Redmond*, 1994 WL 687544 (N.D.Ill.), *aff'd*, 54 F.3d 1262 (7th Cir. 1995) (applying Illinois law).

[5] Gary Glaser & Patrick McMurray, *Inevitable Disclosure Still Not Settled*, Nat'l Law Journal, Aug. 29, 2005, at S10.

[6] *Id.*

[7] William Lynch Schaller, *Trade Secret Inevitable Disclosure: Substantive, Procedural & Practical Implications of An Evolving Doctrine*, 86 J. Pat. & Trademark. Off. Soc'y 336 (2004).

[8] Hanna Bui–Eve, *To Hire or Not to Hire: What Silicon Valley Companies Should Know About Hiring Competitors' Employees*, 48 Hast. L.J. 981 (1997); Ronald J. Gilson, *The Legal Infrastructure of High Technology Industrial Districts: Silicon Valley, Route 128, and Covenants not to Compete*, 74 N.Y.U. L. Rev. 575 (1999); Alan Hyde, *Working in Silicon Valley: Economic and Legal Analysis of a High–Velocity Labor* Market 27–89 (2003); Robert P. Merges, *The Law and Economics of Employee Inventions*, 13 Harv. J.L. & Tech. 1 (1999); Susan Street Whaley, *The Inevitable Disaster of Inevitable Disclosure*, 67 U. Cin. L. Rev. 809 (1999); Lawrence I. Weinstein, *Revisiting the Inevitability Doctrine: When Can a Former Employee Who Never Signed a Non–Compete Agreement Nor Threatened to Use or Disclose Trade Secrets Be Prohibited from Working for a Competitor?*, 21 Am. J. Trial Advoc. 211 (1997).

journey to the origins of *Redmond* may cast some light on them all the same.

Even the briefest of definitions of the doctrine of "inevitable disclosure" must note that it can figure in at least three different aspects of trade secrets litigation: identifying a trade secret; "threatened misappropriation"; and the scope of any injunction. *PepsiCo v. Redmond* involved all three.

First, in trade secrets litigation, the plaintiff normally must identify the precise secret for which it fears disclosure. This requirement is itself a significant disincentive to litigation. Some technology corporations do not want their rivals to know even the general areas in which the company is conducting research. As applied in *Redmond*, the doctrine of "inevitable disclosure" permitted PepsiCo to complain about potential disclosure of its strategic plan, annual operating plan and sales methods, without having to be any more specific than that. "Trade secrets" of this type are known to every corporate manager.

Second, the Uniform Trade Secrets Act (UTSA), in effect in over forty jurisdictions and applied in *Redmond*, requires plaintiffs to allege the "actual or threatened misappropriation" of their trade secrets.[9] The doctrine of "inevitable disclosure" turns this into a simple requirement that plaintiff show that its manager has moved to a competitor where he will work on similar problems. After this uncontested showing, the doctrine of "inevitable disclosure"—which has already been used to make all of that manager's knowledge a "trade secret"—now can be used to jump over any requirement that the plaintiff show "actual or threatened misappropriation." If he takes the job, he will "inevitably disclose" something.

Third, a plaintiff who proves actual or threatened misappropriation of an identified trade secret most frequently obtains an injunction against this misappropriation. *Redmond*, unusually, involved an injunction also forbidding Bill Redmond from taking the job that he had been offered at Quaker. He was enjoined for six months from "assuming or performing any duties for Quaker relating in any way to the pricing of beverages" or "the development or implementation of any marketing or sales programs for the sale of beverages."[10]

We owe the doctrine of "inevitable disclosure" to a handful of lawyers, working long hours under enormous pressure to put together, by Thanksgiving 1994, a preliminary injunction hearing. Their inspirations and mistakes, and not precedent or policy, gave us the doctrine.

---

[9] UTSA § 2.

[10] *PepsiCo, Inc. v. Redmond*, 1994 WL 687544, at *92 (N.D. Ill).

Tiny facts, not necessarily significant to participants at the time, eventually led two courts to legal innovation.

But to understand how lawyers on both sides came to be under such pressure, we must look at Gatorade, a beverage that is a kind of metaphor for the new American economy, and at PepsiCo, one of America's best-known companies, whose decades-long obsession with Gatorade resembles Captain Ahab's for the white whale—except for its ending. Bill Redmond's case is the only part of that obsession to yield legal change. But, in the big picture of PepsiCo's obsessive pursuit of Gatorade, Redmond was only a very small fish.

Social and Legal Background

GATORADE

Gatorade is the first really successful sports drink, which has outlived rival after rival to hold down 80 percent of that huge market.[11] Its expensive sponsorship of numerous sports leagues and events guarantees it a presence on the sidelines and on television screens. One out of every twenty Americans will buy a bottle today. It has been the subject of a book,[12] whose author maintains a website.[13]

Gatorade is basically water, enhanced with sodium and potassium and sweetened. Designed to replace quickly the fluids and chemicals lost in sweat, it was developed at the University of Florida medical school after a weekend in August 1965 when 25 freshman football players had been admitted to the hospital because of heat exhaustion and dehydration. The hospital's chief of security, Dewayne Douglas, was a former University of Florida football player who was also an assistant coach of the team. He knew a research fellow at the medical school working on a team that studied sodium levels in rats, and told him about the team's problem. Their efforts resulted in the earliest versions of Gatorade.

Once before, Gatorade nearly made intellectual property law in a dispute between an employer and an employee. That time, the employees created the dispute. In 1967, they had formed a trust to sell their recipe to the food company Stokely–Van Camp, identified through personal contacts, for $5000 and a royalty of 5 cents on every gallon sold. They had not informed their employer, the University of Florida, which claimed ownership invoking legal doctrines under which the employer

---

[11] Bob Condor, *First Ade Drinking It or Pouring It—Gatorade Has Received Plenty of Exposure in 40 Years of Football*, Seattle Post–Intelligencer, Jan. 30, 2006, at E1.

[12] Darren Rovell, *First in Thirst: How Gatorade Turned the Science of Sweat into a Cultural Phenomenon* (AMACOM 2005). Rovell's account is the source for much of the information about Gatorade in this section.

[13] www.firstinthirst.typepad.com.

holds the rights to inventions by employees hired to invent.[14] The lawsuit would have made an interesting decision, but settled in 1972 when the university accepted 20 percent of the trust's royalties. The settlement, described by the press at the time as "used dental floss," was by 2004 worth almost $100 million. Stokely was acquired by Quaker Oats in 1983.

By 1990, Gatorade sales were $900 million annually. It was the only successful sports drink. Its dominance did not reflect the secrecy of its chemical formula, which is not difficult to replicate, but its powerful image and association with athletes. The following year, it passed Quaker oatmeal in sales and signed a ten-year, $13.5 million deal with the basketball star Michael Jordan, which would lead to an advertising campaign in which customers were urged to "Be Like Mike" by drinking Gatorade. The large cola companies had previously introduced sports drinks that were not very successful. By the 1990s, they were prepared to wage war for that growing market.

PepsiCo

The kind of competition to which Quaker was accustomed in the breakfast cereal business was quite different from the intense competition that had become known as the "cola wars." By the 1990s, PepsiCo and rival Coca–Cola had developed an intensely competitive style, revolving around enormous promotional expenditures and celebrity marketing campaigns but occasionally involving pricing. It is almost impossible to find any journalism on this competition that does not invoke the metaphor of "war."[15]

"By 1992, the soft drink market was worth approximately $40 billion, while the sports drink market was on an upward climb toward $1 billion. While the sports drink market seemed small, it was growing faster, and it had greater potential for profit. Gatorade essentially sold for twice as much as a similar volume of Coke and used half the amount of sugar (the expensive ingredient) that soft drinks did."[16] In that year, talks between Coca–Cola and Quaker for a joint venture collapsed. Pepsi brought out a sports drink called Mountain Dew Sport, soon renamed AllSport. Coke followed with PowerAde. A new front had opened in the

---

[14] Catherine L. Fisk, *Removing the "Fuel of Interest" from the "Fire of Genius": Law and the Employee–Inventor, 1830–1930*, 65 U. Chi. L. Rev. 1127 (1998); Robert P. Merges, *The Law and Economics of Employee Inventions*, 13 Harv. J.L. & Tech. 1 (1999). See also Professor Fisk's chapter in this volume.

[15] A vivid picture of PepsiCo culture can be found in Roger Enrico & Jesse Kornbluth, *The Other Guy Blinked: How Pepsi Won the Cola Wars* (1986).

[16] Darren Rovell, *First in Thirst: How Gatorade Turned the Science of Sweat into a Cultural Phenomenon* 126 (ANACOM 2005).

cola wars. "Many thought that the powerful push of the two soft drink giants ... would push Gatorade to the back of the refrigerator."[17]

Factual Background

At the risk of oversimplification, it will be simplest to recount Bill Redmond's leaving PepsiCo for Quaker through the eyes of the four individuals who later testified, and one who did not. Early in 1994, all of the four witnesses worked for PepsiCo, specifically its operating division Pepsi–Cola North America (PCNA), and all had responsibilities for all its beverages, principally Pepsi–Cola, but including other carbonated beverages, AllSport, and other products such as juices and teas. Craig Weatherup was President and Chief Executive Officer of PCNA. Brenda Barnes was Chief Operating Officer of PCNA. They would eventually testify for PepsiCo. Early in 1994, Donald Uzzi was promoted to Senior Vice President and Chief Customer Officer of PCNA, although he had already been offered, and accepted, the position of President of Gatorade. Gatorade was owned by Quaker Oats. Uzzi went to Quaker in March 1994 to run Gatorade. One of his bosses there was Philip A. Marineau, Quaker's President and Chief Operating Officer.

In light of the looming sports drink "war," and in particular the November 1994 lawsuit against Redmond, it is interesting that Uzzi's leaving PepsiCo for Gatorade eight months earlier did not result in litigation. PepsiCo was content to have Pam McGuire, one of its in-house lawyers (later involved in the Redmond litigation), brief Uzzi on the importance of maintaining secrets, and send a letter to Quaker reminding them not to make use of any PepsiCo trade secrets.[18] Of course, Uzzi's departure left some hard feelings. PepsiCo would later point out to the court in the *Redmond* litigation that, as noted, Uzzi actually accepted a promotion from PepsiCo after he had already accepted Quaker's offer. If the relevance of this fact to trade secrets doctrine is not clear, it soon will be.

In early 1994, Redmond was not, on paper at least, at this level. He was 34 years old and was PepsiCo's General Manager of the Northern California Business Unit. Redmond grew up in Albany and graduated from Siena College there. Right out of college he joined Proctor and Gamble, then moved to PepsiCo, where he had been for ten years. Despite his youth, he had been successful in California and was regarded

---

[17] *Id.* The pending "war" over sports drinks was evident to contemporaneous observers. *See, e.g., Cola Wars Continue: Coke vs. Pepsi in the 1990s*, Harvard Bus. Sch. Case 9–794–055 (1994), at 11–12; Kristine Portnoy Kelley, *They Want to Be Like Don (Gatorade President Don Uzzi)*, *Beverage Industry*, June 1, 1994.

[18] Telephone interview with Pam McGuire, PepsiCo. (Feb. 16, 2006). McGuire is still at PepsiCo.

as a rising star at PepsiCo, someone whose importance to the future of the organization might not have been reflected in his title. Brenda Barnes in particular was a supporter of Redmond's, and promoted him in July 1994 to be PepsiCo's General Manager for all of California, Pepsi-Co's most profitable regional unit. This was the first time that the entire state would be unified under one manager. His responsibilities mainly concerned carbonated beverages. Redmond estimates that 98% of the unit's sales were cola and other carbonated soft drinks. At that time, AllSport and Lipton iced tea sales were "peanuts." Redmond's job involved overseeing sales, marketing and pricing, mainly for cola and carbonated soft drinks. In the spring before this promotion, Weatherup, PCNA's President and CEO, took Redmond out to dinner at a restaurant in San Francisco to discuss his future with PepsiCo. Redmond learned that the next posting would probably be overseas. Since he did not want to leave the country, he began thinking of changing employers.[19]

Uzzi, his former PepsiCo boss, moved to Quaker in March 1994 and in May took Redmond out to dinner in San Francisco to try to recruit him. Redmond met in August with Uzzi (Gatorade President), Marineau (Quaker President), and two other Quaker executives. It would have been tempting in August 1994 to see this meeting as a kind of confrontation between the old and new markets for managers. Quaker President Phil Marineau had been with Quaker consistently for the 22 years since he had returned from Vietnam in 1972, working his way up to President of the company. He had run Gatorade since Quaker acquired Stokely–Van Camp. Now he was sitting with the former PepsiCo executive whom he had recruited eight months earlier to manage his old brand, trying to recruit another outsider.

On October 24, Quaker offered Redmond a position that he turned down, wanting more money and responsibility. On Tuesday, November 8, Redmond was offered the position of Vice President—Field Operations for Gatorade, which he accepted "on the spot early in the day."[20] This was a hectic time at Quaker. Six days earlier, on Wednesday, November 2, Quaker announced that it was acquiring Snapple Beverage Corp., a manufacturer of iced tea, from its founders, known to scholars of labor law as the owners of First National Maintenance Corp., the subject of a famous Supreme Court labor case over a decade earlier.[21]

Redmond, as his lawyer told the story a few years later,

---

[19] Telephone interview with Bill Redmond (Feb. 6, 2006).

[20] Bradford P. Lyerla, *Thirteen Rules for Inevitable Disclosure Trials*, 15 Computer Lawyer (No. 6) 10, 15 (June 1998).

[21] Alan Hyde, *The Story of* First National Maintenance Corp. v. NLRB: *Eliminating Bargaining for Low–Wage Service Workers*, in *Labor Law Stories* 281, 284, 310 (Laura J. Cooper & Catherine L. Fisk eds. 2005).

tried to call his boss, Brenda Barnes, but she was out of town. Instead, he told Pepsi's Senior VP of HR, who was named Bensyl, of Quaker's offer and the compensation. Then he made a mistake. Instead of telling Bensyl that he had already accepted Quaker's offer, he said that he favored accepting the offer ("60/40"). He also exaggerated the responsibilities of the position, telling Bensyl that he would be the [Chief Operating Officer of Gatorade]. Bill's real title was to be VP of Field Operations, the closest thing that Quaker had to a COO in that part of its business, but still not a true Chief Operating Officer.

That all took place on Tuesday. Barnes was not due back in Pepsi's office until Thursday. On Thursday, Redmond met with Barnes and repeated what he had told Bensyl. He also repeated the same story, including the inaccuracies, to Pepsi's CEO Craig Weatherup over the telephone. Weatherup and Barnes tried to talk Redmond out of leaving and pointedly told him that his long-term prospects at Pepsi were excellent, reminding him that Pepsi is a much bigger fish in the beverage pond than Quaker. However, they did not do the one thing that might have interested Redmond. They did not try to out-bid Quaker. On Thursday afternoon, two days after accepting Quaker's offer, Redmond told Pepsi that he was going to take the Quaker offer. Bensyl escorted Redmond out of the building and Pepsi sued him six days later.

Why did Redmond lie to Pepsi? Because he was young and clumsy. A more polished businessman would have found a way to "shop" the Quaker offer without being untruthful. No one, however, ever suggested that the lies had any connection to or imperiled Pepsi's trade secrets. They were completely innocuous to Pepsi's trade secrets.[22]

The trial judge was later to be quite upset by Redmond's conduct. He eventually concluded, somewhat ambiguously, that "Redmond did not, in his own mind, distinguish that job [Vice President—Field Operations] from the job of 'Chief Operating Officer.' "[23] But, as we shall see, he placed more significance on Redmond's failure to say that he had actually accepted the Quaker offer.

Weatherup and Barnes fired Redmond on November 10. Weatherup—much more so than Barnes—wanted to sue Redmond.[24] He told Jerry Carey, an in-house lawyer, to call their outside counsel, Roger Pascal, then as now a partner in the Chicago firm of Schiff Hardin.

---

[22] Lyerla, *Thirteen Rules.*

[23] *PepsiCo, Inc. v. Redmond*, 1996 WL 3965 (N.D.Ill.).

[24] Telephone interview with PepsiCo outside counsel Roger Pascal (Jan. 23, 2006).

Proceedings in the District Court

PLAINTIFFS BREW "INEVITABLE DISCLOSURE"

Why were Weatherup and his subordinates at PepsiCo, who did nothing to prevent Uzzi's departure for Gatorade eight months earlier, so intent on litigation against Redmond, who would rank below Uzzi at Gatorade, as he had at PepsiCo? Roger Pascal mentioned two reasons. First, he said, PepsiCo wanted to send a message to Quaker. Second, they wanted to send a message to their own employees.[25]

I confess that I was stunned by this response. I waited for more, but that was clearly the end of the sentence. I asked Pascal: "Did trade secrets have nothing to do with it?"

Pascal said that, for PepsiCo, protecting information was "not the top priority." PepsiCo was actually upset about Uzzi's raiding their employees. Redmond was not the first to be recruited by Uzzi for Gatorade. Weatherup and Barnes thought that Uzzi was targeting their employees.[26] They wanted to get Quaker to stop, and to signal strongly to those employees that they could not expect to depart to a rival without litigation.[27]

Pascal reviewed the file, and was not optimistic about success. "I gave them an estimate of success that was well below fifty percent." Redmond had never signed a covenant not to compete. He had signed an agreement to maintain information confidential, but Pascal thought it was "garden variety." Redmond had not taken a single PepsiCo document with him.

It was Pascal, the outside lawyer, not the PepsiCo executives, who hit on the idea that PepsiCo would have a better chance if its lawsuit complained, not about raiding of executives, but about the danger to its trade secrets.[28] While Weatherup and Barnes had initially expressed no concern that Redmond's departure would endanger their trade secrets, in subsequent conversation with their lawyers, "the more they thought about it, the more concerned they were. PepsiCo really did believe that

---

[25] *Id.*

[26] Discovery later revealed that "all three of the people interviewed for the position Redmond ultimately accepted worked at PCNA." *PepsiCo v. Redmond*, 54 F.3d at 1271.

[27] Pascal's recollection, that Weatherup and Barnes were not initially concerned that Redmond's departure for Gatorade would lead to loss of trade secrets, is confirmed by Redmond's recollection of his final meeting with them. As retold by Redmond's lawyer, *supra* n.20, Weatherup and Barnes expressed no concern at that interview that Redmond's departure would endanger PepsiCo trade secrets.

[28] In-house counsel Pam McGuire confirmed this. Weatherup and Barnes "wanted to sue about raiding. Roger came up with theft of trade secrets."

Redmond's knowledge of their pricing of Lipton teas, juices, and sports drinks could do them harm."[29]

Pascal and the other lawyers still thought the case was weak, even if brought as a trade secrets case. The problem was not in showing that Redmond knew PepsiCo secrets. He was one of just over a dozen executives with access to all company plans. Indeed, throughout the litigation, Quaker did just what Pascal had predicted. Quaker conceded that Redmond had knowledge of PepsiCo trade secrets. It simply denied having any interest in those secrets.

Indeed, there were several holes in the story that Quaker was interested in PepsiCo secrets. First, Gatorade dominated the sports drink market. AllSport was an insignificant factor in the sports drink market. AllSport, teas and juices were a relatively insignificant part of PepsiCo's beverage business. Why on earth would Quaker care about PepsiCo secrets? Second, the pricing of beverages is a trade secret only during the brief period of time before the product hits the stores, at which time anyone can see how it is priced. In technical terms, Quaker would have a strong case that acquisition of PepsiCo secrets was neither "actual" nor "threatened."

It was thus in "desperation"[30] that the lawyers turned to the theory of "inevitable disclosure." Although the concept had been used in earlier trade secret cases, it had not been used in all the senses that Pascal needed. As mentioned, Pascal needed a doctrine that would do three things. First, PepsiCo could not be required to identify a single particular trade secret, the misappropriation of which it feared. Second, PepsiCo would have to show that the "inevitability" of disclosure could meet the statutory requirement that plaintiff show "actual or threatened" misappropriation. Finally, PepsiCo would have to argue that an injunction merely forbidding Redmond from misappropriation would be inadequate, that instead he had to be kept off the job at Gatorade.

As of 1994, the doctrine of inevitable disclosure supported only the third. *Eastman Kodak Co. v. Powers Film Products* is perhaps the best-known example of a case in which a court enjoined a trade secrets defendant from taking a job, rather than simply enjoining him from disclosing trade secrets, on the theory that: "[I]f he is permitted to enter this employ, injunctive relief in form against the imparting of such special knowledge is more than likely to prove inefficient. The mere rendition of the service along the lines of his training would almost necessarily impart such knowledge to some degree."[31] So the concept

---

[29] Telephone interview with Roger Pascal (Jan. 23, 2006).

[30] *Id.*

[31] 179 N.Y.S. 325, 330 (App.Div. 1919).

that an employee might find that the duties of a new job called on knowledge gained on the old was not new. Nevertheless, there were big differences between cases like *Kodak* and *PepsiCo*. First, *Kodak*, like nearly all trade secrets cases until recently, enforced a covenant not to compete. The employee's access to trade secrets made its enforcement "reasonable." Redmond, by contrast, had signed no such covenant. Second, Kodak, unlike PepsiCo, identified the precise industrial process with which it was concerned. Third, Kodak, unlike PepsiCo, was able to show that the employee had actually made use of its secrets before litigation started.

The first problem for each side's lawyers was determining the relevant scope of legal authority. Trade secret suits in Illinois, as in most U.S. jurisdictions, are governed by the local version of the Uniform Trade Secrets Act.[32] The Uniform Act was approved in 1979, amended in 1985, and effective in Illinois only in 1988, fewer than seven years before the briefs were written in *Redmond*. The Illinois version follows the Uniform Act in stating: "Actual or threatened misappropriation may be enjoined."[33] Neither statute defines "threatened," and no Illinois state cases interpreted that section of the Act. It is not entirely clear where a lawyer or court should turn for law in a case like that. Perhaps the most common strategy, one adopted by the defense in *Redmond*, is to turn to the state common law of trade secrets that predated the adoption of the Uniform Act. Many courts treat the Uniform Act as merely a codification of earlier common law and equity, and the Court of Appeals in *Redmond* repeated this view,[34] though the statute is arguably to the contrary.[35] A second permissible strategy, though uncommon, might be to assume that a Uniform Act is intended to create nationally uniform law, and attempt to construe it consistently with other states that have adopted it.

Pascal adopted a third approach. He concluded, correctly as it turned out, that the federal courts would be interested only in Illinois federal cases. This is not what law students are taught in the first year. *Redmond* was in federal court only because of the diversity of citizenship between the parties, and the only applicable law was the law of Illinois. Yet the Seventh Circuit ultimately paid little attention to defendants' cases from state court, distinguishing each on its facts and not examining any for general principles of trade secret law. The Seventh Circuit

---

[32] UTSA, 14 ULA at 529 et seq. (2005); Illinois Trade Secrets Act, 765 ILCS 1065.

[33] 765 ILCS 1065/3(a), UTSA § 2(a).

[34] 54 F.3d at 1269.

[35] UTSA § 7, 765 ILCS 1065/8(a) ("... this Act is intended to displace conflicting tort, restitutionary, unfair competition, and other laws of this State providing civil remedies for misappropriation of a trade secret.").

has frequently been criticized for its perfunctory efforts at discerning state law by which it is purportedly bound.[36]

There were only two federal cases from Illinois to interpret "threatened" misappropriation, *Teradyne v. Clear Communications*, interpreting the Uniform Act, and *AMP v. Fleischhacker*, which predated it. Both denied any relief to plaintiffs.[37]

Teradyne, the case under the Act, was a difficult case for Pascal, but the court's dictum was to provide the inevitable disclosure doctrine in the form in which PepsiCo needed it. The actual holding of *Teradyne* is, however, flatly inconsistent with the later *Redmond* case. The facts are indistinguishable: departure of top executives to a rival company. The complaint was dismissed for failure to state a claim. "Here there is no allegation that defendants have in fact threatened to use Teradyne's secrets or that they will inevitably do so. An allegation that the defendants said they would use secrets or disavowed their confidentiality agreements would serve this purpose. An allegation that Clear could not operate without Teradyne's secrets because Teradyne's secret technology is the only one that will work would suffice though more technical facts may be necessarily included in such a pleading. The defendants' claimed acts, working for Teradyne, knowing its business, leaving its business, hiring employees from Teradyne and entering the same field (though in a market not yet serviced by Teradyne) do not state a claim of threatened misappropriation. All that is alleged, at bottom, is that defendants could misuse plaintiff's secrets, and plaintiffs fear they will. This is not enough. It may be that little more is needed, but falling a little short is still falling short."[38]

PepsiCo could not make (and did not make) any of the allegations that *Teradyne* suggested in dictum might suffice. It did not allege that Quaker had threatened to use its secrets, or had disavowed Redmond's obligation of confidentiality, or could not operate without PepsiCo secrets. PepsiCo relied on *Teradyne* merely because it used the word "inevitable." "Threatened misappropriation can be enjoined under Illinois law" where there is a "high degree of probability of inevitable and immediate ... use of ... trade secrets."[39] As we shall see, the Seventh Circuit, too, would rely on this dictum. Today, of course, the facts, analysis, and holding of *Teradyne* have all been forgotten, and the case is routinely miscited as a case "applying the inevitable disclosure doc-

---

[36] *See, e.g.,* Stewart Macaulay et al., *Contracts: Law in Action* 486, 685 (1995).

[37] *AMP Inc. v. Fleischhacker,* 823 F.2d 1199 (7th Cir. 1987); *Teradyne, Inc. v. Clear Communications Corp.,* 707 F.Supp. 353 (N.D. Ill. 1989).

[38] 707 F.Supp. at 356–57.

[39] *Teradyne,* 707 F.Supp. at 356.

trine."[40] Only the dictum—the use of the word "inevitable," really—survives. This slenderest of reeds would, in *Redmond*, become the "doctrine of inevitable disclosure."

But not without some help from the defense.

DEFENDANTS DRINK KOOL-AID

Redmond was fired on Thursday, November 10. After a weekend of feverish work, PepsiCo's lawyers on the following Wednesday, November 16—a week before Thanksgiving—filed a complaint against Redmond and Quaker, alleging Redmond's inevitable threatened disclosure of their trade secrets and seeking a temporary restraining order (TRO) preventing him from working in beverage sales at Quaker. The case was assigned to Judge George W. Lindberg, who issued the TRO that afternoon. Judge Lindberg was appointed to the federal bench in 1989 by the first President Bush after service on the Illinois appellate court, elected positions as state Comptroller and State Representative, and as general counsel to a lie detector company. In 1994 he was 62 years old and, according to a lawyer involved in PepsiCo, who obviously does not wish to be identified, "not the most hard-working or energetic judge in Chicago."

Quaker was represented by Michael Sheehan of Connelly, Sheehan & Moran in Chicago, its regular employment counsel. Sheehan was only 35 in 1994. He remembers the day vividly. "I thought it would be a calm day for a litigator. I had nothing scheduled in court and thought I would get some work done. Then a fax started coming in with a hearing set for that afternoon." He walked to Quaker headquarters at 10:30 that morning, then to federal court at 2 that afternoon where he was unable to prevent the issuance of a TRO.[41] That night, Sheehan and his associate Jimmy Oh prepared declarations by Redmond and Uzzi that explained Redmond's proposed duties at Quaker and how these would in no way put him into the position of having to disclose any secrets about PepsiCo marketing or pricing plans. Redmond felt completely confident. He had not seen the lawsuit coming and never understood any relationship between selling cola in California through bottlers owned by the corporation, and selling Gatorade nationally directly to stores.[42] The lawyers were up all that night preparing to go back to court the next day.

---

[40] See, e.g., Linda K. Stevens, *Trade Secrets and Inevitable Disclosure*, 36 Tort & Ins. L.J. 917, 930 (2001).

[41] Telephone interview with Michael Sheehan (Feb. 2, 2006).

[42] Telephone interview with Bill Redmond (Feb. 6, 2006).

At one level, the declarations were a success. The next day, Thursday, November 17, Sheehan moved to dissolve the TRO. Judge Lindberg, after reading the declarations, did just this on Friday, November 18.[43] But this apparent victory for the defense laid the foundation for its ultimate defeat in two ways unexpected by either side at the time.

First, the TRO's dissolution accomplished little except to give Pepsi-Co an argument, which the judge also accepted, for accelerated discovery and hearing on a request for a preliminary injunction. Quaker did not immediately put Redmond to work marketing beverages just because the TRO was dissolved. The continuing legal uncertainty made it prudent for Quaker to act as if the restraint were still in effect. Redmond drew his paycheck and learned about the company, but performed no work. Dissolving the TRO thus accomplished nothing for defendants. By contrast, the accelerated schedule put everyone under pressure and contributed to further slips.

More importantly, however, both Redmond's and Uzzi's declarations, hastily prepared in order to get the TRO dissolved, contained an overstatement that would soon be fatal to their position. As summarized by Judge Lindberg in his November 18 Memorandum and Order dissolving the TRO:

> In the declarations, Redmond and Uzzi describe Redmond's duties with Quaker as consisting of the execution of existing plans, strategies and programs. The declarants state that each plan was fully developed prior to Redmond joining Quaker and that Redmond will only be involved in the execution of the various plans. Redmond's primary responsibility will be managing the integration of the Gatorade/Snapple distribution system. Further, Redmond will be involved in the execution of the previously developed sales and marketing, pricing and promotional programs.[44]

These statements had clearly impressed Judge Lindberg. He relied on them in dissolving the TRO. There was only one problem with them. They weren't true. As Bill Redmond told us, "Nobody is hired to execute a plan."[45] PepsiCo naturally enough sought to discover these "fully developed" "plans, strategies and programs." Not surprisingly, since Snapple had been acquired by Quaker only two weeks before these events, the plans did not exist. As characterized by Judge Lindberg when he issued his preliminary injunction one month later:

> That "business plan" however, consists only of a formal contract among a single Snapple distributor, Select Beverages, Inc., Snapple

---

[43] *PepsiCo, Inc. v. Redmond*, 1994 WL 687544 (N.D. Ill.).

[44] *Id.* at *3.

[45] Telephone interview with Bill Redmond (Feb. 6, 2006).

and Stokely Van Camp, and/or a two page "contract terms summary" that sets forth the changes in the renegotiated Snapple
agreement. Regardless of what Quaker says constitutes the business
plan, in fact Redmond himself has no knowledge of any such
business plan. Although Redmond swears that his new boss—Uzzi—
told him of this plan, Uzzi himself knows of no one who transmitted
such hearsay to Redmond.[46]

Why had Uzzi overstated the extent of Quaker's planning? Carelessness? Failure to appreciate what opposing counsel would do with it?
Desire to stretch the truth to help a friend? None of the lawyers knew
for sure, and we did not interview Uzzi, but, as we shall see, his
subsequent career may provide a partial answer.

All of the lawyers on the case agree that this misrepresentation or
overstatement in the declaration was the pivotal factor in the case that
turned Judge Lindberg against the defendants and led to his unprecedented injunction. On the plaintiffs' side, the partner at Schiff Hardin
who has become their leading trade secrets litigator has written: "It is
impossible to know whether the trial judge would have ruled in Pepsi-
Co's favor absent the misstatements in the defendants' declarations."[47]
The defense agrees. Redmond's lawyer has written: "The defense would
have been far better off to have suffered the indignity of a TRO for a few
more days, than to rush to take a position on the facts that we could not
substantiate at the trial."[48] He was even more pointed in conversation,
stressing the overpromising in the declarations, and Redmond's lack of
candor in conversations with Pepsi superiors, as the two critical factors
that swung Judge Lindberg against Redmond.[49]

But of course this shift by Judge Lindberg didn't just happen. It
required some lack of coordination on the defense team, and some very
effective lawyering by plaintiffs.

The defense team began expanding the day after Sheehan got the
TRO dissolved. Quaker wanted its antitrust counsel, Helene D. Jaffe of
the New York firm of Weil, Gotshal & Manges, involved.[50] Quaker had
long been concerned over potential antitrust liability for Gatorade's
dominance of the market for sports drinks, and wanted to be certain that

---

[46] *PepsiCo, Inc. v. Redmond*, 1994 WL 687544, at *11–12.

[47] Linda K. Stevens, *Trade Secrets and Inevitable Disclosure*, 36 Tort & Ins. L.J. 917,
934 (2001).

[48] Lyerla, *Thirteen Rules*.

[49] Telephone interview with Brad Lyerla, partner at Marshall, Gerstein & Borun, Chi.,
Ill. (Oct. 7, 2005). Lyerla was then at Jenner & Block, also in Chicago.

[50] Jaffe is still a partner at Weil, Gotshal & Manges and is now Co–Chair of its Trade
Practices and Regulatory Law Department.

no record would be made that might be used to establish a definition of the relevant market or improper tactics in its maintenance.[51] Quaker also thought that Redmond should have separate counsel, so it retained Bradford Lyerla, then at Jenner & Block, to represent Redmond. From the time Lyerla joined the team on Saturday, November 19, only he talked to Redmond, so as to ensure that no one else connected to Quaker might come into possession of PepsiCo trade secrets.[52] On Monday, November 21, the defense team moved to dismiss and filed a supplemental memorandum of law on inevitable disclosure.

One lawyer involved in the case thought that the defense was poorly served by this expanded team. At the hearing there were evident signs of lack of coordination on a common story, particularly on the trade secrets issue which by now dominated the proceedings. In truth it would have been hard to recover from the fatal puncturing of the initial defense story, that Redmond was being hired merely to implement an existing plan.

Still, it is hard to figure out the compelling defense narrative. Sheehan and Lyerla had little expertise in trade secrets litigation—to be fair, not many lawyers did in 1994, including PepsiCo's. Sheehan and Lyerla approached the case as employment litigation. For example, there was some attempt by Lyerla to portray Redmond as a kind of small fish who was being pushed around.[53] However, this account didn't seem to fit the actual individual, whose mastery on the witness stand of intimate details of PepsiCo's California operations only confirmed that his role in that corporation exceeded his paper title. Redmond was induced during his testimony to prepare a chart explaining PepsiCo's "Pricing Architecture," which both demonstrated his possession of trade secrets, and helped remove any ability to appear as a little guy caught in a clash of giants.[54] Since Helene Jaffe was aboard, albeit for her expertise in her field of antitrust, the defense decided to have her cross-examine Redmond's immediate boss, Brenda Barnes. Some lawyers who preferred not to be identified thought that this was a disaster. Jaffe attempted to trip Barnes up by questioning her on news articles of questionable relevance. It was pointlessly aggressive cross-examination, that only made Barnes appear more honest, sincere and genuinely concerned about how Redmond's knowledge of trade secrets might harm PepsiCo. What did not

---

[51] Telephone interview with Mike Sheehan (Feb. 2, 2006).

[52] Telephone interview with Brad Lyerla (Oct. 7, 2005). It is hard to evaluate how important this was since Redmond told me he was going to work each day at Quaker's offices.

[53] Mike Sheehan told us this was part of the strategy behind retaining separate counsel for Redmond. Telephone interview with Mike Sheehan (Feb. 2, 2006).

[54] *PepsiCo, Inc. v. Redmond*, 1994 WL 687544, at *32.

emerge from these disparate defense efforts was a coherent story of why trade secrets were not a concern.

Thanksgiving did not really happen for any of the lawyers. All report a blur of activity, a brief wandering home for food and a return to the office.

Monday, November 28 was the first of three days of hearings on PepsiCo's request for a preliminary injunction. PepsiCo focused on Uzzi's and Redmond's untrustworthiness. Roger Pascal, PepsiCo's lead lawyer, recalls that as early as three or four minutes into his cross-examination of Redmond, he was getting him to admit that he had lied to his boss Brenda Barnes about not having accepted the Quaker offer. "I used the word 'lie' in the next 15 questions." The judge asked him to stop, but the point was made.[55]

Brad Lyerla, Redmond's lawyer, has argued that the manner of Redmond's departure, and the overstatements in the early declarations about Quaker's "business plans," were analytically irrelevant.[56] However, the district court and court of appeals treated them as relevant both to the question of whether Redmond "threatened" to misappropriate trade secrets, and what kind of relief would be necessary to protect PepsiCo, and it is hard to say that they were wrong. "PepsiCo highlighted the discrepancies between the declarations and the evidence and argued that the trial judge had been 'snookered' by the defendants into dissolving the TRO with the false declarations. PepsiCo argued that if the defendants could not even tell the truth to the court, how could they be trusted to honor PepsiCo's trade secrets?"[57] Lyerla's strategy was to "keep reminding the court that there was no nexus between the lies and Pepsi's trade secrets," and to rely on one of the two earlier federal cases on threatened misappropriation for the proposition that an employee who lied once his departure became controversial might not necessarily disclose trade secrets.[58] It is hard to fault this strategy, but it did not succeed. Uzzi and Redmond both came across as somewhat slippery. Their hair was slicked back and they appeared very New York, a negative impression exacerbated by Helene Jaffe, also a sharply-dressed New Yorker.

On the other hand, everyone who was there agrees that PepsiCo's witnesses, Craig Weatherup and Brenda Barnes, were superb. The judge was impressed that such high PepsiCo officials testified. Weatherup was

[55] Telephone interview with Roger Pascal (Jan. 23, 2006).

[56] Lyerla, *Thirteen Rules*.

[57] Stevens, *Trade Secrets and Inevitable Disclosure*.

[58] Lyerla, *Thirteen Rules*, discussing *AMP Inc. v. Fleischhacker*, 823 F.2d 1199 (7th Cir. 1987).

an effective speaker who had gone on ABC Nightline a year earlier to explain why Pepsi was not recalling any products after a syringe turned up in a can of Diet Pepsi.[59] Barnes was from Chicago, 40 years old, one of seven children of a factory worker, with a pleasant, next-door-neighbor quality.[60] Roger Pascal attributes PepsiCo's success primarily to its two witnesses, only secondarily to the declarations by Redmond and Uzzi emphasized by his law partner and litigation opponents. They "humanized" a company that could easily have appeared "heartless."[61] They explained the seasonal nature of marketing planning, suggesting that Redmond had left at a particularly vulnerable time when plans had been drawn up for pricing for the next year, but had not yet become public. This subtly suggested a limit on the holding in PepsiCo's favor, perhaps that "inevitable disclosure" might be a concern only for relatively brief periods of time, and might be reflected in the relatively short six-month injunction that Judge Lindberg ultimately issued.

At the conclusion of the hearing, Judge Lindberg asked each side to submit findings, telling them not to be greedy because he would just take one side's. In the words of the Court of Appeals, "the district court adopted PepsiCo's proposed findings of fact and conclusions of law verbatim as the text for most of its opinion."[62] Lindberg found PepsiCo's Strategic Plan, Annual Operating Plan, and Pricing Architecture (all capitalization original) to constitute trade secrets that gain value from their secrecy. A competitor that knew where Pepsi was placing resources would, the court observed, know where Pepsi was placing resources. The court adopted Pepsi's account of this possibility as "the difference between winning and losing," "catastrophic," without explaining how another manufacturer could make any use of marketing information that, by definition, becomes public as soon as it is executed.[63] The district court, in a passage to be passed over in silence by the Court of Appeals, held that Redmond's "performance of his job at Quaker results in *actual misappropriation* [of trade secrets] because he will use PepsiCo's trade secrets and other confidences in order to perform his duties."[64] It also

---

[59] Marcy Magiera, *The Pepsi Crisis: What Went Right*, Advertising Age, July 19, 1993.

[60] Delroy Anderson, *Barnes at Home in CEO Position*, Chicago Tribune, Feb. 11, 2005.

[61] Telephone interview with Roger Pascal (Jan. 23, 2006).

[62] *PepsiCo, Inc. v. Redmond*, 54 F.3d 1262, 1267 n.4 (7th Cir.1995). The Court of Appeals concluded that this did not "alter our basic standard of review" but (somewhat in self-contradiction) required "a closer and harder look" "where, as here, the court changed nothing in a party's submissions and even repeated that party's typographical errors."

[63] *PepsiCo, Inc. v. Redmond*, 1994 WL 687544, at *19, 33.

[64] *Id.* at *45 (emphasis supplied).

ruled, in a holding later affirmed, that the inevitability that Redmond would use such information constituted a *threatened* misappropriation.

Space does not permit discussion of the legal authority relied on by the district court to establish the proposition that proof of "inevitable disclosure" of some unidentified trade secret could substitute for proof of the statutory requirement of "threatened disclosure." The reader who checks those cases will discover that none supports that proposition. I will discuss only two. We have already discussed the curious evolution of *Teradyne*, from a case that denied any relief because "working ... knowing ... leaving ... hiring ... and entering" a field does not constitute a violation of trade secrets absent more specific allegations, to, in the words of the district court, "[t]he only court to consider whether 'inevitable disclosure' constitutes a threatened misappropriation under the ITSA [that] concluded that it does."[65] Even shabbier was the court's treatment of the first case in its string citation, cited for the precise opposite of its holding.[66] The court enjoined Redmond from working in beverage marketing, sales, or pricing for six months and from using any PepsiCo trade secrets forever.[67]

The Seventh Circuit's Decision

The appeal was argued on April 5, 1995, and the decision issued on May 11, affirming the district court in full. None of the lawyers could recall any amusing anecdotes about the argument or appeal. As mentioned, Judge Flaum, writing for the Court, referred sarcastically to the district court's verbatim adoption of PepsiCo's submission; passed over its baffling finding that Redmond had actually misappropriated trade

---

[65] 1994 WL 687544, at *48–49.

[66] *IBM Corp. v. Seagate Tech., Inc.*, 1991 WL 757821 (D. Minn. 1991), *rev'd*, 962 F.2d 12 (8th Cir. 1992), *dismissed*, 941 F. Supp. 98 (D. Minn. 1992). In the actual case, IBM got a preliminary injunction against a scientist's departure for Seagate; the Court of Appeals reversed on the grounds that IBM had not demonstrated either actual trade secrets or a threat to disclose them; and, on remand, the district court dismissed. The district court noted on remand that the Eighth Circuit had neither accepted nor rejected "inevitable disclosure," but that IBM had not shown anything to warrant an injunction under that or traditional theories: "A trade secret will not be protected by the extraordinary remedy of injunction on mere suspicion or apprehension of injury. There must be a substantial threat of impending injury before an injunction will issue. Merely showing the existence of trade secrets is not enough.... Merely possessing trade secrets and holding a comparable position with a competitor does not justify an injunction." *IBM*, 941 F.Supp. at 101.

Judge Lindberg's *PepsiCo* opinion cites the unpublished preliminary injunction opinion in *IBM* as support for the doctrine of "inevitable disclosure"; describes the Court of Appeals decision as "remanded for more specific statement of relief," which is not true; and fails completely to mention the published opinion of the district court, dismissing the case.

[67] 1994 WL 687544, at *91–93.

secrets merely by taking a job with a competitor; and disapproved its reliance on common law.

Otherwise, the Court of Appeals closely tracked the district court. It agreed, as all parties basically had, that Redmond knew PepsiCo secrets. It found threatened misappropriation by invoking the doctrine of inevitable disclosure, which it derived from the Uniform Trade Secrets Act (which does not mention it) and two earlier federal cases that dismissed trade secrets suits in their entirety. "The ITSA [Illinois Trade Secrets Act], *Teradyne*, and *AMP* lead to the same conclusion: a plaintiff may prove a claim of trade secret misappropriation by demonstrating that a defendant's new employment will inevitably lead him to rely on the plaintiff's trade secrets."[68] It is a nice trick for a silent statute and two defense victories to lead so ineluctably to a single, plaintiff's, conclusion. It approved the district court's determination that Redmond's decisions about Quaker's beverages would necessarily take advantage of his knowledge of PepsiCo's targets and prices, without explaining, or offering any example, how such information would even be useful. Instead, it accepted a PepsiCo analogy that has since become "classic":[69] "PepsiCo finds itself in the position of a coach, one of whose players has left, playbook in hand, to join the opposing team before the big game."[70] While the decision had the effect of affirming the injunction against Redmond's working in beverages, that injunction was due to expire by its own terms in the middle of June, and the Court of Appeals did not specifically discuss the duration of the injunction.

The Immediate Impact of PepsiCo, Inc. v. Redmond

The Impact on the Beverage Wars

Probably the only impact of the injunction was that Quaker did indeed stop recruiting Pepsi executives. None of our interviewees could remember any others who were even interviewed.[71]

Other than that, it is difficult to find any impact of the injunction on either the beverage wars, or the individuals affected. Accounts of the beverage wars in trade publications following 1994 fail to disclose any advantage, even faint, that Gatorade might have attained by employing former PepsiCo executives. That "playbook" so important in litigation never appears in other sources. All the sports drinks aggressively pursued endorsements from athletic teams and leagues, signed athletes as endorsers, advertised heavily, emphasized their distinctive tastes, made

---

[68] *PepsiCo, Inc. v. Redmond*, 54 F.3d at 1269.

[69] Lyerla, *Thirteen Rules*.

[70] *PepsiCo, Inc. v. Redmond*, 54 F.3d at 1270.

[71] Interviews with Pam McGuire, Roger Pascal, Bill Redmond.

constant price adjustments (as would be predicted by the classical model of a market found in any Economics 1 textbook, but apparently not known at the United States Court of Appeals for the Seventh Circuit). By the end of 1995, Coke's and Pepsi's entry into sports drinks had an effect on Gatorade. Gatorade's market share had slipped from 80 to 72.3 percent; Coke's POWERade had 12.1 percent, and Pepsi's AllSport had 9.8 percent.[72]

By 1997, Brenda Barnes had succeeded Craig Weatherup as President and CEO of Pepsi–Cola North America. In that year, she made headline news by resigning all her corporate jobs in order to spend more time with her children.[73] As her successor, PepsiCo named Phil Marineau, former President of Quaker Oats, the man who started at Quaker in 1972, built Gatorade, and recruited Uzzi and Redmond from PepsiCo. Marineau had left Quaker in late 1995, the year the Seventh Circuit decided *Redmond*, as part of the shake-up following the disaster of the Snapple acquisition. He had a one-year covenant not to compete with Quaker in beverages, so spent less than a year as President of Dean Foods (which did not sell beverages), then moved to PepsiCo in September 1997—with no complaint from Quaker about loss of trade secrets.[74] "PepsiCo Inc., long known for exporting managers to other companies, is counting on an outsider for new ideas and to rally the troops against Coca–Cola Co.," read the lead in *Wall Street Journal*. It quoted a beverage consultant ("The most positive aspect is that the people at Pepsi brought in an outsider—it shows they're ready to play the game differently") and a Pepsi bottler ("If he does for Pepsi what he did for Gatorade, that would be wonderful.")[75] The transformation of the market for executives by 1997 was essentially complete. Even a company like PepsiCo would now recruit from without, and even a man like Marineau, who spent his first twenty-five years with a single company, would spend his next ten quickly moving among several more. The doctrine of "inevitable disclosure," however, remained on the beach after the tide of one-career managers had receded forever.

---

[72] Darren Rovell, *First in Thirst: How Gatorade Turned the Science of Sweat into a Cultural Phenomenon* 126–38 (AMACOM 2005).

[73] Nikhil Deogun, *Top PepsiCo Executive Picks Family Over Job*, Wall Street Journal, Sept. 24, 1997, at B1. Barnes later returned to the corporate world and today is CEO at Sara Lee Corporation. Delroy Anderson, *Barnes at Home in CEO Position*, Chicago Tribune, Feb. 11, 2005.

[74] Lawyers for PepsiCo confirmed that there was no legal difficulty in hiring Marineau.

[75] Nikhil Deogun, *PepsiCo Looks to Outsider Marineau to Supply New Ideas and Inspiration*, Wall Street Journal, Sept. 25, 1997, at B2. Marineau lasted only twenty months at PepsiCo. Today he is CEO at Levi Strauss. Andrew Edgecliffe–Johns, *Tightening Levi's Belt: Essential Guide to Phil Marineau*, Financial Times, Feb. 28, 2000.

Not even "the man who built Gatorade," however, could rescue AllSport. In the final absurd plot twist, PepsiCo in 2000 acquired the entire Quaker Oats company for $13.4 billion, outbidding rival Coca–Cola. It thus acquired Gatorade and 81 percent of the U.S. sports drink market. Like Ahab, its obsession with Gatorade had ended. Unlike Ahab, PepsiCo was able to swallow its white whale.[76] The argument that Gatorade, with 80 percent of the market, would have any interest in the "Pricing Architecture" of a product that never had more than 9 percent, ludicrous in 1994, was a historic relic six years later. PepsiCo had spent a great deal of money to keep a former employee off the job for six months, to send a message to its employees and to a competitor, and to establish a legal principle that might have caused it harm three years later, when it joined the crowd and began recruiting the occasional executive from outside its company.

The Impact of PepsiCo, Inc. v. Redmond on Individuals

It is hard to find any impact of the *Redmond* case on the affected individuals, with the possible exception of a hypothetical PepsiCo employee who had hoped to follow Redmond and Uzzi to Gatorade.

Bill Redmond drew a paycheck from Quaker during the six months of the injunction. He spent that time learning about other aspects of Quaker's organization and going to the gym. His job was waiting for him when the injunction against taking it expired. The only effect of the injunction on his life was that none of his old friends from PepsiCo would talk to him. None of his duties at Quaker involved any use of PepsiCo secrets and nobody ever referred to them, or to the continuing injunction.[77]

The biggest factor shaping the careers of Marineau, Uzzi and Redmond at Quaker was what turned out to be the disastrous purchase of Snapple from the First National Maintenance owners. Marineau and Uzzi had engineered the purchase of the brand in 1994 for $1.7 billion. The market was soon flooded with competing bottled teas and juices, and the Snapple brand proved to carry no particular cachet. Quaker eventually sold the brand in March 1997 for $300 million. By then, Marineau, Uzzi and Redmond were all gone. Marineau, as mentioned, camped out

---

[76] Even news articles that stressed Quaker's other brands all assumed that the company was of interest to PepsiCo primarily for Gatorade, e.g. Greg Winter, *PepsiCo sets a new course with deal for Quaker Oats* , New York Times, Dec. 5, 2000. As part of the acquisition, PepsiCo sold AllSport to Monarch Beverages. As of this writing, Gatorade continues to hold over 80 percent of the U.S. sports drink market, and is PepsiCo's fastest-growing brand. Chad Terhune, *PepsiCo Net Rises on Solid Sales; Gatorade Grows,* Wall Street Journal, Feb. 9, 2006.

[77] Telephone interview with Bill Redmond (February 6, 2006).

at Dean Foods for less than a year before becoming president and CEO of Pepsi–Cola North America.

Donald Uzzi was fired (permitted to resign) from Quaker in July 1996 because of the failure of Snapple.[78] He next was executive vice-president of Sunbeam, then run by "Chainsaw Al" Dunlap, who fired him in April 1998. Uzzi apparently then turned on Dunlap and was a source for a book critical of Dunlap.[79] The Securities and Exchange Commission (SEC) brought charges against Dunlap, Uzzi, and Sunbeam's former CFO, alleging massive financial fraud at Sunbeam, including sham transactions, improperly recognized revenue and improperly recorded reserves. Uzzi settled the charges by paying $100,000 to the SEC without admitting or denying wrongdoing.[80] By then, Uzzi was serving Ross Perot's Electronic Data Systems as Senior Vice–President of Global Advertising, Marketing and Communication. He has since moved to other ventures. Uzzi has been a front-page example of a corporate executive who has survived decisions ranging from poor to corrupt.[81]

Bill Redmond, of course, had nothing to do with Quaker's buying Snapple, a deal that Marineau and Uzzi had done before he arrived there. In fact, he even ran Snapple for a while after Uzzi was fired in July 1996.[82] By that December, he had returned home to upstate New York to the first of a series of jobs as CEO turning around companies that are in bankruptcy.[83] He likes this work and thinks he is good at it. He told us that the only lasting impact of the litigation is that it left him with less respect for the legal process.[84]

"They were careless people, Tom and Daisy—they smashed up things and creatures and then retreated back into their money or their vast carelessness or whatever it was that kept them together, and let other people clean up the mess they made. . . . "[85]

---

[78] Barnaby J. Feder, *Resignation at Quaker Oats Over Snapple's Poor Sales*, New York Times, July 20, 1996, at 41.

[79] John A. Byrne, *Chainsaw* (1999). On Uzzi as a source, see the review of the book by Greg Burns, Chicago Tribune, Nov. 21, 1999 at C7.

[80] *SEC settles with ex-Andersen partner in Sunbeam probe*, The Accountant, Feb. 18, 2003.

[81] Matt Krantz, *The Nine Lives of Ousted Corporate Fat Cats* , USA Today, July 18, 2002, at B1.

[82] Feder, *Resignation at Quaker Oats*.

[83] Janiss Denn, *Albany native heads up Garden Way*, Albany Times–Union, Dec. 20, 1996 at E1.

[84] Telephone interview with Bill Redmond (Feb. 6, 2006).

[85] F. Scott Fitzgerald, *The Great Gatsby*.

The Continuing Legal Importance of PepsiCo v. Redmond

But what puts *PepsiCo v. Redmond* into this anthology is not a forgotten skirmish in the beverage wars, but the genie of inevitable disclosure that escaped that long-ago discarded bottle of AllSport. Whenever an employee moves to a competitor, the potential is there for a lawsuit to be threatened on the theory that the employee, merely by working in the same area, will inevitably disclose some trade secret that she or he knows. The threat far exceeds the actual application of the doctrine. As of September 2005, 117 court decisions cited *PepsiCo v. Redmond*, but of these only 14 issued any kind of injunction against a former employee, one of which was reversed on appeal without opinion. There is some faintness of purpose in attempting to review the case law. Other articles have done so in more space and will in the future, and the law is too unsettled to make any analysis more than temporary. However, since most articles, in our view, overstate the willingness of courts to enjoin employees, a brief discussion of some case development may be helpful.

PepsiCo v. Redmond represents, not only the modern origin of inevitable disclosure, but also its high-water mark. There are no subsequent cases that enjoin employees from taking jobs with competitors merely because of their knowledge of their old employer's annual operating plan or strategic plans. The few successful injunctions involve considerably more specific allegations both of particular trade secrets, and of the likelihood of threatened disclosure.

The author could find only three appellate courts to adopt inevitable disclosure, citing *Redmond*, and actually affirm an injunction or otherwise make the doctrine part of its holding. The only state supreme court is Arkansas. Managers of a trucking company that bids with companies that outsource trucking services left for a competitor. The court affirmed an injunction against their taking that job. The court, however, was clearly concerned about the information they had on specific existing customer contracts, which they might use to underbid their old employer. This seems more like a case in which the court correctly found "threatened disclosure" of actual identified trade secrets, rather than "inevitable disclosure" of something from a mass of corporate plans. However, the Arkansas court, like the *Redmond* court, was clearly beguiled by the magic of "corporate strategy," and thus might reach the same result in a case that involved only strategic plans.[86] The only other state appellate court to adopt the doctrine is in Illinois. Reversing a dismissal by the trial court, the court held that the plaintiffs should be permitted to show that the new employer could not function without the

---

[86] *Cardinal Freight Carriers, Inc. v. J.B. Hunt Transp. Servs.*, 987 S.W.2d 642 (Ark. 1999).

secrets it would learn from its new employee.[87] Finally, the Third Circuit, in an unpublished opinion not for citation, has predicted that Pennsylvania would adopt inevitable disclosure.[88]

On the other hand, at least two states have squarely rejected inevitable disclosure. The intermediate appellate court in California rested on that state's statutory refusal to enforce covenants not to compete. It reasoned that, on facts like *Redmond*'s, the doctrine of inevitable disclosure was just a covenant not to compete with a different name, and required plaintiff to show the statutory "actual or threatened" misappropriation.[89] This reasoning persuaded Maryland's highest court to reject inevitable disclosure and require plaintiffs to show "actual or threatened" misappropriation, which meant no injunction in the case presented.[90]

The uncertainty in the law has probably led firms that hire from outside into a more pro-active posture. Mike Sheehan, the attorney who represented Quaker, for example, said that he advises such firms, successfully so far, to send fairly detailed communication to the old employer about the employee's precise job title and duties, why disclosure of trade secrets is not a fear, what steps have been taken to ensure that they will not be disclosed—ending with an invitation that the old employer make any proposal that it feels is still needed in order to protect its secrets.[91] The next round of scholarship on trade secrets might attempt more systematically to delve into firm practice in avoiding litigation.

Conclusion

It is hard to believe that courts will really stand in the way of the new market for managers and the increased propensity to hire from outside the organization. *Redmond* may someday be seen as an oddity. However, that conclusion is premature. The case sends shadows over managerial recruitment, forcing firms into defensive action and, though very rarely, restricting personnel mobility. How odd that this comes out of a lawsuit in which a corporation, angered about "raiding," had to be talked into consciousness of trade secrets by very able lawyers. How odd that a judge adopted the doctrine, not because the law compelled it, not because anyone argued that it was good policy, but because he looked into the eyes of the defendant before him and thought that he had been lied to.

---

[87] *Strata Mktg. v. Murphy*, 740 N.E.2d 1166 (Ill. App. 2000).

[88] *Doeblers Pa. Hybrids, Inc. v. Doebler Seeds*, LLC, 88 Fed.Appx. 520 (3d Cir. 2004).

[89] *Whyte v. Schlage Lock Co.*, 125 Cal. Rptr.2d 277 (Ct. App. 2002).

[90] *LeJeune v. Coin Acceptors, Inc.*, 849 A.2d 451, 467–70 (Md. 2004).

[91] Telephone interview with Mike Sheehan (Feb. 2, 2006).

*

6

The Story of *Ingersoll–Rand v. Ciavatta*: Employee Inventors in Corporate Research & Development– Reconciling Innovation with Entrepreneurship

Catherine L. Fisk[*]

Armand Ciavatta, the son of a working-class Italian–American family from New England, was a born inventor. Interviewed at age 76, he said he still has ideas for inventions that he hasn't found the time to develop. While working as a research program manager for Ingersoll–Rand, a New Jersey-based manufacturer of heavy equipment, he submitted a dozen ideas for new products to the hierarchy at the research facility where he worked. The company rejected all of them. After Ciavatta was fired in a dispute with a higher-up over the quality of the mine roof stabilizer for which Ciavatta was the manufacturing manager, he had an idea for an improved stabilizer. Now unemployed, Ciavatta went back to tinkering in his home. He developed a prototype stabilizer with kitchen utensils borrowed from his wife and the assistance of a neighborhood boy. Investing his life savings along with money borrowed from a bank and from his brother, Ciavatta patented his stabilizer and he started his own small business to market his invention. When Ciavatta's invention proved a success in the marketplace, Ingersoll–Rand sued to force him to relinquish the patent. Though Ingersoll–Rand claimed that Ciavatta had improperly used information gained during his employment there, Ciavatta eventually won the litigation battle in a unanimous decision of the New Jersey Supreme Court.[1] But he lost the

* The author wishes to thank Amin Aminfar, Duke Law class of 2007, for exceptional research and editorial assistance in the preparation of this chapter and Armand Ciavatta for sharing the story of his invention and his case.

[1] *Ingersoll–Rand Co. v. Ciavatta*, 542 A.2d 879 (N.J. 1988).

war, as Ingersoll–Rand sales representatives waged a successful campaign to persuade their clients not to switch to Ciavatta's product. The struggle to keep his business afloat consumed much of the rest of Ciavatta's career, and he suffered the fate of long-term unemployment not uncommon for a middle-aged engineer who suddenly found himself out of work. As for Ingersoll–Rand, the denouement of the story isn't much happier. The company eventually disbanded the research and development facility where Ciavatta had worked and ultimately gave up most of its mining business.

Ciavatta's story is not unique. Many inventors believe that their former employers have unfairly claimed their ideas and refused to share the profit or the credit for the invention. Some tell a story of a bureaucratic research and development culture that fails to stimulate, support, or reward innovation. Some become frustrated and go out on their own to work on a promising idea. When the idea succeeds, as the employees tell it, the employer suddenly decides that the invention should be pursued and demands the former employee assign the patent to the firm. These employees understandably see the employer's behavior as opportunistic, and regard contractual provisions that would enable the employer to claim the invention as unconscionable.[2]

Petr Taborsky, for example, made national headlines in 1997 when he went to prison rather than comply with a court order that he hand over his laboratory notebooks and his patents to an invention he devel-

---

[2] Other leading cases raising similar issues include: *Wommack v. Durham Pecan Co.,* 715 F.2d 962 (5th Cir. 1983) (granting shop right to employer of general laborer whose duties included unloading trucks and sweeping floors for an invention for removing worms from pecans because laborer developed patented process at work); *Francklyn v. Guilford Packing Co.,* 695 F.2d 1158 (9th Cir. 1983) (granting employer shop right to device for harvesting clams invented by fisherman); *Dewey v. American Stair Glide Corp.,* 557 S.W.2d 643 (Mo. Ct. App. 1977) (rejecting employer's claim to shop right due to evidence of an express prohibition against working on a device for solving a problem of falling Stair Glide chair elevators and evidence that the invention was devised entirely at home and during employee's lunch hour); *Waterjet Tech., Inc. v. Flow Int'l Co.,* 996 P.2d 598 (Wash. 2000) (entitling employer to a patent over the method and apparatus for using high-pressure waterjet developed by former lab technician and associate engineer); *Hewett v. Samsonite Corp.,* 507 P.2d 1119 (Colo. Ct. App. 1973) (granting employer shop right to patents for improved luggage invented by foreman who designed inventions on work time using company material but denying employer ownership of the patent because employee was not hired to invent); *Crowe v. M&M/Mars,* 577 A.2d 1278 (N.J. Super. App. Div. 1990) (granting candy manufacturer shop right to an improved pump that could be used for spraying coating on chocolate candy invented by mechanical engineer employed as independent contractor). *See* Paul C. Van Slyke & Mark M. Friedman, *Employer's Rights to Inventions and Patents of its Officers, Directors, and Employees,* 18 AIPLA Q.J. 127 (1990); Steven Cherensky, Comment, *A Penny for Their Thoughts: Employee–Inventors, Preinvention Assignment Agreements, Property, and Personhood,* 81 Cal. L. Rev. 595 (1993); Marc B. Hershovitz, Note, *Unhitching the Trailer Clause: The Rights of Inventive Employees and Their Employers,* 3 J. Intell. Prop. L. 187 (1995).

oped in his spare time while a student at the University of South Florida. Taborsky had taken a job in 1987 for $8.50 an hour working as a lab technician at the university to help pay his tuition. He was originally assigned to work on a project in which the university had contracted with the local power company to develop a process for removing ammonia from a clay used to filter water. The power company terminated the project when the university was unable to solve the problem, and Taborsky was reassigned to menial jobs around the lab paid for by sources other than the power company contract. But Taborsky was determined to solve the problem even without the support of his employer. Working after hours for months without pay, Taborsky eventually devised a solution to the problem. Unsurprisingly, both the university and the power company became interested and insisted that the power company owned the process. Because he worked as an employee of the university, Taborsky would get nothing for his discovery. Taborsky took his lab notebooks and dropped out of school. The professor who ran the lab got the university police to confiscate Taborsky's lab notebooks and Taborsky was criminally prosecuted and convicted of theft of the notebooks and of the data and ideas that he had developed. Undaunted, Taborsky patented his invention. In his view, it was not theft to steal his own ideas and the results of work he had done on his own time after the laboratory director had abandoned the project. The trial judge saw it differently, and sentenced Taborsky to prison, where he worked on a chain gang for two months.[3]

Though their circumstances are in important ways quite different, the common intensity of Petr Taborsky's and Armand Ciavatta's convictions about owning their ideas reflects how far patent ownership extends beyond simple economic analysis. It is about dignitary and autonomy issues as well. For these and other inventors, control over their patents is control over their creativity, and owning their patents is often as much about receiving credit for that creativity as it is about money. Just as employment for most people is as much about dignity, self-respect and autonomy as it is about a paycheck, so, too, is control over intellectual property rights.

From the employer's point of view, of course, it's a different story. Innovation is notoriously expensive and difficult, particularly in those

---

[3] Leon Jaroff, *Intellectual Chain Gang*, Time Magazine, Feb. 10, 1997, at 64 (detailing Taborsky's invention and incarceration); *Dateline: Taking Liberty? Man Goes to Prison to Fight His Right* (NBC television broadcast Dec. 12, 1999) (recounting Taborsky's story); Greg Saitz, *Inventor Squares Off with Employer*, Times–Picayune, Jan. 10, 2002, at 3 (reporting on employee inventor fired from M&M/Mars candy company for refusing to assign patent to invention for spray paint can). *See generally* David F. Noble, *America By Design: Science, Technology, and the Rise of Corporate Capitalism* (1977) (recounting criticisms of alleged anti-competitive and innovation-stifling consequences of corporate control of patents to employee inventions).

fields where complex modern technology requires the sustained inventive efforts of many people to develop new products. When one employee claims as his own all the profit and all the credit for an invention to which many of his co-workers and predecessors at the firm contributed, the firm is entitled to resist that opportunism by insisting that the patent and the profits should belong to the firm that fostered the culture and financed the work. From the point of view of the University of South Florida's general counsel, the contract between Taborsky and the university entitled the university to all his inventions. As she put it, "It is irrelevant to us who invented the process. We own it." Employers are worried that if employees can claim the results of their inventions, no employee would ever admit to having an inventive idea during working hours. Any employee who developed an idea on the job, even with the financial assistance of the firm and the creative and technical assistance of co-workers, would quit as soon as the invention appeared to be possibly profitable, claiming sole credit for work when it should be shared with the company and other employees. Employers tend to doubt the veracity of employee claims (though not necessarily Taborsky's or Ciavatta's claims) to have done their work after hours or after quitting or being fired. Moreover, aside from a university's concerns as employer, there is the question of a university's concerns as a producer of scientific knowledge. Should individual scientists who produce major break-throughs in important scientific problems be able to claim their work for themselves, thereby using intellectual property law to exclude other scientists from benefiting from their work?

As these disputes filter through litigation, employment contracts become increasingly important. In addition to their significance to the legal issues, interpretation and enforcement of these contracts will shape the ethical, economic, and political debates about reconciling individual creativity with collaborative work, about how credit and profit for creativity should be allocated, and about desirable incentives for individual entrepreneurship and corporate investment in research and development (R & D). Most inventors work as employees for the majority of their careers and are often required as a condition of employment to sign a contract drafted by the firm's lawyers giving the firm exclusive control over as broad a range of economically valuable information and innovation that the lawyers think is legally feasible. Such contracts typically claim as firm property—both during and after an employee's term of employment—the nebulous category of "proprietary information," along with the slightly more clearly (though still poorly) defined category of "trade secrets." These contracts, variously known as "invention assignment agreements" or "holdover clauses" or "trailer clauses," also claim as firm property any invention the employee might make that has any relationship to the firm's business or, less frequently, to the business of the firm's subsidiaries and affiliated companies. Armand Ciavatta's contract, for example, claimed for Ingersoll–Rand all inventions that might have anything to do with the company's twenty diverse subsidiaries and affiliates, regardless of whether Ciavatta had any contact with the affiliates or their work. In other words, since one Ingersoll–Rand subsidiary manufactured the Kryptonite bicycle lock, if Ciavatta had invented a new bike lock, the contract would have covered it even though Ciavatta never had a thing to do with that line of business. In short, opportunistic behavior by employees is confronted by contractual overreaching by employers.

Reluctant simply to let the market power of one party or the other dictate who wins and who loses these disputes when they come to litigation, many courts have tried to carve a middle path by insisting that reasonable contracts will be enforced. *Ingersoll–Rand v. Ciavatta* was one such case.

Social Background

Among the statutes enacted by the first Congress of the United States was the Patent Act of 1790. Congress accorded patent protection high priority because of the widespread belief that intellectual property protections were essential to stimulate invention, and invention was necessary to economic development. Many, perhaps most, early nineteenth century inventors worked alone or with a few others in a small workshop in a town or village or on a farm. Most technology was relatively simple and thus it was possible for skilled craftspeople and ordinary laborers to understand the technology behind the devices that they used and to find the tools they would need to develop improvements to them. Invention was both democratic and entrepreneurial in the sense that many people with inventive talent had a realistic chance of becoming inventors, owning a patent, and being able to profit from their patented invention by either manufacturing and selling it themselves or by assigning or licensing the patent to someone who could.[4]

---

[4] The history of American technological innovation and corporate R & D in this and following paragraphs is drawn from Thomas Hughes, *American Genesis: A Century of Innovation and Technological Enthusiasm, 1870–1970* (1989); Joel Mokyr, *The Lever of Riches: Technological Creativity and Economic Progress* (1990); Doron S. Ben–Atar, *Trade Secrets: Intellectual Piracy and the Origins of American Industrial Power* (2004); B. Zorina Khan, *The Democratization of Invention: Patents and Copyrights in American Economic Development, 1790–1920* (2005); Steven Lubar, *The Transformation of Antebellum Patent Law*, 32 Tech. & Culture 932 (1991); Walter Licht, *Industrializing America: The Nineteenth Century* (1995); David A. Hounshell & John Kenly Smith, Jr., *Science and Corporate Strategy: Du Pont R & D, 1902–1980* (1980); Naomi R. Lamoreaux & Kenneth L. Sokoloff, *Inventors, Firms, and the Market for Technology in the Late Nineteenth and Early Twentieth Century United States*, in *Learning By Doing in Markets, Firms, and Countries* (Naomi R. Lamoreaux, Daniel M.G. Raff & Peter Temin eds., 1999); David F. Noble,

The early United States was a country obsessed with the need for and benefits of innovation. Compared to Europe, America was rich in natural resources and land but poor in skilled labor, technological sophistication and investment capital. Acquisition of technology, whether by importation from Europe or invention in America, and immigration of people skilled enough to use and develop technology were widely considered to be essential to the development of the country. Both political leaders and local business folk thought that encouraging invention would lead to economic development that would dramatically improve the lives of ordinary people and increase the wealth of the nation. Consequently, the Framers of the Constitution empowered Congress to enact patent and copyright laws "To promote the Progress of Science and useful Arts, by securing for limited Times to Authors and Inventors the exclusive Right to their respective Writings and Discoveries." Technological innovation, both in the form of new inventions made in the U.S. or patented technologies imported from Europe, were eagerly sought by every possible means. And by the late nineteenth century, the efforts paid off. The U.S. went from being technologically backward and a net consumer of intellectual property to a technological leader and exporter of intellectual property to Europe and the world.

As the nineteenth century wore on, technology grew more complex and required greater resources to innovate in economically significant ways. While many people with some inventive ability, education, skill and access to a workshop might have been able to design and patent an improvement to the relatively simple steam engines of the early nineteenth century, by the end of the century only those with highly specialized knowledge of metals and mechanical engineering who had access to a locomotive and several miles of railroad track would be in a position to patent a major improvement. While crucial technology grew exponentially more complex, firms and factories grew larger. Opportunities for individual invention and entrepreneurship based on individual patent ownership became less prevalent. Instead, it was far more likely in the early twentieth century that an inventor would be an employee of a large corporation and work with other employees using the tools and material of his employer to develop a patent. Invention became less democratic and entrepreneurial at the individual level. Both invention and entrepreneurship became corporate.

America By Design: Science, Technology, and the Rise of Corporate Capitalism (1977); Leonard S. Reich, *The Making of American Industrial Research: Science and Business at GE and Bell, 1876–1926* (1985). For a full history of the law governing employee inventors see Catherine L. Fisk, *Removing the "Fuel of Interest" from the "Fire of Genius": Law and the Employee–Inventor, 1830–1930*, 65 U. Chi. L. Rev. 1127 (1998); Catherine L. Fisk, *Working Knowledge: Trade Secrets, Restrictive Covenants in Employment, and the Rise of Corporate Intellectual Property, 1800–1920*, 52 Hastings L.J. 441 (2001).

In the two decades bracketing the turn of the twentieth century, many large American firms founded research and development facilities. In 1902, Du Pont founded a sophisticated R & D operation that produced innovations in explosives (the company's original business) and eventually in plastics, artificial fibers, and chemicals. In the same period, Bell Telephone founded the famed Bell Laboratories, the Eastman–Kodak Company established a lab that produced major innovations in photographic film and printing, and General Electric instituted a research facility that produced major innovations in electricity. Many other firms similarly approached research and development with a degree of sophistication that was unprecedented in the U.S. Along with a transformation in industrial research came a transformation in how research and development employees were managed. Between 1870 and 1910, patentees became more likely to assign away rights to their patents at the time the patent was issued than they were before. Assignments to corporations jumped from 24% of recorded assignments in 1870 to 64% of recorded assignments in 1910.[5] Contracts between firms and their employees requiring employees to assign all patents to the firm were relatively rare until World War I but became routine in the twentieth century. The explosive growth of corporate research and development dramatically changed both the environment in which workplace innovation occurred and how the lay and legal public imagined invention. In the popular and judicial imagination, perhaps more than in actual fact, the hero inventor experimenting alone in his laboratory or workshop ceded his place to company men in laboratory coats working collaboratively—and on a corporate payroll—to advance the progress of technology. Legal doctrine changed accordingly, with twentieth century courts becoming far more likely than their nineteenth century predecessors to conclude either that employees were hired to invent, and the firm therefore owned all employee patents, or that the employee and the firm had validly contracted for assignment of employee patents.

The growth of corporate R & D was but one facet of a dramatic change in American business generally over the course of the early twentieth century. Corporations grew exponentially in size. As a result, the management of the tens of thousands of blue collar and white collar workers employed in the behemoth firms became ever more systematic and bureaucratic. The rise of managerial capitalism in the mid-century meant that inventive employees were even less likely to be entrepreneurs founding their own small firms, tending instead to be mid-level quasi-managerial employees of a research division of a large corporation. But the era when employees were not expected to be individually entrepreneurial did not last.

---

[5] Noble, *supra.*

By the mid–1980s, the link between job stability and innovation began to be severed. The stability of corporate jobs was disappearing as firms faced new global competition and unprecedented pressure from Wall Street to reduce labor costs. Suddenly, firms that had once offered stable jobs in exchange for the long-term loyalty of their employees began laying off massive numbers of employees and insisting that workers should be much more entrepreneurial. As the Vice President of Human Resources at AT & T said in 1996 when eliminating 40,000 jobs, "People need to look at themselves as self-employed, as vendors who come to this company to sell their skills. . . . [W]e have to promote the whole concept of the work force being contingent."[6]

By the late 1980s, scholars of innovation and economic development had begun to worry about the ability of managerial capitalism and corporate R & D to continue to deliver innovation and economic growth. Firms had long worried about how to provide incentives for employees to innovate since individual employees, who typically were required to assign patents to the firm, no longer stood to profit from their patents. Beginning in the 1940s, firms adopted a variety of bonus systems that promised modest financial rewards for employees whose work produced patents, but these bonus schemes often were either too small or too arbitrary to provide adequate incentives. As anxiety about the success of R & D at large corporations grew, a new, different, and wildly successful phenomenon emerged in Silicon Valley. Silicon Valley was characterized by rapid innovation, extraordinary levels of mobility among highly educated technology workers, constant start-ups of new firms, and a degree of entrepreneurship among technology employees that had not been seen since the nineteenth century. The Silicon Valley phenomenon caused both scholars and business people to wonder whether the days of R & D at large and bureaucratic firms were numbered.[7]

Thus, Armand Ciavatta's fight against Ingersoll–Rand occurred in the early 1980s at the convergence of a number of significant real-world, academic, and public policy developments. He was the company man who was fired by a firm at a time at which stable corporate jobs for middle-aged employees were becoming harder to find and long-term unemployment was likely to be a particularly severe problem for a group who had

---

[6] Edmund L. Andrews, *Don't Go Away Mad, Just Go Away: Can AT & T Be the Nice Guy As It Cuts 40,000 Jobs?* N.Y. Times, Feb. 13, 1996, at D1, D6. *See also* Catherine L. Fisk, *Knowledge Work: New Metaphors for a New Economy*, 80 Chi.-Kent L. Rev. 839 (2005).

[7] *See* Eric Von Hippel, *Democratizing Innovation* (2005); Eric Von Hippel, *The Sources of Innovation* (1988); Joel Mokyr, *The Lever of Riches: Technological Creativity and Economic Progress* (1990); David C. Mowery & Nathan Rosenberg, *Technology and the Pursuit of Economic Growth* (1989); AnnaLee Saxenian, *Regional Advantage: Culture and Competition in Silicon Valley and Route 128* (1994).

not expected to become or remain unemployed mid-career.[8] Layoffs occurred because firms were beginning to feel significant pressure from Wall Street to reduce labor costs in order to boost share prices. Corporate R & D departments were often targeted because they were perceived by cost-cutters to have become too bureaucratic, too cautious, and insufficiently creative and entrepreneurial. The impact of these job losses was exacerbated by the contracts departing employees had signed. Although the holdover agreements, restrictive covenants and other contractual devices used by firms for security were well-suited to prevent opportunistic quits in a workplace characterized by internal labor markets and implicit promises of job security, those same devices conceivably gummed up the works of the highly mobile and productive labor market that seemed to drive rapid innovation in Silicon Valley. The plight of the unemployed middle-aged engineer who sought to remake himself as an entrepreneur competing with one of the giants of American industry presented a particularly juicy challenge for a court to sort out. The case invited the court to craft legal doctrine capable of dealing with some of the most salient and pressing issues at the intersection of American business and technology.

Legal Background

Although United States patent laws have been revised significantly since the first Patent Act of 1790, most of the basics have not changed. The government may, upon application, issue a patent for an invention it deems new and useful. Patentable inventions can be devices (such as a better mousetrap) as well as processes (such as a recipe). A patent application must describe the invention with reasonable specificity, must explain how the invention meets the statutory requirements of being novel, useful and non-obvious, and must identify the true inventor. A patent lasts for a term of years and entitles the patent owner to a monopoly for the manufacture of the patented device. The patent application is a public disclosure designed to enable any person to read the patent and see how the patented device or process works, thereby allowing later inventors to come up with new ideas for improvements over existing patents.[9]

Federal patent law says nothing about ownership of patents produced by employees. While the Patent Act provides for the assignment of a patent upon issuance, state law governs the validity of assignments.

---

[8] On the phenomenon of restructuring or opportunistic firings unsettling the individual and social expectations of the career employee, see chapter one in this volume by Professor Grodin.

[9] On the general requirements of modern patent law, see Janice M. Mueller, *An Introduction to Patent Law* (2003); Roger E. Schechter & John R. Thomas, *Principles of Patent Law* (2004).

When the patentee or the person identified in the patent application as
the true inventor is an employee, the law of employment governs the
rights to the patent. Beginning in the late eighteenth century, the patent
law requirement that the "true inventor" be listed in the application
encouraged the notion that an individual person was both the inventor
and the proper owner of the patent. One of the common grounds for
attacking either the Patent Office's decision to award a patent or the
patent's validity when defending against a claim of patent infringement
was to assert that the patentee was not the true or first inventor. The
legal structure thus invited patentees to identify, in their legal documents and in their own minds, an invention as the product of one
individual's effort rather than the collective creation of a collaborative
workshop. For this and other reasons the default rule during the
nineteenth century was that any invention that an employee patented
belonged to the employee, regardless of whether the employee had made
the invention at work. Occasionally, employers and employees thought to
agree in advance on who would own patents to workplace inventions.
Courts often either very narrowly interpreted or declined to enforce
agreements to assign future inventions to the employer. The rationale
for both the default rule of employee ownership and the narrow interpretation of pre-invention assignment agreements was a sense of both the
intrinsic justice and instrumental benefit of a rule of individual ownership of valuable ideas. The pro-employee character of the nineteenth
century law of employee inventions may be attributed both to the pre-
industrial tradition of craft autonomy and control over craft knowledge
and to the early Industrial Revolution's ideology that the genius inventor
was the catalyst of technological change and economic growth.[10]

In the latter half of the century, courts made limited incursions on
the relatively pro-employee law. First, courts developed a doctrine that
eventually became known as the "shop right" rule. An employee who
developed an invention at work using the employer's tools was still
entitled to the patent, but the law gave the employer a shop right—a free
license to use and to manufacture the invention. Originally, the shop
right was a sort of equitable estoppel, existing only where the employee
had allowed the employer to use the invention in the business and then
later tried to restrict its use. Eventually, the employee's acquiescence
was no longer required. The shop right also expanded over time. When
first conceived, the right was non-transferable, such that an employer
could not sell the shop right, and if the business were sold or liquidated,
the shop right was not transferred with the other business assets. In the
twentieth century, the shop right became a transferable asset.

---

[10] The legal change described in this and the following paragraphs is detailed in
Catherine L. Fisk, *Removing the "Fuel of Interest" from the "Fire of Genius": Law and the
Employee–Inventor, 1830–1930*, 65 U. Chi. L. Rev. 1127 (1998).

Around the turn of the twentieth century, courts became more willing to conclude that employers owned employee patents based either on a finding that an employee had been hired to invent or on a contract assigning future inventions. Undergirding this judicial receptivity was the thought that, even where an employee was clearly the originator of an idea, employers could still justly own employee patents because the employee's idea would be worth little without the firm's investment that created value in the idea and brought it to market. Reasoning that invention is a long and arduous endeavor to which many employees contribute while on the firm's payroll and not solely the product of a stroke of individual genius, courts tended to find the public interest to lie not in the individual employee owning the patent but in corporate control. "Protection for the future requires that inventions already controlled [by a firm] be not undermined and diverted by other inventions along the same line."[11]

Over the course of the twentieth century, the law of employee inventors stabilized into three doctrinal categories. First, the default rule was that employees not hired specifically to invent owned the patents to all their inventions, regardless of when or where the employee conceived or developed the invention. Second, if the employee used work time or the employer's facilities to develop the invention, the law gave the employer a shop right to the invention, but the employee could still license or sell the patent to others or manufacture or market the invention herself. Third, firms and employees could contract around the default rules of employee ownership and shop right in two ways. First, an employer who hired an employee specifically on the understanding that the employee's job was to invent would be entitled to all patents produced in the scope of the employment contract. In this sense, the employment contract of a hiring to invent was deemed to overcome the default rule. Alternatively, the employer could contract around the default rule by requiring that all patents or inventions the employee might make during or for some period after the employment would be the employer's property and that the employee would be obligated to assign them. This last category affords the employer the broadest rights to employee inventions, for the obligation to assign the patents would not be limited to inventions made during the employment or even to those relating directly to the employee's work. *Ingersoll–Rand v. Ciavatta* presented a question about the limits on such pre-invention assignment agreements. Could an employer require an employee to assign the patent to any invention on any topic the employee might ever acquire for the rest of his or her life? If not, what are the limits of such contracts?

---

[11] *National Wire Bound Box Co. v. Healy*, 189 F. 49, 55 (7th Cir. 1911).

The law of employee inventors developed on a parallel track with two other bodies of law governing rights to economically valuable workplace knowledge: the law of trade secrets and the law of restrictive covenants. As explained in chapter six of this book, courts will prevent an employee from using economically valuable knowledge in subsequent or competitive employment when the knowledge qualifies as a trade secret. In addition, an employer may enter into a "restrictive covenant" or "noncompete agreement" with an employee to prevent the employee from engaging in competitive employment. In both the trade secret and the restrictive covenant areas, courts recognize that excessively broad protection for the employer's desire to prevent former employees from using knowledge gained at work can stifle competition, prevent the employee from finding employment, and retard the economic development and innovation that comes from the diffusion of talent and knowledge throughout the economy. On the other hand, courts also recognize that, to provide adequate incentives for firms to invest in the development of human capital and to invest in new technologies, the law should allow some contractual or default rule protection against employees opportunistically quitting their jobs before the employer has had the chance to recoup its investment in the employee's training or other development of human capital.

Most twentieth-century courts developed a variety of multi-factor balancing tests to mediate the disputes over trade secrets and non-compete agreements, and the balancing tests generally focus on the nature and extent of the employer's legitimate interest in restricting employees' use of knowledge, the proper geographic, temporal and occupational scope of the restriction on competitive work, the hardship on the employee of limiting his or her employment opportunities, and the public interest in either the free diffusion of knowledge through employee mobility or the restriction on competition. Some courts treat contracts regarding employee inventions, however, without the special reasonableness and public policy restrictions that dominate in trade secret and non-compete cases; contracts to assign future inventions in these courts are enforced like any other contract.[12] Some courts refuse on public policy grounds to enforce pre-invention assignment agreements that are without time limit and without limit on the subject matter of inventions covered.[13] A few states have statutes limiting the enforceability of pre-invention assignment agreements; under such statutes only inventions

---

[12] *See, e.g., Cubic Corp. v. Marty,* 229 Cal. Rptr. 828 (Cal. Ct. App. 1986) (enforcing agreement to assign invention developed during term of employment and relating to employee's work); *Shaw v. Regents of Univ. of Calif.,* 67 Cal. Rptr. 2d 850 (Cal. Ct. App. 1997) (stating that invention assignment agreement is a contract and therefore, unlike other employment policies, it cannot be unilaterally modified).

[13] *See, e.g., Guth v. Minnesota Mining & Mfg. Co.,* 72 F.2d 385, 388 (7th Cir. 1934).

relating to the employee's job may be subject to compulsory assignment.[14] In most states, the law of trade secrets, the law of restrictive covenants and the law of employee inventions have little explicit doctrinal overlap. Indeed, one of the novel features of the New Jersey Supreme Court's decision in *Ingersoll–Rand v. Ciavatta* was its liberal borrowing from the law of trade secrets and restrictive covenants in devising a rule about the permissible scope of invention assignment agreements. Whether explicitly, as in *Ingersoll–Rand v. Ciavatta*, or implicitly, as in many other states, all three areas of law attempt to devise rules to regulate the labor market with an eye toward fostering the optimal level of innovation consistent with the dignitary and economic interests of the inventive employee.

Factual Background

The Ingersoll–Rand Company, headquartered in New Jersey, is a large and diversified company that manufactures heavy equipment, power tools, locks, and a wide array of machinery and parts for the auto, construction, and industrial equipment industries. "We are not a glamorous company," quipped the company chairman to *Forbes* in 1993.[15] But when the company was founded, its emphasis on designing and building drills and construction and mining equipment seemed quite glamorous, as it furnished the machines that built the infrastructure of America and some of the rest of the world. As the *New York Times* obituary of one company founder breathlessly explained, "It was his development of the drill which made possible many of the great engineering feats of the last century and those now in progress."[16]

The company was founded in the late nineteenth century by a number of inventor-entrepreneurs who parlayed their inventions and business acumen into a very successful business based on new technology using compressed air. Simon Ingersoll invented and patented a rock drill that became the foundation of the company's business. He sold the patents to the firm he founded in 1871. He himself never enjoyed a large share of the wealth generated by the company that bore his name because he had sold his patents to the firm. Henry Clark Sergeant received over sixty patents for various inventions and is credited with the innovation that made the rock-drill successful. He formed his own company to market his inventions, and that company eventually merged with the Ingersoll Drill Company in 1888; the Ingersoll–Sergeant Com-

---

[14] *See, e.g.*, Cal. Lab. Code § 2870 (assignment agreement covering inventions developed without employer resources or unconnected to employer's work is, with some exceptions, unenforceable).

[15] Paul Klebnikov, *A Traumatic Experience*, Forbes, Jan. 18, 1993, at 83.

[16] Obituary, *Henry C. Sergeant*, N.Y. Times, Feb. 1, 1907, at 9.

pany specialized in tunnel driving and quarrying. Meanwhile, brothers Albert, Jasper, and Addison Rand founded a firm specializing in mining work based on their own, independent drill technology. When Ingersoll–Sergeant merged with Rand in 1905, the announcement of the merger focused on the uniting of the patents as much as anything else.[17]

The early history of the companies that eventually united to form Ingersoll–Rand was characterized by the ability of each firm to combine the mechanical ingenuity of its founder with the business acumen necessary to make the patented inventions a success in the marketplace. For decades, it was a firm that prided itself on its employees' and leadership's strong combination of engineering talent and business savvy. And there was reason for the corporate pride: An 1887 *Scientific American* article on the construction of the New York Aqueduct reads like an advertisement for Ingersoll drills. Ingersoll–Rand drills were used on the construction of the New York Subway, the Panama Canal, the Hoover Dam, the Cascade Tunnel (then the longest mountain railroad tunnel on the North American continent), and on Mt. Rushmore. Just as notably, Ingersoll–Rand patented the original jackhammer.[18]

If the early success of the firm exemplified the happy marriage between invention and entrepreneurship that characterized many nineteenth century technology businesses, the history of the firm in the middle decades of the twentieth century exemplified the life story of the large, vertically-integrated, and massively diversified manufacturing corporation whose fate was linked to the fortunes of American manufacturing, construction and mining. The company employed about 47,000 people and reported sales of $3.4 billion in 1982. It enjoyed a solid return on equity even as its stock price fluctuated a bit (along with the American economy as a whole) in the 1970s. The men who ran the company had spent their careers there, rising through the ranks.[19] It was the kind of place where white-collar workers like Armand Ciavatta enjoyed an implicit understanding of lifetime employment so long as they performed competently.

---

[17] George Koether, *The Building of Men, Machines, and a Company* (1971); Obituary, *Henry C. Sergeant*, N.Y. Times, Feb. 1, 1907, at 9; Johannes H. Wisby, *Compressed Air*, L.A. Times, Nov. 19, 1899, at A10.

[18] Ingersoll–Rand Co., *The Story of the Hoover Dam* (1932–1936); Charles W. Hobart, *The Cascade Tunnel and the Man That Made It*, 13 Mag. W. Hist. 534 (1991); Johannes H. Wisby, *Compressed Air*, L.A Times, Nov. 19, 1899, at A10; *New York Water Supply*, Sci. Am., June 4, 1887 at 351 (describing the use of Ingersoll drills in the construction of the New York aqueduct).

[19] John A. Byrne, *And Then the Bottom Fell Out*, Forbes, Feb. 14, 1983, at 142; Paul Klebnikov, *A Traumatic Experience*, Forbes, Jan. 18, 1993, at 83.

In the early 1980s, that abruptly changed. In 1981, Ingersoll–Rand enjoyed record earnings of $9.71 per share, which was up 21 percent over 1980. But the company had a bad year in 1982. Its stock price tumbled and orders fell. In 12 months in 1982 and early 1983, the company laid off 11,900 employees (so that it was down to 35,500) and shut down 11 plants. A corporate culture that favored a stable, if unglamorous, career in research and development, marketing, or manufacturing collided with the rapid change in the business environment of the 1980s. Armand Ciavatta was a company man of the 1960s who suddenly found himself without a company.

The company had a research and development division in Princeton, New Jersey, where Armand Ciavatta worked as a program manager. The research division, known as Ingersoll–Rand Research, employed researchers with doctoral degrees from top science and engineering programs like the Massachusetts Institute of Technology and the California Institute of Technology. Along with the stability and solidity of the large American corporation came a bureaucratic culture that perhaps did not make the most of the research and development talent it employed. Cautious managers may have found it easier to nix innovative product development ideas than to pursue them and risk the embarrassment and career setback of a flop. As one leader of a major corporate R & D facility commented years later, "If a rising corporate star brings forth a risky innovation that ends up failing, his or her career is apt to be damaged considerably more than that of the executive who squelches an innovation that could have been a winner."[20] Ingersoll–Rand's research culture, like that of many corporate R & D facilities, was designed to weed out poor ideas. It was less concerned with the possibility that a good idea would go undeveloped than that resources would be invested in development of a bad idea that would fail when it hit the market. But as a consequence, the product development process had become a cumbersome affair that could last three or four years from idea to market. As one engineer described it, the marketing department might dream up a product and "toss the idea over the wall" separating marketing and engineering. Engineering would work up a design and toss it over another wall to the manufacturing department that would make the product and then heave it over yet another wall to sales. Too often, however, engineering would toss an idea back to marketing because the engineers thought the idea was unworkable, or manufacturing would return an idea to engineering for reworking when they thought the design or prototype was flawed. By the late 1980s, the company thought

---

[20] John Seely Brown, *Foreword* to Henry W. Chesbrough, *Open Innovation: The New Imperative for Creating and Profiting from Technology* (2003).

product design had become so problematic that it initiated a major overhaul to try to reunite the innovative and the entrepreneurial.[21]

Armand Ciavatta was born into a working class Italian–American family in New England. He graduated from Rhode Island School of Design in 1953 with a B.S. in machine design. He served in the National Guard in an engineering battalion as a training officer and company commander. Later he took classes in mining, tunneling and heavy construction engineering. Before coming to Ingersoll–Rand in 1972, he spent twenty years working as an engineer for major firms in various capacities; he conducted quality control tests for instrumentation used in the first commercial nuclear reactor; he was chief project engineer for the Revere Corporation, where he worked with transducers and other force-measuring devices; and he served as Vice President of Engineering and Quality Control for Iona Corporation, where he was responsible for engineering, development and testing of the company's line of kitchen and consumer appliances. He had also been an inventor: while employed by Revere Corporation, Ciavatta invented and patented a force transducer using strain gauge.[22]

Ciavatta served as the Director of Engineering and Quality Control of a division of Ingersoll–Rand from 1972 to 1974 before becoming Program Manager for the research division of Ingersoll–Rand in 1974. Shortly after joining the research division, Ciavatta signed Ingersoll–Rand's form "Agreement Relating to Proprietary Matter," which broadly restricted his rights to use certain knowledge. In exchange for the symbolic consideration of one dollar and, of course, employment by the company "during such time as may be mutually agreeable to the COMPANY and myself," the agreement obligated Ciavatta not to "divulge, either during my employment or thereafter ... any secret, confidential or other proprietary information" of Ingersoll–Rand or of any of its many affiliates. In addition, he agreed:

> To assign and I hereby do assign, to the COMPANY, its successors and assigns, my entire right, title and interest in and to all inventions, copyrights and/or designs I have made or may hereafter make, conceive, develop or perfect, either solely or jointly with others either (a) during the period of such employment, if such inventions, copyrights and/or designs are related, directly or indirectly, to the business of, or to the research or development work of the COMPANY or its affiliates, or (b) with the use of the time, materials or facilities of the COMPANY or any of its affiliates; or (c) within one year after termination of such employment if conceived as a result of

---

[21] N. R. Kleinfeld, *How "Strykeforce" Beat the Clock*, N.Y. Times, Mar. 25, 1990, at section 3 p.1 (Mar. 25, 1990).

[22] *Ciavatta*, 542 A.2d at 881.

and is attributable to work done during such employment and relates to a method, substance, machine, article of manufacture or improvements therein within the scope of the business of the COMPANY or any of its affiliates.[23]

In the summer of 1974, the Director of Research, Dr. McGahan, assigned Ciavatta to investigate methods of coal haulage, which sparked Ciavatta's interest in underground mining. During his four years at Ingersoll–Rand Research, Ciavatta worked on a variety of development projects in the mining field. Ciavatta became interested in underground mining and read extensively in the literature on the subject. He was never formally involved in research or development relevant to Ingersoll–Rand's product for stabilizing mine roofs, which was a "friction stabilizer." Nevertheless, his boss, Dr. McGahan, the Director of Research, "encouraged the research staff to be creative, to discuss ideas for projects or potential projects beyond those to which they had been assigned." The office's system for handling invention ideas was typical of research facilities: employees were to submit any invention ideas to superiors on "disclosure forms." In his first two years at Ingersoll–Rand Research, Ciavatta bubbled with ideas. He submitted thirteen disclosures for mining technology and instrumentation, several of which were proposals for devices to support or stabilize roofs of underground mines. Most of them used a different principle than Ingersoll–Rand's friction stabilizer; only one disclosure was an improvement to Ingersoll–Rand's "split-set friction stabilizer." Ingersoll–Rand chose not to pursue any of his concepts. Concluding that Ingersoll–Rand was not interested in his innovations, Ciavatta lost his motivation to invent and did not submit any further disclosures.[24]

In March 1978, Ciavatta became the manufacturing manager of the Ingersoll–Rand split-set friction stabilizer. The stabilizer was a 4–foot length of steel tube that was split down its length such that when viewed from the end it looked like a C rather than an O. A steel band was welded around the circumference of the tube at one end for extra strength. Ingersoll–Rand customers had been complaining that the stabilizers, particularly the ring at the end, had a tendency to split and peel while being driven into the rock roof of a mine. McGahan was convinced that the problem was with the steel used to make the stabilizer. Ciavatta disagreed. He thought the problem was in the design of the tube and the welded ring. They argued about it for awhile, but McGahan prevailed and assigned Ciavatta and metallurgists to study the problem. A few months of study produced no answer. In a staff meeting Ciavatta

---

[23] *Id.* at 615; Agreement Relating to Proprietary Matter (copy on file with author).

[24] *Ciavatta*, 542 A.2d at 882; Telephone Interview with Armand Ciavatta, August 3, 2005.

reiterated his belief that the cause of the problem was the radius of the driver, but again McGahan refused to listen. According to Ciavatta, McGahan insisted that if Ciavatta continued to defy him he would be fired. Frustrated, Ciavatta went to the rock pile at the back of the Ingersoll–Rand Research laboratory and drove stabilizers into granite with two different drivers to prove his point. The test confirmed Ciavatta's suspicion: the problem was in the design, not in the metal. He wrote a memo to McGahan and to McGahan's superiors describing the results of the futile months of testing the metal, documenting his own experiments in the yard, and proposing a solution. He was fired the next day.[25] According to the facts as found by the New Jersey courts, the apparent motivation for his abrupt firing was unrelated to the memo: Ciavatta tried to stop shipments of the stabilizer because of his concerns about quality control problems. Ciavatta's superior in the manufacturing program, John Irwin, countermanded Ciavatta's order. According to Ingersoll–Rand, Ciavatta was fired "because of unsatisfactory performance and his poor relations with fellow employees."[26]

While looking for a new job, Ciavatta spent his spare time experimenting with ideas for inventions, just as he always had. One day in the summer of 1979, Ciavatta got the idea for the invention that sparked the litigation, literally by having a light bulb turn on over his head. He had his eureka moment while installing an overhead light fixture in the ceiling of his home in August of 1979, about two months after being fired from Ingersoll–Rand. His wife had picked out a new light fixture, and Ciavatta was up on a ladder hanging the fixture from the ceiling when he got an idea for a new mine roof stabilizer. Stabilizers are pounded into holes drilled in the roof of a mine and use the friction between the metal and the rock surrounding it to reduce separation of the rock strata. Ciavatta's idea was to use a tube that was not split along its length and which had a cross-section shaped like an ellipse.

While working on his invention, Ciavatta looked diligently for work but found few offers, a situation not unusual for a middle-aged engineer in a recessionary economy. He took a job with a firm in Michigan in the winter of 1979–1980, but quit when he learned that the people running the company were engaged in business practices that Ciavatta considered unethical or at least unsavory. Ciavatta returned to New Jersey, but still could not find a job. He found it humiliating to have to rely on his wife's income to support the family, but he felt himself fortunate to have that.[27]

---

[25] *Ingersoll–Rand Co. v. Ciavatta*, 509 A.2d 821, 824 (N.J. Super. Ct. Ch. Div. 1986); Telephone Interview with Armand Ciavatta (August 3, 2005).

[26] *Ingersoll–Rand Co. v. Ciavatta*, 542 A.2d 879, 883 (N.J. 1988).

[27] Telephone Interview with Armand Ciavatta (August 3, 2005).

Ciavatta made a sketch of his idea and, to test it, borrowed some canoli tubes from his wife to stand in for the stabilizers. He drilled holes in a wooden board and had a neighborhood boy stand on a bathroom scale holding the board while Ciavatta pushed the tubes into the holes and measured the reaction force on the scale.[28] When his idea seemed to work, he tried building a prototype with supplies purchased from a hardware store. When that worked, he sought the advice of counsel about whether the invention was patentable and whether the Ingersoll–Rand Proprietary Agreement would require him to assign it to the company. The patent lawyer whom Ciavatta consulted advised him in October 1979 that the patent would belong to Ciavatta. In March 1980, Ciavatta filed for a patent, which was granted in February 1982, for a "tubular shank [that] can be employed either for fastening or for stable mounting in unconsolidated underground strata." According to the patent, when driven into a hole, "the shank is compressed from its oblate shape into a nearly circular shape" which "renders the shank relatively immune to vibration or shifting of strata" around the hole.[29] Ciavatta received a second patent for an improvement to the first patent in March 1982.[30]

While his patents were pending, Ciavatta prepared a business plan and sought venture capital. Finding none, he used his life savings plus $125,000 borrowed from his brother and from a bank to begin manufacturing the device. In October 1982, shortly after the patents were issued, he exhibited his device at the annual mining equipment trade show, and a few months after that he made his first sale. Ciavatta's invention began to catch on in the market, and, by June 1985, his total sales were about $270,000.

Prior Proceedings

When Ingersoll–Rand learned of Ciavatta's invention in December 1981, various Ingersoll–Rand employees exchanged memoranda about whether his device was feasible, whether it was a competitive threat to any Ingersoll–Rand products, and whether it infringed any of the company's patents to the split-set stabilizer. About seven months later, in July of 1982, Ingersoll–Rand's lawyer wrote to Ciavatta demanding that he assign the patent to the company. Ciavatta refused. As Ciavatta's stabilizer caught on in the market, Ingersoll–Rand began to perceive it as a competitive threat. Ingersoll–Rand lowered the price of its split-set stabilizer to reflect Ciavatta's lower price and, in April 1984, filed a suit

---

[28] *Id.*

[29] U.S. Patent No. 4,316,677 (filed Mar. 7, 1980).

[30] U.S. Patent No. 4,322,183 (filed Mar. 4, 1981).

in the Chancery Division of the New Jersey Superior Court for Somerset County.

Ingersoll–Rand was represented by its corporate counsel and patent lawyers in New York and New Jersey, Mark S. Anderson (now a name partner at Woolson, Guterl, Sutphen & Anderson), and James M. Rhodes, Jr. and John M. Calimafde of Hopgood, Calimafde, Kalil, Blaustein & Judlowe. Ciavatta was represented at the trial level by Charles J. Walsh, a respected trial lawyer in the Newark area who later served as a New Jersey Superior Court judge for a number of years before his death in 2005. On appeal, Walsh was joined by Stuart M. Feinblatt of the New Jersey firm of Sills, Beck, Cummis, Zuckerman, Radin & Tischman.

In the trial court, notwithstanding what Ciavatta recalled as a very effective trial performance by Walsh, Ingersoll–Rand prevailed. After a bench trial, the trial judge, William D'Annunzio, found that the Proprietary Agreement covered the invention and concluded that the agreement was enforceable under the only relevant New Jersey law, a line of cases governing the enforceability of contracts restricting post-employment competition by employees.

Throughout the litigation, both Ciavatta and Ingersoll–Rand relied heavily on two decisions of the New Jersey Supreme Court, *Solari Industries, Inc. v. Malady*[31] and *Whitmyer Brothers, Inc. v. Doyle.*[32] This pair of decisions had held that covenants restricting former employees from competing are enforceable only if reasonable and are reasonable only to the extent that they prevent an employee from using trade secrets (including customer relationships) and confidential information. In *Solari*, the court held that a non-competition agreement by which a firm sought to restrict a former employee from obtaining a franchise to sell a competing firm's product in the United States was enforceable only to the extent "reasonably necessary to protect [the employer's] legitimate interests, will cause no undue hardship on the defendant, and will not impair the public interest."[33] In *Whitmyer*, the state high court reversed a preliminary injunction, finding unreasonable an agreement that prevented a plaintiff from starting a business that competed with his former employer's government contracting business. The employee would use no trade secrets, the court held, and a restrictive covenant could not be used to prevent an employee from using general knowledge and trade skills acquired in prior employment.[34]

---

[31] 264 A.2d 53 (N.J. 1970).

[32] 274 A.2d 577 (N.J. 1971).

[33] 264 A.2d at 61.

[34] 274 A.2d at 31.

Judge D'Annunzio interpreted the *Solari–Whitmyer* restrictions on the enforcement of restrictive covenants as being designed to "protect the right of an employee to change employment and to use his skill, knowledge and experience to further his employment prospects in the job market," and "to promote the public interest in the most effective and widespread use of an employee's skills and limitations." Patent assignment agreements, by contrast, have no comparable adverse effect on the employee's ability to find another job or on the public's interest in the use of employee talent.[35] Rather, according to the trial judge, the principal rationale for enforcing a patent assignment agreement is "recognition of the sometime unstructured, informal and serendipitous processes that lead to invention. Processes that receive their impetus and inspiration from exposure to a subject and interaction with one's colleagues, co-employees and superiors. [sic] A process in which neither secrets nor confidential information plays a part."[36] Thus, where *Solari-Whitmyer* might be read to validate the economic benefits of information spillovers associated with employee mobility, the trial judge viewed Ciavatta's case as one involving an employee opportunistically claiming as his own the results of a collaborative and collective invention process thought to characterize the modern research lab.

Having determined that the *Solari-Whitmyer* reasonableness test did not apply to holdover agreements and that an employee's use of trade secrets was not necessary to enforce a holdover agreement, Judge D'Annunzio applied a multifactor reasonableness test to assess the contract. The factors were:

- the degree of relationship between the invention and the former employment
- whether the invention was based on knowledge acquired in the former job
- the extent of collaborative sharing of knowledge and ideas in the former job
- whether enforcement of the agreement would restrict the employee from finding another job
- whether enforcement of the agreement would "violate any legitimate expectations of the defendant" or would come as a surprise
- whether the invention used confidential information of the former employer.

In the trial judge's estimation, only the last factor favored Ciavatta. He rejected Ingersoll–Rand's argument that Ciavatta had used two

---

[35] 509 A.2d at 828.

[36] *Id.* at 829.

allegedly confidential drawings done by James Scott, the inventor of the
Ingersoll–Rand split set stabilizer, and Dr. McGahan, the Ingersoll–Rand
research division director. These were sketches of alternative possible
designs for stabilizers including some elliptical shapes. Although the
drawings had been kept in a file cabinet to which Ciavatta had access
during his employment, the trial judge found insufficient evidence that
Ciavatta had seen or copied them. He also tartly observed that the
information contained in them was no secret: "There is nothing proprietary about an ellipse. It is also clear that Dr. Scott was very open and
communicative about his ideas." Moreover, continued the judge, "plaintiff's manufacturing process has been in existence for over 50 years. . . .
There does not appear to be anything secret about it or the principles it
utilizes."

What the judge found far more significant in assessing the enforceability of the holdover agreement was Ingersoll–Rand's portrayal of
Ciavatta as having learned everything he knew about mine roof stabilizers under the company's tutelage. The invention grew directly out of
Ciavatta's work, and he owed everything he knew on the subject to
Ingersoll–Rand. "Defendant was enriched through his experience with
[Ingersoll–Rand]. . . . His enrichment was particularly relevant to the
invention in question and came at the hands of an employer possessed of
a wealth of experience in designing and producing underground mining
equipment." Moreover, the judge reasoned that enforcement of the
contract "would not constitute a significant deterrent to a change of
employment by Ciavatta" because, prior to working for Ingersoll–Rand
research, he had worked for a number of firms on a variety of different
engineering projects.

The trial judge also rejected Ciavatta's defenses that Ingersoll–Rand
was barred by equitable doctrines of estoppel, laches and unclean hands
from an injunction ordering Ciavatta to assign the patent. Ciavatta
argued that Ingersoll–Rand had waited nearly five years after firing him,
and nearly four years after learning of his patent application, to file suit
claiming the invention. He argued that it would be inequitable to allow
them to claim the patent after they had watched him invest so much
time and money into it. The trial judge found that Ciavatta had not
relied on Ingersoll–Rand's inaction when he decided to go forward with
the invention and that Ingersoll–Rand had good reason for delaying suit
until Ciavatta's invention became a competitive threat. "Plaintiff should
not be penalized because it exercised restraint and waited until there
was some practical advantage to be gained from litigation."

Ciavatta appealed. The appellate division reversed and ordered Ingersoll–Rand's complaint dismissed. The appellate court held that the
proper analysis was the three-part reasonableness test of *Solari* and
Whitmyer. Under that test, the agreement was unenforceable because

Ingersoll–Rand had no legitimate interest in enforcing it and the hardship on Ciavatta was considerable. The invention, the court explained, did not rely on Ingersoll–Rand trade secrets or confidential information. As to hardship, the court said that "an engineer in his 50's who for one year is required to assign to his former employer any inventions which might be conceived by him 'as a result of and attributable to work done during his former employment['] ... most probably will remain unemployed in the same field for the proscribed period."[37] If Ingersoll–Rand could claim the fruits of Ciavatta's creativity, "it is not difficult to appreciate ... why defendant had such difficulty in locating other employment following his dismissal by plaintiff. The net effect of the agreement is to impose upon the employee a prohibition, effective for one year ... from working on mine supports for any company in the mining industry. If an employee does not possess sufficient wealth to bridge the one-year period, he may be forced into a different industry...."

Finally, the appellate division emphasized that Ciavatta did not seek to invalidate the holdover clause in order "to bring to fruition for his own benefit an invention substantially developed by him or his coemployees during his prior employment." The court recognized that the employer has a legitimate interest in using holdover clauses "to foster the free exchange of ideas by its employees without fear that the employees will use trade secrets or confidential information learned during such interchange to the employer's disadvantage" after the end of the employment. Here, by contrast, Ciavatta was fired, suggesting that he had not acted opportunistically by quitting as soon as he conceived of an invention and that he used no confidential information. Summing up, the appellate division portrayed Ciavatta as using general knowledge and "our free-enterprise system" to bring a new technology to market after he was fired. Such use, the court held, could not be restrained by contract.

This time, Ingersoll–Rand appealed.

The New Jersey Supreme Court Decision

The New Jersey Supreme Court ruled unanimously to affirm the Appellate Division. The opinion was written by Justice Marie Garibaldi. Justice Garibaldi was appointed to the Court by Republican Governor Thomas Kean in 1982 when she was nearly 48 years old. A 1959 graduate of Columbia Law School with a master's degree in tax from NYU School of Law, Garibaldi had been a lawyer for the IRS in New York for seven years immediately after graduation, a lawyer in private practice with two Newark, New Jersey law firms for fifteen years, and a

---

[37] *Ingersoll–Rand v. Ciavatta*, 524 A.2d 866, 869 (N.J. Super. Ct. App. Div. 1987).

municipal court judge for two years. The *New Jersey Law Journal's* guide to the state supreme court described her as "the conservative bulwark of a Court whose other members are distinguishable only by shades of liberality." Yet the paper also described her as an "enigmatic presence" who seldom dissented, and whose "opinions show a careful deference to the Legislature, to precedent, and to administrative agency interpretations." She was "a staunch protector of contractual rights" who generally came down "on the side of business interests," though notably not in *Ingersoll–Rand v. Ciavatta*. Justice Garibaldi wrote opinions in a number of cases besides *Ingersoll–Rand v. Ciavatta* showing sensitivity to the rights of employees and other historically disadvantaged groups. She wrote the opinion for the court forcing the all-male eating clubs at Princeton University to admit women. She wrote another opinion finding compensable under the Workers' Compensation Act claims of psychiatric disability due to fear of having been exposed to toxic substances in the workplace. Her opinions both for the Court and in dissent showed some sensitivity to civil liberties; the *New Jersey Law Journal* remarked that she "generally comes down on the side of the First Amendment" in cases involving freedom of the press. She wrote the opinions for the Court in a 1987 trilogy of cases establishing a right to withdraw life-sustaining treatments in cases of grave illness or brain death, and she dissented from the Court's decision in *In re T.L.O.*, a 1983 decision upholding searches of student lockers without probable cause.[38]

Justice Garibaldi's opinion for the New Jersey Supreme Court was long, scholarly and thoughtful, but also characteristically pragmatic. The opinion began by noting the default rule that an employee's inventions are his own, absent an agreement to the contrary. After citing cases, the court went on to observe that the default rule seldom applies to inventive employees because, as the court deduced from its survey of case law and law review literature on the issue, "most large, technologically advanced companies today require their employees by contract to assign their patents to their employers."

The court then turned to the policy issues associated with enforcement of such contracts. Here, the court perceived a "dichotomy of our views on the rights of an inventor and rights of an employer" and on the

---

[38] Ronald J. Fleury, *Garibaldi: A Liberal Dose of Restraint*, N.J. L.J., Feb. 17, 1982, at 12. See also *Frank v. Ivy Club*, 576 A.2d 241 (N.J. 1990) (holding that Princeton eating club's exclusion of women violates the New Jersey Law Against Discrimination); *Saunderlin v. E.I. du Pont Co.*, 508 A.2d 1095 (N.J. 1986) (holding that fear of exposure to workplace toxins is a compensable injury under workers compensation); *In re Farrell*, 529 A.2d 404 (N.J. 1987) (affirming a right to die when suffering from a terminal illness); *In re Subpoena Issued to Schuman*, 552 A.2d 602 (N.J. 1989) (finding state shield law prevented subpoenaing reporter to whom a crime had been confessed).

public interest in providing incentives for employees to invent and employers to invest in invention. On the employee side of the dichotomy, the court particularly emphasized the need to provide incentives for invention. The opinion discussed the concern expressed by some scholars about a decline in patenting by Americans and cited a *Wall Street Journal* article stating that Japan "witnessed a dramatic increase in the number of inventions generated by employed inventors" after the country began tying employed inventors' compensation to the market value of inventions in 1959. The employer side of the balance was characterized in terms of the employer's investment in research: "It is becoming a more collective research process, the collaborative product of corporate and government research laboratories instead of the identifiable work of one or two individuals. Employers, therefore, have the right to protect their trade secrets, confidential information, and customer relations."

The court then canvassed New Jersey law, focusing primarily on the *Solari–Whitmyer* rules for restrictive covenants, and the law of other jurisdictions on holdover clauses. The court found the law of other jurisdictions consistent with the three-part *Solari–Whitmyer* test in that it focused on the employee's interest in "enjoying the benefits of his or her own creation," the employer's interest "in protecting confidential information, trade secrets, and, more generally, its time and expenditures in training and imparting skills and knowledge to its paid work force," and the public's "enormously strong interest in both fostering ingenuity and innovation of the inventor and maintaining adequate protection and incentives to corporations to undertake long-range and extremely costly research and development programs."

After discussing in general how the employee's interest, employer's interest and public interest should be assessed under the three-factor *Solari-Whitmyer* test in the holdover invention context, the court turned to the facts of the case. The analysis of the facts was quite brief. The court began by noting that Ciavatta was not hired to invent or to work on design improvements for the stabilizer. "Ingersoll–Rand did not assign Ciavatta to a 'think tank' division in which he would likely have encountered on a daily basis the ideas of fellow Ingersoll–Rand personnel regarding how the split set stabilizer could be improved or how a more desirable alternative stabilizer might be designed." Not only had he not been directed to invent improvements to the Ingersoll–Rand stabilizer, the court noted, but all his efforts to suggest inventions had been rejected. The court also explained that nothing in the Ingersoll–Rand stabilizer was a trade secret or was a product of company research program. In addition, Ciavatta had not left Ingersoll–Rand in order to capitalize upon an invention. Cautioning that "the manner of an employee's departure" is not dispositive, the court nevertheless stated that it is a factor to be weighed and, on these facts, it weighed in Ciavatta's favor.

He was fired, and he later developed the product based on his general skill and knowledge. Drawing an analogy to the law of trade secrets, which prohibits employees from using their employer's economically valuable secrets in competitive employment, the court noted that Ciavatta's invention was not the product of any recent Ingersoll–Rand research and, indeed, "the technology Ciavatta employed was developed over fifty years ago and was well known in the industry." Based on this, the court concluded that the holdover agreement was unenforceable. Having found such a dearth of evidence to support the employer's interest in claiming the employee's invention, the court did not need to balance the employer's interest against the employee's interest or the public interest.

The court concluded its discussion with two pieces of guidance for future cases. First, the court specifically stated that "the range of the employer's proprietary information that may be protected by contract may narrowly exceed the specific types of information covered by the law of trade secrets and confidential information." Second, the court pointed out that the Ingersoll–Rand contract was significantly overbroad in that it claimed for the company any invention "within the scope of the company or any of its affiliates," and since Ingersoll–Rand was a diversified firm with thirty divisions worldwide, such a provision was substantially broader than justified to achieve the purpose of protecting information that the employee would have had access to and learned in the course of his employment.

A number of questions were explicitly or implicitly left unanswered. First, the nature of the employer's legally cognizable interest in preventing employees from using workplace knowledge in post-employment inventions was left undefined. Suggesting that the employer's interest may "narrowly exceed" that which is a trade secret or "confidential information" does little to clarify the situation, inasmuch as the boundaries of trade secret law are somewhat uncertain, and the legal status of "confidential information" that does not qualify as a trade secret is entirely unclear. Although the opinion suggested that a holdover clause would be enforceable to the extent it required assignment of post-employment inventions that use trade secrets (which was not the case with Ciavatta's stabilizer), it left unclear whether a former employee could patent an invention that uses information that the employer claims as proprietary but does not qualify as a trade secret.

Second, the case leaves uncertain the significance of the nature of the departing employee's job. That Ciavatta did not work in R & D clearly mattered to the court, but how much? Recent research has shown that many firms get some of their innovations not from their own R & D employees but from users of their products who modify the products to suit their own needs.[39] The manufacturer then will incorporate the users' modifications into improved versions of the product. Would an employee who worked to implement the users' modifications into a new version be treated as a "think tank" sort of person or as a regular employee like Armand Ciavatta? A third open question is the significance of the employee's reason for leaving for other employment. The New Jersey Supreme Court noted that Ciavatta did not leave to capitalize on his idea; he was fired, and he may have been fired unjustly (though that was specifically left undecided). What if Ciavatta had quit out of frustration or boredom after the company rejected all his product ideas? What if the employee promptly went to work for a competitor or promptly licensed his inventive idea to another firm rather than, as Ciavatta did, slowly and laboriously developing his product and his own little company to market it at considerable personal expense?

The Impact and Importance of *Ingersoll–Rand v. Ciavatta*

Although inventions are a subject of considerable popular interest, the law governing employee inventors is somewhat technical and often falls through the disciplinary gap between employment law and intellectual property law. Employment lawyers often regard invention assignment agreements as being part of the arcane specialty of patent law, and patent or intellectual property lawyers tend to think of the issue as being simply a particular application of the law of employment contracts. As a consequence, the law governing invention assignments is a topic that intellectual property and employment lawyers tend vaguely to gesture at, uniformly acknowledging its importance yet still essentially ignoring it because they assume it falls into someone else's bailiwick. The fate of the *Ingersoll–Rand v. Ciavatta* decision after it was handed down in June of 1988 perfectly illustrates this phenomenon.

One obstacle to the greater salience of the law of ownership of employee inventions is the disparate sources of law governing the issue. Federal law governs patent validity, but ownership of employee inventions is governed exclusively by state law, and the law varies from state to state. As noted above, several states have statutes regulating the enforceability of employment agreements governing employee inventions, while most rely on common law. Some states, like New Jersey in *Ingersoll–Rand*, have explicitly blended the employee invention doctrine with law governing trade secrets and restrictive covenants in a way that creates an overarching body of rules regulating ownership of workplace knowledge. But most states have distinct legal doctrines regulating the different areas. Thus, although in some states the law of invention assignment agreements has certain similarities to the law of trade

---

[39] Eric Von Hippel, *Democratizing Innovation* (2005).

secrets and restrictive covenants, few states have attempted explicitly to link the three areas in the way that Justice Garibaldi did in *Ingersoll–Rand*. For all these reasons, no one single decision is likely to have a large impact and *Ingersoll–Rand v. Ciavatta* has not, at least as measured by the number or length of law review or judicial discussions of it.

Nevertheless, in the quotidian world of inventors and their employers and the lawyers who represent them, the enforceability of holdover clauses is important and the case is a significant precedent. Not surprisingly, therefore, both the Appellate Division and the Supreme Court's decisions were reported in the *New Jersey Law Journal* and the *Newark Star–Ledger*, though it was hardly front-page news.[40] In the year or so after the state high court handed down its decision, one student published a case note on it, and in the following years a few other notes mentioned it.[41]

Although the immediate impact of the case for people other than the parties was neither sensational nor substantial, the long-term importance of the case was greater than a simple citation count might suggest. The case remains a leading citation in New Jersey courts on the enforceability of both invention assignment agreements and non-compete agreements, with fifteen New Jersey cases relying on it since 1988. It has been cited as well in nine other decisions from around the country and the Federal Circuit (the federal court of appeals with exclusive jurisdiction over appeals from Patent Office decisions). It has been followed by state supreme courts in Iowa, Maine, and Washington. Judges have tended to regard the case as most significant for its development of the multi-factor test for the enforceability of both invention assignment agreements and restrictive covenants, whereas law review articles have emphasized the aspect of the opinion that arguably broadened the employer's legitimate interest in preventing employees from patenting in areas where the employer has valuable proprietary information.[42]

---

[40] Kathy Barrett Carter, *Inventor Wins Ruling Against Former Employer*, Newark Star–Ledger (n.d.); Kathy Barrett Carter, *State Court Voids Pact Restricting Ex–Employee's Use of Information*, Newark Star–Ledger, June 23, 1988, at 39; Kathy Barrett Carter, *When the Good News Arrives a Bit Too Late*, N.J. L.J., July 21, 1988, at 12.

[41] Hanna Bui–Eve, Note, *To Hire or Not to Hire: What Silicon Valley Companies Should Know About Hiring Competitors' Employees*, 48 Hastings L.J. 981 (1997); Kenneth F. D'Amato, Note, *Employer Not Entitled to Enforcement of Holdover Agreement Where He Does Not Have a Proprietary Interest in Conceiving the Invention*—Ingersoll Rand v. Ciavatta, 19 Seton Hall L. Rev. 947 (1988); Marc Hershovitz, Note, *Unhitching the Trailer Clause: The Rights of Inventive Employees and Their Employers*, 3 J. Intell. Prop. L. 187 (1995); Domenick Carmagnola, *The Changing Landscape of Restrictive Covenants*, N.J. L.J., June 24, 1996, at 10.

[42] *See, e.g., Maw v. Advanced Clinical Commc'ns*, 846 A.2d 604 (N.J. 2004) (holding that graphic designer fired for refusing to sign a 2–year non-compete not entitled to relief

One of the principal jurisprudential accomplishments of the *Ciavatta* decision was its melding of the law of holdover clauses with the law of restrictive covenants and trade secrets. The court's multi-factor reasonableness analysis, which explicitly relied on the *Solari* and *Whitmyer* decisions in the restrictive covenant area, attempted to create a unified reasonableness rule to govern a wide range of disputes between employees and firms over the control of economically valuable workplace knowledge. That approach has meant that *Ciavatta* has been as significant for its contribution to the law of restrictive covenants (an area that produces more published decisions) as it has been to the law of holdover agreements (an area of law that produces fewer published decisions).

On the merits of the court's approach, as opposed to simply the breadth of its impact, reasonable minds might differ, but the court's approach reflects the majority view. Multifactor reasonableness tests are particularly appealing to judges who are unprepared to take an extreme view in one direction or another. For example, judges with an extremely expansive view of employer rights could take a bright-line position that all holdover agreements are enforceable; those with an extremely expansive view of employee rights could adopt an equally clear and easily administrable rule that such agreements are never enforceable. But this is an area where most judges (and the handful of legislatures that have weighed in on the problem) believe that a middle course is preferable, and that the justice of enforcing such agreements must depend on the facts. Even California's statute, which appears to create a clear rule that

under New Jersey's "Conscientious Employee Protection Act"); *Lamorte Burns & Co. v. Walters*, 770 A.2d 1158 (N.J. 2001) (finding marine insurance investigative firm had legally protectable interest in client names and information and therefore was entitled to summary judgment on non-compete, duty of loyalty and trade secret claims); *Johnson v. Benjamin Moore & Co.*, 788 A.2d 906 (N.J. Super. Ct. App. Div. 2002) (holding paint company not liable to person who submitted a new product idea, citing *Ciavatta* for the proposition that novelty is not a requirement for a trade secret but that novelty is a requirement for a claim for misappropriation of a submitted idea); *Morris Silverman Mgt. Corp. v. Western Union Fin. Servs.*, 284 F. Supp. 2d 964 (N.D. Ill. 2003); *Freedom Wireless v. Boston Commc'ns*, 220 F. Supp. 2d 16 (D. Mass. 2002) (pre-invention assignment agreements should be construed narrowly, therefore space technology company not entitled to patent to a pre-paid cellular calling card system developed by former employee); *Campbell Soup Co. v. Desatnick*, 58 F. Supp. 2d 477 (D.N.J. 1999); *Laidlaw v. Student Transp. Inc.*, 20 F. Supp. 2d 727 (D.N.J. 1998); *Neveux v. Webcraft Techs.*, Inc., 921 F. Supp. 1568 (E.D. Mich. 1996); *Campbell Soup v. ConAgra, Inc.*, 801 F. Supp. 1298 (D.N.J. 1991) (upholding a holdover contract against a former product development technologist, but concluding that the patented techniques for a new frozen chicken product were not covered by the contract), *vacated on other grounds*, 977 F.2d 86 (3d Cir. 1992); *Revere Transducers, Inc. v. Deere & Co.*, 595 N.W.2d 751 (Iowa 1999) (upholding claim against former employees who prepared designs that incorporated Revere's confidential information and disclosed that information to Deere, a Revere customer, after going to work for Revere); *Bernier v. Merrill Air Eng'rs*, 770 A.2d 97 (Me. 2001); *Waterjet Tech., Inc. v. Flow Int'l Corp.*, 996 P.2d 598 (Wash. 2000).

holdover clauses are unenforceable except when the employee uses the employer's materials *or* the invention relates to the employer's current or possible R & D, may not be as clear a rule as it seems. Under California law, the court would have to decide whether Ciavatta's stabilizer is sufficiently closely related to Ingersoll–Rand's business. One imagines that a court might bring in the same fairness concerns that the New Jersey court considered in deciding whether the relationship between Ciavatta's invention and Ingersoll–Rand's business was close enough to enforce the agreement. The effort to do justice in the particular case, however, has made this is an area of law that has proven remarkably resistant over the years to efforts to clarify and simplify. However, what a multifactor reasonableness test lacks in the way of certainty, it makes up for in its explicit focus on the need to accommodate conflicting policies. To the extent that the opinion's analytic approach has caught on in other jurisdictions, it has brought greater coherence and pragmatism to the effort to identify the employer, employee, and public interests in the enforcement of these contracts. That is a worthy accomplishment in a field of law that was previously characterized, at least in some states, by uncertain standards and archaic formalism.[43]

Controversy remains both in New Jersey and elsewhere about where to draw the line between the knowledge that employees gain on the job which they should be free to use in subsequent employment, including in the development of post-employment patents, and that knowledge which the prior employer may claim as proprietary. Many of the reported decisions resolve the issue, as the New Jersey Supreme Court did, based on particular facts of the case, and the various results reached by different decisions often can be explained by factual distinctions about the circumstances of the invention and the employment. Yet fundamental policy debates persist. As recently as 2004, the New Jersey Supreme Court sharply divided over whether an employee who was fired for refusing to sign a possibly overbroad non-compete agreement could recover under a New Jersey statute prohibiting some forms of wrongful termination that violate public policy.[44] The majority concluded, over a sharp dissent, that a refusal to sign an overbroad non-compete agree-

---

[43] For a survey of the legal doctrine on the enforceability of non-compete agreements, see Brian M. Malsberger, *Covenants Not to Compete: A State-by-State Survey* (3d ed.2002). For an example of legislation regulating the enforcement of pre-invention assignment agreements, see Cal. Lab. Code § 2870 (2005) and *Cubic Corp. v. Marty*, 229 Cal. Rptr. 828 (Ct. App. 1986). Under the California statute, a pre-invention assignment agreement is unenforceable if the employee did not use the employer's equipment or information, the employee developed the invention on his or her own time, and the invention does not relate to the employer's business. That standard largely replicates the common law rule.

[44] See *Maw*, cited in note 42 supra.

ment was a purely private dispute that did not implicate public policy, although the court also noted that the particular provision in question was not incompatible with a clear mandate of public policy. The court also stated that if the employee could not negotiate a narrower non-compete agreement, she could have signed it anyway and then disputed its enforceability when and if the employer attempted to enforce it against her. This suggests that at least some members of the court regarded overbroad non-compete agreements as being less obnoxious to the public interest than other illegal contract terms might be.

Conclusion

More than twenty-five years after Armand Ciavatta invented his friction stabilizer and seventeen years after the New Jersey Supreme Court ruled in his favor, Ciavatta remained resolute about the justice of his position but disappointed by the failure of the courts to do real justice. Though he said he would do the same thing again, his disaffection with the law is clear: "unfortunately for me and others the law is used to punish the creative and productive elements in our society." In his view, the "sole purpose of the litigation was to put me out of business. I won the verdict. I lost my business with a better product. This will not stop until the financial penalties for this kind of litigation [are] significant."[45] Petr Taborsky, the University of South Florida lab technician who went to jail rather than relinquish his invention of an improved method for using clay to extract ammonia from water, told a similar story. After defying the court order to relinquish his ideas and losing the appeal of his criminal conviction, he even refused to accept a pardon from the Florida governor because to do so, he said, would be an implicit admission of his guilt. The endless legal wrangling prompted his wife to leave him, about which Taborsky bitterly remarked, "I decided that the case was more important than our marriage."[46]

Ciavatta's lament about the failures of law to do justice in his case, or in his life, identifies one of the most significant failings in our system of civil litigation, at least in the field of employment. Litigation is often ruinously expensive for the small business and the individual litigant. Remedies, when they come at all, often come too late. The problem is not unique to employment litigation. Stories of creative inventors whose lives were ruined and fortunes squandered in patent litigation are as old as Eli Whitney, who is said to have spent most of the money he made from his patents on the cotton gin prosecuting dozens of patent infringement cases that brought him no relief from his fear that others were pirating his ideas. The dogged determination of these inventors to claim

---

[45] Letter from Armand Ciavatta to Catherine Fisk (undated; summer 2005).

[46] Leon Jaroff, *Intellectual Chain Gang*, Time, Feb. 10, 1997, at 64.

both the credit and the control over their ideas suggests that what is at stake is more than money. At a basic level, these inventors and others feel that their creativity is essential to who they are and that intellectual property rights confirm the importance of the mark they have made in the world.

Of course, the Ciavattas and Taborskys of this world may or may not be right about whether protecting their rights to patents serves the long-term interest of the country by encouraging more inventions. Although the circumstances of Ciavatta and Taborsky differed in significant respects, in neither case did the heart of their arguments rest on the long-term national interest in encouraging innovation as much as their own strong attachment to their own inventive work. The law cannot ignore the psychic and emotional costs suffered by employees who feel that depriving them of their patents is akin to depriving them of parts of themselves. But their tenacity is revealing. Fundamentally, the law governing employee innovators and regulating the control over workplace knowledge has influenced and will continue to influence where innovation comes from and how society balances entrepreneurship and innovation, security and free inquiry.

7

The Story of *NLRB v. Washington Aluminum*: Labor Law as Employment Law

Cynthia Estlund

Seven workers in a non-union machine shop, after complaining of unusually cold conditions in the shop, walk off the job without permission, in clear violation of a rule prohibiting just that. They are fired. Does the employer violate the law in doing so?

If you put this question to reasonably sophisticated observers of the law—say, upperclass law students—the overwhelming majority will say no. Or so I have found when I have polled students on a variety of discharge scenarios before they begin a course in employment law. Most of those students, while generally aware of the American regime of employment at will, already realize that there are exceptions to at-will employment—exceptions for status-based discrimination and for whistle-blower retaliation, for example; they correctly identify many discharges that are unlawful on those grounds either nationwide or in many states. (And, unlike the less sophisticated laypersons surveyed by Professor Pauline Kim in her eye-opening studies, most of my students correctly identify many discharges that are lawful even though they appear unjustified.)[1] Yet nearly all of these same students believe that it is lawful, perhaps even justified, to fire employees who defy the most basic demands of the job by walking out on the employer. My more informal inquiries suggest that most lawyers who do not specialize in labor and employment law share this belief.

But they are wrong. For in *NLRB v. Washington Aluminum*,[2] the Supreme Court in 1962 unanimously held that these discharges were unlawful under the National Labor Relations Act of 1935 ("NLRA" or

---

[1] Pauline T. Kim, *Bargaining with Imperfect Information: A Study of Worker Perceptions of Legal Protection in an At–Will World*, 83 Cornell L. Rev. 105 (1997); Pauline T. Kim, *Norms, Learning, and Law: Exploring the Influences on Workers' Legal Knowledge*, 1999 U. Ill. L. Rev. 447 (1999).

[2] 370 U.S. 9 (1962).

"Act"), which prohibits employer interference with "concerted activities for the purpose of collective bargaining or other mutual aid or protection," including the cessation of work in protest of unsatisfactory working conditions.[3] *Washington Aluminum* is conventionally classified as a "labor law" case; it does not appear in most employment law casebooks. That is unfortunate, for the case offers a dramatic illustration of how "labor law" reaches beyond the unionized workplace and beyond the process of union organizing to up-end traditional and powerful assumptions about employer discretion within the non-union workplace. The NLRA is the first and arguably the most radical of wrongful discharge laws. Yet *Washington Aluminum* also helps to illustrate the chasm that can exist between the law on the books and the law in action—between what the law provides in principle and what it accomplishes in reality.

In reality, of course, few non-union workers walk off the job to protest poor working conditions. What they do far more often is talk— among their co-workers, sometimes with management or supervisors. When they talk about wages, benefits, working conditions, workplace rules, disciplinary actions, or other shared concerns, they are often engaged in "concerted activity" protected by the NLRA. It is probably the free speech protections of the NLRA that take the biggest potential bite—in principle, that is—out of employment at will in the non-union workplace.

Most familiarly, the Act protects the speech by which employees seek to recruit their co-workers to join a union. An early decision, *Republic Aviation Corp. v. NLRB*,[4] held that the employer not only is prohibited from enforcing a no-solicitation policy against union recruiting, but is obliged to permit such activity on its own property—in non-work areas of the workplace during non-work time. But it is not only union talk that the Act protects. For example, in *Timekeeping Systems, Inc.*,[5] an employee in a non-union workplace was fired for sending a series of e-mails criticizing the employer's new proposed vacation plan in terms that the employer deemed "inappropriate and intentionally provocative" and that the National Labor Relations Board ("NLRB") characterized as "flippant and rather grating language."[6] There was no great and overriding public interest in the employee's speech; indeed, the employee's conduct bordered on insubordination and offended the employer's civility norms. Surely an at-will employee can be fired for such conduct? In fact, he cannot. In a fairly routine decision, the NLRB held

---

[3] 29 U.S.C. §§ 151–169 (2000).

[4] 324 U.S. 793 (1945).

[5] *Timekeeping Systems, Inc.*, 323 N.L.R.B. 244 (1997).

[6] *Id.* at 247.

that the employer had violated the Act, and ordered the employee's reinstatement.

Republic Aviation and *Timekeeping Systems* illustrate the Act's enactment of a kind of First Amendment for the private sector workplace. The speech that it protects is confined in various ways. But for a wide range of communication among co-workers or between workers and managers about workplace issues, the NLRA made the workplace itself— or at least non-work areas of the workplace during non-work hours—a kind of "public forum" for employees in which they are entitled to discuss not only union organizing activity, which is at the core of protected speech under the NLRA, but more or less whatever matters to them at work. While perhaps less dramatic than *Washington Aluminum*'s protection of a spontaneous work stoppage, the free speech protection of the Act has a more sweeping impact on employers, for the conduct that is protected by this aspect of the law on the books is far more common.

But what about the law in action? Do employees in fact feel free to talk about their shared grievances at work, or about the possibility of joining together with a union to improve their conditions? They most definitely do not.[7] Do reasonably sophisticated people—those familiar with the background rule of employment at will—even know that employees have these rights? My own informal inquiries suggest that they do not. The yawning gap between the sweeping conceptual reach of the Act and its limited practical impact on the workplace poses intriguing puzzles and teaches important lessons about the landscape of employment law, both on the books and in action.

The NLRA as a Wrongful Discharge Law

The National Labor Relations Act creates a framework—a "constitution" of sorts—for labor relations in most of the private sector labor market. It establishes a process by which a majority of workers in an appropriate subset of the employer's operations can choose to be represented by a labor organization—a union; it requires employers to bargain in good faith with such a representative; and it establishes the rules of engagement between unions and employers in the course of collective bargaining and labor disputes.

If we think of these as the structural provisions of the NLRA's "constitution of the workplace," we can recognize Section 7 of the Act as its "bill of rights." Like the federal Constitution's Bill of Rights, Section 7 declares employee rights that were regarded as both intrinsic to full personhood and instrumentally necessary for the governance structures created by the rest of the document. Section 7 declares that "Employees

---

[7] Richard B. Freeman & Joel Rogers, *What Workers Want* 20–24 (1999).

shall have the right to self-organization, to form, join or assist labor organizations, to bargain collectively through representatives of their own choosing, and to engage in concerted activities for the purpose of collective bargaining or other mutual aid or protection." It is this last clause—"to engage in concerted activities for the purpose of . . . mutual aid or protection"—that extends the NLRA's reach well beyond the context of union organizing and collective bargaining into the daily routines of the vast majority of private sector workplaces in the U.S.

Section 7 rights (and other components of the Act) are enforced through a set of "unfair labor practices," (ULPs) which the NLRB is charged with preventing and remedying. Most important for present purposes, Section 8(a)(1) of the NLRA makes it an ULP to "interfere with, restrain, or coerce" employees in the exercise of their Section 7 rights; and Section 8(a)(3) makes it a ULP to discriminate against employees based on union membership or activity. Under these provisions, it is illegal for an employer to discharge (or otherwise penalize) an employee for supporting a union, or for engaging in protected "concerted activities for the purpose of . . . mutual aid or protection." These are the basic wrongful discharge provisions of the NLRA. The Act prohibits far more than terminations based on protected conduct. Demotions, punitive transfers, or other adverse actions, as well as threats and bare prohibitions of protected activity, count as "interference" and "discrimination" under Section 8. For example, it is unlawful for employers to broadly ban employee "solicitation" in the workplace,[8] or to prohibit employees from discussing their wages with each other.[9] Discharge is simply the most egregious form of interference and discrimination. In that sense, the NLRA goes well beyond many of the newer wrongful discharge doctrines.

The scope of Section 7 rights beyond the realm of traditional union activity—and that will be our focus here—is defined largely by two statutory requirements: The employee's activity must be "concerted," and it must be for "mutual aid or protection." Speech or conduct is "concerted activity" if it is taken as a group (that is, by two or more employees), or on behalf of a group, or with an eye to stimulating group action.[10] It is for "mutual aid or protection" if it bears on terms and conditions of employment (compensation, hours, safety, vacations, work

---

[8] *See Garfield Electric Co. and Indecon, Inc.*, 326 N.L.R.B. 1103, 1107 (1998) ("Since employees are presumptively privileged to solicit union support in nonworking areas on company property during their break-times," a no-solicitation rule that purports to prohibit such activity is unlawful); *Our Way, Inc.*, 268 N.L.R.B. 394 (1983) ("The governing principle is that a rule is presumptively invalid if it prohibits solicitation on the employees' own time.").

[9] *Timekeeping Systems, Inc.*, 323 N.L.R.B. 244, 248 n. 11 (1997).

[10] *See Mushroom Transp. Co. v. NLRB*, 330 F.2d 683, 685 (1964); *Meyers Industries, Inc.*, 268 N.L.R.B. 493, 497 (1984).

rules, or simply how supervisors treat employees, for example) or other matters that concern "employees as employees."[11] That may include political and legal issues that extend beyond the particular workplace, as well as issues such as product quality, patient care, or consumer safety, if those concerns are sufficiently linked to working conditions or job security.[12]

The quintessential "concerted activit[y] for . . . mutual aid or protection" is union organizing activity. But both statutory requirements are satisfied by forms of employee protest or simple conversation that have nothing to do with unionization, as was the case in both *Washington Aluminum* and *Timekeeping Systems*. A great deal of activity that many employers would like to prohibit and punish among their non-union workers (perhaps precisely because it is seen as a precursor to union organizing) is in fact protected by Section 7.

These broad protections are, to be sure, hemmed in by some substantive limitations. Some employee activity that is concerted is not protected because it is too altruistic—for example, motivated by concerns for patients rather than fellow workers—or because it is too narrowly focused on the complaining employee's own concerns.[13] Some activity that is both concerted and for mutual aid or protection is nonetheless held to be beyond the pale and unprotected: Violence against persons or property, occupation of the employer's property as in a sit-down strike, or public disparagement of the employer's product are some examples of unprotected concerted activity.[14] A strike in breach of a no-strike clause

---

[11] *Eastex, Inc. v. NLRB*, 437 U.S. 556, 569–70 (1978).

[12] *Id. See, e.g., Kaiser Engineers*, 213 N.L.R.B. 752 (1974) (protecting engineers who wrote to legislators about immigration laws that they feared would affect the supply of engineers); *NLRB v. Oakes Mach. Corp.*, 897 F.2d 84, 89 (2d Cir. 1990) (protecting employees' protest of company president's diversion of resources to personal projects because of effect on profitability and compensation); *Squier Distrib. Co. v. Local 7, Int'l Bhd. of Teamsters*, 801 F.2d 238, 241 (6th Cir. 1986) (protecting employees fired for reporting embezzlement of company funds because "[t]he employees' overriding concern was clearly for their job security"); *Cordura Publications*, 280 N.L.R.B. 230, 231–32 (1986) (protecting employees' letter to the chairman of the board, despite its focus on the quality of the employer's product (automobile research), because such issues related to the poor treatment of employees); *Professional Porter & Window Cleaning Co.*, 263 N.L.R.B. 136, 138–39 (1982) (protecting maids' complaints to building management about deteriorated building conditions and poor cleaning materials because they were related to a dispute over conditions of employment).

[13] *Holling Press, Inc.*, 343 N.L.R.B. No. 45 (2004) (no protection for employee who solicited co-worker to testify in support of her sexual harassment complaint; activity intended to advance her own case and not interests shared with others).

[14] *See, e.g., NLRB v. Ohio Calcium Co.*, 133 F.2d 721 (6th Cir. 1943) (employer not required to reinstate workers who had rocks in their hands at picket line where new employees and managers were attacked by thrown rocks); *NLRB v. Fansteel Metallurgical*

of a collective bargaining agreement is another.[15] Moreover, some employer actions that clearly "interfere" with protected activity are nonetheless permitted as a form of lawful economic pressure against employees' concerted activity. Most important of these is the much-criticized right of employers to permanently replace most strikers.[16] The statute itself also prohibits some concerted activities, such as some "secondary" pressures that target an employer that is deemed legally neutral in the underlying labor dispute.[17]

These restrictions on employees' rights are important, and they are mostly judge-made. Observers have criticized many of these doctrines as both unjustified and partly responsible for the sapping of organized labor's strength since the 1950s.[18] But they should not obscure the still-enormous bite that the NLRA takes out of the venerable right of employers, absent an agreement to the contrary, to fire employees for good reason, bad reason, or no reason at all.

This, of course, is all about the law on the books—and mostly the judicial reporters rather than the statute books. In fact, the Act's bark is much worse than its bite. To explore both the formal and the practical reach of the Act into the non-union workplace, let us turn to our principal case, *Washington Aluminum.*

Factual Background

The facts of *Washington Aluminum* are very simple. Monday, January 5, 1959, was an unusually cold day in Baltimore. "The temperature at 8:00 A.M. was but 15 degrees, the high reading for the entire day was only 22 degrees and the low reached 11 degrees for an average reading of 17 degrees, which was a minus 18 degrees deviation from normal readings for the month. The low temperatures were additionally accentu-

---

Co., 306 U.S. 240 (1939) (holding that the NLRA. does not protect illegal seizure of employer's buildings); *NLRB v. Local Union No. 1229, Int'l Bhd. of Electrical Workers*, 346 U.S. 464, 477 (1953) (television station technicians who engaged in public disparagement of the station's programming had "deprived [themselves] of the protection" of § 7).

[15] *See NLRB v. Sands Mfg. Co.*, 306 U.S. 332, 344 (1939).

[16] *See NLRB v. Mackay Radio & Tel. Co.*, 304 U.S. 333, 345 (1938). For a tiny sample of critical commentary, see Julius Getman, *The Betrayal of Local 14*, pp. 224–28 (1998); William B. Gould IV, *Agenda for Reform* 185–88, 202–03 (1993); Paul C. Weiler, *Governing the Workplace: The Future of Labor and Employment Law* 264–69 (1990); Michael H. Gottesman, *Union Summer: A Reawakened Interest in the Law of Labor?*, 1996 Sup. Ct. Rev. 285, 293–96; compare Samuel Estreicher, *Collective Bargaining or "Collective Begging": Reflections on Antistrikebreaker Legislation*, 93 Mich. L. Rev. 577 (1994).

[17] *See NLRA § 8(b)(4), 29 U.S.C. § 158(b)(4).

[18] *See Karl E. Klare, *Judicial Deradicalization of the Wagner Act and the Origins of Modern Legal Consciousness, 1937–1941*, 62 Minn. L. Rev. 265, 265–70 (1978); James B. Atleson, *Values and Assumptions in American Labor Law* 9–10 (1983).

ated by the highest wind velocities recorded for the whole month."[19] These conditions created a particular problem in the machine shop at Washington Aluminum, a Baltimore manufacturer of aluminum products; the doors of the shop were often opened and the shop was uninsulated. When one of the machine shop employees, William George, Jr., arrived that morning, he "found that ice had formed on the drain pipe of the spotwelder he operated in the machine shop."[20]

A "lead worker" at the machine shop, J. Alfred R. Caron, stopped by the office of the foreman, David Jarvis, when he arrived for work around 7:10 a.m. They discussed "how cold it was and miserable," and observed two other employees walking by the office window, which looked into the plant, "huddled" against the cold.[21] In what the company later characterized as a "jocular or facetious statement,"[22] Jarvis remarked, "If those fellows had any guts at all they would go home." Caron then returned to the machine shop, where six of his fellow machinists were standing together "shaking a little, cold."[23] According to his later testimony:

> I told them, I said, "Dave told me that if we had any guts at all, we would go home." And I said, "I am going home." I said, "What are you fellows going to do?"
>
> Then they started talking among themselves saying, "Well, let's go."
>
> And I started out first. And they were following behind me.[24]

Caron later testified that he said to Jarvis as he passed by, "Dave it is too cold, I am going home." He did not seek permission to leave, although he knew of "the standing company rule which required that permission of a foreman was required in order to leave the plant."[25]

As Jarvis told the story, when he saw several of the machine shop workers heading toward the exit, he approached one of the men, Tafelmaier, and asked him to stay on the job; Tafelmaier obliged.[26] According to Jarvis, by the time he had spoken to Tafelmaier, "the seven other men had gone out of the shop and, consequently, he had no opportunity

---

[19] *NLRB v. Washington Aluminum Co.*, 291 F.2d 869, 871 (4th Cir. 1961).

[20] *Washington Aluminum Co.*, 126 N.L.R.B. 1410, 1416 (1960) [hereinafter NLRB I].

[21] *Id.* at 1415.

[22] Brief for Respondent in Opposition to Petition for Writ of Certiorari, at 5.

[23] NLRB I, at 1415–16.

[24] *Id.*

[25] *Id.*

[26] *NLRB v. Washington Aluminum Co.*, 291 F.2d at 872.

to inquire as to their reasons for leaving or to request them also to remain." That left just Tafelmaier and Jarvis in the machine shop. "In order to complete what general plant foreman Wampler termed 'critical' jobs that were at the time being processed in the machine shop, Wampler supplied Jarvis with two temporary workers who had to be taken from their normal assignments in other departments of the plant."[27]

The six employees who left the plant with Caron all agreed with him "that the plant was extremely cold, that they had no permission to leave, and that they knew it was forbidden by plant rules to leave the plant without a foreman's permission. . . . [They] left the plant after Carson [sic] talked to them and after they had discussed the matter among themselves." One of the employees later explained why he had left the plant: "Well, they said it was extremely cold. And we had all got together and thought it would be a good idea to go home; maybe we could get some heat brought into the plant that way."[28]

The issue was not exactly getting "some heat into the plant"; it was getting enough heat into the machine shop on that unusually cold day. The machine shop, "a rectangular structure with floor space measuring approximately forty by seventy-five feet," contained two gas space heaters. In the adjacent shop, a very large oil-fired furnace carried heated air through ducts directly into the machine shop area; an additional furnace had recently been installed in that adjacent shop, "and the two top rows of windows in the partition separating this shop from the machine shop were removed to allow additional heat from this new furnace to flow into the machine shop building."[29] But the unusually cold temperatures in Baltimore that day proved too much for these measures.

The employer's supervisors and managers were aware of the problem and were in the process of addressing it. The company president, Fred Rushton, himself was on the case. The heat in the plant was normally shut off during the night and turned on again at 5 a.m. But because unusually cold weather was expected for the next day, Rushton visited the plant at 10 p.m. on Sunday, January 4: "I had to talk to the watchman to make sure we get the heat on and see that things are as good as we can get them and normal. Certainly you want to have a warm shop. Plus the fact that we have pipes in there that may break if we are not careful." After hearing from the president, the night watchman, Vincent Battaglia, tried to turn on the "big furnace" at 1 a.m. on Sunday night. But it "would not operate nor could he get it into operation at 5 a.m. when he again tried." Battaglia reported this to the

---

[27] *Id.*

[28] NLRB I, at 1416.

[29] *NLRB v. Washington Aluminum Co.,* 291 F.2d at 870.

maintenance man, Roy Rose, when the latter arrived in the morning around 7:15 a.m., around the time Caron and his co-workers were arriving.[30] Rose discovered

> "that a control switch in the back of the furnace was in a certain position which, though it would permit the blower fans to function, would keep the electrodes from igniting the furnace fire. He immediately manipulated the control to its automatic position and the furnace shortly thereafter commenced to heat up in its normal manner. This mechanical adjustment had been made by approximately 7:30 A.M. and by the time the work whistle first sounded calling the employees to work."[31]

Rose knew that it would take "2 1/2 to 3 1/2 hours for the furnace to warm an area within a 50–foot radius of it after it began operating."[32] In the meantime, until after lunch time, the men still working in the machine shop bundled themselves up with extra jackets.

But Caron and his six co-workers were long gone by then. They had not made any explicit demands for more heat; they had not asked, and perhaps did not know, whether something was being done about the cold; they had not asked to take off a few hours until the plant had warmed up. They had simply walked out.

Around 8:30 a.m., President Rushton arrived back at the plant. He testified later:

> [W]hen I came back in B shop again I noticed all the people were out of the shop.

> So Dave Jarvis was there. And I said, "Dave, where is everybody?"

> He said, "They have all walked off."

> I said, "We can't have that, Dave."

> "Well," he said, "they have all gone."

> I said, "Dave, if they have all gone, we are going to terminate them."[33]

A little later—9:00 a.m. or so—one of the workers who had walked out, Augustine Affayroux, apparently had second thoughts. He "returned to the plant, told [Jarvis] he had only gone for coffee, and asked to be returned to work but that [Jarvis] told Affayroux he had already been discharged on President Rushton's orders." Jarvis proceeded to call

---

[30] NLRB I, at 1416–17.

[31] *NLRB v. Washington Aluminum Co.*, 291 F.2d at 871.

[32] NLRB I, at 1416 (1960).

[33] *Id.* at 1417.

"those of the seven men who had telephones and sent telegrams to the others informing them they were discharged." At about 9:30 a.m., Jarvis phoned Caron at his home to tell him that, on orders of Rushton, all seven men who had left the plant that morning were discharged. Later that day Caron went back to the plant and got his toolbox.[34]

That would normally be the end of the story. Non-union workers employed at will are fired—not for "no reason" or for any obvious "bad reason," but for refusing to do their jobs and violating plant rules. But it was just the beginning, for the workers found their way to the regional office of the NLRB, and, on February 26, 1959, they filed a charge claiming that their discharges constituted an unfair labor practice (ULP) under the NLRA—that the employer had "interfere[d] with, coerce[d], or restrain[ed] employees" in the exercise of their "right to engage in concerted activities for the purpose of collective bargaining or other mutual aid or protection."[35] A charge simply initiates administrative proceedings under the Act. It is entirely within the discretion of the NLRB's General Counsel whether to proceed on the basis of the charge, initially by filing a complaint.

Prior Proceedings
BEFORE THE NLRB

Before tracing the progression of the charge through the machinery of the NLRB, we might pause to ask: How did these non-union employees find their way to the NLRB in the first place? A clue may lie in another intersecting set of proceedings that had begun winding its way through the Board as well: On the very same day that the employees filed their ULP charge, about seven weeks after the discharges took place, the employer Washington Aluminum Co, Inc. and the Industrial Union of Maritime and Shipbuilding Workers, AFL–CIO, signed a "stipulation for certification upon consent election."[36] That is, they agreed that the Board should hold an election to determine whether the Union would represent the employer's production and maintenance workers. It turns out that on February 2, 1959, four weeks after the discharges, the Union filed a petition to represent the Washington Aluminum workers.[37] Under Board law, the Union's petition would have had to be backed up by evidence of support from at least 30 percent of the relevant workers at Washington Aluminum. It is unclear whether organizing activity was already underway when the Washington Aluminum workers were fired,

---

[34] *Id.* at 1416–17.

[35] *Id.* at 1414.

[36] *Id.*

[37] *Washington Aluminum Co.*, 128 N.L.R.B. 643, 644 (1960) [hereinafter NLRB II].

or whether the discharges had somehow galvanized discontent among the workers and led to the organizing campaign.[38] In any event, however, it seems very likely that in the aftermath of the incident the discharged Washington Aluminum workers turned to the Union, and that the Union led them to the Board and to a potential legal remedy.

Just a few weeks after the agreement to proceed to a consent election, on March 17, 1959, an election was held under the supervision of the Regional Director for the Baltimore office of the NLRB. The vote was 68 for the Union and 70 against the Union. But there were also 5 challenged ballots, which were unopened and impounded. Four of those were among the seven workers who had been discharged two and a half months earlier and whose ULP charges were pending.[39] If they had been lawfully fired, they were ineligible to vote and the Union would lose the election. If they were found to have been fired unlawfully, however, they would be eligible to vote in the representation election and their ballots, enough to swing the election, would be opened.

On May 15, the Regional Director issued a complaint in the workers' discrimination case alleging that the workers were unlawfully discharged for engaging in protected concerted activity. On June 11, he recommended to the Board that the representation case and the ULP case be consolidated, insofar as "the eligibility to vote of these four voters depends . . . upon the resolution of the unfair labor practice case." The Board agreed, and on June 30 the Board ordered a hearing before a Trial Examiner "to resolve the issues raised on the eligibility to vote of Robert A. Heinlein, Frank Olshinsky, Augustine Affayroux, Sr., and Warren A. Hovis."[40] The hearing was held on August 3 and 4, 1959, before a Trial Examiner in Baltimore, Maryland.

The Trial Examiner found in his decision of September 11, 1959, that the four individuals "had been unlawfully discharged and that they were therefore entitled to vote."[41] It is worth pausing to observe that only eight months had elapsed between the very cold January day when the workers were fired and the much warmer September day when the factfinder's decision was issued, after a full hearing at which the workers were represented not only by their own counsel but by the General Counsel of the NLRB.

The testimony, summarized above, had created little dispute about the facts. The only quibble addressed by the Trial Examiner was over

---

[38] A detailed summary of the archived files of the Union reveals no files relevant to these events or legal disputes at Washington Aluminum.

[39] NLRB I, at 1414.

[40] *Id.*

[41] NLRB II, at 645.

the precise reasons for firing the men, which were expressed in slightly varying terms. Rushton testified that "[t]he real reason is because they didn't inform the foreman of the action they were taking." This the Trial Examiner described as "merely the statement of an afterthought." He credited instead the testimony of Jarvis, who testified that Rushton told him to fire the men because "they had left the premises unauthorized. And this curtailed our operation." Another party to the discussions, Arthur Wampler, the general foreman, similarly testified that the men were discharged "for violating plant rules, leaving the plant without permission, and to maintain discipline."[42] But these all boiled down to one reason: They had left the plant without permission, in violation of plant rules.

Of course, that is precisely what workers do when they go on strike, and the Act protects strikers. As the NLRB's Trial Examiner saw it, these workers were simply "economic strikers"—they had gone on strike to improve their working conditions.[43] That they had done so without the involvement of a union made their case unusual but no less clear under the law, which protects concerted activity by workers, including strikes, with or without a union connection. They could not be discharged for that activity. They could have been replaced—even "permanently replaced"—under long-established (if highly controversial) precedent. In that case, they would only have been entitled to stand first in line for the next job opening at Washington Aluminum for which they were qualified. But because they were not replaced before their dismissal, they were entitled to immediate reinstatement.

The decision of the Trial Examiner—now it would be an administrative law judge—takes the form of a recommendation, and must be approved by the NLRB itself. After several months, but no additional hearings, the Board agreed with the Trial Examiner in its decision of March 31, 1960:

> The Trial Examiner found, and we agree, that the Respondent violated Section 8(a)(1) in terminating the employment of the seven complainants who were engaged in protected concerted activity under the Act. We rely, inter alia, upon the following: The credited testimony of employee Hovis that "We all got together and thought it would be a good idea to go home; maybe we could get some heat brought into the plant that way"; the credited testimony of employees Heinlein, Caron, and George as to previous complaints made to [Jarvis] over the cold working conditions, and to the effect that the men left on the morning of January 5 in protest of the coldness at

---

[42] NLRB I, at 1417.

[43] *Id.* at 1418.

the plant; and the evidence that the seven complainants left the shop at approximately the same time.[44]

These observations underscore the concerted nature of the activity—that the employees left together—and the fact that it was for "mutual aid or protection"—that is, that the walkout was a response to, and an effort to improve, cold working conditions. The Board, like the Trial Examiner, saw this case as entirely straightforward: The Act protects strikers; the employer had fired employees for striking. The fact that there was a rule prohibiting employees from leaving the plant without permission could make no difference, for violation of such is virtually inherent in the protected activity of striking.

The remedy, too, was routine. Apart from an order to "cease and desist" from violating the Act in like manner, the Board ordered the following "affirmative action which the Board finds will effectuate the policies of the Act":

> (a) Offer to Robert A. Heinlein, Frank J. Adams, Frank Olshin-sky, Warren A. Hovis, Augustine Affayroux, Sr., William George, Jr., and J. Alfred R. Caron immediate and full reinstatement to their former or substantially equivalent positions without prejudice to their seniority or other rights and privileges discharging if necessary any employees hired to replace them.

> (b) Make whole said employees ... for any loss of pay they may have suffered by reason of Respondent's discrimination against them.[45]

In addition, the employer was ordered to produce the records necessary to determine how much backpay was due, and to post official Board notices in its plant describing the adjudicated ULPs and the employer's commitment to cease and desist.[46] The sole economic cost to Washington Aluminum of its ULP, putting aside its own attorneys' fees, was the backpay award. Yet the stakes in this case were larger for the company, for they meant the difference between continuing to operate non-union and being thrust into the world of collective bargaining.

Given the outcome in the discharge cases, the Board ordered the challenged ballots to be opened. The Regional Director issued a revised tally of ballots on April 7, 1960. Not too surprisingly, the discharged (and now reinstated) employees had voted for the Union, giving the Union a

---

[44] *Id.* at 1411.

[45] *Id.* at 1412.

[46] *Id.*

razor-thin majority. The Union was therefore certified as exclusive bargaining representative for the production and maintenance employees of Washington Aluminum on April 13, 1960.[47]

Now that it was clear that the unionized status of its employees turned on the legality of the earlier discharges, it was perhaps inevitable that the employer would carry on its fight in the discharge case. (One suspects that the company might not have appealed the discharge case at all, much less up to the Supreme Court, if the stakes had been limited to reinstatement and backpay for a few employees.) In response to the Union's request to bargain, Washington Aluminum's management took the position, in a letter of April 21, that the Board's decision in the discharge case was wrong—that their discharge of the seven men had been lawful—and that it planned to seek review of that decision in the U.S. Court of Appeals for the Fourth Circuit. As a consequence, the "Company is not in a position to sit down with the Union and negotiate a contract covering wages and working conditions for the reason that, if the Fourth Circuit ultimately decides the case in favor of the Company, the Company would be under no duty to recognize the Union as the bargaining representative for the Company's employees."[48] That letter generated a second ULP charge against Washington Aluminum, this time by the Union, for refusal to bargain with the certified bargaining representative of its employees, proscribed by Section 8(a)(5) of the Act.[49]

The "refusal to bargain" case, like the underlying representation case, turned entirely on the outcome of the wrongful discharge case and the eligibility of the discharged employees, which was now before the Fourth Circuit. Given the Board's earlier decision, the "refusal to bargain" proceedings were essentially formalities (authorized by the Act to enable the employer to obtain judicial review of the agency's order). The NLRB General Counsel issued a complaint on May 5. The parties stipulated to the facts and waived proceedings before the Trial Examiner, pushing the case straight up to the Board, which issued its inevitable decision on August 16, 1960: "[T]he Respondent, by its admitted refusal to bargain with the Union, as the certified bargaining representative of its employees, on and after April 21, 1960, has violated . . . the Act."[50] But the outcome of the resulting order to bargain, as well as that of the reinstatement and backpay orders, were all contingent on the Board's success before the Fourth Circuit.

---

[47] NLRB II, at 645.

[48] *Id.*

[49] *Id.*

[50] *Id.* at 643–45.

IN THE COURT OF APPEALS

The Fourth Circuit panel consisted of the court's three Eisenhower appointees: Chief Judge Simon E. Sobeloff and Judges Herbert S. Boreman and Clement F. Haynsworth, Jr. All were fairly new to the court in 1961, when *Washington Aluminum* came before them. But in general the Fourth Circuit was not a friendly forum for the Board or for workers at odds with their employers. Indeed, it has a longstanding "reputation as the most anti-union court of appeals in the nation."[51] That reputation was stoked by the first Fourth Circuit judge ever nominated to the Supreme Court: Judge John J. Parker in 1930. Judge Parker met vehement labor opposition on the basis of his role in upholding injunctions against union organizing that were based on so-called "yellow-dog contracts," by which workers promised not to join a union as a condition of employment. The most notorious of those injunctions, the 1927 "Red Jacket" injunction[52] against the United Mine Workers, became a rallying cry against Parker (and incidentally for federal anti-injunction legislation).[53] When his racist speeches during a past gubernatorial campaign became public and further inflamed opposition, Judge Parker's nomination was rejected by the Senate, and he remained on the Fourth Circuit.[54]

When Judge Parker died in 1958, his seat was filled by Judge Haynsworth, who went on to become the only other Fourth Circuit judge ever to be nominated to the Supreme Court when President Nixon tapped him in 1969. Haynsworth, like Parker, encountered strong opposition from organized labor. Unions cited in particular his holding in the *Darlington Industries* case (largely sustained by the Supreme Court) that it was an employer's "absolute prerogative," and no violation of the Act, to close its business, even if for the purpose of retaliating against

---

[51] Adam M. Gershowitz, *Supreme Court Nominees and the Fourth Circuit Curse*, available at http://library.findlaw.com/2003/Mar/31/132667.html.

[52] *International Org., United Mine Workers of America v. Red Jacket Consol. Coal and Coke Co.*, 18 F.2d 839 (4th Cir. 1927).

[53] *Opposes Parker on Supreme Bench*, N.Y. Times, March 26, 1930 at 26; *Sharp Protests Hit Parker as Justice*, N.Y. Times, March 30, 1930 at 3. Congress ultimately enacted the Norris LaGuardia Act of 1932, 29 U.S.C. §§ 101–115, to outlaw yellow-dog contracts and restrict use of injunctions in labor disputes brought in federal courts.

[54] *Nominee's Career Assailed*, N.Y. Times, May 8, 1930 at 1. Judge P had said:

The Negro as a class does not desire to enter politics. The Republican Party of North Carolina does not desire him to do so. We recognize the fact that he has not yet reached that stage in his development when he can share the burdens and responsibilities of government. The participation of the Negro in politics is a source of evil and danger to both races and is not desired by the wise men in either race or by the Republican Party of North Carolina.

Donald E. Lively, *The Supreme Court Appointment Process: In Search of Constitutional Roles and Responsibilities*, 59 S. Cal. L. Rev. 551, 567 n. 88 (1986).

workers who had voted to unionize.[55] Haynsworth, like Parker, was also rejected by the Senate, albeit mainly on the basis of ethics concerns: As a Fourth Circuit judge, he had ruled in favor of a company that had a business relationship with another company in which he was part owner. These concerns were unearthed and voiced chiefly by union opponents.[56]

The second member of the *Washington Aluminum* panel, Judge Boreman, never achieved quite the public profile that Judge Haynsworth did, but he showed a strong penchant for reversing pro-labor decisions by the NLRB. In one such case—argued just before *Washington Aluminum* and decided just after—he reached deep into the record and reversed the Board's credibility determinations in order to overturn its finding that a worker had been discharged because of his union activity.[57] Better known was his decision for the Fourth Circuit in *Griggs v. Duke Power*,[58] which had rejected the disparate impact theory under the Civil Rights Act of 1964, and which was reversed by the Supreme Court.

The Supreme Court's landmark decision in *Griggs* drew heavily upon the dissent filed by Judge Boreman's colleague, Judge Sobeloff, the third member of the *Washington Aluminum* panel.[59] Judge Sobeloff had served as Solicitor General of the United States under Eisenhower and in that capacity had been the legal voice of the federal government in desegregation litigation, a role that delayed Senate confirmation of his appointment to the Fourth Circuit.[60] He was the most liberal member of the court and a frequent dissenter, as indeed he was in the *Washington Aluminum* case.

The split Fourth Circuit panel reversed the Board in *Washington Aluminum*.[61] Writing for himself and Judge Haynsworth, Judge Boreman

---

[55] *Darlington Mfg. Co. v. NLRB*, 325 F.2d 682 (4th Cir. 1963), *aff'd in part and rev'd in part*, 380 U.S. 263 (1965). The Supreme Court largely agreed, but remanded for a determination of whether the closing was motivated in part by a desire to chill union sentiment in other operations in which the employer had an interest. The Board found that it was, and Judge Haynsworth concurred in his court's enforcement of the Board's order. *Darlington Mfg. Co.*, 165 N.L.R.B. 1074 (1967), *enforced*, 397 F.2d 760 (4th Cir. 1968).

[56] James Wooten, *Judge Haynsworth Had Stock in Supplier to Concern in Suit*, N.Y. Times, Aug. 24, 1969 at 61; Fred P. Graham, *Haynworth's Ethics Criticized by 3 Labor Leaders at Hearing*, N.Y. Times, Sept. 25, 1969 at 23; Warren Weaver, Jr., *Roll Call is Tense: Dissidents of G.O.P. Join 38 Democrats in the Rejection*, Nov. 22, 1969 at 1.

[57] *NLRB v. United Brass Works, Inc.*, 287 F.2d 689 (4th Cir. 1961).

[58] 420 F.2d 1225 (4th Cir. 1970), *rev'd*, 401 U.S. 424 (1971).

[59] *See* 401 U.S. at 430–31 (citing 420 F.2d at 1237–48); see also Samuel Estreicher, *The Story of* Griggs v. Duke Power Co., in Employment Discrimination Stories 153–171 (Joel W. Friedman ed. 2006).

[60] *See* Herbert Browne, *Civil Rights in the 1950s*, 69 Tul. L. Rev. 781, 788–89 (1995).

[61] *NLRB v. Washington Aluminum Co.*, 291 F.2d 869 (4th Cir. 1961).

emphasized several aspects of the case that the company had pressed upon the court but that the Board had not stressed. First, the majority took pains to underscore just how unusually cold it was that day in Baltimore. Second, the court elaborated at some length upon the measures taken by the company to heat the plant—both the various pieces of heating equipment in place, including their size and location, and the particular measures taken on January 5 to heat the plant. Third, the court noted—as the Board had not—the company's claim that the workers had left "critical jobs" undone. Finally, and crucially in the eyes of the panel majority, the opinion emphasized the workers' failure to present any explicit demands to the employer.

The court found "a conspicuous and total absence of any action on the part of the employees to attempt to make inquiry concerning the causes of their physical discomfort or to present their claims or demands to the company prior to the walkout." According to the majority, a strike " 'is the act of quitting work by a body of workmen for the purpose of coercing their employer to accede to some demand they have made upon him, and which he has refused.' An important and necessary qualification of the right to exert pressure on an employer through work stoppages is that such pressure be exerted in support of a demand or request made to the employer." The wisdom of this qualification was illustrated by this very case, in the court's view; for, had the Washington Aluminum workers "made some effort to request improvement of the condition in the machine shop prior to abandoning work, it is evident from the record their efforts would have been rewarded."

In short, the majority portrayed the company as acting entirely reasonably and conscientiously in the face of extraordinary weather conditions over which they had no control; and the workers as acting precipitously, impatiently and unreasonably in failing to give the employer a chance to address their complaints:

> [T]he purpose of the act was not to guarantee to the employees the right to do as they please under any given set of circumstances and in total disregard of the obligations of their employment. In the instant case, regular production schedules involving "critical" purchase orders were disrupted; to do the work of those who absented themselves, employees were transferred from their regular jobs in other departments and there is no evidence that any of those so substituting suffered any ill effects other than temporary discomfort. With no reasonable justification, the employees left their jobs without first having obtained the necessary permission. ... Under these circumstances, we conclude that the discharges were not, in any sense, discriminatory and were not without justification.

Indeed, the majority seems to have concluded that the discharges were not discriminatory *because* they were not without justification.

The discharge case was the linchpin of the remaining cases before the court: Because the workers had been discharged lawfully, they were not eligible to vote in the representation election. The union therefore did not gain a majority in the election, and the company was not required to bargain with the union. The court thus set aside not only the reinstatement orders but also the certification of the union and the Board's decision on the company's refusal to bargain.

Judge Sobeloff dissented.[62] In response to the majority's requirement of a specific demand, Judge Sobeloff observed that the workers had hardly left the employer guessing about the reasons for their departure. Indeed, the issue was not new, for on "a number of earlier occasions complaints had been made about the lack of heat in the shop." The foreman himself had virtually taunted the workers to leave—"if they had any guts at all," that is. In short, said Judge Sobeloff, "[t]he Labor Board's position is neither unsupported by the record nor unreasonable, and I find no warrant for refusing enforcement of its order."

Perhaps emboldened by Judge Sobeloff's dissent, the Board determined to press on. On behalf of the Board, the petition for certiorari was filed by Archibald Cox, then Solicitor General of the United States, a former Harvard Law School professor and the preeminent labor law scholar of his generation. The petition rested partly on the lack of deference shown by the court of appeals to the Board's interpretation of the NLRA, and partly upon a simple circuit split. The petition featured a nicely opposing decision by the Sixth Circuit nearly a decade earlier, in which the court had enforced, *per curiam*, a Board order reinstating several employees who had been fired for engaging in "spontaneous walk-outs and temporary work stoppages ... in protest against what they not unreasonably considered *excessive heat* in the factory building."[63] But this was hardly an issue that was roiling the courts of appeals. The subtext of the petition for certiorari was that the Fourth Circuit was simply wrong and out of line in its stingy interpretation of federal labor law protections.

The Supreme Court Decision

The Court granted the petition and just six weeks after the oral argument, on May 28, 1962, the Court reversed the Fourth Circuit 7–0.[64]

---

[62] *Id.* at 879.

[63] *NLRB v. Southern Silk Mills*, 209 F.2d 155 (6th Cir. 1953) (emphasis added), *rehearing denied*, 210 F.2d 824, *cert. denied*, 347 U.S. 976 (1954).

[64] *NLRB v. Washington Aluminum Co.*, 370 U.S. 9 (1962).

(Justices Frankfurter and White did not participate). Like the Board and Judge Sobeloff, the Court saw this as a straightforward case of concerted activity for mutual aid or protection. As for the lack of a specific prior demand, Justice Black, writing for the Court, said:

> We cannot agree that employees necessarily lose their right to engage in concerted activities under [Section] 7 merely because they do not present a specific demand upon their employer to remedy a condition they find objectionable. The language of [Section] 7 is broad enough to protect concerted activities whether they take place before, after, or at the same time such a demand is made. To compel the Board to interpret and apply that language in the restricted fashion suggested by the respondent here would only tend to frustrate the policy of the Act to protect the right of workers to act together to better their working conditions.

Whereas the Fourth Circuit had faulted the workers for not acting enough like ordinary unionized strikers by presenting a demand, the Supreme Court highlighted their unrepresented status as a reason for giving them more latitude: "The seven employees here were part of a small group of employees who were wholly unorganized. They had no bargaining representative and, in fact, no representative of any kind to present their grievances to their employer. Under these circumstances, they had to speak for themselves as best they could." They had complained before about the cold; but

> These had been more or less spontaneous individual pleas, unsupported by any threat of concerted protest, to which the company apparently gave little consideration.... The bitter cold of January 5, however, finally brought these workers' individual complaints into concert so that some more effective action could be considered. Having no bargaining representative and no established procedure by which they could take full advantage of their unanimity of opinion in negotiations with the company, the men took the most direct course to let the company know that they wanted a warmer place in which to work. So, after talking among themselves, they walked out together in the hope that this action might spotlight their complaint and bring about some improvement in what they considered to be the "miserable" conditions of their employment.

At least given what the Court called "a running dispute between the machine shop employees and the company over the heating of the shop of cold days," no more specific demand was required to earn Section 7 protection. A question remained, however, whether the protections of *Washington Aluminum* would be available absent a history of complaints.

The Fourth Circuit had been impressed, too, by what it saw as the conscientious attentions of the employer to the heat problem and the precipitous and impatient response of the workers. The Supreme Court initially brushed aside considerations of reasonableness and unreasonableness:

> The fact that the company was already making every effort to repair the furnace and bring heat into the shop that morning does not change the nature of the controversy that caused the walkout. At the very most, that fact might tend to indicate that the conduct of the men in leaving was unnecessary and unwise, and it has long been settled that the reasonableness of workers' decisions to engage in concerted activity is irrelevant to the determination of whether a labor dispute exists or not.

"Reasonableness" was therefore irrelevant to whether the employees' conduct was protected by Section 7.

The Court immediately went on, however, to sympathize with the workers' predicament and to affirm the reasonableness of their response:

> Moreover, the evidence here shows that the conduct of these workers was far from unjustified under the circumstances. The company's own foreman expressed the opinion that the shop was so cold that the men should go home. This statement by the foreman but emphasizes the obvious—that is, that the conditions of coldness about which complaint had been made before had been so aggravated on the day of the walkout that the concerted action of the men in leaving their jobs seemed like a perfectly natural and reasonable thing to do.

The Court thus muddied the waters again: Does concerted activity have to be justified or not? Does it have to "seem[] like a perfectly natural and reasonable thing to do"—perhaps by the lights of future judges sitting in their climate-controlled chambers—or not?

The Court was more categorical in its rejection of "the company's contention that because it admittedly had an established plant rule which forbade employees to leave their work without permission of the foreman, there was justifiable 'cause' for discharging these employees." It is true that the Act explicitly permits employees to be fired "for cause." But that provision must be interpreted consistent with the rest of the Act:

> [It] cannot mean that an employer is at liberty to punish a man by discharging him for engaging in concerted activities which [Section] 7 ... protects. And the plant rule in question here purports to permit the company to do just that for it would prohibit even the

most plainly protected kinds of concerted work stoppages until and unless the permission of the company's foreman was obtained.

Workers cannot, in other words, be required to beg the employer's permission to strike. Were the law otherwise, employers could nullify the Act by maintaining work rules that prohibited what the Act protects.

Finally, the Court rejected the claim that these workers' walkout, albeit concerted and for mutual protection, was unprotected because it was simply beyond the pale—"indefensible," in the language of a then-recent Court decision, known as *Jefferson Standard*.[65] The Court had held that workers' public disparagement of their employer's services, with no explicit link to terms and conditions of employment or to any labor dispute, was disloyal and "indefensible." Of course, many employers are inclined to view all forms of economic pressure, protest, or even unionization itself as disloyal. Washington Aluminum so claimed here: The workers had left the employer high and dry, with "critical orders" pending. But the Court explained that this was not the kind of "disloyalty" that took concerted activity out of the Act's protections.[66] Indeed, such "disloyalty" is inherent in even the most obviously protected concerted activity; every economic strike, for example, is intended to pressure the employer by inflicting economic harm. What made the conduct in *Jefferson Standard* "indefensible," said the Court in *Washington Aluminum*, was that the workers had shown "a disloyalty to the workers' employer which this Court deemed *unnecessary* to carry on the workers' legitimate concerted activities." Implicit in this statement, and crucial to an understanding of the NLRA, is the fact that some conduct that employers might reasonably regard as "disloyal" is necessary "to carry on the workers' legitimate concerted activities," and is protected. That, in a nutshell, is what makes the NLRA arguably the most radical restriction of employer prerogatives ever enacted. We will return to this point.

Far from "indefensible," said the Court in closing,

> concerted activities by employees for the purpose of trying to protect themselves from working conditions as uncomfortable as the [evidence] showed them to be in this case are unquestionably activities to correct conditions which modern labor-management legislation treats as too bad to have to be tolerated in a humane and civilized society like ours.

With that final volley, the Court imparted further ambiguity about just how bad working conditions have to be to justify employees' concerted

---

[65] *NLRB v. Local Union No. 1229, Int'l Bhd. of Electrical Workers*, 346 U.S. 464 (1953). The case is known by the name of the employer, responding party to the charges below.

[66] *Washington Aluminum Co.*, 370 U.S. at 17.

efforts to improve them. To be sure, the Court never described the conditions as dangerous—merely as "bitterly cold" and very "uncomfortable." Still, this closing phrase seemed to open the door to future employers' claims that the conditions protested by their employees, unlike those in *Washington Aluminum*, were not "too bad to have to be tolerated in a humane and civilized society like ours," and that their protest was therefore unprotected.

Before taking stock of *Washington Aluminum*'s legacy, let us pause to take note of two things that the Court did not discuss: First, somewhat curiously, the Court, unlike both the Board and the Fourth Circuit judges, never used the term "strike" to describe the workers' protest. "Work stoppage," yes; but not "strike." The Fourth Circuit majority had gone astray, in part, by fixating too closely on whether the workers' activity fit what it regarded as the conventional definition of a strike; its analysis essentially begged the question whether the activity nonetheless constituted "concerted activity for . . . mutual aid or protection" under Section 7. The Court's avoidance of the term "strike" seems calculated to emphasize that the NLRA's protections are not confined to the conventional labor-management conflicts associated with unions and collective bargaining.

Second, the unionization effort that began very close in time to the discharges in question, the success of which turned on the Court's decision, played no role whatsoever in the Court's opinion. The Court dropped a footnote early in the opinion to point out that its decision in the discharge case would determine the ultimate outcome of both the union election and the Board's refusal-to-bargain charge. But it almost studiously avoided any mention of a union presence at Washington Aluminum.[67] The lack of union involvement made the case a first: the Supreme Court's first encounter with concerted activity under the Act that lacked any union involvement. Perhaps the Court wished to underscore the fact that the Act's protections were not contingent on a link to traditional organizing activity. Or perhaps the Court wished to emphasize the vulnerability of these unrepresented workers. Such workers "had to speak for themselves as best they could," and could not be expected to make formal demands or follow any particular procedures as a prerequisite to gaining the Act's protections. In effect, the Court seemed inclined to construe the Act liberally to protect these unrepresented workers.

---

[67] It is possible that a union was already behind the scenes at Washington Aluminum on January 5, 1959, given the filing of the representation petition a mere four weeks later. I have found no direct evidence that this was the case; nor would it have been of any direct legal relevance. But the proximity of union activity at the time of the concerted protest would be at least suggestive of the practical implications of the case for workers in the complete absence of a union. We will return to the issue below.

The Large Outlines of the NLRA's Wrongful Discharge Protections and the Small Shadow They Cast

What were the Washington Aluminum workers thinking? What were they after when they walked off the job in defiance of their employer? We have the official version: The employees had some thought of gaining some leverage over workplace conditions through collective action. In the words of one of the employees, credited by the Board and weighed heavily by the Supreme Court, "we had all got together and thought it would be a good idea to go home; maybe we could get some heat brought into the plant that way."[68] Given the time and the place—unions were active in industrial Baltimore in the late 1950s—and given the advent of a union on the scene near the time of the walkout, the workers may have had at least an inchoate desire for union representation.

Consider first how the Washington Aluminum workers' fate would have differed if they *had* been represented by a union and covered by a typical collective bargaining agreement at the time of their protest. Suppose they had encountered the same bitterly cold (but not imminently dangerous) conditions, had walked off the job in protest, and had been fired in response. Unlike non-union workers, who are typically employed at-will and relegated to whatever protections the labor and employment laws afford, these union workers would have been covered by a "just cause" requirement, ubiquitous in union contracts. The employer would therefore have had to justify any discipline or discharge. So the workers could have brought, through their union, a grievance claiming discharge without "just cause." Their grievance, assuming their union agreed with them, would then be the subject of negotiations between management and the union—initially through a shop steward, later perhaps a higher union official—and would culminate, if they could not agree on a resolution, in a hearing before a neutral arbitrator chosen by both the employer and the union.

So would there have been "just cause" for discharge under the CBA (even though there was not "cause" within the meaning of the Act)? That is where the workers' fortunes start to look bleak. The walkout would presumably be deemed a "strike"; and it would be the employer this time who would argue for this characterization, for a strike would violate the no-strike clause of the CBA. ("No strike" clauses are as ubiquitous in CBAs as "just cause" clauses.) That contract violation would supply "just cause" for the discharge under the CBA. Moreover, it would render the walk-out unprotected under the Act.[69]

---

[68] 370 U.S. at 12.

[69] *See NLRB v. Sands Mfg. Co.*, 306 U.S. 332, 344 (1939).

Does this mean that these workers would be in worse shape after unionizing than they were before? Not unless they valued the right to protest workplace conditions that are determined unilaterally by management (and the right to reinstatement in the event of discharge) more than the power to negotiate over those conditions both prospectively through the formation of the CBA and thereafter through formal and informal grievance and arbitration procedures. The Washington Aluminum workers, had they been represented by a union, might have succeeded in negotiating for more effective heating of the shop before January 5. Even in the face of the bitter cold of January 5, they might not have felt so powerless to affect their working conditions, and they would in any event have had a mechanism readily at hand for making their demands. Had they used that mechanism, they would have been protected against retaliation (and against arbitrary or ill-considered discipline) by the "just cause" provision of their contract as well as by the union's collective muscle.

Workers who succeed in organizing and negotiating a collective bargaining agreement essentially trade their legal right to engage in disruptive concerted activity for a share in the governance of the workplace. They trade off some of their rights of protest and disruption in exchange for a form of democratic participation. That is a tradeoff that many workers today would be happy to make.[70] And it is a tradeoff that the nation's labor laws were intended to permit workers to make.

THE ENORMITY (IN PRINCIPLE) OF THE NLRA'S EXCEPTION TO EMPLOYMENT AT WILL

Had the NLRA worked as its New Deal proponents hoped, and promoted the stable and widespread unionization of the economy, "employment law" as we have come to know it would look very different today. Much of it arguably would not exist, for employees would have had recourse through collective bargaining and grievance procedures against many of the abuses of employer power that a great deal of employment law aims to curb. Employees would also have had something that the entire sprawling hodgepodge of employment law does not purport to give them: a collective role in the governance of the workplace and in determining their own terms and conditions of employment. But

---

[70] The most in-depth recent survey of worker attitudes finds that one-third of non-union workers would vote for a union if they had the chance. Richard Freeman & Joel Rogers, *What Workers Want* 68–69 (1999). But far higher numbers said they would like an organization in the workplace with elected worker representatives (59%), and would like to have an arbitrator rather than management settle disputes in cases of disagreement (59%). *Id.* at 142. Most workers would prefer to have "joint management committees that discuss problems," a form of workplace organization that U.S. labor law arguably prohibits. *Id.* at 152.

that was not to be, except for a shrinking minority of the private sector workforce.

But *Washington Aluminum* also encapsulates that part of the labor law that is central to employment law. For the case nicely illustrates the enormity of what the Act does, and what it did in 1935, in the last throes of "liberty of contract," to employment at will and the employer sovereignty that it embodied. In its heyday, liberty of contract meant, above all, the right to choose whether to contract at all—whether to hire a worker and whether to continue to employ the worker. That is why Justice Harlan, who had dissented from the Court's 1905 decision in *Lochner v. New York*[71] striking down a maximum hours law for bakers, wrote the majority opinion in *Adair v. United States*,[72] which struck down Congress' prohibition of "yellow dog contracts" and the discharge of workers based on union activity. Even if it was legitimate in Justice Harlan's view to regulate workers' hours on (tenuous) health and safety grounds, it was "not within the functions of government—at least, in the absence of contract between the parties—to compel any person, in the course of his business and against his will, to accept or retain the personal services of another. . . ."[73] Under *Adair*, wrongful discharge legislation was, it seemed, flatly unconstitutional. That position, had it remained the law, would have doomed not only the NLRA but the Civil Rights Act of 1964 and the entire edifice of wrongful discharge law that has evolved since then.

So even after the Court in *West Coast Hotel v. Parrish*[74] revealed its famous "switch in time," upholding a minimum wage law and signaling the demise of "liberty of contract" as a robust constitutional barrier to legislation, the NLRA and its wrongful discharge provisions posed a distinct "liberty of contract" challenge. The Court—or rather the newly-formed bare majority that cast its lot with the New Deal—did not hesitate to cross that threshold, just two weeks after *West Coast Hotel*, in *NLRB v. Jones & Laughlin Steel*.[75] But it did feel compelled to say a few words by way of justification:

> [T]he statute goes no further than to safeguard the right of employees to self-organization and to select representatives of their own choosing for collective bargaining or other mutual protection without restraint or coercion by their employer.

---

[71] 198 U.S. 45 (1905).

[72] 208 U.S. 161 (1908).

[73] *Id.* at 174.

[74] 300 U.S. 379 (1937).

[75] 301 U.S. 1, 33 (1937).

That is a fundamental right. Employees have as clear a right to organize and select their representatives for lawful purposes as the respondent has to organize its business and select its own officers and agents. ... Congress was not required to ignore this right but could safeguard it.

The Court not only denominates the right of self-organization as fundamental; it implies that the right preexisted congressional action—that Congress had not created the right but had recognized and safeguarded it. From where did that right emanate? The Constitution?[76] The Court left unarticulated and unexplored the implications of a constitutional right of worker self-organization. It was enough in the New Deal to dismantle the barriers that "liberty of contract" had set up against legislative efforts to protect union activity, and to uphold the NLRA.

In safeguarding the right of employees to form a union, Congress thus carved a sizable chunk out of employers' heretofore constitutionally protected prerogatives under employment at will. Almost incidentally, it imposed a major restriction on employers' right to exclude others from their property. The NLRA represented a major imposition on employers' sovereignty—their right to control who enters onto their property and what they do while there. The Supreme Court, in giving its constitutional blessing to this law, made it the nation's first significant wrongful discharge law and the precursor to both the Civil Rights Act of 1964 and the multitude of antidiscrimination and antiretaliation laws and doctrines that followed.

It is one of the great ironies of American employment law that the very first significant exception to the venerable doctrine of employment at will was also the most radical and far-reaching in its conception. To appreciate the importance of that exception, one must look at the dissident pro-union employee from the standpoint of the employer. Suppose you are the head of a medium-sized firm. You currently run your business as you and your fellow managers believe best serves its owners (yourself perhaps among them), and you hire and fire people to help your firm succeed in the market. You operate on a non-union basis, and you believe, as most non-union employers do, that remaining non-union (or "union-free") is important to your firm's success, even survival, in today's highly competitive product and capital markets.

---

[76] That is most logical and historically likely source of any pre-statutory fundamental right was the Thirteenth Amendment, seen by some in the labor movement as a charter of labor's freedom and a better basis than the Commerce Clause for Congress' power to protect labor rights in the NLRA. For a lengthy and engaging exploration of this idea, see James Gray Pope, *The Thirteenth Amendment Versus the Commerce Clause: Labor and the Shaping of American Constitutional Law, 1921–1957,* 102 Colum. L. Rev. 1 (2002).

Now you learn that one or more of your employees—individuals whom you are paying to contribute to your economic success—are seeking to sow discontent with your regime, and to recruit other employees to an organization that will demand limits on your unilateral authority in the workplace and a greater share of the firm's revenues. And that organization will seek to enforce its demands—demands that you believe will injure or even doom the firm—by threatening and perhaps inflicting serious economic harm by disrupting the supply of labor and relations with suppliers, customers, and the public.

That is not the only way for an employer to view the prospect of unionization. An organized collective voice for employees, operating in a cooperative partnership with management, can contribute to a firm's fortunes. But the negative view prevails, at least among non-union employers. Unions do seek a greater share of profits (and historically have succeeded); they do back up their demands with the threat of economic disruption, often a strike along with efforts to induce consumers and suppliers to cease doing business with the employer for the duration of the strike; and strikes are costly. That is the future you might envision if your activist employees have their way.

Yet federal law prohibits you from firing, disciplining, or even reprimanding the employees who are seeking to bring this about. You must in fact allow them to use the workplace—your property, that is—during breaks and the like, to foment discontent about your policies and practices—wages, hours, fringe benefits, supervisors' treatment of workers, the comfort and safety of the workplace environment. You cannot even punish them for walking off the job in protest.

Washington Aluminum underscores the surprising scope of the NLRA's wrongful discharge provisions: They reach into employer prerogatives and take away part of employers' right to control and manage their workforce, not only when a union enters the scene but whenever two or more employees act together in support of shared workplace interests, even when their actions are disruptive and arguably unreasonable.

The NLRA aims chiefly to protect employees' right to choose unionization and collective bargaining. So why does it protect concerted activity that has nothing to do with unionization? It does so for the same reason that employers often view such activity with alarm: Because union sentiment does not always spring full-blown from the workforce; it often originates in more inchoate, less structured collective reactions to shared grievances. One thing leads to another. If employers could lawfully squelch the early manifestations of the collective impulse among workers, they might never reach the point of seeking unionization. (On the other hand, employers' efforts to suppress employee protest might sometimes embolden employees to take the next step and contact a union, as might have happened in *Washington Aluminum* itself.)

So while the Court in *Washington Aluminum* hedged a bit at the edges—emphasizing the extreme conditions faced by the workers and their history of complaints—it underscored just how deeply the NLRA cuts into managerial prerogatives. Employers cannot necessarily enforce entirely rational work rules such as a prohibition on leaving the job without permission. They cannot penalize workers who refuse to perform their job duties, and who leave the employer shorthanded in the face of "critical orders," if the refusal, and the walkout, was a form of protest against poor working conditions. And these restrictions are in place to leave "breathing room" for the even more threatening development of full-blown union sentiment and the surrender of cherished managerial prerogatives.

Describing union organizing in the language of "treachery" and "rebellion" may capture the perspective of many anti-union managers, and drives home the depth of the Act's intrusion into managerial prerogatives and employment at will. But for its proponents, and for the proponents of the Act in 1935, unionization and self-organization are better captured by the language of democracy and freedom: The Act gave workers the right to dissent and to challenge workplace managers so that they could effectively exercise their right of collective self-governance—the right not to dislodge and replace the current regime of managers but to elect worker representatives and to establish a regime of negotiated co-governance of workplace matters.

Section 7 and the right to engage in concerted activity, free from employer interference and discrimination, functions in part as a kind of First Amendment for the private sector workplace. Much as a core function of the First Amendment's freedom of expression is to enable public debate and democratic self-governance, a core function of Section 7 is to foster workplace debate and "industrial democracy." And much as the First Amendment requires incumbent officials to tolerate dissent and criticism within their jurisdiction even when it aims and tends to undermine their authority, Section 7 requires employers to tolerate dissent and criticism within the workplace even when it tends to undermine their authority. Section 7 thus creates a "workplace forum" that parallels the First Amendment's "public forum": During appropriate times and places within the workplace, workers have the right to discuss and debate shared work-related concerns, free from employer restriction. At least to that extent, workers' speech and association rights trump employers' managerial and property rights.

Timekeeping Systems, Inc.[77] offers a nice modern illustration: The chief operating officer of Timekeeping Systems, Inc., Barry Markwitz, sent an e-mail message to all of the company's employees alerting them to proposed changes in the vacation time policy; employees were told that comments were welcome and that they should "Please give me your comments (send me an e-mail or stop in and talk to me)." A software engineer at the company, Larry Leinweber, responded to another employee's enthusiastic e-mail response with his own claim that the proposed changes would actually create less flexible vacation time and therefore harm employees. Leinweber addressed his e-mail to his "Fellow Travelers" and, based upon his "assum[ption that] anyone actually cares about the company and being productive on the job," went on to emphasize that he would "prove" Markwitz's e-mail to be "false." This e-mail, which included some "flippant and rather grating language," was sent to all employees at the company. Markwitz demanded an apology from Leinweber, which Markwitz planned to forward to the other employees; when Leinweber refused, Markwitz fired him.

The Board held that Leinweber's e-mail was protected concerted activity: It was commentary about the terms or conditions of employment designed to inform and mobilize his fellow employees. The concerted nature of the action was not only known to the employer, but was the "principal" reason why Leinweber was discharged.[78] Finally, even though the e-mail's language was somewhat obnoxious, it was not disruptive enough to lose status as "protected" activity.[79] The employer was ordered to reinstate Leinweber with backpay.[80]

In other cases, too, Section 7 has protected employee speech on a variety of topics. Most frequent are concerns related to pay and hours: The Act has been held to protect a nursing home employee's discussion of wage-related problems with co-workers and complaints to her supervisor;[81] and a nurse's memorandum to management outlining her and her coworkers' concerns with a newly-introduced pay and hours system

---

[77] 323 N.L.R.B. 244, 246–48 (1997).

[78] This is more than the law requires. The NLRA requires proof that the activity was concerted, that the employer was motivated by the activity, and that the employer knew of the concerted nature of the activity. It does not require proof that the employer was motivated by the concerted nature of the activity as such. So it would have been enough in *Timekeeping Systems* that Markwitz fired Leinweber because of the e-mail, and knew of its workplace-wide circulation, even if the fact of wider circulation—of its "concerted" nature—had been irrelevant to Markwitz's decision.

[79] *Id.* at 248–49.

[80] *Id.* at 250.

[81] *NLRB v. Main Street Terrace Care Center*, 218 F.3d 531 (6th Cir. 2000).

which resulted in short-staffed shifts and less money per hour.[82] Protection extends as well to speech about break policy or hiring practices.[83] Much of the speech that Section 7 protects is within the firm and among co-workers. But Section 7 also protects discussion of these issues with clients, as in the case of an employee of a sub-contractor who threatened to meet with the contractor's client about concerns such as inadequate preparation time and failure to pay overtime; the employer was barred from disciplining the employee or from imposing a work rule prohibiting employees from discussing work issues with third parties.[84]

The NLRA protects speech that wrongful discharge doctrines based on public policy do not. And vice versa. In particular, the NLRA protects shared self-interest among workers, not sheer altruism.[85] There has been occasional recognition that, for many workers, one of the most important conditions of their employment is the quality of care, service, or education that they can extend to their patients, clients, or students.[86] But health care professionals, teachers and others are often found to be insufficiently self interested in their concerns to claim Section 7's protections. So a nursing home employee who called a state hotline to complain about the heat in the building was found not to have engaged in protected activity because she sought to ease the suffering of the patients in her care, not to address working conditions.[87] Employees of a home for troubled youth who complained about managerial incompetence and its impact on the " 'quality of care,' 'the quality of the program' and the 'welfare of the children' " were similarly unprotected.[88] Occupational therapists who complained about hospital management and the effect on the quality of care were unprotected because they were "in

---

[82] *Short v. Community Memorial Hospital*, 2004 WL 2616293 (Cal. Ct. App. 2004) (dismissing nurse's wrongful termination case because her activity was concerted and protected and therefore preempted by the NLRA).

[83] *NLRB v. Caval Tool Division, Chromalloy Gas Turbine Corp.*, 262 F.3d 184 (2d Cir. 2001) (break policy); *NLRB v. Phoenix Mut. Life Ins. Co.*, 167 F.2d 983 (7th Cir. 1948) (hiring policy).

[84] *Compuware Corp. v. NLRB*, 134 F.3d 1285 (6th Cir. 1998).

[85] *See generally* Cynthia Estlund, *What Do Workers Want? Employee Interests, Public Interests, and Freedom of Expression Under the National Labor Relations Act*, 140 U. Pa. L. Rev. 921 (1992).

[86] *Dominican Sisters of Ontario*, 264 N.L.R.B. 1205, 1210 (1982) (nurses who hired outside counsel to protest proposed changes in emergency room staffing, while "primarily concerned with the effect on patient care," were still protected by Section 7 because "to a health care professional, such as a registered nurse, the handling of patient care is a condition of employment.").

[87] *Waters of Orchard Park*, 341 N.L.R.B. 642 (2004).

[88] *Lutheran Social Service of Minnesota*, 250 N.L.R.B. 35, 42 (1980).

no way disturbed or troubled by any personal demands that may have been imposed on them."[89] Employees are on firmer ground if they claim to be concerned about their own work schedules than about their patients' survival.

Still, Section 7 protects a wide range of speech on matters that undeniably do matter to employees. When they speak on these matters, employees are protected even if they confront company officers with "flippant and rather grating language," or in a "loud and boisterous" manner.[90] Employees may lose protection if they use particularly egregious language, or if they express their concerns in a manner that is "so violent or of such serious character as to render [them] unfit for future service."[91] But the law mandates tolerance for the strong language and strong sentiments that labor disputes can elicit.

Of course, as *Washington Aluminum* shows, it is not only speech that is protected. The law has protected employee walk-outs to protest an overbearing supervisor who was interfering with productivity;[92] a co-worker's sexual harassment and a supervisor's general incompetence;[93] or unsafe working conditions, such as noxious ammonia fumes in the work area[94] or a lack of the appropriate safety devices on their equipment;[95] or disagreeable job requirements, such as having to make weekly trips to corporate headquarters.[96]

Compare these cases to some of the breakthrough "public policy" wrongful discharge cases, in which employees were fired for refusing to

---

[89] *Good Samaritan Hospital & Health Center,* 265 N.L.R.B. 618, 626 (1982); *Damon House,* 270 N.L.R.B. 143, 143 (1984) (no protection for counselors at a drug treatment center who sent a letter attacking the center's executive director and his impact on adolescent residents); *Autumn Manor,* 268 N.L.R.B. 239 (1983) (no protection for nursing home employees who testified at nursing home's relicensing hearing about alleged patient abuse; testimony "had no direct relationship to the working conditions of employees").

[90] *NLRB v. Air Contact Transport Inc.,* 403 F.3d 206, 208–9 (4th Cir. 2005) (internal quotations omitted). *See also NLRB v. Waco Insulation, Inc.,* 567 F.2d 596, 599 (4th Cir. 1977).

[91] *Sullair P.T.O., Inc. v. NLRB,* 641 F.2d 500, 502 (7th Cir. 1981) (internal citations omitted). *See also Media General Operations, Inc. v. NLRB,* 394 F.3d 207, 213 (4th Cir. 2005).

[92] *Arrow Electric Co. v. NLRB,* 155 F.3d 762 (6th Cir. 1998).

[93] *Trompler, Inc. v. NLRB,* 338 F.3d 747 (7th Cir. 2003). *Cf. Bob Evans Farms, Inc. v. NLRB,* 163 F.3d 1012 (7th Cir. 1998) (walk-out of employees in a restaurant was not reasonable because of negative impact on employer's business and lasting reputational damage).

[94] *NLRB v. Tamara Foods, Inc.,* 692 F.2d 1171 (8th Cir. 1982).

[95] *Elam v. NLRB,* 395 F.2d 611 (D.C. Cir. 1968).

[96] *Vic Tanny Int'l, Inc. v. NLRB,* 622 F.2d 237 (6th Cir. 1980).

commit a crime,[97] for exposing illegal and life-threatening conduct,[98] for doing their civic duty by serving on a jury,[99] or for filing a workers compensation claim as they had a right to do.[100] Those decisions protect employee conduct that more or less directly advances the public interest against employers engaged in socially harmful and often illegal conduct. They tend to protect employee conduct that is out of the ordinary, outside of the workplace routine, and usually triggered by some kind of employer malfeasance. The impact on employer discretion is episodic and comparatively minor. By contrast, the NLRA constrains employers' power to respond to routine workplace conflicts and to discipline disruptive employees; and it does so without any obvious public stake in the particular conduct that is protected. The public stake is large and lofty— it is the goal of promoting workplace democracy and freedom of association among workers—but it is at least one step removed from the immediate dispute, in which little more than worker self-interest—albeit collective self-interest—seems to be at stake.

The point of this comparison is certainly not to criticize the NLRA's wrongful discharge protections, but rather to highlight their distinctive nature and their surprising reach. They reflect the NLRA's aspiration to reconfigure the distribution of power and the shape of everyday relations in the workplace. The nation's oldest wrongful discharge law is still among the most far-reaching in its intrusion into traditional managerial prerogatives.

THE REALITY OF THE NLRA IN THE NON-UNION
WORKPLACE: OBSCURITY AND NEGLECT

So how is it that the NLRA's constraints on employment at will are so obscure a feature of the employment law landscape as it is conventionally painted? The NLRA's protections in the non-union workplace, including its wrongful discharge provisions, are largely unknown to non-specialists, even to most lawyers. And beyond the well-known but much-flouted prohibition on firing union supporters, these protections have barely penetrated the consciousness of employers. Evidence to that effect is found in the newsletters and advice memos that employment lawyers and human relations experts send to employers. Periodically in one of

---

[97] *Petermann v. International Bhd. of Teamsters*, 344 P.2d 25 (Cal. Ct. App. 1959).

[98] *White v. General Motors Corp.*, 908 F.2d 669 (10th Cir. 1990) (recognizing public policy claim by employees fired for complaining about use of defective brakes in automobile manufacturing plant); *Garibaldi v. Lucky Food Stores, Inc.*, 726 F.2d 1367 (9th Cir. 1964) (recognizing claim by employee discharged for reporting employer's illegal distribution of spoiled milk).

[99] *Nees v. Hocks*, 536 P.2d 512 (Or. 1975).

[100] *Frampton v. Central Indiana Gas Co.*, 297 N.E.2d 425 (Ind. 1973).

these publications, one can read warnings to employers such as: "Non-union employers may be surprised to learn that the National Labor Relations Act (NLRA), the federal law giving employees the right to join unions and engage in collective activity, does not limit protection to employees who participate in traditional union activities."[101] And it surely does come as a surprise. For employers commonly prohibit employees from discussing their wages with each other, for example, even though that is a violation of the NLRA. Employers would likely not hesitate to fire employees who walk off the job as the *Washington Aluminum* workers did, or who openly and sarcastically criticize the employer's vacation policies to fellow employees as the employee in *Timekeeping Systems* did. Indeed, they might not even go to the trouble of concocting another reason for firing the employees, convinced as they likely are by their right to discipline such troublemakers.

Given this state of affairs, it is not surprising that few non-union employees who are fired or disciplined outside the context of union organizing make their way to the NLRB, where they would have to file their claim.[102] (Informal inquiries suggest that rather few such claims are filed; it is possible but unlikely, in my view, that this is because employers rarely discipline employees for discussing workplace concerns with co-workers or for fomenting discontent among them.) Recall that the employees in *Washington Aluminum* filed their charges after a union had already entered the picture and gained enough support within the workforce to seek a representation election. Unions are highly attuned to the NLRB's ambit; non-union workers are not. Ironically, if the employees in *Washington Aluminum* had not had a union to turn to, this landmark case of labor law in the non-union workplace might never have arisen.

We might simply conclude that employers and employees do not know much about the law generally. But contrast this state of unconsciousness about the NLRA's protections with popular knowledge of

---

[101] Personnel Policy Service, Inc., *Employers Beware: NLRA Protects Nonunion Activity, Too, available at* http://www.ppspublishers.com/articles/nlra.htm. *See also* Employment Law Department of Gibbons, Del Deo, Dolan, Griffinger & Vecchione, *Sixth Circuit Finds Employer Committed Unfair Labor Practice by Terminating Non–Union Truck Drivers Who Engaged in Protected Concerted Activity, available at* http://www.gibbonslaw.com/publications/articlesuser2.cfm?pubid=1200; Kirsten Heaton, Allen Kato, and Thomas Moyer, *Weekly Employment Brief, available at* http://www.fenwick.com/docstore/publications/Employment/WEB_09–24–01.pdf ("It is important to note that the federal National Labor Relations Act protects employees who engage in concerted activity even in non-union worksites.").

[102] Charles J. Morris, *NLRB Protection in the Nonunion Workplace: A Glimpse at a General Theory of Section 7 Conduct,* 137 U. Pa. L. Rev. 1673, 1675 (1989) ("Many employers, perhaps most, and certainly most employees, are totally oblivious of the existence of this important body of law [the NLRA].").

antidiscrimination law. Employment discrimination on the basis of race
and sex, for example, has hardly been obliterated. But it is almost
universally and vociferously repudiated by employers, and it is the
announced target of employer-created equal employment offices, anti-
harassment policies, grievance procedures, and other EEO compliance
machinery. Antidiscrimination law has produced a rash of other more
and less salutary "liability avoidance" measures, ranging from training
of supervisors to avoid racially or sexually-charged language, to "sanitiz-
ing" of personnel files to remove such language after the fact.[103] There is
no evidence that the NLRA has produced any such liability avoidance
effort.

The most obvious explanation is that the NLRA creates very little
liability to be avoided. Its prohibitions and protections are impressively
broad in principle, but they are backed by the puniest of sanctions: No
punitive sanctions of any kind and no compensatory damages, only
backpay; and even backpay liability is discounted by wages actually
earned by the employee in the interim. And the exclusive procedural
avenue for securing these limited remedies is administrative: No juries,
no hungry plaintiffs' attorneys, no class actions, no party-controlled
discovery, no costly litigation. If an employee files a charge, a government agent will be assigned to investigate the employee's charges. But if
the facts are murky, overburdened agency officials might decide to
dismiss the charge or to settle for even less than the law allows. And the
employee in that event has no recourse under the Act. [104]

Nor can states come to the rescue with their own supplemental
remedies—as some might well have done by way of common law or even
statutory remedies for wrongful discharge in violation of public policy;
for the doctrines of federal labor preemption have barred states from
regulating or protecting private sector union or other concerted activity.[105] Federal law does not merely fail to afford a private right of action
and fully compensatory damages for a wrongful discharge for protected
labor activity; it precludes such remedies.[106]

In practical terms, the NLRA is the least fearsome of employment
laws. Indeed, preemption doctrine makes it as much a shield for employers as it is a sword for employees. The result, in the words of one human

---

[103] Susan Bisom–Rapp, *Bulletproofing the Workplace: Symbol and Substance in Employment Discrimination Law Practice*, 26 Fla. St. U. L. Rev. 959 (1999).

[104] Cynthia Estlund, *The Ossification of American Labor Law*, 102 Colum. L. Rev.
1527, 1551–54 (2002) [hereinafter Estlund, *Ossification*].

[105] *Id.* at 1554.

[106] That is not to say that states may not protect individual employees who complain of
illegal conduct or refuse to engage in such conduct, simply because the employee happens
to have acted in concert with others.

rights organization, is "a culture of near-impunity," in which a determined anti-union employer can affort to regard the labor law's sanctions
as a tolerable cost of doing business.[107] That may help to explain many
employees' perception that, whatever the law says, it will not prevent or
deter their employer from firing them if they support unionization or
other collective protest. And that is among the reasons why a proposal to
repeal the NLRA (and with it the preemption of state protections of
union activity) might meet more resistance these days from employers
than from some unions and employee advocates.

Litigation is no panacea for employees. It is a lousy mechanism for
resolution of most workplace disputes. But employers' fear of litigation
can be an excellent stimulus for internal reforms designed to curtail
litigation—partly by avoiding the conduct that gives rise to litigation,
partly by anticipating and resolving disputes before litigation arises.
Fear of antidiscrimination litigation, for example, has led to the proliferation of "self-regulatory" measures by which many discrimination claims
are avoided or resolved without litigation.[108] The NLRA inspires none of
this fear.

So there is a rather simple explanation for the relative invisibility of
the NLRA on the employment law landscape. But that explanation
seems to beg another question: Why is this wrongful discharge law
virtually alone, and at odds with much of the growing body of wrongful
discharge laws and doctrines, in the limited nature of the remedial and
procedural arsenal backing it up?

A partial answer lies in the peculiar history of the Act: Its provisions
were initially fixed at a time when employees saw few allies in the
courts, and preferred to place their hopes with a federal agency charged
with their protection. (Its exceptionally broad implied preemption doctrine, which ousts states from any supplemental role, was seen at the
time as providing necessary insulation from reactionary state interference with the federal scheme.)[109] The expectation that federal agencies
rather than private lawsuits would provide greater protection to employees prevailed even in 1964, when both the hopes of proponents and the
fears of opponents were focused on the role of the EEOC.[110] But the

---

[107] Lance Compa, *Unfair Advantage: Workers' Freedom of Association in the United States under International Human Rights Standards* 8 (2000), available at http://www.hrw.org/reports/2000/uslabor/USLBR008–02.htm.

[108] *See* Cynthia Estlund, *Rebuilding the Law of the Workplace in an Era of Self–Regulation*, 105 Colum. L. Rev. 319 (2005). By the same token, defusing the fear of litigation, as some seek to do through mandatory arbitration, threatens to stall the engines of reform. But that is for another day.

[109] Estlund, *Ossification* at 1552.

[110] Title VII's proponents originally sought to create an agency like the NLRB, the rulings of which would be binding subject to limited judicial review and which could seek

framers of the Civil Rights Act of 1964, in the wake of the desegregation decisions, had enough confidence in courts and in private lawsuits as potential engines of reform to create a private right of action; and there was by that time enough progressive antidiscrimination law in operation in the states for Congress to make explicit its intent that the federal law should be a floor and not a ceiling—an option and not an exclusive avenue—for discrimination claims. In subsequent decades, the proliferation of state and federal antidiscrimination litigation has had an enormous impact on workplace policies and practices.

Labor law reformers might have learned from this experience. But the exclusively federal, exclusively administrative approach of federal labor law was by then fixed, and has been surprisingly entrenched against significant changes of any kind.[111] In particular, efforts to beef up the Act's remedial scheme over the past several decades have either failed to get a majority or failed to surmount the Congress's supermajority requirements, which allow a committed minority to defeat legislation favored by a not-quite-large-enough majority.

Which brings us to more profound questions: Why has opposition to serious labor law remedies been so committed, and why has support for those remedies not reached a veto-and filibuster-proof majority? This is not the place for extended reflection on these questions, except to suggest that the answers are linked to the impunity with which many employers still violate the NLRA's protections,[112] and to the public's unawareness of those protections. The wrongfulness of these illegal discharges—of firing employees for supporting a union or for spurring collective dissent—has not, at least for the past several decades, enjoyed anything like the universal public assent that the antidiscrimination principle has enjoyed. The basic rights of association and self-organization among workers that were established by the NLRA in 1935, and that are now inscribed in international human rights law, have not captured (or maintained their hold on) public consciousness nor shaped public norms as fully as has the right to be free from discrimination on the basis of race and sex.

Perhaps that is because the rights of association and self-organization are inextricably linked in the public consciousness to the particular institutions through which employees have exercised those rights—to labor unions. Unions have not only been the primary source of support

---

judicial enforcement of its orders; opponents succeeded in weakening the EEOC. ALFRED W. BLUMROSEN, MODERN LAW: THE LAW TRANSMISSION SYSTEM AND EQUAL EMPLOYMENT OPPORTUNITY 48 (1993).

[111] For a full treatment of this proposition, see *id.* at 1535–36.

[112] See Lance Compa, *Unfair Advantage: Workers' Freedom of Association in the United States under International Human Rights Standards* 8–10 (2000).

and public education about Section 7 rights; they embody the value of self-organization. Unions' role as advocates and as examples of the values underlying the NLRA is undermined by the decline of union membership and power. That role is also compromised by the checkered history of some unions; indeed, it is when unions are accused of corruption, engage in some disorderly dispute, or disrupt commerce that they are most likely to get mass media coverage. But there is a deeper problem: The point of protecting workers' freedom of expression and association was to facilitate workers' self-governance through the formation of unions. The decline of union membership may foster a perception that unions (whether desirable or not) are fading into history. And if that is so, then what exactly is the point of protecting workers' concerted protest and discussion?

The point is this: Workers' ability to exercise "voice" at work—to participate in the decisions that matter to them in their working lives— is a matter of enduring social import, even if the traditional institutions for worker voice have been battered and diminished by economic and social changes, ineffectual labor laws and recalcitrant employers. If unions are to rebound or to remake themselves for the new workplace, or if some new institutional vehicle for worker voice is to emerge in their place, that will depend on unorganized workers being protected in their nascent and multifarious efforts to make common cause with each other, within or across workplaces. We cannot be as sure as Senator Wagner was where those efforts might lead and what institutional form they might eventually take. But we can be quite sure that no effective vehicles of employee voice are going to spring full-blown from the minds of reformers. Rather, they will have to grow at least in part out of workers' own experiences and experiments, their own efforts to improve their lot. As long as Section 7 persists in the statute books—even as an artifact of a labor law regime that is ineffectual and outdated—it has a critical role to play in protecting those nascent efforts.

*

8

The Story of *Gilmer v. Interstate/Johnson Lane Corp.*: The Emergence of Employment Arbitration

Samuel Estreicher

On May 13, 1991, the Supreme Court held in *Gilmer v. Interstate/Johnson Lane Corp.*[1] that employees could enter into binding pre-dispute arbitration agreements encompassing claims they have against employers under the Age Discrimination in Employment Act of 1967 (ADEA)[2] and by extension other federal and state employment laws. Although the ADEA and other federal statutes, viewed on their own terms, contemplate actions in court, the Federal Arbitration Act of 1925 (FAA),[3] as interpreted by the Court, requires the enforcement of arbitration agreements covering statutory as well as common law claims. The ruling did not come out of the blue. It had been prefigured by a series of decisions broadening the reach of the FAA, including the Court's 1987 *Perry v. Thomas*[4] holding that an employee's arbitration agreement with his securities-industry employer preempted a state statute requiring that wage payment claims be heard in court and not be subject to arbitration. *Perry* seems to have slipped in under the radar screen, not then eliciting *amici* briefs from plaintiff groups or the kind of widespread attention that *Gilmer* evoked. Moreover, as *Perry* involved a state law claim, the plaintiff community might still have harbored the hope that the Court would rule differently when confronted with a claim arising under one of the hallmark federal anti-discrimination laws.

Gilmer dashed those hopes. However, the Court did not decide the meaning of the exclusion in § 1 of the FAA for "contracts of employment of seamen, railroad employees or any other class of workers engaged in

---

[1] 500 U.S. 20 (1991).

[2] 29 U.S.C. §§ 621–633(a) (2005).

[3] 9 U.S.C. §§ 1–16 (2005).

[4] 482 U.S. 483 (1987).

foreign or interstate commerce."[5] It was able to avoid this question because, although it was fully briefed by some of the *amici*, the issue had not been raised below, identified among the questions presented, or even briefed by Gilmer's counsel. Justice White, writing for a 7–2 majority, was able to say that the § 1 exclusionary clause did not apply because Gilmer's arbitration agreement was part of a registration process with the New York Stock Exchange (NYSE), rather than a contract of employment directly entered into with his former employer. Ten years later, in *Circuit City Stores, Inc. v. Adams*[6] the Court decided the question left open in *Gilmer*, reading the exclusion to "exempt[] from the FAA only contracts of employment of transportation workers."[7] *Gilmer* ushered in a new era of arbitration of employment disputes.

Factual Background and Prior Proceedings

Robert Dickerson Gilmer, a Davidson College graduate who previously worked in the securities industry, was hired as Manager of Financial Services by Interstate Securities Corporation (later, Interstate/Johnson Lane Corporation, or Interstate) on May 18, 1981 in its Charlotte, North Carolina office.[8] With more than 1000 employees, Interstate was one of the largest brokerage firms in the southeast. One week after his hiring,[9] Gilmer was required to register as a securities representative (or "registered representative") with several stock exchanges, including the NYSE. He was quite familiar with this procedure, having worked for 11 years with a Richmond, Virginia securities firm as a manager of its mutual fund department.[10] He also appears to have previously taken and passed several registration examinations with both the NYSE and the National Association of Securities Dealers. Gilmer's lawyer stated at the hearing on Interstate's motion to compel arbitration: "he had already been registered and had been for some fifteen, twenty years. He was

---

[5] 9 U.S.C. § 1 (2005).

[6] 532 U.S. 105 (2001). The author was co-counsel for petitioner in this case.

[7] *Id.* at 119.

[8] The business culture in the Charlotte office, reflecting a new managerial philosophy resulting in considerable turnover, is captured well in Martin Donsky, *Craig Redwine's Struggle to Reshape Interstate*, Business/North Carolina (Nov. 1987), pp. 17 ff.

[9] This was apparently an important point to Gilmer's counsel who wanted to argue lack of consideration for the arbitration agreement contained in the Form U–4: "But he was already employed at the time he signed that, and he was already a representative and duly licensed to sign securities in North Carolina." Transcript of November 2, 1988 hearing on Interstate's motion to compel arbitration, reprinted in Joint Appendix, *Gilmer*, 500 U.S. 20 (No. 90–18) [hereinafter "JA"], 22.

[10] See Gilmer's employment application with Interstate, as reprinted in JA 13–14.

registered in 1959. . . ."[11]

Gilmer's registration application, entitled "Uniform Application for Securities Industry Registration or Transfer," or "Form U–4," was (and still is) used throughout the securities industry. The U–4 required, among other things, that Gilmer "agreed to arbitrate any dispute, claim, or controversy" arising between him and Interstate "that is required to be arbitrated under the rules, constitutions or by-laws of the organizations with which I register." NYSE Rule 347, which had been approved by the Securities and Exchange Commission (SEC), provided that

> Any controversy between a registered representative and any member or member organization arising out of the employment or termination of employment of such registered representative by and with such member or member organization shall be settled by arbitration, at the instance of any such party, in accordance with the arbitration procedure prescribed elsewhere in these rules.[12]

Interstate terminated Gilmer's employment on November 13, 1987, at which time he was 62 years of age. He was then a Senior Vice President and Manager of Interstate's Mutual Fund Department receiving, according to his lawyer, a salary of $70,000 plus commissions of around $75,000.[13] Gilmer filed a charge of age discrimination with the Equal Employment Opportunity Commission (EEOC). He then brought suit in 1988 in the U.S. District Court for the Western District of North Carolina claiming his discharge was due to age bias in violation of the ADEA. He was represented by John T. Allred of the Charlotte firm Petree Stockton & Robinson. Allred, a distinguished practitioner now retired from Kilpatrick Stockton, took the case because Gilmer was a longstanding friend, going back "to our bachelor days"; Gilmer was a godfather to Allred's son. Allred handled employment cases but was a general litigator, "learning my way around courtrooms by representing insurance companies and such."[14]

Gilmer's complaint alleged no "pattern and practice" or class claims:

---

[11] *Id.* at 22.

[12] NYSE 347, as reprinted in App., Br. for Respondent, *Gilmer,* 500 U.S. 20 (No. 90–18) [hereinafter "Br. for Respondent"].

[13] Complaint § I, *Robert D. Gilmer v. Interstate Securities Corporation,* Civil Action No. C–C–88–0396–M (W.D. N.C.), filed Aug. 29, 1988 [hereinafter "Complaint"], reprinted in JA, 4. Salary information is from the transcript of the hearing on Interstate's motion to compel arbitration, reprinted in JA, 20–21. Gilmer's W–2 for 1987 stated a total income, including commissions, of $118,742.65.

[14] Telephone interview with John T. Allred (Aug. 24, 2005).

Plaintiff is a former employee of the defendant Interstate Securities Corporation and brings this action under the [ADEA] to secure reinstatement and full reinstatement and full restitution and payment of all lost wages and benefits resulting from defendant's violation. . . .[15]

Gilmer claimed that he received regular promotions and pay increases and was told at the time of his termination: "You have done a superior job promoting the product line and the department has been very profitable. We have no complaints. You have done the best job of all department heads."[16] Three days later, his supervisor sent the following message to all branch offices:

BOB GILMER HAS LEFT THE FIRM TO PURSUE OTHER INTERESTS. WE APPRECIATE THE FINE JOB HE HAS DONE FOR US IN THE PAST AND WISH HIM THE BEST OF LUCK IN THE FUTURE.

CARLA GRIFFIN WILL BE THE DIRECTOR OF MUTUAL FUND MARKETING. . . . PLEASE JOIN ME IN CONGRATULATING CARLA ON HER NEW POSITION.[17]

Gilmer alleged that Carla was younger and less qualified, that he had not left of his own accord and that he was not given an opportunity for reassignment to other positions within Interstate.[18]

Interstate was represented by another Charlotte attorney, James B. Spears, Jr. of Haynsworth, Baldwin, Johnson and Greaves. Spears, a prominent practitioner, is an employment lawyer. He also argued, though lost, another ADEA case in the Supreme Court, *O'Connor v. Consolidated Coin Caterers Corp.*[19] The "Haynsworth" in the firm name is Knox Haynsworth, the nephew of Judge Clement Haynsworth, whose

---

[15] Complaint, § VII, reprinted in JA, 5–6.

[16] *Id.* § VIII, reprinted in JA, 6. During the EEOC investigation, Interstate stated that Gilmer "was unable to [improve sales performance in his department] and that was solely the reason for his termination." Letter from Interstate to William H. Convey, Jr. of the EEOC office in Charlotte NC dated May 27, 1988, p,4. The Company's "Employee Termination Form" stated, however, that the reason for Gilmer's termination was "job elimination due to cost containment."

[17] *Id.*, Exh. A, reprinted in JA, 9 (capitalization in original).

[18] Interestingly, Griffin was not required to sign a Form U–4 because she "was assigned responsibility for only the administrative portion of Mr. Gilmer's former position. This new responsibility . . . did not include Mr. Gilmer's former responsibilities for mutual fund trading as regulated by the National Security Exchanges." Affidavit of Franklin C. Golden in Support of Defendant's Motion to Compel Arbitration and Motion to Dismiss Complaint, ¶ 2, filed Nov. 4, 1988, reprinted in JA,75.

[19] 517 U.S. 308 (1996). Telephone interview with James B. Spears, Jr., Aug. 25, 2005.

appointment by President Nixon to the Supreme Court did not get through the Senate. Spears' firm later merged into Ogletree Deakins.

In response to the complaint, Interstate moved to compel arbitration of the ADEA claim, relying on the arbitration agreement in the U–4 and the FAA.[20] Senior District Judge James B. McMillan denied the motion, concluding that "Congress intended to protect ADEA claims from the waiver of a judicial forum. Plaintiff is entitled to a jury trial on any factual issues for recovery of damages for violation of ADEA."[21] The District Court relied on *Alexander v. Gardner–Denver Co.*[22] for the proposition that claims arising under the federal anti-discrimination statutes were not subject to mandatory arbitration: "The Supreme Court reasoned that arbitration procedures were not well suited to the final resolution of rights created by Title VII. This reasoning is applicable to claims under the ADEA."

On appeal, the U.S. Court of Appeals (2–1) reversed.[23] The majority opinion was authored by Judge J. Harvie Wilkinson. Judge Wilkinson, a former member of the University of Virginia law faculty, had previously clerked for Justice Lewis F. Powell, Jr. of the Supreme Court, the author of the opinion for the Court in *Alexander v. Gardner–Denver*. Judge Wilkerson's opinion maintained that the Supreme Court had made clear in a recent trilogy of cases—Mitsubishi *Motors Corp. v. Soler Chrysler– Plymouth, Inc.*,[24] *Shearson/American Express, Inc. v. McMahon*[25] and *Rodriquez de Quijas v. Shearson/American Express, Inc.*[26]—that the FAA "established a 'federal policy favoring arbitration,' " and that an arbitration agreement is unenforceable "only if Congress has evinced an intention to preclude waiver of the judicial forum for a particular right, or if the agreement was procured by fraud or use of excessive economic power." The court saw no evidence of such a congressional intention in the ADEA context, which "involve(s) in the main simple, factual inqui-

---

[20] Defendant's Motion to Compel Arbitration and to Dismiss Complaint, filed Sept. 27, 1988, reprinted in JA, 10 ff. Annexed to the Motion was an affidavit from Gloria Gibson, Interstate's Director of Personnel, attaching as an exhibit a copy of Gilmer's U–4 application.

[21] Findings of Fact and Conclusions of Law, Conclusion of Law No. 4, filed Jan. 17, 1989, reprinted in JA, 87.

[22] 415 U.S. 36 (1974).

[23] 895 F.2d 195 (4th Cir. 1990). The case was argued on November 2, 1989, and decided on February 6, 1990. Spears argued for the appellant Interstate; W. R. Loftis, Jr., of the Petree firm, argued for the appellee Gilmer.

[24] 473 U.S. 614 (1985).

[25] 482 U.S. 220 (1987).

[26] 490 U.S. 477 (1989).

ries" and that "[s]o long as arbitrators possess the equitable power to redress individual claims of discrimination, there is no reason to reject their role in the resolution of ADEA disputes." The *Gardner-Denver* line of cases was distinguished as involving arbitration under collective bargaining agreements where there was a concern that individual rights of employees might not receive full protection from their collective bargaining agent. Judge Widener dissented on the view that *Gardner-Denver* controlled arbitration pursuant to individual employment contracts.

The Supreme Court Decision

Because of a conflict between this ruling and the 2–1 decision of the Third Circuit in *Nicholson v. CPC Int'l Inc.*[27] (over Judge Edward Becker's strong dissent), the Supreme Court granted Gilmer's petition for writ of certiorari on October 1, 1990. The grant was expressly limited to the first question in the petition: "Are claims brought pursuant to the Age Discrimination in Employment Act ... subject to compulsory arbitration?"[28] Gilmer and Interstate were represented in the Supreme Court by their respective trial counsel. A number of organizations filed *amicus curiae* briefs: The organizations supporting Gilmer were the AFL–CIO, the American Associations of Retired Persons, and the Lawyers' Committee for Civil Rights Under Law; those supporting Interstate were the Center for Public Resources, the U.S. Chamber of Commerce, the Equal Employment Advisory Council, and the Securities Industry Association.

Gilmer and his counsel, although successful in convincing the Court to hear the case, faced an uphill climb. The Court was not writing on a clear slate. It had already decided that the FAA, whatever Congress's initial intentions may have been, established a federal substantive rule in favor of arbitration,[29] erecting a powerful presumption of arbitrability reaching all claims arguably within the scope of an arbitration agreement. This presumption applied even when arbitration was sought of federal or state statutory claims. The burden was on the party opposing arbitration to show that Congress intended to preclude arbitration of claims under a particular federal statute. Express no-waiver provisions in the securities laws had been held insufficient in view of the fact that

---

[27] 877 F.2d 221 (3d Cir. 1989). The author was co-counsel for appellee in this case.

[28] Petition for Writ of Certiorari at 2, *Gilmer*, 500 U.S. 20 (No. 90–18). Gilmer's second question, not within the grant, stated: "Is an arbitration clause executed six years before any claim arises under the ADEA an invalid prospective waiver." *Id.*

[29] This view of the FAA essentially begins with *Prima Paint Corp. v. Flood & Conklin Mfg. Co.*, 388 U.S. 395 (1967) (FAA is a Commerce Clause enactment establishing a federal substantive rule of arbitrability requiring the arbitrator, not the court, to consider a claim of fraud in the inducement of a contract).

arbitration constituted only a change of forum, not a waiver of any substantive right.[30] In the trilogy referenced by the Fourth Circuit, the Court had held that the FAA required enforcement of private arbitration agreements covering claims under the Sherman Act, under the federal securities laws, and under the Racketeer Influenced Corrupt Organizations Act (RICO)—even though these laws expressed important public policies and provided for injunctive relief and, in the case of the Sherman Act and RICO, trebled damages in order to promote deterrence. In *Perry v. Thomas*, and in the earlier decision on which it relies, *Southland Corp. v. Keating*,[31] the Court had made clear that the FAA-based presumption reaches state statutes and overrides any no-arbitration strictures under state law. Justice O'Connor had issued a strong dissent in *Southland*, but she later joined the Court's opinion in *Mitsubishi* and *Rodriguez* and authored the opinion for the Court in *McMahon*. Her dissent in *Perry* suggested that her problem with the FAA was limited to its preemptive effect on state public policies; her concern did not seem to extend to federal regulation.

Gilmer's counsel apparently placed his hope on the Court's continued adherence to *Gardner-Denver* and its progeny.[32] This was not entirely unwarranted. Allred had convinced District Judge McMillan and dissenting Circuit Judge Widener that this line of cases was still intact. Indeed, as late as 1987, two years after *Mitsubishi* came down and the same term as *Perry v. Thomas*, the Court had stated in *Atchison, Topeka & Santa Fe Railway Co. v. Buell*:

> This Court has, on numerous occasions, declined to hold that individual employees are, because of the availability of arbitration, barred from bringing claims under federal statutes [citing *Gardner-Denver* and later cases]. Although the analysis of the question under each statute is distinct, the theory running through these cases is that notwithstanding the strong policies encouraging arbitration,

---

[30] In *McMahon*, the Court confronted § 29(a) of the Securities Exchange Act of 1934, 15 U.S.C. § 78cc(a), which declares void "any condition, stipulation, or provision binding any person to waive compliance with any provisions" of the Act; Section 29(a) was viewed as dealing only with stipulations seeking a waiver of compliance with the substantive terms of the Act, and did not provide a basis for barring enforcement of waivers of certain procedural provisions, as would entailed in pre-dispute arbitration agreements. *See* 482 U.S. at 230 ff. In *Rodriguez*, the Court dealt with § 14 of the Securities Act of 1933, 15 U.S.C. § 77n, which bars agreements "to waive compliance with any provision" of that statute, and similarly read § 14 as not barring private arbitration agreements modifying certain procedural provisions of the Securities Act. *See* 490 U.S. at 482–83.

[31] 465 U.S. 1 (1984).

[32] *See Barrentine v. Arkansas–Best Freight System*, 450 U.S. 728 (1981); *McDonald v. City of West Branch*, 466 U.S. 284 (1984); *Atchison, Topeka & Santa Fe Railway Co. v. Buell*, 480 U.S. 557 (1987).

"different considerations apply where the employee's claim is based on rights arising out of a statute designed to provide minimum substantive guarantees to individual workers."[33]

The Court did not, however, discuss the FAA cases in the *Gardner-Denver* line of decisions, effectively treating the two as distinct lines of authority.

Interstate's counsel insisted that the *Gardner-Denver* decisions were plainly distinguishable:

> [N]one of these cases involved the *enforcement* of a written individual agreement to arbitrate that would have encompassed the statutory issues in the case. *Alexander, Barrentine and McDonald* all focused on whether a prior arbitral award was *preclusive* of particular statutory claims. Each decision probably needed to go no further than its recognition that the statutory claims were not decided in the collective bargaining arbitration that *preceded* the court action. In fact, the Court recognized in each case that the statutory claim could not have been decided by the labor arbitrators, since each arbitrator's authority was clearly limited to interpreting and applying the terms of the various collective bargaining agreements. The issue of preclusion is not presented in this case. This case involves only the threshold question of whether the court should enforce an individual arbitration agreement. The issue of preclusion should await the completion of the arbitration. . . .
>
> *Buell* similarly dealt with a different issue. . . . That case resolved whether the Railway Labor Act ("RLA") provided the exclusive remedy for the plaintiff's [Federal Employers Liability Act ("FELA")] claim. The Court held that the RLA procedures were not the plaintiff's exclusive remedy. The Court noted that FELA provided the plaintiff with a damages claim for "negligent conduct that is independent of the employer's obligations under its collective bargaining agreements. . . ." 480 U.S. at 565. The "minor dispute" provisions, on the other hand, did not address the damages issue presented by the plaintiff's FELA claim. Since the RLA did not provide the means to resolve the plaintiff's FELA claim, the Court found no conflict between the RLA and FELA warranting a holding that the RLA repealed any part of the FELA.[34]

Hindsight always provides 20–20 vision, but it was unlikely that the *Gilmer* Court, having granted a decision to resolve the tension between these two line of cases, would have opted to have the *Gardner–Denver*

---

[33] 480 U.S. 557, 564–65 (1987) (quoting *Barrentine v. Arkansas–Best Freight System*, 450 U.S. 728, 737 (1981)).

[34] Br. for Respondent 35–37 (citations omitted; emphasis in original).

line simply supersede the FAA line in cases involving statutory claims by employees. A good part of the reasoning in the *Gardner–Denver* line involved the limited authority of the labor arbitrator, deciding disputes arising under a collective bargaining agreement, to address individual statutory claims of employees, and reflected skepticism about the competence of arbitrators generally to address statutory issues. The Court in the FAA context had flatly repudiated this skepticism, first announced by the Court in its 1953 ruling *Wilko v. Swan*,[35] over a strong dissent by Justice Felix Frankfurter,[36] even to the point of overruling *Wilko* itself in the 1989 *Rodriguez* decision.[37]

In any event, we know that Justice White's opinion for the Court in *Gilmer* largely adopted the approach offered by Interstate's counsel for distinguishing the *Gardner-Denver* and its progeny. These were arbitration cases under collective bargaining agreements where "we stressed that an employee's contractual rights under a collective-bargaining agreement are distinct from an employee's statutory Title VII rights"; where "[w]e also noted that a labor arbitrator has authority only to resolve questions of contractual rights"; where "[w]e further expressed concern that in the collective-bargaining arbitration, 'the interests of the individual employee may be subordinated to the collective interests of all employees in the bargaining unit'"; and which "involved the quite different issue of whether arbitration of contract-based claims precluded subsequent judicial resolution of statutory claims."[38]

Gilmer's counsel tried to argue that the *Gardner-Denver* line of cases was the one applicable to statutory claims, whereas the FAA

---

[35] 346 U.S. 427 (1953).

[36] *Id.* at 439 ff.

[37] Justice Kennedy's opinion for the *Rodriguez* Court states in relevant part: "The Court's characterization of the arbitration process in *Wilko* is pervaded by what Judge Jerome Frank called 'the old judicial hostility to arbitration.' That view has been steadily eroded over the years, beginning in the lower courts. The erosion intensified in our most recent decisions upholding agreements to arbitrate federal claims under the Securities Exchange Act of 1934, under the Racketeer Influenced and Corrupt Organizations (RICO) statutes, and under the antitrust laws.... To the extent that *Wilko* rested on suspicion of arbitration as a method of weakening the protections afforded in the substantive law to would-be complainants, it has fallen far out of step with our current strong endorsement of the federal statutes favoring this method of resolving disputes." 490 U.S. at 480–81 (citations omitted).

[38] These quotations are taken from Part IV of Justice White's opinion for the Court. 500 U.S. at 33–35. The Court later pried open even the *Gardner-Denver* line of cases. In *Wright v. Universal Martime Service Corp.*, 525 U.S. 70 (1998), while holding that the presumption of arbitrability under collective bargaining agreements did not apply to statutory as opposed to contractual claims of employees, it suggested that unions might be able to negotiate express waivers of the right of represented employees to go to court to pursue their individual statutory rights.

decisions involved "commercial" agreements by businessmen, but he had obvious difficulty, ultimately resting his cause on the absence of a knowing waiver of Gilmer's statutory rights:

> QUESTION: What about other kinds of rights? Is it all statutory rights that are not covered by the Arbitration Act, or what? What is your position?
>
> MR. ALLRED: Well, . . . as I read the cases, Your Honor, it's those cases in which the—when the Congress has passed laws protecting employees with minimum statutory standards, minimum rights, like—
>
> QUESTION: But just employees? Nobody else? What about the Sherman Act, for example, a dispute about whether there has been a violation of the Sherman Act? Two businessmen—
>
> MR. ALLRED: Well, that's covered by the law—by the FAA. If the two businessmen have agreed to arbitrate, then it's therefore enforceable.
>
> QUESTION: But that's a public policy. People shouldn't be able to get out of that any easier than they get out of employment discrimination. I guess. Should they?
>
> MR. ALLRED: Well, what the—they agreed to arbitrate those cases.
>
> QUESTION: Your client agreed here.
>
> MR. ALLRED: Well, . . . he agreed, in my judgment, to arbitrate disputes with respect to the New York Stock Exchange rules, with respect to things of that nature, but not his civil rights. And I just don't think . . . that was a knowing waiver.[39]

Gilmer could not easily argue that he had not knowingly agreed to arbitration—in view of his having signed the U–4 and his extensive prior experience in the securities industry. Rather, the contention was that there was no specific agreement to arbitrate future statutory claims. Although this "knowing waiver" argument would be later picked up in post-*Gilmer* decisions in the Ninth Circuit,[40] it was not briefed as a discrete argument in the *Gilmer* case, and in any event would have been difficult to square with *Mitsubishi*, where the Court had flatly rejected the position that because a claimant "falls within the class for whose benefit the federal and local antitrust laws and dealers' Acts were passed, but the arbitration clause at issue does not mention these

---

[39] Transcript of Oral Argument at *22–23, *Gilmer*, 500 U.S. 20 (No. 90–18), 1991 WL 636282 (hereafter "Oral Argument").

[40] *See infra* text accompanying note 57 & note 76.

statutes or statutes in general, the clause cannot be read to contemplate arbitration of these claims."[41]

The task for Gilmer's counsel was to develop an argument that either the FAA did not apply to Gilmer's situation or that the ADEA's regulatory and remedial scheme was so inconsistent with arbitration that the Court should find an implied exclusion from the FAA's reach for ADEA claims. As to the former, there were two conceivable arguments for the FAA's non-applicability: (1) Gilmer's employment with Interstate did not "involv[e] commerce" within the meaning of § 2, the coverage provision of the FAA; and (2) Gilmer's U–4 agreement to arbitrate was a "contract of employment" within the meaning of § 1's exclusionary clause. Unfortunately, for Gilmer, neither argument had been raised below or even briefed by his counsel.

The coverage argument under § 2 could have taken one of two forms. The broader one—that an employment contract could never "evidenc[e] a transaction involving commerce"[42]—would be difficult, though not impossible, to sustain in light of the presence of the exclusionary clause in § 1; one would have to argue that Congress inserted the exclusion out of an abundance of caution that the FAA might be misconstrued to reach employment contracts at all. (On this score, see Justice Souter's dissent in *Circuit City Stores, Inc. v. Adams*.[43]) The narrower argument would be that this particular employment contract did not evidence such a transaction; however, since Gilmer's job involved managing the sale of mutual funds over interstate exchanges, this point would have been difficult to sustain on the particular facts of the case. Either version of the argument, moreover, would seem to require overruling *Perry v. Thomas*. The Court later in *Allied-Bruce Terminix Cos. v. Dobson*[44] would reject any narrowing potential in § 2, holding that Congress intended the coverage of the FAA to be coextensive with Congress's power to legislate under the Commerce Clause.

---

[41] 473 U.S. at 625. Justice Blackmun's opinion responds in part: "Just last Term in *Southland Corp., supra,* where we held that § 2 of the [FAA] declared a national policy applicable equally in state as well as federal courts, we construed an arbitration clause to encompass the dispute at issue without pausing at the source in a state statute of the rights asserted by the parties resisting arbitration." *Id.* at 627.

[42] In *Bernhardt v. Polygraphic Co. of America*, 350 U.S. 198, 200, 201 n.3 (1956), its first brush with the FAA, the Court seemed to say that an employment contract did not "evidence 'a transaction involving commerce' within the meaning of § 2 of the Act," and therefore did not "reach the further question whether in any event petitioner would be included in 'any other class of workers' within the exceptions of § 1 of the Act." This passage is relied upon by Justice Stevens, dissenting in *Circuit City Stores, Inc. v. Adams,* 532 U.S. 105, 128 (2001). The *Circuit City* majority did not address *Bernhardt.*

[43] 532 U.S. at 140.

[44] 513 U.S. 265 (1995).

THE FAILURE TO RAISE AND PRESERVE THE § 1 ISSUE

The better prospect for Gilmer was to argue that his arbitration agreement was part of an application process amounting to a "contract of employment" within the scope of the § 1 exclusion for "contracts of employment of seamen, railroad employees, or any other class of workers engaged in foreign or interstate commerce." Remarkably, until the *amicus* filings in this case, plaintiff lawyers appear not to have read closely the text of the FAA; the § 1 argument is glaring by its absence in all of the leading pre-*Gilmer* lower court decisions involving individual employee claims. And even though *amici* AFL–CIO and others had briefed the point, Gilmer's counsel had some difficulty presenting the argument, which required a theory of the relationship between "involving" commerce under the coverage provision and "engaged in" commerce under the exclusion:

QUESTION: What would be your submission as to why your client was engaged in interstate commerce?

MR. ALLRED: . . . Well, that he was managing a group of people that bought and—that sold mutual funds . . .

QUESTION: In 1925 do you think he would have been held to have been involved in interstate commerce?

MR. ALLRED: I don't know the answer to that, Your Honor.

QUESTION: Maybe his actions would have—might affect interstate commerce—maybe Congress these days has the power to regulate what he's doing. But does that mean in 1925 he was engaged in—

MR. ALLRED: Well, now, if you looked at it from a narrow standpoint that engaged meant you had to be physically engaged, you had to be driving a bus or a truck or in the transportation industry, I would agree with you. But I don't—but it seems to me that if you were in the New York Stock Exchange and you were selling General Motors stock that emanated from Detroit, that that broker, that the people in the investment banking industry were engaged in commerce.

QUESTION: But there was no evidence taken in the trial court on this point?

MR. ALLRED: That is correct.

QUESTION: Because you hadn't raised it?

MR. ALLRED: That is correct, Your Honor. We just—we read the Gardner–Denver line of cases and saw that this Court has held that whenever employment discrimination is at issue, that arbitration is inappropriate. . . .[45]

Allred ultimately gets to the point:

> QUESTION: . . . Now, why would Congress say involving commerce in section 2, and say engaged in commerce in section 1, without intending a distinction between the two?
>
> MR. ALLRED: Well, Your Honor, there's a good answer to that—
>
> QUESTION: I hope so.
>
> MR. ALLRED: in one of the briefs. The—but I think you can't, on the one hand, have the situation that says that you are going to allow transactions in commerce to be subjected to compulsory arbitration, and then eliminate those who are engaged in same activity. It seems to me that the—that you have to read both of those together. . . .

Interstate's lawyer also had difficulty navigating the argument:

> QUESTION: He is a person engaged in commerce?
>
> MR. SPEARS: He is not only—he—his contract, his agreement to be bound by the arbitration and all the other rules of the Exchange is the contract involved in the transaction involving commerce.
>
> QUESTION: And it involves commerce because he then becomes a person engaged in commerce, as I understand it[?]
>
> MR. SPEARS: If he relates to a transaction involving commerce.
>
> QUESTION: Which then brings him squarely within the language of section 1.
>
> MR. SPEARS: Well, section 2.
>
> QUESTION: And section 1.
>
> MR. SPEARS: Well, with regard to that, I think, the difference in the language that was noted intends a broad application of section 2, and a narrow, restrictive application of section 1. . . .
>
> QUESTION: Yeah, but not the way you just described it and explained it to me. . . . You want to change your explanation, I guess[?]
>
> MR. SPEARS: Well, I guess I'll have to. . . .

DODGING THE § 1 ISSUE

Should the Court have reached the § 1 issue? It is always a difficult enterprise for the Court to reach out and decide a question that was not properly framed below, and the above colloquy may have left an impres-

---

[45] Oral Argument *10–11.

sion with a few of the Justices that some factual issues remained unexplored or that, perhaps, these lawyers were not fully prepared to engage the issue. Moreover, as a formal matter, as counsel for Interstate reminded the Court, Gilmer's arbitration agreement was not part of an employment contract as such:

> QUESTION: Well, I thought you were relying on the arbitration clause in the employment agreement. And I think you are now telling me you're not.

> MR. SPEARS: The arbitration clause is in his registration agreement. There is no separate written employment agreement. . . .

This gambit may have won the case for Interstate, for it gave the Justices a way of deciding the case without at that point entering the thicket of the § 1 issue. Thus, Justice White writes in the opening footnote of the opinion for the Court:

> The FAA requires that the arbitration agreement being enforced be in writing. See 9 U.S.C. §§ 2, 3. The record before us does not show, and the parties do not contend, that Gilmer's employment agreement with Interstate contained a written arbitration clause. Rather, the arbitration clause at issue is a contract with the securities exchanges, not with Interstate. The lower courts addressing the issue uniformly have concluded that the exclusionary clause in § 1 of the FAA is inapplicable to arbitration clauses contained in such registration applications. We implicitly assumed as much in *Perry v. Thomas*, 482 U.S. 483 (1987), where we held that the FAA required a former employee of a securities firm to arbitrate his statutory wage claim against his former employer, pursuant to an arbitration clause in his registration application. Unlike the dissent, we choose to follow the plain language of the FAA and the weight of authority, and we therefore hold that § 1's exclusionary clause does not apply to Gilmer's arbitration agreement. Consequently, we leave for another day the issue raised by *amici curiae*.

The Court was being somewhat formalistic and was hardly following "the weight of authority".[46] Until this case, no lawyer had thought to suggest that the U–4 application process did not amount to a contract of employment. Yet, there was some logic to the position. Even though it should not make a difference for § 1 purposes that a group of employers have gotten together and required their employees to arbitrate employment disputes,[47] here the arbitration requirement is the product of the

---

[46] I criticized this reasoning in a postscript to a contemporaneous article that I was hoping, to no avail, would reach the Court in time. *See* Samuel Estreicher, *Arbitration of Employment Disputes Without Unions*, 66 Chi.-Kent L. Rev. 753 (1990) (author's note).

[47] *See* Samuel Estreicher, *Predispute Agreements to Arbitrate Statutory Employment Claims*, 72 N.Y.U. L. Rev. 1344, 1364 & n.66 (1997).

rules of the securities exchange, is part of a process that also includes customer complaints against securities firms and their registered representatives, and at least since 1975 has entailed active SEC oversight of the arbitration rules and procedures of the various exchanges (emphasized recently in the *McMahon* ruling[48]).

Would it have made a difference if the Court had decided the § 1 issue in *Gilmer*? Here, we enter the realm of sheer speculation. From the standpoint of the quality of briefing on the issue, the *amici* supporting Gilmer's position would seem to have been at a higher point on the learning curve (concerning the intricacies of the history of the § 1 exclusion) than the lawyer or *amici* supporting Interstate. Doctrinally, it may have been harder to argue against FAA enforcement of statutory employment claims in 2001 once the Court decided age bias claims were arbitrable at least in the securities industry context. The intervening decade permitted, as we shall see below, widespread improvements in employer-promulgated arbitration programs (prodded in part by court decisions and concerned organizations). It also yielded the decision in *Allied–Bruce Terminix*, which by adopting a broad view of the coverage provision facilitated the argument, later found persuasive in *Circuit City Stores, Inc. v. Adams*, that Congress intended a narrower scope for the § 1 exclusion. Also, it is at least arguable that what has come to be a dominant "textualist" view of statutory interpretation among the Justices was not as fully developed in 1991 as it would later become.

Arguments Available to Gilmer's Counsel

In any event, shorn of the § 1 exclusion, Gilmer's counsel was left with one remaining argument: Congress intended in the ADEA to guarantee a right of action in the courts before a jury on disputed questions of fact that could not be bargained away in private agreements. This was a difficult argument to make—given the stream of precedent, which rejected the equation of arbitration with a waiver of substantive rights, and essentially placed the burden on the party opposing arbitration to show a Congressional intention to preclude waiver of a judicial forum for ADEA claims, "discoverable in the text of the ADEA, its legislative history, or an 'inherent conflict between arbitration and the ADEA's underlying purposes.'"[49] There was no obvious textual[50] or legislative history[51] hook for such a contention. What

---

[48] *See* 481 U.S at 233–34.

[49] *Gilmer*, 500 U.S. at 26.

[50] In a footnote appended to a discussion of post-dispute settlement agreements, *id.* at 29 & n.3, the Court noted that Congress in the Older Workers Benefit Protection Act (OWBPA), Pub. L. 101–433, 104 Stat. 978, amended the ADEA to provide, in § 7(f)(1)(C), 29 U.S.C. § 626(f)(1), that "an individual may not waive any right or claim under this

remained was an "inherent conflict" argument that was unsustainable in view of prior decisions (notably, *Mitsubishi*, *McMahon*, *Rodriguez* and *Perry*) compelling arbitration of claims arising under statutes, like the ADEA, with an agency enforcement role, the availability of a jury trial, exemplary damages to deter violations, limited judicial review, and the like.

Gilmer's counsel did argue that securities industry panels were likely to be biased and that the procedures were likely to be inadequate to address statutory claims. This contention was bereft entirely of support in the record. Moreover, a facial challenge was rendered all the more difficult by amendments to NYSE arbitration rules (highlighted by counsel for Interstate and its supporting *amici*) to provide for greater involvement of arbitrators from outside the industry, expanded discovery, and written arbitration awards that would be publicly available.[52]

Ultimately, Gilmer's counsel was left with the contention that securities industry employees faced "unequal bargaining power" in dealing with their employers. Noting that its earlier decisions involving arbitration of customer claims (in *McMahon* and *Rodriguez*) rejected similar assertions, the Court, per Justice White, answered: "Mere inequality of bargaining power ... is not a sufficient reason to hold that arbitration agreements are never enforceable in the employment context." A facial challenge was ruled out; but under Section 2 of the FAA, "courts should remain attuned to well-supported claims that the agreement to arbitrate resulted from the sort of fraud or overwhelming economic power that would provide grounds 'for the revocation of any contract.' " Reinforcing the point, Justice White observed: "There is no indication in this case, however, that Gilmer, an experienced businessman, was coerced or defrauded into agreeing to the arbitration clause in his registration application.[53] As with the claimed procedural inadequacies discussed above, this claim of unequal bargaining power is best left for resolution in specific cases."

---

unless the waiver is knowing and voluntary." Although the provision speaks in terms of "any right," its context in the statute makes clear that it is referring to a post-dispute waiver of substantive rights, not what the *Gilmer* Court would consider a procedural right to pursue a claim in court as opposed to arbitration. This is the unanimous reading of the post-*Gilmer* decisions in the lower courts. *See Rosenberg v. Merrill Lynch, Pierce, Fenner & Smith*, 170 F.3d 1, 12–14 (1st Cir. 1999); *Seus v. John Nuveen & Inc.*, 146 F.3d 175, 181–82 (3d Cir. 1998); *Williams v. Cigna Fin. Advisors, Inc.*, 56 F.3d 656, 660–61 (5th Cir. 1995) (all interpreting OWBPA not to affect the *Gilmer* holding).

[51] I discuss below an aspect of the legislative history concerning the Civil Rights Act of 1991, which amended both the ADEA and Title VII. *See infra* text accompanying note 78.

[52] *See Gilmer*, 500 U.S. at 30–32; Br. for Respondent 17–26; Br. of *Amicus Curiae* Securities Industry Association in Support of the Respondent, No. 90–18, O.T. 1990.

[53] Gilmer conceded no fraud was involved. *See* Oral Argument at *16.

The Immediate Impact of Gilmer

What was the upshot of the decision for Robert Gilmer? He submitted his claim to a NYSE arbitration panel and recovered $250,000, approximately two years' compensation.[54] His lawyer says he did not work again because he was "devastated" by his termination from Interstate.

In the larger community, *Gilmer* generated extensive critical commentary from academics and the plaintiff bar. Although supportive of mediation, the EEOC issued a policy statement opposing enforcement of pre-dispute employment arbitration agreements.[55] A dominant theme of critics was that pre-dispute arbitration agreements extracted as a condition of employment are not consensual, but really are a modern-day "yellow dog" contract forcing hungry workers to sell their rights to get or keep a job.[56] As San Francisco's Cliff Palefsky, a prominent plaintiff lawyer, put it, "an intellectual and legal scandal ... is occurring in broad daylight."[57]

The imagery is vivid but does not quite fit the facts. What was wrong with "yellow dog" contracts in our earlier labor history was that they were used by employers as purely strategic devices to blunt unionization. These agreements served no interest of employers other than that of thwarting the associational freedom of their employees. Employers sought by these clauses to lay a predicate for obtaining injunctions against labor unions who, by the mere act of attempting even peacefully to organize their workforce, could be found to have engaged in tortious inducement of breach of contract. Once public policy evolved in support

---

[54] John Allred, his counsel, claims that Gilmer should have recovered $1.8 million but that the arbitrators (it was a tripartite panel) were reluctant to award liquidated damages for a "willful" violation under ADEA, 29 U.S.C. § 626(b). Telephone interview with John T. Allred (Aug. 24, 2005).

[55] *See* EEOC, *Policy Statement on Mandatory Binding Arbitration of Employment Discrimination Disputes as a Condition of Employment* (EEOC Notice 915.002, 1997), reprinted in *Daily Lab. Rep. (BNA)*, No. 133, July 11, 1997, E–4 ff. The Government also filed a brief in support of the respondent in *Circuit City Stores, Inc. v. Adams. See* Br. for the United States as Amicus Curiae Supporting Respondent, in *Circuit City*, 532 U.S. 105 (No. 99–1379).

[56] For commentary in this vein, *see, e.g.*, Judith P. Vladeck, *'Yellow Dog Contracts' Revisited*, N.Y.L.J. July 24, 1995, p.7, col. 2; Katherine Van Wezel Stone, *Mandatory Arbitration of Individual Employment Rights: The Yellow Dog Contract of the 1990s*, 73 Den. U. L. Rev. 1017 (1996). The most coherent statement of this view is Joseph R. Grodin, *Arbitration of Employment Discrimination Claims: Doctrine and Policy in the Wake of Gilmer*, 14 Hofstra Lab.L.J. 1, 29 (1996).

[57] Joyce E. Culter, *Arbitration: Suits Challenging Mandatory Arbitration as Depriving Employees of their Rights*, Daily Lab. Rep. (BNA), Mar. 3, 1995, available in LEXIS, BNA Library, DLABRT File (quoting Cliff Palefksy of McGuinn, Hillsman & Palefsky).

of the right of workers to form independent organizations—or, as of the enactment of the Norris–LaGuardia Act of 1932, 29 U.S.C. §§ 101–15, the right at least to be free of court injunctions in the peaceful pursuit of organizing objectives—these clauses were properly deemed to serve no legitimate interest of employers. By contrast, pre-dispute arbitration, if properly designed, can offer ex ante advantages for both parties to the contract.[58]

There were also developments supportive of employment arbitration. While not going so far as to endorse agreements obtained as a condition of employment, President Clinton's Dunlop Commission on the Future of Worker–Management Relations issued a report recommending essential safeguards for arbitration.[59] In 1994, the American Bar Association in conjunction with leading employer, plaintiff and union representatives developed a "Due Process Protocol for Mediation and Arbitration of Statutory Employment Disputes," which has been very influential. Effective June 1, 1996, the American Arbitration Association (AAA) issued new national rules for the resolution of employment disputes adhering to the Due Process Protocol.[60] JAMS, another leading ADR services provider, followed suit with a "minimum set of procedures or standards of procedural fairness".[61] These safeguards (drawing largely from the Dunlop Commission report) include:

- No restriction on the right to file charges with the appropriate administrative agencies;

- A reasonable place for the holding of the arbitration[62];

- A competent arbitrator who knows the laws in question;

- A fair and simple method for exchange of information;

---

[58] See Samuel Estreicher, *Saturns for Rickshaws: The Stakes in the Debate over Predispute Employment Arbitration Agreements*, 16 Ohio St. J. on Disp. Res. 559 (2001); David Sherwyn, Samuel Estreicher & Michael Heise, *Assessing the Case for Employment Arbitration: A New Path for Empirical Research*, 57 Stan. L. Rev. 1557 (2005).

[59] See U.S. Depts. of Commerce and Labor, Commission on the Future of Worker–Management Relations, *Report and Recommendations* 31 (Dec. 1994). For the author's testimony before the Dunlop Commission, see "Statement by Professor Samuel Estreicher to the Commission on the Future of Worker–Management Relations Panel on Private Dispute Resolution Alternatives," reprinted in Daily Lab. Rep. (BNA), Sept. 30, 1994, available in LEXIS, BNA Library, DLABRT File.

[60] American Arbitration Assn., National Rules for the Resolution of Employment Disputes (initially promulgated in 1996), available at www.adr.org.

[61] J.A.M.S./Endispute Arbitration Policy, in 9A Lab. Rel. Rep. (BNA), Mar. 26, 1996, at 534:521, current version of rules available at www.jams.org.

[62] This item is not mentioned in the Dunlop report. See Samuel Estreicher, *Predispute Agreements to Arbitrate Statutory Employment Claims*, 72 N.Y.U. L. Rev. 1344, 1349, n.18.

- A fair method of cost sharing to ensure affordable access to the system for all employees;

- The right to independent representation if sought by the employee;

- A range of remedies equal to those available through litigation;

- A written award explaining the arbitrator's rationale for the result; and

- Limited judicial review sufficient to ensure that the result is consistent with applicable law.[63]

Many large employers have followed these guidelines in the design of their employment arbitration programs.[64]

POST-*GILMER* ISSUES IN THE COURTS

On the litigation front, the scope of the § 1 exclusion was the most important open question after *Gilmer*. Ten years later, the Court in *Circuit City Stores, Inc. v. Adams* held (5–4) that § 1's exclusion of "contracts of employment of contracts of seamen, railroad employee, or any other class of workers engaged in foreign or interstate commerce" extended to the enumerated classes of employees and others similarly directly engaged in interstate commerce, i.e., employees in the transportation industry. Justice Kennedy's opinion reasoned that since Congress used narrower language in the exclusion clause ("engaged in" in interstate commerce) than it used in the coverage provision (transactions "involving" interstate commerce), it intended a narrower exclusion limited to seamen and railroad employees for whom there was existing arbitration legislation, with a catch-all ("any other class of workers") to cover other transportation workers for whom similar legislation would (and in the case of airline workers, did) follow.[65] Justices Stevens and Souter penned strong dissents, taking issue with the majority's textual

---

[63] " '[A]lthough judicial scrutiny of arbitration awards necessarily is limited, such review is sufficient to ensure that arbitrators comply with the requirements of the statute' at issue." *Gilmer*, 500 U.S. at 32 n.4 (quoting *McMahon*, 482 U.S. at 232). *See generally*, Aleta G. Estreicher, *Judicial Review of Arbitration Awards Resolving Statutory Claims*, in *Alternative Dispute Resolution in the Employment Arena: Proc. NYU 53d Ann. Conf. on Labor*, ch. 28 (Samuel Estreicher & David Sherwyn eds. 2004).

[64] *See, e.g.*, Br. of Credit Suisse First Boston as *Amicus Curiae* in Support of Petitioner at 1–5, in *Circuit City*, 532 U.S. 105 (No. 99–1379); William L. Bedman, *Alternative Dispute Resolution: The Haliburton Experience*, ch. 3 in *Alternative Dispute Resolution in the Employment Arena*; Eric Taussig, *Predispute Arbitration Agreements: The Philip Morris Program*, ch. 4 in *id.*; Elizabeth W. Millard, *Credit Suisse First Boston Employment Dispute Program*, ch. 5 in *id.*; and Eugence Clark, *The Citigroup Corporate and Investment Bank's Dispute Resolution Procedure*, ch. 6 in *id.*

[65] *See Circuit City*, 532 U.S. at 121.

reading and failure fully to take account of the legislative history of the provision.[66]

Aside from the § 1 issue, the plaintiff bar leveled a number of challenges to pre-dispute employment arbitration. On two issues, some, short-lived success was achieved in the Ninth Circuit. The first was presaged by Gilmer's argument that there cannot be a "knowing" waiver of the right to a judicial forum unless the employee is told he is giving up his rights under specified statutes prior to his execution of the agreement. The argument enjoyed support for a time in cases involving securities brokers because the Form U–4 had not stated expressly that arbitration would be required of employment claims.[67] After the form was amended to cure this problem, this avenue of challenge largely closed up, although clear notice to the employee that he is giving up the right to go to a jury is still required by lower court decisions.[68]

A second approach was to argue that Title VII of the Civil Rights Act of 1964 was not subject to *Gilmer* because in 1991 amendments Congress inserted legislative history stating that it opposed mandatory arbitration of Title VII claims.[69] This argument was problematic because

---

[66] This is not the place to rehearse this debate. Compare, e.g., Matthew Finkin, *"Workers' Contracts' Under the United States Arbitration Act: An Essay in Historical Clarification,"* 17 Berkeley J. Emp. & Lab. L. 282 (1996), with Samuel Estreicher, *Predispute Agreements to Arbitrate Statutory Employment Claims*, 72 N.Y.U. L. Rev. 1344, 1365–71.

[67] The Ninth Circuit in *Prudential Ins. Co. of Am. v. Lai*, 42 F.3d 1299 (9th Cir. 1994), held that a waiver of the judicial forum must be knowing and voluntary, and because the rules of the National Association of Securities Dealers (NASD) at the time did not expressly refer to arbitration of employment claims there was no knowing waiver in that case. The issue in the NASD context was largely mooted when on October 1, 1993, the SEC amended its NASD Code to provide "for the arbitration of any dispute, claim or controversy arising out of or in connection with the business of any member of [NASD] or arising out of the employment or termination of employment of associated person(s) with any member." *See* Uniform Application for Securities Industry Registration or Transfer, Blue *Sky Rep. (CCH)*, ¶ 5118 (1996); *Williams v. Cigna Financial Advisors, Inc.*, 56 F.3d 656, 658 (5th Cir. 1995) (quoting amended NASD rule); *Kuehner v. Dickinson & Co.*, 84 F.3d 316, 320–21 (9th Cir. 1996) (enforcing arbitration under the new rule); cf. *Renteria v. Prudential Ins. Co. of Am.*, 113 F.3d 1104, 1106–08 (9th Cir. 1997) (registered representative did not make a "knowing waiver" because she signed the U–4 prior to the 1993 amendment even though the form required plaintiff to arbitrate all disputes listed in the NASD Code "as may be amended from time to time").

[68] *See, e.g.*, *Campbell v. General Dynamics Government Systems Corp.*, 407 F.3d 546 (1st Cir. 2005).

[69] In explaining § 118 of the Civil Rights Act of 1991, the Conference Report, S. Conf. Rep. No. 2104, 101st Cong., 2d Sess., reprinted in 136 Cong. Rec. H8050 (daily ed. Sept. 26, 1990), states (pre-*Gilmer*):

The Conferees emphasize ... that the use of alternative dispute resolution mechanisms is intended to supplement, not supplant, the remedies provided by Title VII.

the language actually enacted, § 118 of the Civil Rights Act of 1991, was by its terms supportive of arbitration:

> Where appropriate and to the extent authorized by law, the use of alternative means of dispute resolution, including settlement negotiations, conciliation, facilitation, mediation, factfinding, minitrials, and arbitration, is encouraged to resolved disputes arising under the Acts or provisions of Federal law amended by this title.

In an *en banc* ruling in *EEOC v. Luce, Forward, Hamilton & Scripps*,[70] the Ninth Circuit ultimately abandoned its earlier view that *Gilmer* was inapplicable to Title VII claims, bringing it in line with the other circuits.

Several issues do remain unresolved. One is the issue of costs. Although arbitration may in general be a more informal, less costly means of resolving disputes than litigation, forum and arbitrator fees may create a significant hurdle for claimants of average income. Many companies have addressed this issue in their arbitration programs by either picking up these costs minus a nominal filing fee, or providing an employee benefit that absorbs those costs.[71] Some court rulings, like then Chief Judge Harry Edwards of the D.C. Circuit's opinion in *Cole v. Burns Intl. Sec. Serv.*[72] have construed employer programs or the rules of arbitration organizations to similar effect. In *Green Tree Financial Corp. v. Randolph*,[73] involving a consumer dispute under the Truth in Lending Act,[74] the Supreme Court reversed a lower court's refusal to order arbitration:

Thus, for example, the Conferees believe that any agreement to submit disputed issues to arbitration, whether in the context of a collective bargaining agreement or in an employment context, does not preclude the affected person from seeking relief under the enforcement provisions of Title VII. This view is consistent with the Supreme Court's interpretation of Title VII in *Alexander v. Gardner–Denver*.... The Conferees do not intend this Section to be used to preclude rights and remedies that would otherwise be available.

In the debates over the 1991 law, some legislators were supportive of *Gilmer*, *see* 137 Cong. Rec. H9548 (daily ed. Nov. 7, 1991) (remarks of Rep. Hyde); *id.* at S15, 478 (daily ed. Oct. 30, 1991) (remarks of Sen. Dole); others were disapproving, *see id.* at H9530 (daily ed. Nov. 7, 1991) (remarks of Rep. Edwards).

[70] 345 F.3d 742 (9th Cir. 2003) (en banc).

[71] For a description of Brown & Root /Halliburton's program, see Samuel Estreicher, *Predispute Agreements to Arbitrate Statutory Employment Claims*, 72 N.Y.U. L. Rev. 1344, 1350 n.20.

[72] 105 F.3d 1465, 1483–85 (D.C. Cir. 1997).

[73] 531 U.S. 79 (2000).

[74] 15 U.S.C. § 1601.

It may well be that the existence of large arbitration costs could preclude a litigant such as Randolph from effectively vindicating her federal statutory rights in the arbitral forum. But the record does not show that Randolph will bear such costs.... The record reveals only the arbitration agreement's silence on the subject, and that fact alone is plainly insufficient to render it unenforceable....

... We have held that the party seeking to avoid arbitration bears the burden of establishing that Congress intended to preclude arbitration of the statutory claims at issue. See *Gilmer, supra....* Similarly, we believe that where, as here, a party seeks to invalidate an arbitration agreement on the ground that arbitration would be prohibitively expensive, that party bears the burden of showing the likelihood of such costs. Randolph did not meet that burden....[75]

A second open issue involves the availability of class actions. The Supreme Court has yet to decide whether an employee who has signed an otherwise valid pre-dispute arbitration agreement can serve as a named representative, or share in the recovery obtained, in a class action asserting statutory employment rights. It has ruled, however, that courts lack authority to compel class-wide arbitration of claims where the underlying agreement is silent on the question; rather, this is a matter to be decided in the first instance by the arbitrator.[76] Some employers have responded by expressly requiring employees to waive their right to bring a class action, whether in court or arbitration, and have run up against judicial resistance.[77]

A third open question concerns the role of generally applicable state law in voiding agreements for unconscionability or duress. It is clear from decisions like *Southland* that state laws that subject arbitration agreements to special requirements are preempted by the FAA. Under § 2 of the FAA, arbitration agreements must stand on the same footing as other agreements. However, they do not enjoy any different status than other agreements; they are "valid, irrevocable, and enforceable, save upon such grounds as exist at law or in equity for the revocation of any contract." Some courts, like the California Supreme Court, have seized upon this language to develop an active unconscionability jurisprudence to curb perceived employer overreaching in employment arbitration agreements.[78]

---

[75] 531 U.S. at 90–92.

[76] See *Green Tree Fin. Corp. v. Bazzle*, 539 U.S. 444 (2003).

[77] See, e.g., *Discover Bank v. Superior Court of Los Angeles*, 36 Cal. 4th 148 (Cal. 2005). The applicability of *Discover Bank* to employment arbitration is the subject of *Gentry v. Superior Court*, 135 P.3d 1 (petition for review granted—Calif. Sup. Ct. 2006).

[78] See, e.g., *Armendariz v. Foundation Health Psychcare Servs., Inc.*, 6 P.3d 669 (Cal. 2000) (holding that arbitration agreement lacking parallel promises was unconscionable absent reasonable justifications based on business realities).

Conclusion

The Court's decision in *Gilmer* was pivotal to these developments because it essentially changed the background assumption that discrimination and other statutory claims were impervious to private adjustment of procedures through contract. The Court held that the new pro-arbitration jurisprudence it was developing under the FAA applied with full force to statutory employment claims. The Court's path was eased by omissions of the lawyers involved, but whether the decision would have come out differently if the FAA's applicability to employment contracts had been developed below and properly preserved on appeal is anyone's guess. There is no question, however, that *Gilmer* has changed the way we think about the field and the way lawyers must proceed on behalf of their clients.

*

9

The Story of the Montana Wrongful Discharge from Employment Act: A Drama in 5 Acts

Andrew P. Morriss[*]

In 1987, the Montana legislature passed the Wrongful Discharge from Employment Act (WDEA or Act),[1] creating the first generally applicable good cause wrongful discharge standard for non-union employees in the United States. Although no state has yet followed Montana's lead, the WDEA both influenced the still-unenacted Model Employment Termination Act[2] (META) and generated enormous interest among legal commentators.

Montana is distinctive not only for being the first state to replace the at-will rule with a statute but also for being one of six states (California, the Dakotas, Georgia, Louisiana, and Montana) to have codified the at-will rule rather than adopting it through the common law. The story of the WDEA thus has its roots in an earlier statutory story. As a result, the evolution of Montana wrongful discharge law takes the state from statute to statute, with an intervening period of common law dominance. And the tale is one of competition between the courts and the legislature, over which institution will determine the law of employment, raising important general questions about the role of common law courts. In recounting the story of the WDEA we will take a look at the history of the statute as well as at the history of its predecessors. Finally, we will examine the impact of the WDEA on the practice of law in Montana and on discharged employees' claims, using statistics, to see if

[*] Thanks to Dean Gerald Korngold for research support, to Sam Estreicher and Gillian Lester for helpful edits, and to the Montana State Law Library for research assistance.

[1] Mont. Code Ann. § 39–2–901 et seq.

[2] *See* Leonard Bierman & Stuart A. Youngblood, *Interpreting Montana's Pathbreaking Wrongful Discharge from Employment Act: A Preliminary Analysis,* 53 Mont. L. Rev. 53, 53–54 & n. 5 (1992).

the statute has lived up to the claims made by its proponents and fears expressed by its opponents before its passage.

The story of Montana's employment law has five phases. In the first, employment termination claims in Montana were governed by Montana Code § 39–2–503, first enacted in 1895 as part of Montana's adoption of a comprehensive Civil Code modeled on the French Code Napoleon. For almost a hundred years, Montana employment law was built around a codified at-will rule, similar to other states' common law at-will rule.

The second phase began in January 1982 with the Montana Supreme Court's decision in *Gates v. Life Montana Insurance Co.*,[3] which recognized employers' liability for breach of an implied covenant of good faith and fair dealing in the wrongful discharge context. From 1982 to 1985, the Montana Supreme Court steadily broadened wrongful discharge claims in spite of the statutory at-will rule. In most cases, the court simply ignored Civil Code § 39–2–503. The effect was dramatic, however, as the court effectively transformed Montana from an at-will state to one in which virtually any discharge could be challenged in court. In particular, the court steadily increased the scope of the implied covenant theory until it could plausibly be claimed in nearly all wrongful discharge cases. Having created a wide-ranging wrongful discharge theory, however, the court pulled back slightly. Beginning in 1985, the Montana Supreme Court "became much less predictable" in wrongful discharge cases and began to intermittently reject employee claims.[4] Nonetheless, a number of substantial jury verdicts under these theories were upheld by the state supreme court during this time. To take just one example, in *Flanagan v. Prudential Federal Savings*[5] the court upheld an award of $1.3 million in punitive damages, out of a total $1.5 million award, for a bank's discharge of an assistant loan officer. By the end of the 1980s, the Montana court's decisions "left open the possibility of a legal challenge to almost any discharge,"[6] although whether any particular plaintiff would succeed was still open to question.

In response to employer concerns over wrongful discharge litigation,[7] the Montana legislature passed the WDEA in 1987. The governor signed the WDEA into law on May 11, 1987[8] and the new statute became

---

[3] 638 P.2d 1063 (Mont. 1982).

[4] LeRoy H. Schramm, *Montana Employment Law and the 1987 Wrongful Discharge from Employment Act: A New Order Begins*, 51 Mont. L. Rev. 94, 95 (1990).

[5] 720 P.2d 257 (Mont. 1986).

[6] Schramm, *New Order* at 104.

[7] *See* Alan Krueger, *The Evolution of Unjust Dismissal Legislation in the United States*, 44 Indus. & Lab. Rel. Rev. 644, 647–648 (1991); Schramm, *New Order* at 108–112.

[8] Schramm, *New Order* at 113.

effective on July 1, 1987, beginning the third phase of Montana employment law. The WDEA was immediately challenged by plaintiff lawyers
on state constitutional grounds, however, and the constitutionality of the
Act remained uncertain until a sharply divided state supreme court
upheld the act on June 29, 1989 in *Meech v. Hillhaven West, Inc.*[9] In
addition, during this time uncertainty over the common law of wrongful
discharge in Montana also increased, as the Montana Supreme Court
issued a series of opinions that displayed what one author termed "the
shifting standards that have bedeviled this area of law".[10] Further
"[f]rom 1982 to 1989 almost every major decision had, if not a vigorous
dissent, a concurrence expressing philosophical reservations."[11]

The fourth phase was the attempt by the plaintiffs' bar to overturn
the WDEA on constitutional grounds that led to the *Meech* decision. The
fifth, and so far final, act is the post-*Meech* experience under the statute.
The WDEA in practice has proven to be different from the WDEA in
theory, and in the discussion of this period of Montana's legal history
this chapter will review some empirical evidence gathered from case files
in the Montana courts about how the statute operates in practice.

Finally, there may be new acts in this continuing drama, for the
viability of *Meech*, and so the constitutionality of the WDEA, has been
called into question by later decisions involving the same constitutional
provisions, raising the possibility that Montana might return to a common law of wrongful discharge at some point in the future.

The story of the WDEA is thus not merely the story of the passage
of a single statute. Rather it is a drama that extends over more than 100
years, from the initial, statutory at-will rule, which was first drafted as
part of a 1862 law reform effort in New York before Montana even
existed as a separate jurisdiction, to the final repeal of the at-will statute
in 2001, fourteen years after the passage of the WDEA. It is a story that
raises fundamental questions about the roles of courts and legislatures,
about efforts at comprehensive legal reforms, and about the effectiveness
of legislation at accomplishing its goals. In short, the story of the WDEA
is a microcosm of the story of many of the larger issues in our legal
system.

Act One: The Civil Code At–Will Rule

The employment-at-will rule forms the starting point for indefinite
employment contracts in every state, except Montana after the passage

---

[9] *Meech v. Hillhaven West, Inc.*, 776 P.2d 488 (Mont. 1989).

[10] Schramm, *New Order*, at 103 (discussing problems with interpreting case law in the late 1980s).

[11] *Id.* at 107.

of the WDEA. In most states the rule is a common law rule.[12] In Montana, however, the at-will rule was first adopted as part of the Montana Civil Code in 1895.[13] The Montana Civil Code originated in a draft code prepared for New York by prominent nineteenth century lawyer David Dudley Field. California (in 1872) and Dakota Territory (in 1866) also adopted statutory at-will rules when they adopted versions of the same Civil Code. The story of the Montana at-will rule, a crucial piece of the larger story of the WDEA, thus starts in New York in 1846, where a new state constitution mandated a codification commission.

CREATING THE CODIFIED RULE

New York's interest in codification in the 1840s grew out of decades of debate over the relative merits of statutory and common law. Jeremy Bentham, the English utilitarian philosopher, wrote to President James Madison in 1811 to offer to draft for the United States a "complete body of proposed law, in the form of Statute law, say in one word a Pannomion-including a succedaneum to that mass of foreign law, the yoke of which in the wordless, as well as boundless, and shapeless shape of common, alias unwritten law, remains still about your necks."[14] Madison, soon occupied with the War of 1812 during which the British burned the White House, politely declined in 1816 the offer to have an Englishman revise American law. Bentham also made his offer to various state governors, all of whom ultimately declined as well.

But Bentham's offer, together with American admiration for the Napoleonic Code, a set of laws which spread with French armies across Europe, and lingering hostility to the common law as an imported British institution, planted the seeds of codification in American soil early in the nation's history. The idea of replacing the common law with a civil code was taken seriously enough that Massachusetts commissioned a study of the possibility in the 1830s. The result was a report, authored principally by famed jurist Joseph Story, which concluded that

---

[12] An extended discussion of the adoption of the at-will rule in American jurisdictions is available at Andrew P. Morriss, *Exploding Myths: An Empirical and Economic Reassessment of the Rise of Employment At–Will*, 59 Missouri L. Rev. 679 (1994).

[13] A detailed history of the history of the Montana codification movement is available in Andrew P. Morriss, *"This State Will Soon Have Plenty of Laws"—Lessons from One Hundred Years of Codification in Montana*, 56 Mont. L. Rev. 359 (1995). The University of Montana sponsored a debate over repealing the Civil Code on the 105th anniversary of the Code, which was published as Andrew P. Morriss, Scott J. Burnham & James C. Nelson, *Debating the Field Civil Code 105 Years Late*, 61 Montana L. Rev. 371 (2000). For information on the nineteenth century codification movement generally, see Andrew P. Morriss, *Codification and Right Answers*, 74 Chi.-Kent L. Rev. 355 (1999).

[14] Letter to James Madison (Oct. 30, 1811), in 8 The Correspondence of Jeremy Bentham 182 (Timothy L.S. Sprigge ed., 1988).

while codification was possible in some areas of the law the time was not right for a comprehensive effort.[15]

The idea of codification continued to be popular, in part because it resonated with Jacksonian concerns over the legitimacy of judge-made law. David Dudley Field, then a young lawyer in New York state and a prominent Jacksonian Democrat, picked up the codification torch and lobbied relentlessly for a code commission in New York. (Field went on to become one of the most famous, and most financially successful, lawyers in nineteenth century America, while gaining notoriety through his representation of controversial clients such as New York political machine leader "Boss" Tweed and financier Jay Gould.)

Field succeeded in gaining the inclusion of a provision establishing a code commission in the 1846 New York constitution, although he failed to get himself appointed to the resulting body. It may be that Field's zeal for codification kept him from the commission; in any event, lacking his enthusiasm, the commission produced little in its first decade. Field occupied himself with rewriting New York's procedure rules in the interim, creating a Code of Civil Procedure that influenced many later procedural reforms, including the Federal Rules of Civil Procedure. Finally succeeding in gaining appointment to the commission in 1857, Field then produced, along with two fellow commissioners, drafts of a Civil Code (1862), a Political Code (1859), and a Penal Code (1864). After collecting comments on each, the commissioners published final drafts a few years later.

Critically for our story, both the 1862 draft Civil Code and the 1865 final proposed Civil Code included at-will provisions. Section 830 of the 1862 draft provided that "An employment having no specified term may be terminated at the will of either party on notice to the other." The 1865 final draft changed this language, now renumbered as section 1029, slightly to "An employment having no specified term may be terminated by either party, on notice to the other, except where otherwise provided by this title." The 1865 draft also included two new related sections, which created presumed terms for particular employments: Under section 1035, "a servant" was "presumed to have been hired for such length of time as the parties adopt for the estimation of wages. A hiring at a yearly rate is presumed to be for one year; a hiring at a daily rate, for one day; a hiring by piece work, for no specified term." Under section 1036, domestic servants were presumed hired by the month, clerks or "other servant not merely mechanical, or agricultural" were presumed hired by the year, and other servants "for no specified term."

---

[15] Joseph Story et al., Codification of the Common Law, in The Miscellaneous Writings of Joseph Story 698, 734 (William W. Story ed., 1852).

New York did not embrace Field's proposals. Indeed, his drafts languished there until the 1870s, when the state came very close to adopting the proposed codes on several occasions (a part of the story to which we will return to shortly). The drafts circulated widely, however, and found almost immediate favor in the newly formed Dakota Territory (from which present day North and South Dakota were later created). The Dakota Territorial Supreme Court judges were "favorably impressed by the codes," and, so, "the bench and bar of the territory united upon recommending" repeal of the existing laws adopted in 1862 and adoption of the New York drafts in their place.[16] Perhaps most amazingly, the Dakota Territorial Legislature barely altered the draft beyond substituting the words "territory" and "Dakota" for the words "state" and "New York". The employment contract provisions in particular did not change. The appeal to frontier judges of a comprehensive law drafted for New York may have had more to do with the convenience of a single volume of laws that could be carried with them as they road circuit than the appropriateness of the text. Nonetheless, Dakota Territory found itself with a comprehensive civil code in 1866, complete with a statutory at-will rule.

Field's drafts also found favor in California a few years later, where Stephen Field, David's brother, had made his fortune in the Gold Rush and served as a state Supreme Court Justice before being appointed to the United States Supreme Court in 1863. After a lengthy and at times acrimonious review process, California adopted a heavily revised version of Field's draft Civil Code in 1872. With respect to employment law, section 1999 provided "An employment having no specified term may be terminated at the will of either party, on notice to the other, except where otherwise provided by this Title." California sections 2010–11 provided the cross-references: section 2010 copied the New York draft on presumed terms and section 2011 expanded the monthly term presumption to cover all "servants" rather than only domestic servants and deleted the specific terms presumed for other categories of employees.

There was some additional activity surrounding Field's drafts in New York; they passed both houses of the state legislature twice and individual houses several times during the late 1870s and 1880s. The story of the Field Codes in New York through the 1880s is itself complex and we can only briefly describe it here. In 1876, Field became embroiled in a dispute with a procedure revision commission, chaired by Montgomery Throop, another prominent lawyer, which had proposed a complete overhaul of the procedure code drafted earlier by Field. There are a number of explanations for Field's opposition to the Throop revisions;

---

[16] 1 George W. Kingsbury, History of Dakota Territory: South Dakota, Its History and Its People 430 (George Martin Smith ed., 1915).

some contemporaries suggested that the most likely was that the code of civil procedure would henceforth likely be called the Throop Code rather than the Field Code. Whatever the rationale, with roughly half the Throop revisions passed by the legislature, Field managed to block progress on the remainder through his allies in Albany. To persuade Field to lift his opposition, legislative leaders offered him a deal: agree to the procedure revisions and they would support passage of the other codes, including the Civil Code. Both houses of the New York legislature then quickly passed both the codes and the Throop revisions, only to have the governor veto the civil code bill to allow further study of such a radical change. As James C. Carter, a leading code opponent in New York and one of the top lawyers in the United States, put it: "Never was the executive veto more beneficently employed; but it has only 'scotched the snake, not killed it.' "[17] Field fought on and the code came up almost annually thereafter for more than a decade. Code opponents organized around the Association of the Bar of the City of New York to fight Field's efforts and ultimately succeeded in preventing New York from adopting it.

There was also renewed activity in Dakota Territory, where the legislature enacted a revised code, based on California's version, in 1877. Importantly for employment law, in all the various versions in New York, which were regularly altered by Field to respond to his critics, the at-will provisions remained untouched. (Some critics suggested that Field would consent to strike all the substance of the code if only its cover with his name would be enacted.)[18] By the 1890s, three states (California and the two new Dakotas) had at-will rules based on codes and the rest had common law at will rules. (Louisiana and Georgia separately adopted codes during the nineteenth century; both included at-will rules.) Montana, granted statehood in 1889, took up the question along with the larger issue of codification, in 1895.

THE MONTANA CODE

The state was formed out of Idaho Territory in 1864 amid a gold rush in Bannack and Virginia City; its statutes were in a state of almost total confusion from the start. Partisan wrangling between the mostly Democratic Montana Territorial Legislature and the increasingly radical Republican Congress led to Congressional repeal of many of Montana's statutes in 1867; a bungled attempt to collect statutes in force created rather than resolved confusion in 1872; and the unavailability of printed copies of the laws made things even worse. By 1889, as the Territory prepared for statehood, the final Territorial Legislature called for codifi-

---

[17] James C. Carter, *The Proposed Codification of Our Common Law* 10 (1884).

[18] Carter, *Proposed Codification*, at 11–12.

cation in response to a petition from the Montana Bar Association and the governor to resolve the "chaotic condition" of the statutes.[19]

In 1892, the Montana code commission reported a variation on California's modification of Field's 1865 draft for New York. (They also reported Political, Civil Procedure, and Penal Codes). The Third Legislature took up the codes in 1893 but immediately set them aside to wrangle over the appointment to one of Montana's Senate seats. Nothing else was accomplished that session and the legislature adjourned without considering the codes further.

1895 brought a new legislature, with a new Republican majority determined to show it could get things done. The Fourth Legislature took up the codes with enthusiasm, holding hearings on them and setting aside most of the procedures that threatened to obstruct passage: adopting a bar on amendments, waiving the reading of the massive proposals, and creating a special committee to consider the codes. Interestingly, the only amendments which the legislative leaders allowed to a vote before the codes' passage concerned restoring the privilege of free rail travel to members of the legislature, returning the power to choose school text books to the legislature from the state board of education (a power which news accounts suggested was highly lucrative for the education committee members), and several changes sought by the livestock interests. With virtually complete press support and no organized opposition, the codes' passage was assured. The codes sailed through the legislature in only forty-two days. A prominent attorney and member of the legislature later wrote Field's biographer and brother, Henry, that "I consider the Montana Codes substantially the legislation prepared by (David Dudley Field)."[20]

Code proponents were jubilant. Col. Wilbur F. Sanders, a colorful character who was prominent code advocate, former vigilante and political powerhouse in Montana politics for decades, enthused that:

> (A) citizen of Montana, who has but little money to spend on books, needs to have lying on his table but three: an English Dictionary to teach the knowledge of his mother tongue; this Book of the Law (the Codes), to show him his rights as a member of civilized society; and the good old Family Bible to teach him his duties to God and to man.[21]

Code proponents also were certain that Montana had demonstrated her progressive attitude toward legal reform, putting her ahead of a "back-

---

[19] *The Legislature*, Daily Independent (Helena), Mar. 2, 1889, at 4.

[20] Letter to Henry Field, Jan. 24, 1896, in Henry Field, The Life of David Dudley Field 92 (1898).

[21] Letter to Henry Field, Jan. 24, 1896, at 92.

ward" New York, which still refused to adopt the Field codes. The rest of the state was not so sure that adopting such a massive set of statutes had been a good idea, however, and over the next few years the state's newspapers began to question many of the new statute's provisions. Legislators introduced hundreds of amendments in the next few years, often to correct mistakes or restore pre-Code laws on particular points.

Nineteenth century codification advocates repeatedly made Col. Sanders' argument that reducing legal rules to statutes would make them easier for the general population to understand. They also asserted that legislatures' greater democratic legitimacy meant that legislatures should be the source of all "new" law, restricting courts to interpreting existing laws. It is worth considering these claims in the context of Montana's adoption of the at-will rule through the Civil Code. It seems clear that the Code overwhelmed the new state's legislature. No meaningful review or consideration was given by the legislature as a whole to individual provisions such as the at-will rule. Nonetheless, the Civil Code gave Montana an at-will rule endorsed by the state legislature. Should a rule adopted under such circumstances receive greater deference from the courts than a common law version of the at-will rule? Did the legislature's endorsement, however unreflective it might have been, elevate the Montana at-will rule above the version judicially adopted the same year in New York, for example?[22] Ironically, in modern times the New York courts have given far more weight to their judicially-created at-will rule than the Montana courts did to their statutory rule.

Montana's adoption of the statutory at-will rule is an important part of the WDEA story, and the story of employment law more generally, for three reasons. First, the history of the at-will provisions in Field's codes, from his 1862 draft through the Dakota, California, and Montana versions and various drafts proposed in New York, undercuts the oft-repeated claim that the at-will rule was created by treatise writer Horace Wood in his 1877 treatise on master and servant law.

Second, Montana's 1895 "reform" of the law through the Civil Code suggests a need to look more closely at how statutes are adopted. Far from a purely high-minded law reform effort as its backers claimed, Montana's codification was the result of a complex mix of bare-knuckle politics, law reform efforts, and a desire to establish the state as a "progressive" standard bearer. Moreover, the at-will rule, which would dominate Montana employment law for more than eighty years, appeared in Montana jurisprudence as an incidental byproduct of the general codification effort. There is no evidence that the 1895 Montana legislature paid any attention to the at-will provision (or very many

[22] New York first recognized the at-will rule in *Martin v. New York Life Ins. Co.,* 148 N.Y. 117 (1895).

other code provisions) and the rule, designed for New York in the 1860s, became law in Montana with little consideration to its appropriateness to the new environment.

Third, following the statutory at-will rule through the era of its dominance until the rise of the common law of wrongful discharge and the passage of the WDEA in the 1980s will tell us a great deal about how courts, legislatures, and lawyers use statutes.

Act Two: The Common Law of Wrongful Discharge

The Montana courts did not pay much attention to the new codified employment rules at first. In the first Montana opinion to address the question of the term of an indefinite employment contract, the 1923 case of *Weir v. Ryan*,[23] the court simply did not mention the code provisions in the course of determining that the combination of a monthly rate of pay and an oral statement that "I will give you work the year round" created a contract for a year rather than a monthly contract. A 1935 case produced a similar result.[24] The codified rule, if the court was even aware of its existence, thus established an extremely weak default at-will rule from which little evidence was needed to escape. Indeed, the codified rules played little role in published court opinions through 1980.

There are a number of possible explanations for why Montana courts hardly ever mentioned the at-will statutory provisions. It may have been that the rules were so clear that cases simply were not brought, suggesting that Col. Sanders may have been right that an ordinary citizen could look up the law and determine his or her rights without resort to courts or lawyers. Indeed, a key component of Field's vision of the benefits of codification had been to make the law comprehensible to laypeople, preventing litigation from arising in many instances. If so, the codified at-will rule served its purpose. Of course, this does not explain why the statutory provision did not appear prominently in court opinions when such an issue did arise. (Ironically, one of the modern criticisms of the at-will rule is that ordinary people are not aware of the rule when contracting for employment.)

Another, and I believe more likely, explanation lies in the nature of the Montana economy. Montana was, and remains, relatively remote from the rest of the nation and the state's economy has historically centered largely on resource extraction (especially copper mining and timber), cattle and feed crop production, and tourism. None of these industries, except mining, are ones in which long-term employment relations are the norm. Agricultural employment, for example, tends to

---

[23] 218 P. 947 (Mont. 1923).

[24] *Harrington v. Deloraine Refining Co.*, 43 P.2d 660 (Mont. 1935).

be seasonal, and well developed cultural norms regarding cowboys' employment were present in the cattle industry long before Montana adopted her Civil Code.[25]

The mining sector was heavily unionized, effectively taking a large segment of the workforce out of the code rules' coverage through collective bargaining agreements. Federal, state, and local governments are also major employers in most Montana counties, in part because approximately a third of the state is public land (approximately 27% is federal public land; 5% is state public land). Even today, government at various levels is the major employer in many Montana counties. For the latter portion of the twentieth century, public employees were not under the code's default rules because of civil service and due process protections. Many of the remaining jobs, such as working on cattle ranches or in tourism, tended to be seasonal, limiting the potential for employment claims. From 1895 to 1980, the Montana courts likely simply had fewer opportunities to consider the at-will rule, as codified in the Civil Code, than more industrialized states' courts.

On those few occasions where the Montana courts might have addressed the issue, however, the codified rule played little role in their decisions. The at-will rule, however, was hardly the only provision ignored after the codes' passage. Subsequent analyses have found a number of areas where the Montana courts developed common law doctrines in conflict with code language—only to later discover the conflicting provisions.[26] The Montana courts (and quite likely the Montana bar as well) thus ignored much of the code, not simply the at-will provisions. Why? One explanation might lie with the incompatibility of a code approach to law with a common law legal culture. The fate of the western states' Field Codes generally supports such an interpretation, since none of the code states' courts distinguished themselves in code interpretation. Indeed, California almost immediately adopted an interpretative approach that virtually guaranteed that state's code would not displace the courts as a source of legal innovations. Both California and South Dakota also went on to develop broad common law exceptions to the at-will rule despite their own codified versions of the at-will rule. The lack of impact of the codified rule in these jurisdictions raises important questions about the effectiveness of statutes in constraining courts' ability to innovate.

---

[25] See Andrew P. Morriss, *Miners, Vigilantes & Cattlemen: Overcoming Free Rider Problems in the Private Provision of Law*, 33 Land & Water L. Rev. 581, 652–678 (1998) (describing plains cattle industry).

[26] See, e.g., Robert G. Natelson, *Running with the Land in Montana*, 51 Mont. L. Rev. 17, 92 (1990); Morriss, Burnham & Nelson, *supra*.

The erosion of the statutory at-will rule began with the Montana Supreme Court's decision in *Keneally v. Orgain*,[27] which did not even mention the at-will code provision. After simply labeling the employment contract in question an at-will contract, the court proceeded to discuss a growing national trend toward recognition of a public policy exception to the at-will rule. Although the court concluded that the plaintiff in *Keneally* had not alleged facts that could support such a claim, the court hinted strongly that it would recognize such a claim in a future case, noting that "[w]e do not disagree at this juncture that in a proper case a cause for wrongful discharge could be made out by an employee." The court made no mention of the difference between a statutory at-will rule and the common law version of the rule present in most other states.

Even when the state high court did cite the statutory rule, as it did in *Reiter v. Yellowstone County*,[28] decided five months after *Keneally,* a case in which the court used the statutory at-will rule as the basis for denying the existence of a property interest in public employment, it did not address the full set of employment law code provisions. Relying on the statutory at-will rule, the court simply ignored the implied duration sections, which formed at least a colorable basis for a property interest claim.

At the start of the 1980s, lawyers pondering the role of Montana's codified at-will rule—like many of the other provisions of the 1895 Civil Code—occupied a position akin to a swimmer confronting a partially submerged log in a pond: there was something there but it was far from clear what it was. Sometimes the court would rely on the rule, in other cases it would not mention it at all. Nonetheless, there were still relatively few wrongful discharge cases. All that changed in January 1982, when the state supreme court issued its first decision in *Gates v. Life Montana Insurance Co. (Gates I)*,[29] recognizing an employer's liability for breach of the implied covenant of good faith and fair dealing in the wrongful discharge context.

It can often be tricky to date changes in the common law.[30] Care is always needed in relying on courts' versions of legal history because courts write such histories with a purpose in mind. There is little doubt, however, that *Gates I* signaled a major change in the law. The employer's brief in *Gates I* leaves no doubt that it did not anticipate the vast

---

[27] 606 P.2d 127 (Mont. 1980).

[28] 627 P.2d 845 (Mont. 1981).

[29] 638 P.2d 1063 (Mont. 1982).

[30] *See* Andrew P. Morriss, *Developing a Framework for Empirical Research On the Common Law: General Principles and Case Studies of the Decline of Employment At Will,* 45 Case Western Reserve L. Rev. 999 (1995).

expansion of liability the case would produce, explicitly relying on the codified at-will rule as conclusively determining the result.[31] (Somewhat oddly, the appellant's brief cited the at-will rule as supporting its claim that employees were entitled to prior notice before being discharged.)[32] In short, the submerged log of the codified at will rule suddenly sank without a trace, leaving a clear path for common law wrongful discharge claims. The Montana bar responded enthusiastically to *Gates'* invitation and brought new claims to the court.

From 1982 to 1985, the Montana Supreme Court regularly liberalized employment law (mostly simply ignoring Civil Code § 39–2–503). "The court refused to acknowledge that, by qualifying the right to terminate without cause and by adding a requirement of good faith, it effectively eliminated at-will employment."[33] During this period, the court steadily increased the scope of the implied covenant theory until, "[b]y 1985, the Montana Supreme Court had defined the covenant so broadly that it incorporated all extant theories" of wrongful discharge.[34] More than the scope expanded: in a second decision in the *Gates* case (*Gates II*), the court held that punitive damages were available in implied covenant cases.[35] This substantially increased the potential rewards from a wrongful discharge suit.

Let us consider the state of Montana wrongful discharge law in the mid–1980s from the perspectives of a discharged employee, a plaintiffs' attorney, and an employer. For the discharged employee, a wrongful discharge action offered something akin to a lottery ticket. Some discharged employees, and it was hard to predict exactly which ones, would receive substantial rewards if they prevailed in a wrongful discharge suit. The tort damages made available, including punitive damages, meant that even employees in relatively low-status, low-wage jobs might receive substantial recoveries. Recall the 1986 case discussed earlier in which an assistant bank manager received award of $1.3 million in punitive damages, $100,000 for emotional distress, and $93,000 in economic losses.[36] Assuming they could find an attorney willing to bear the upfront costs of litigation, discharged employees had little reason not to file suit.

---

[31] Brief of Respondent, *Gates v. Life of Montana Insurance Co.*, No. 81–219 (July 15, 1981).

[32] Appellant's Brief, *Gates v. Life of Montana Insurance Co.*, No. 81–219 (June 12, 1981) at 16.

[33] Schramm, *New Order* at 105.

[34] *Id*. at 97.

[35] *Gates v. Life of Montana Insurance Co.*, 668 P.2d 213 (Mont. 1983).

[36] *Flanigan v. Prudential Federal Savings*, 720 P.2d 257 (Mont. 1986).

Plaintiffs' attorneys also had powerful incentives to file wrongful discharge suits. Not every suit would yield million dollar plus awards, of course, but large recoveries were frequent enough to make filing wrongful discharge claims worthwhile. Moreover, compared to many areas of the law, wrongful discharge claims were relatively cheap to litigate. Expensive experts were rarely necessary (as they would be in toxic tort cases, for example) and the issues were straight-forward. The common law of wrongful discharge was not predictable enough to enable routine valuation of individual claims, but it was generous enough when the discharged employees won to offset the losses.[37]

From the employer's perspective, every discharge now brought with it a potential law suit. Unlike plaintiffs' attorneys, however, there was no offset for their losses when they won victories. Regardless of whether they won or lost, employers ended up footing the bill for their legal defense. Each wrongful discharge claim was thus a sure loss, with the only question being how much the employer would lose. The impact of this on employer's behavior was signficant: A recent empirical examination of the impact of the appearance of the common law wrongful discharge claims in Montana estimated that it reduced employment in Montana by 0.46 percent per year.[38]

By the late 1980s, both plaintiffs and defendants had complaints about the state of Montana wrongful discharge law. Just as had happened with industrial accident litigation in the early twentieth century, when some plaintiffs won large awards but many received nothing, the lottery-like character offered a chance for both groups to benefit from a compromise. Defendants wanted to limit the damage awards; plaintiffs wanted more assured compensation. The only interest group who would suffer from such a *quid pro quo* was the plaintiff's bar, who would lose their share of the large awards won by a minority of plaintiffs.

Act Three: The WDEA and the Challenge to its Constitutionality

Reacting to these decisions, and to fears among Montana employers that large judgments in wrongful discharge suits were harming the state's economy, some members of the legislature proposed legislation in 1985 to limit suits. This did not make it out of the lower chamber and even a proposed study commission failed to attract funding. When the legislature next met in 1987, the Montana Association of Defense Counsel ("MADC"), backed by the broader, tort-reform Montana Liability Coalition, proposed the Wrongful Discharge from Employment Act. Supporters stressed the importance of clarifying the standard for wrongful

---

[37] Schramm, *New Order*, at 95.

[38] Bradley T. Ewing, et al., *The Employment Effects of a "Good Cause" Discharge Standard in Montana*, 59 Ind. Lab. Rel. Rev. 17 (2005).

discharge suits. As one employer wrote in a Billings Chamber of Commerce pamphlet on issues before the legislature, the law provided

> no meaningful guidelines ... to tell employers when and how they may terminate or demote employees. We do not know what notice is required, how many warnings of improper conduct are required, how much severance pay is required, how the notice should be given or many other factors that may later be used as evidence of "bad faith." Every termination or demotion in Montana is now subject to review by a court and jury. Unless an employer is willing to settle the claim, he must pay between $20,000 and $100,000 in attorneys' fees and costs to defend himself in court.[39]

Although it is difficult to determine the exact source of the ideas contained in the MADC proposal, the legislative file on the bill includes a "labor notes" newsletter from a Washington state law firm concerning a similar bill proposed in that state, a bill which contained many provisions close to the substance of the Montana statute.[40] Moreover, there was more general discussion in the mid–1980s of replacing the common law combination of the at-will rule and the judicially-created exceptions with a comprehensive approach.

The bill proposed by the MADC eliminated the common law causes of action for wrongful discharge as well as all discharge-related tort claims for intentional or negligent interference with contractual rights, intentional or negligent infliction of emotional distress, fraud, defamation, breach of fiduciary duty, negligent or intentional misrepresentation, loss of consortium, and negligence.[41] It allowed a wrongful discharge claim only for cases where employees were discharged for refusing to violate public policy or for reporting a violation of public policy or were discharged without good cause and had been working for an employer for at least 1,000 hours per year for at least five consecutive years immediately preceding the discharge. The bill capped damages at two years' lost wages, less interim earnings and unemployment compensation insurance payments. Punitive damages were not specifically mentioned; by implication, they were not allowed. Employment discrimination claims, which were covered by the Montana Human Rights Act and Title VII of the Civil Rights Act of 1964 were, in any event, exempted from the statutory scheme. Finally, the proposal created incentives for arbitration by granting attorney's fees to a prevailing party whose offer of arbitration was rejected by the other side.

---

[39] Jim Jones, *Wrongful Discharge*, Senate Exhibit 6, March 10, 1987, at 27.

[40] *Proposed Fair Employment Act, Senate Bill 5965,* Schweppe, Krug & Tausend, P.S., March 2, 1987, Exhibit 9A, Senate Judiciary File, March 10, 1987.

[41] All references to the various versions of the act considered by the legislature are to copies contained in the Montana Senate file on HB 241.

The MADC bill was modified in the House. Coverage was extended to employees with at least three, rather than five, years of employment, damages were limited to three years' lost wages and fringe benefits, not two years' lost wages. So modified, the bill passed the Montana House by a vote of 73–27.

The bill provoked howls of outrage from the plaintiffs' bar. For example, Bozeman plaintiff's attorney Mike Cok told the *Bozeman Chronicle* that "This is back to the days of slavery. You're an employer's property—bought and sold and used up." Monte Beck, another attorney from Bozeman, commented that "I can state to you unequivocally that wrongful discharge is in effect dead in Montana, because no lawyer will take a case" because of the damages limitations.[42] The bill had drawn wide support in the House, including from representatives whose support for it "shock[ed] the hell" out of the bill's opponents.[43] As the backlash among the plaintiffs bar appeared, however, some of the House members who voted for the bill suggested in comments to the *Chronicle* that the bill "still needs amending" and the bill's sponsor conceded that it might be "a little harsher than it should be."[44]

The bill did not produce a large number of official comments from interest groups, however. The Montana Health Care Association, the Montana Solid Waste Contractors, and Town Pump Food Stores registered their support. Only the health care group offered a rationale for its support, stating that its members needed the ability to discharge health care workers, without fear of lawsuits, to protect their patients. The Montana Women's Lobbyist Fund and Montana Employers Group, a group of unionized companies, registered objections. The women's group opposed the bill because "the injury of wrongful discharge falls most heavily on women" and because of the restriction of remedies for part-time workers, who were more likely to be female. The unionized employers argued that the bill would help unions "entice" non-union workers into unions to gain job security.

When the bill got to the Montana Senate, there was a concerted effort to amend it. Both Rep. Gary Spaeth, the bill's House sponsor, working with the Montana Association of Defense Counsel, and an ad hoc committee of six lawyers, including both plaintiffs' and defense counsel, proposed modifications to the House version. Both Spaeth and the ad hoc group suggested a broad array of substantive changes, as well as some minor clarifications. All of the ad hoc committee's substantive

---

[42] Terry Sacks, *Fired: Wrongful Discharge Bill Raises Questions About Job Protections in the Workplace*, Bozeman Chronicle, March 1, 1987, at 25.

[43] *Id.*

[44] *Id.*

proposals would have weakened the bill's attempts to limit liability and most were rejected by the Senate committee considering the bill. Some of the Spaeth amendments appear to have been efforts to offer compromises on particular points, perhaps to prevent other amendments from weakening the proposal even more. (Intriguingly, the subcommittee's minutes note that a representative of the Montana Trial Lawyers, a plaintiffs' bar association, "acted as secretary for the committee during its deliberations.")

Seven of the more minor of Spaeth proposals were accepted by the ad hoc committee and by the Senate Judiciary Committee's Subcommittee of Wrongful Discharge with little discussion.

First, the ad hoc committee proposed expanding the definition of constructive discharge to include a failure to recall laid-off workers. The rationale for this proposal was a concern that employers would release workers and fail to rehire older workers "with good work records simply because of their age or pension benefits, etc. and in violation of the employer's personnel policy assuring recall rights to laid off employees, before hiring new employees."[45] The Senate Judiciary Committee did not adopt the proposed language but did add failure to rehire to the definition of constructive discharge.

Second, the definition of "good cause" drew considerable attention from both the MADC and the ad hoc committee. The original MADC-proposed bill had defined "good cause" as "a legitimate business reason." The House had substituted for this language "reasonable, job-related grounds for dismissal based on a failure to satisfactorily perform job duties or disruption of the employer's operation." The MADC found this too narrow "because it would not allow employers to discharge employees for legitimate business reasons such as lack of work, elimination of the job, etc." The MADC thus attempted to restore the original definition, arguing that under it, "the employee's interest in job security would be protected by requiring that the employer in fact have a *legitimate* reason for discharge. At the same time, the employer's interest in management discretion would be protected by allowing businesses to make employment decisions for business reasons."

The ad hoc committee, however, proposed changing the definition of good cause by adding the following language: " 'Good cause' means a fair and honest cause or reason regulated by good faith on the part of the employer in his decision to terminate an employee. Managerial discretion must be taken in to consideration by the trier of fact in applying the 'good cause' standard." The ad hoc committee argued that this would "provide the courts with a strict definition of 'good cause' " and that the

---

[45] The discussion in this section is based on Rationale *of Proposed Amendments to HB 241 and Proposed Amendments to HB 241*, Senate Judiciary Exhibit 10, March 24, 1987.

proposed language "had been recognized by both courts and arbitrators for many years." Since this language would have defeated a primary purpose of the legislation by reimporting the good-faith language into wrongful discharge cases, it is not surprising that the Senate subcommittee did not adopt the proposal. By a 3–1 vote, the Senate subcommittee rejected the ad hoc committee's proposal. It also rejected the MADC proposal, but agreed to a formulation emphasizing the need to defer to managerial discretion.

Third, the ad hoc committee sought to expand the definition of "public policy" to include an "established custom, practice, or law which recognizes the performance of an act that public policy would encourage or the refusal to perform an act that public policy would condemn." In addition, the ad hoc committee proposed to expand the circumstances under which a discharged employee could sue for violation of public policy by deleting the requirement that an employee be discharged in retaliation for a refusal to violate public policy and replacing it with only the requirement that no statutory remedy exist for the public-policy violation. The ad hoc committee argued that this was necessary to cover "situations in which an employee is discharged for insisting upon compliance with established and accepted industry safety practices which are recognized by the employer himself. Further, it does not allow for situations where an employee is discharged or engaging in a civic duty (e.g., jury service, voting, etc.)." The Senate Judiciary subcommittee rejected these proposals as well. Again, this decision is not surprising since the proposed language would have significantly expanded the circumstances under which a discharged employee could have brought a claim, and so decreased the certainty the bill's drafters sought to provide to employers.

Fourth, the ad hoc committee proposed eliminating the restriction of "good cause" claims to full-time employees with at least three years of employment with the employer and providing a claim for employees discharged without good cause who had completed the employers' probationary period. The ad hoc committee pointed to three problems with the "1,000 hours for 3 years" approach of the bill. With respect to part-time workers, the committee argued that excluding them was unfair. Given the seasonal nature of many Montana jobs, this was an important point. Moreover, the committee argued that employers would be given an incentive by the precise numbers to reduce employees' hours to below the 1,000 hour threshold to claim the exemption. Finally, the ad hoc committee suggested that the three-year provision would have "a double-edged effect of creating an implication of 'tenure' for employees who have been employed for more than three years" and create an incentive to discharge employees short of the three year mark to avoid future claims. Rep. Spaeth agreed with this proposal, suggesting that the ad hoc committee's rationale had persuaded the MADC of the possible problems with the original approach. Since both the defense and plaintiffs' bars accepted the proposal, it is no surprise that the Senate Judiciary subcommittee also accepted this amendment.

Fifth, the ad hoc committee attempted to expand the claim for violation of employer's personnel policies by eliminating the requirement that the policies be "express" and written. As with the public policy proposal, the ad hoc committee's argument was based on perverse incentives created by the statute. By limiting claims to express, written policies, the ad hoc committee contended, the bill would "provide a great temptation for employers who have written policies to tear them up and use unwritten, *sub rosa* policies, simply to avoid discharge suits." This would be problematic for both employers and employees. The MADC proposed simply eliminating the cause of action for violations of personnel policies entirely. After this proposal failed on a 2–2 vote, the Senate subcommittee appears to have compromised on a 3–1 vote by deleting the word written, but retaining the word "express," thus limiting claims to where "the employer violated the express provisions of its own personnel policies." Although the record does not tell us why the committee differentiated between the two words, its action is consistent with the overall concern about giving the Montana Supreme Court as little discretion as possible to expand wrongful discharge claims while recognizing the perverse incentive for eliminating written policies created if the statute restricted claims to written policies.

Sixth, the ad hoc committee proposed expanding damages by eliminating the damages cap entirely for public policy claims and where the employee was a member of the age-protected employees under federal or state anti-discrimination law (e.g., those forty or older) and had been employed for ten or more years. Further, the committee proposed explicitly allowing punitive damages "if it is established by clear and convincing evidence that the employer has engaged in actual fraud or actual malice in the discharge" and to state that "general damages shall be as otherwise allowed by law." The ad hoc committee argued that the damages cap was unfair to older employees who would be unlikely to find new employment at their previous level.

> The example situation is an employee of 57 years of age who has worked for the employer for 30 years. An employee who has reached that age, and has limited his employment skills to the specialized needs of his employer, should be allowed to show that it is unlikely that he can become re-employed at age 57 in a similar job, if that is the evidence presented.

The punitive damages language was intended by the ad hoc committee as both a limit on when such damages would be allowed and to punish "the unjustified and malicious taking of a citizen's livelihood." The general damages language was intended to make the WDEA consistent with a more general proposed statute, then pending, that would limit damages in all lawsuits. Of course, if the other statute did not pass or if the Montana Supreme Court struck it down, the effect would have been to expand the damages available under the WDEA. The MADC agreed to the punitive damages change but not to the general damages or age-related lifting of the cap.

Not surprisingly, the Senate Judiciary subcommittee rejected the elimination of the cap and the addition of the "general damages" language, both of which would defeat an important goal of the legislation in limiting damages. The subcommittee did accept the explicit recognition of punitive damages. While this appears to expand the damages available, the subcommittee (and the MADC) may have had in mind the Montana Supreme Court's history of expanding remedies and thus may have believed that the combination of the "clear and convincing" standard with the requirement of "actual fraud or actual malice" would limit the court's possible interpretation of statutory silence on punitive damages.

Seventh, the ad hoc committee proposed expanding the statute of limitations from one to two years, arguing that this would be more consistent with the limitations period for "other property damage claims" and that the one-year period gave "suits involving loss of livelihood" a "second class" status. The Senate subcommittee rejected this amendment.

Finally, the ad hoc committee proposed eliminating the arbitration provisions entirely. The ad hoc committee's opposition was quite clearly based on lawyers' antipathy to arbitration. The ad hoc committee argued that the WDEA repealed "the historically established notion that arbitration should always be a mutual and consensual procedure, not one unilaterally imposed by one party," that employers would unilaterally create arbitration policies whenever a claim was made, that the arbitration provisions were "an unfair (if not unconstitutional) deprivation of access to the courts" and that claims over "the loss of a job should not be relegated to a 'second class' legal status." This was rejected by the Senate subcommittee. The subcommittee instead removed the requirement that the employer have a policy requiring arbitration, broadening the applicability of the arbitration provisions.

The WDEA made sweeping changes in Montana law, fundamentally altering the law governing employment termination in four areas. First, it effectively replaced (but did not explicitly repeal) the at-will rule, substituting a requirement of "good cause" for termination of a non-probationary employee.[46] Second, it capped compensatory damages at four years' lost wages and benefits less interim earnings and limited punitive damages to cases where the employee could prove actual malice or fraud by clear and convincing evidence, which substantially reduced the damages potentially available.[47] Third, it preempted all tort claims relating to wrongful discharge.[48] Finally it created an arbitration mechanism for employment disputes and provided incentives to agree to arbitration through a fee-shifting provision for cases in which one party refused an offer of arbitration from the other.[49] Despite its radical changes in employment law, the passage of the WDEA received little attention in the Montana press, however, going almost unmentioned in contemporary press coverage of that legislative session.

Each of these changes alone would have been significant; together they represented a fundamental remaking of the law of wrongful discharge. Let us briefly consider what changed and what did not with the passage of the WDEA. The WDEA implicitly repealed the Civil Code's at-will provision, although there was no mention of the codified rule in the statute. This is not surprising. Given the Montana Supreme Court's irregular recognition of the statutory rule, it might be unreasonable to expect the legislature to be more careful than the courts in researching the existing law before launching such radical changes. Indeed, when first confronted with the conflict between the code rule and the WDEA, the Montana Supreme Court simply stated that neither the WDEA "nor any other action by the Montana legislature or this Court has nullified the 'at will' designation or § 39–2–503."[50] Not until 1999 did the court give the matter an in-depth consideration and it then held that the WDEA "superseded and impliedly repealed the at-will act."[51] The Montana legislature finally explicitly repealed the code provision in 2001.[52] This history of Montana's codified at-will rule is a lesson in the looseness of the constraints imposed by statutes on courts.

The compensatory and punitive damages provisions provided the *quid* for the good cause *quo*. The cap on damages meant that employers no longer faced the potential of a ruinous award. In particular, the set-

---

[46] Mont. Code Ann. §§ 39–2–903(5), 39–2–904(2).

[47] Mont. Code Ann. § 39–2–905.

[48] Mont. Code Ann. §§ 39–2–905(3); 39–2–913.

[49] Mont. Code Ann. §§ 39–2–914, 39–2–915.

[50] *Medicine Horse v. Trustees, Big Horn County School District No. 27*, 823 P.2d 230, 232 (Mont. 1991).

[51] *Whidden v. John S. Nerison, Inc.*, 981 P.2d 271, 275 (Mont. 1999).

[52] § 4, Ch. 583, L. 2001.

off for earnings in the ex-employee's new job cut potential damage awards significantly. Under the WDEA, for example, the almost $1.5 million award in the 1986 case of *Flanigan v. Prudential Federal Savings*[53] would have been no more than $93,000 (the economic losses) and most likely significantly less once the mitigation of damages provisions were applied.

The arbitration provisions offered an alternative means of handling cases. Given that the damages were now restricted to an amount readily calculable and the bar lowered for the employee to prevail, there was some hope that the arbitration provisions might result in lower overall attorney's fees.

Not everyone was happy with the WDEA. The plaintiffs' bar, in particular, stood to lose because of the elimination of tort damages and its corresponding effect on their large contingency fees. The statute's constitutionality under Article II, Section 16 of the Montana Constitution was promptly challenged in a wrongful discharge action filed in state court and then removed by the defendant to federal court. That court certified the question of the statute's constitutionality to the Montana Supreme Court in 1989. The case came to the court in the midst of a long-running struggle between the court and the state legislature over broader issues of tort reform and the role of the judiciary. These conflicts set the stage for the constitutional challenge to WDEA.[54]

These conflicts can be readily seen in the court's opinions arising out of the state legislature's efforts to limit governmental tort liability. This topic was closely related to the wrongful discharge law issue, since the largest recoveries were in tort-theory cases and the state and local governments were (and are) among the most important employers in much of Montana. We must therefore briefly discuss the larger conflict to understand the opinion upholding the WDEA.

Montana revised its state constitution in 1972, replacing the original 1889 constitution adopted at statehood with a quite different document. Although the 1889 constitution did not directly address governmental tort liability, the courts interpreted its provisions to significantly limit liability for the state and counties, as well as for local governments engaged in certain activities.[55]

---

[53] 720 P.2d 257 (Mont. 1986).

[54] This section draws on an interview with Professor Betsy Griffing, University of Montana School of Law, who served as a clerk on the court during this period. The interview was conducted in April 2005 by my research assistant, Kai Lee.

[55] This history is discussed in detail in *Pfost v. State*, 713 P.2d 495 (Mont. 1985).

The new constitution took a different approach, eliminating governmental immunity entirely. In 1974, however, Montana voters passed a constitutional amendment that authorized the legislature to provide governmental immunity for the state and its subdivisions through a two-thirds vote. In 1977, the state legislature did just that, limiting the economic damages available in actions against the state to $300,000 per claimant and $1,000,000 per occurrence and eliminating punitive damages against the state and its subdivisions.

The Montana Supreme Court invalidated the statute's limitations on economic damages as unconstitutional in *White v. State of Montana* in 1983.[56] The court found that because the right to bring an action for personal injuries was a fundamental right, strict scrutiny was required of any statute abridging that fundamental right. Two weeks after the court voided the statute, the legislature passed a new immunity statute, giving it retroactive effect to the date of the statute involved in *White*. Once again, the legislature limited economic damages in actions against the state and its subdivisions to $300,000 per claimant and $1,000,000 for each occurrence. The court once again struck down the statute in a 4–3 decision in *Pfost v. State* in 1986.[57] In the course of doing so, the court read a state constitutional provision requiring "full legal redress" to mandate a remedy for every wrong involving employment.

The court and legislature were thus on a collision course before the WDEA's passage over which branch of government would define Montana law. (The court has since engaged in a similar struggle over a variety of referenda issues, striking referenda that were adopted on a variety of technical grounds.[58]) The WDEA should be seen against this larger struggle. The court had defined a new cause of action in the *Gates* decisions, a cause of action that not only swallowed a prior legislatively enacted at-will rule but which threatened Montana governments with large tort awards. At the same time, the court repeatedly had rejected the legislature's attempts to limit liability. Unable to impose a cap on economic damages directly, the legislature attacked the problem at one of its sources through the WDEA's abolition of the underlying causes of action.

Act Four: Meech and the Constitutional Attack on the WDEA

Russell Meech began working for Hillhaven West, Inc., a nursing home operator, in August 1984 in Washington state.[59] He later moved to

---

[56] 661 P.2d 1272 (Mont. 1983).

[57] 713 P.2d 495 (Mont. 1985).

[58] *See, e.g., Marshall v. State ex. rel. Cooney*, 975 P.2d 325 (Mont. 1999).

[59] This section draws on the following documents: Brief of Petitioner Russell E. Meech, *Meech v. Hillhaven West, Inc.*, No. 88–410, October 11, 1988; Brief of Respondents

a Hillhaven facility in Montana, where he was assistant administrator until his termination in October 1987. As Meech's brief noted, he "had every reasonable expectation that his employment with Hillhaven was a life-long career." Once discharged, Meech filed suit seeking damages for a wide range of common law tort actions, including: "breach of the implied covenant of good faith and fair dealing in the employment relationship, wrongful termination, intentional or negligent infliction of emotional distress, and oppressive, malicious and unjustifiable conduct." All of these claims were preempted by the WDEA. After Meech's lawsuit was removed to federal court by Hillhaven, both parties agreed that the question of the WDEA's constitutionality belonged before the Montana Supreme Court and so agreed to the certification of the issue to that court.

Meech's remarkably concise argument (the substance of the main argument makes up less than six double spaced pages of the thirteen-page brief) explicitly placed the case in the context of the court's struggle with the legislature over limits on damages:

> The legislature, as in *White* (sovereign immunity from liability for non-economic damages), and *Pfost* (limitations on dollar values for damages against the state), cannot present a compelling state interest to deprive citizens of the fundamental right to full legal redress, where employees suffer injuries due to wrongful discharge from employment, violation of the covenant of good faith and fair dealing in the employment relationship, intentional infliction of emotional distress and other contractual and tort violations. The Constitutional Amendment [at issue in *Pfost* and *White*] is void, and, therefore, the Act is void.

Remarkably, Meech's argument relied on almost no authority beyond these cases; the brief cites only some pre-WDEA cases to support its characterization of the pre-statute case law and a few cases in a section that launched a preemptive attack on the defendant's argument. The one-paragraph argument that the punitive damages limitation was unconstitutional, for example, did not cite even a single case. The impression given by the brief is that plaintiff (or plaintiff's counsel) anticipated that the case would not be a difficult one.

Meech also made an argument, largely buried in an analysis of *White* and *Pfost,* that the WDEA violated the state constitution's equal protection clause by distinguishing between employees and other victims of torts by denying wrongfully discharged employees the "full legal redress" guaranteed by the Montana Constitution without a compelling

Hillhaven West, Inc. and R. Ron Semingson, No. 88–410, December 12, 1988; Reply Brief of Petitioner, Russell E. Meech, No. 88–410, January 6, 1989.

state interest. This argument was also made without much reliance on case authority.

Hillhaven responded with a lengthier brief which advanced three main counter-arguments. First, the respondents asserted that the legislature had the authority to alter common law causes of action through legislation, drawing on several examples of changes in liability brought about through legislation (e.g., workers' compensation's exclusive remedy for workplace injuries). Second, the respondents argued for a rational basis review rather than strict scrutiny, arguing that the legislature had carefully examined the evidence of the impact of the common law of wrongful discharge on employment and concluded that limits were needed. This argument emphasized the *quid pro quo* of the statute's enshrining the good-cause standard in the law for all employees in exchange for restricting the damages available concluding that "[w]hile Meech may disagree with the wisdom of the Act, it certainly is rationally related to legitimate state interests, and is, therefore, constitutional." Third, the respondents directly attacked the Montana court's holdings in *Pfost* and *White,* arguing that they were incorrect and should be overruled, drawing on decisions from other states interpreting their own constitutions.

Only one amicus curiae filed a brief, the California Employment Law Counsel (CELC), a sixty-member group of California employers who told the court that their interest was in the WDEA as a model for reform in California as well as in assisting its members with their operations in Montana. The CELC's argument was aimed primarily at distinguishing the WDEA from *White* and *Pfost.* Noting that the legislature has been recognized to have "plenary authority" to regulate employment, the CELC enumerated the many aspects of employment regulated by Montana statutes and concluded that the WDEA simply extended that regulation to termination.

A sharply divided Montana court upheld the statute. The majority agreed with the respondents' argument and overruled, in part, *Pfost* and *White.* Reaching back to the Magna Carta, the majority analyzed the "full legal redress" language of the state constitution and found that it was intended as a constraint on the courts, not the legislature. Moreover, the majority held that no one had a vested right in common law claims. Again turning to history, the court noted that the first Montana statutes, known as the Bannock statutes after the first territorial capitol, included a provision adopting the common law of England "so far as it is not repugnant to or inconsistent with the constitution of the United States or the constitution or *laws*" of the jurisdiction. Noting the existence of "flaws" in *White* and *Pfost,* the majority then overruled them with arguments derived from the dissents in those cases. The majority also rejected the equal protection challenge to the punitive damages bar by finding that the legislation represented a reasonable tradeoff of more extensive damages for greater certainty of recovery.[60]

The majority opinion is an impressive piece of legal scholarship, drawing on diverse sources (from Magna Carta to modern law reviews) and which did not merely mimic the parties' briefs. Somewhat remarkably, for a court which has been heavily criticized for its lack of consistent methodology and respect for precedent, the majority opinion carefully built an analytical framework that justified not only the specific result but which also critiqued the court's prior jurisprudence. Given the care and detail in the majority opinion, it seems clear that the court viewed the case as not only about the WDEA but also as an important milestone in the ongoing struggle over the powers of the legislature.

This sense is reinforced by the apocalyptic language with which Justice Sheehy's dissent (in which he was joined by Justice Hunt)[61] opened: "This is the blackest judicial day in the eleven years that I have sat on this Court. Indeed it may be the blackest judicial day in the history of the state.... The decision today cleans the scalpel for the legislature to cut away unrestrainedly at the whole field of tort redress. Perhaps worse by this decision today, the Court throws in the sponge as a co-equal in our tripartite state government."

While *Meech* marked a partial turning point in the running battle between the Montana legislature and supreme court, it did not end the struggle. Throughout the 1990s, the Montana Supreme Court proved to be among the most activist state supreme courts in the nation, aggressively striking both legislation and referenda results it found in conflict with constitutional language through reasoning its critics charged was essentially result-oriented.

Act Five: The WDEA in Action

The Montana Legislature has made several changes to the WDEA since its passage. In 1993 the legislature altered the definition of "good cause" to provide that "the legal use of a lawful product by an individual off the employer's premises during nonworking hours is not a legitimate business reason." This was done as part of the creation of a separate statute forbidding such discrimination. Although the sponsor of the amendment conceded that he was unaware of any problem with Mon-

---

[60] The Montana Supreme Court addressed other challenges to the constitutionality of the WDEA after *Meech: Johnson v. State,* 776 P.2d 1221 (Mont. 1989), and *Allmaras v. Yellowstone Basin Properties,* 812 P.2d 770 (Mont. 1991). These later challenges were not, however, as significant as the challenge in *Meech* and so have received little attention in the legal literature and need not detain us here.

[61] Justice Harrison provided a brief dissent, objecting to the overruling of one prior opinion, while agreeing with "much that is said by the majority" and disagreeing with Justice Sheehy on a number of points.

tana employers discharging employees for such activities, he thought the bill was important "to ward off any problems that could occur." Although the underlying new statute was the subject of some controversy, there was little commentary on the provision amending the WDEA.[62]

Also in 1993, the legislature amended the definition of damages recoverable to give employees credit for money they spent in "searching for, obtaining, or relocating to new employment."[63] Employer groups succeeded in adding the qualifier "reasonable" to the credit but failed to limit the offset to expenses incurred in the first two years of a job search. The bill also overturned a state supreme court decision[64] that had limited employers' ability to collect attorney's fees after making an offer to arbitrate which was rejected by the employee and prevailing in court. The debate notes include suggestions that the amendment "would get the court's attention" and was needed because the decision in question "was a clear example of the courts' unwillingness to enforce the statute that was written."

In 2001, the legislature eliminated the at-will code provision, responding to the Montana Supreme Court's decision in *Whidden v. John S. Nerison, Inc.*[65] The legislation created a presumptive probationary period of six months, since simply eliminating the at-will provision could be construed to make employees of employers without formal probationary periods permanent from the first day they were hired. The only controversy surrounding this essentially technical amendment came when the state university system objected to the six-month probationary period since work-study students could be considered to become "permanent" employees during a single academic year's employment.[66]

How has the WDEA changed employment law in practice in Montana? To answer that question I gathered data on wrongful discharge suits from the courthouses in five Montana counties: Gallatin, Granite, Lake, Missoula, and Silver Bow.[67] Together these counties represent approximately one quarter of Montana employment.[68] The counties were

---

[62] This paragraph is based on the legislative history file for Ch. 193 (1993).

[63] This paragraph is based on the legislative history file for Ch. 442 (1993).

[64] *Hoffman v. Town Pump, Inc.*, 843 P.2d 756 (Mont. 1992).

[65] 981 P.2d 271 (Mont. 1999).

[66] This paragraph is based on the legislative history file for Ch. 583 (2001).

[67] In the case of Granite County I discovered that there had been no wrongful discharge cases filed in that county since 1985 (or ever, to the recollection of court personnel.)

[68] Including all five counties checked, these counties contain 24% of Montana establishments, 29% of Montana employees, and 28% of Montana payroll (using 1997 numbers). Dropping Granite County changes these figures by between one and two percent.

selected because the data were available rather than because they were representative of the state.[69] However, they are representative of the areas of the state with the most economic activity, with four of the five among the top ten counties in total payroll and number of employees. Four include a major "urban" center of employment[70] and these four counties represent most of the major areas of economic activity in the state.[71]

The data set includes data on 496 wrongful discharge cases filed between January 1, 1985 and December 31, 1999.[72] The data was collected by examining the records in each county courthouse.[73] Each county provided a listing of all wrongful discharge cases for at least part of the period in question; in some instances older records had to be reviewed manually to determine whether a case was a wrongful discharge case. The information collected is described in Table 1. The data set thus includes every case denominated a wrongful discharge case by the plaintiff when filed in the Montana state courts. It therefore does *not* include cases originally filed in federal court, either in Montana or elsewhere, over state wrongful discharge law claims. It also includes only limited data on cases originally filed in Montana state courts but later removed to federal court, unless the case was subsequently remanded to the state courts. Finally, it includes only limited data on cases transferred from a court in one of the counties studied to a court in a county not studied. Data on these cases were limited because the original file contained only the original complaint and a notice of transfer or removal.[74]

---

[69] The counties are not representative: the four counties with wrongful discharge cases ranked well ahead of the average Montana county in per capita income, for example, ranking 6, 8, 9, and 12 in 1997 per capita income.

[70] So long as "urban" is treated as a relative term—Montana is a sparsely populated state.

[71] Areas not represented are eastern Montana, where there is significant economic activity around Billings, in Yellowstone County, and the Great Falls area, in Cascade County.

[72] The Gallatin county data includes data only through November 1999.

[73] I collected the data for Gallatin County. The data for the other counties was collected by law students from the University of Montana School of Law.

[74] Gathering such data is time consuming and expensive. Additional data are gradually being collected.

Table 1: Variable Descriptions

Variable	Description
Defendants	
Government	1 if any defendant is a government; 0 otherwise
Out-of-State Corporation	1 if any defendant is an out-of-state corporation; 0 otherwise
Partnership	1 if any defendant is a partnership; 0 otherwise
Individual	1 if any defendant is an individual; 0 otherwise
Montana Corporation	1 if any defendant is a Montana Corporation; 0 otherwise
Number of Defendants	Number of defendants, not including "John Doe" defendants
Plaintiffs	
Managerial	1 if complaint or other pleading describes plaintiff as a manager, supervisor or executive; 0 otherwise
Professional	1 if complaint of other pleading describes plaintiff as a professional; 0 otherwise
Number of Plaintiffs	Number of plaintiffs
Pretrial Practice	
Discovery Disputes	1 if file includes a motion concerning a discovery dispute; 0 otherwise
Depositions	1 if file includes a notice of depositions; 0 otherwise
Merits Motions	1 if file includes a merits motion; 0 otherwise
Location	
Gallatin	1 if case filed in Gallatin County; 0 otherwise
Lake	1 if case filed in Lake County; 0 otherwise
Missoula	1 if case filed in Missoula County; 0 otherwise
Silver Bow	1 if case filed in Silver Bow County; 0 otherwise
Attorneys	
Out of State	1 if an out-of-state attorney appears in the case; 0 otherwise
Same County	1 if all attorneys on case are from the same county; 0 otherwise
Claims	
Total Claims	Total number of separate claims listed in complaint
Counterclaim	1 if a counterclaim is filed by a defendant; 0 otherwise
Substantive claims present	Series of variables, coded 1 if a particular claim is present and 0 otherwise
Other	
File Size	Physical size of file in inches
Duration	Time between filing and closure of file in months

Some of the data concern cases that were either not yet concluded at the time I gathered the data or whose resolution is not known (transferred and removed cases). For these cases, statisticians describe the data as "censored." For them, I have data only on the cases through the date the data were collected. Dealing with censored data introduces some difficulty into assessing the data. For some variables, the fact that a case is not yet concluded can affect the results. If one simply examined the duration of all cases, for example, and compared the mean duration of post-*Meech* and pre-WDEA cases, the former would appear to be shorter simply because more of them would not yet have been concluded, while pre-WDEA cases could have longer durations since they were measured for a longer period.

There are two solutions to this problem. First, when doing simple difference in means tests, I examined the subsets of uncensored data in addition to testing all cases. This is a highly imperfect correction for the problem of censoring and these results still need to be treated with caution. Second, I used a statistical technique known as a "hazard model" to examine the duration of cases. Hazard models, originally developed to address similar problems in examining survival rates in medical studies, correct for censoring without disregarding the data from the censored observations or introducing selection bias problems by not examining those cases. (Since this is not a statistical text, I will not describe the statistical issues in detail.)

The data collected fall into five categories. First, the case file contained information on the parties (number, type). Second, the pleadings identified the claims made (including whether there was a counterclaim). Third, the case file revealed the extent of the activities in the case before the case was settled or decided (discovery disputes, merits motions). Fourth, the file told how the case ended (settled, pretrial merits determination, trial, arbitration). Finally, the pleadings listed the counsel.

Most of the variables are self-explanatory but a few require elaboration. The duration of the case was measured from the time of filing to the time the file was closed. When a case was removed to federal court, transferred to a county not studied, or simply not concluded by the time the data were gathered, the observation was censored. Others, such as whether the plaintiff held a managerial or professional job, were drawn from the complaint's (or other pleadings') description of the plaintiff's job. (Since some complaints did not describe the plaintiff's employment other than to note that he or she had been employed by the defendant, these variables are underinclusive of the actual number of managerial or professional jobs.) The plaintiff was coded as a manager for all employees describing their employment using the word "supervisor" or "manager" as well as for employees describing their job as an executive position (e.g., "vice president"). Plaintiffs were coded as professionals for all employees listing their employment as falling within a specialized profession (nursing, medicine, law, engineering).

In addition to describing the parties and claims, based on the complaint and other pleadings, I examined the file for evidence of how the case proceeded. I looked for documents indicating that depositions had been taken, that there had been discovery disputes, and that pretrial substantive motions had been filed. As these variables were based on the file, I cannot exclude the possibility that the lawyers in the case exchanged documents or had disputes without formally filing them. For example, a lawyer might have sent a letter with a draft motion to opposing counsel in a discovery dispute but then resolved the dispute without formally filing the motion. Similarly, although many cases included notices of depositions, the parties may sometimes agree to conduct discovery without filing the notice. Thus, these variables may also be underinclusive.

As well as recording the presence of documents that indicated a more complex case, I measured the physical size of the file in inches as a proxy for how complex the case was. Although there may be many things that influence the size of a file which are unrelated to the complexity of the case (e.g., how wordy the lawyers are), file size offers a reasonably objective measure of whether the parties have had to resort to the court on a regular basis to resolve disputes. File size is thus an imperfect measure but one that does have the advantage of being objectively measured.

The changes introduced by the WDEA into Montana employment law offer a natural experiment. By capping damages, introducing incentives for arbitration, preempting tort claims, and instituting a "good cause" requirement for discharges, the WDEA ought to affect many aspects of wrongful discharge lawsuits in Montana. We can examine these impacts through two methods: (1) comparing the characteristics of wrongful discharge cases filed in each of three periods (pre-WDEA, post-WDEA and pre-*Meech*), and post-*Meech* and (2) using a statistical technique known as "hazard models" to examine the duration of wrongful discharge cases before and after the statute.

One unambiguous provision of the WDEA was its bar on non-WDEA tort claims arising out of a discharge. Two effects ought to appear from this bar. First, in the post-WDEA, pre-*Meech* period, the number of claims in wrongful discharge complaints should rise slightly, as a careful attorney would plead a WDEA claim as an alternative claim to the common law tort claims.[75] The careful attorney would continue to include the tort claims, despite the WDEA preemption provisions, because of the substantial possibility that the WDEA would be ruled unconstitutional by the Montana Supreme Court. After *Meech*, however, the total number of claims per complaint should decrease as attorneys stopped including preempted claims. Tables 2 and 3 report the means and the results of a difference in means test for the three periods and for the pre-*Meech* and post-*Meech* periods generally.[76] As the tables show, the number of claims dropped significantly between the pre-*Meech* and post-*Meech* periods, from a mean of 3.93 claims to a mean of 2.99 claims, thus confirming the predicted impact of the statute. (There was no statistically significant difference between the pre-WDEA and post-WDEA, pre-*Meech* period, which can be attributed to the combination of the small nature of the change (adding one or two claims) and to the small numbers of observations available.) These results are reassuring, if not earthshattering. If Montana attorneys were paying attention to anything about the WDEA, the preemption provisions should have an impact. Thus although this result is akin to verifying that gravity holds, it is good to know that gravity does indeed apply.

Table 2: Total Claims, Means and Std. Dev.

	All Cases	
Phase	(N)	Mean (SD)
Pre–WDEA	57	3.91 (1.70)
Post–WDEA, Pre-*Meech*	61	3.95 (1.89)
Pre-*Meech*	118	3.93 (1.80)
Post-*Meech*	366	2.99 (2.07)

[75] The practice in Montana is to plead between one and three WDEA claims. One claim is the substantive breach of the WDEA through a discharge. The second and third claims concern punitive damages and allege the employer acted with "actual malice" or committed "fraud" in the discharge. *See* § 39–2–905(2).

[76] Note that censoring is not an issue for this test, as the number of claims is measured by the claims listed on the original complaint and is not dependent on any post-filing activity.

Table 3: Total Claims, t-Statistics for Difference in Means

Phase	Pre–WDEA	Post–WDEA, Pre-*Meech*	Post-*Meech*
Pre–WDEA	—	0.116 (.908)	3.68 (.000)
Post–WDEA, Pre-*Meech*	0.116 (.908)	—	3.61 (.001)
Pre-*Meech*	—	—	–4.76 (.000)
Post-*Meech*	3.68 (.000)	3.61 (.001)	—

The next question is whether cases filed in the different periods have different levels of pre-disposition activity. Here I examined four characteristics of the cases: the taking of depositions, the existence of discovery disputes, the filing of pre-trial merits motions, and the size of the file. Note that censoring is an issue for all of these measures, as cases which have not yet closed might still have a motion filed or a deposition taken in the future. There were no statistically significant differences between the various periods with respect to the taking of depositions, but there were significant increases in the number of discovery disputes and merits motions between the post-WDEA, pre-*Meech* period and both the preceding and following periods.[77] File size decreased significantly after the WDEA compared to all pre-*Meech* cases and the post-WDEA, pre-*Meech* cases.

Even taking into account the need for caution in relying on these results because of the censoring problem, these results tell an interesting story about the impact of the WDEA. The increase in merits motions in the interim period is likely due to defendants' routine filing of motions concerning claims precluded by the WDEA in this period. (This is consistent with what I observed about the substance of the motions while collecting the data.) The spike in discovery disputes during this same period is also likely related to defendants' objection to discovery on non-WDEA claims after the Act's passage. Finally, the spike in file size may simply reflect the increase in discovery disputes and merits motions during the interim period. Notably, none of these indicators are significantly smaller in the post-*Meech* period compared to the pre-WDEA period, suggesting that the WDEA has not permanently altered the need for depositions, the likelihood of discovery disputes, the likelihood of the parties seeking a ruling by the court on a legal issue, or the file size.

---

[77] Because this is a book chapter, rather than an economics paper, I've mostly restricted the presentation of statistical results to giving textual descriptions of the results. Full statistical results are given for selected tests, however, to give you a feel for how such material looks.

The WDEA also changed the rules governing wrongful discharge cases by making it easier for plaintiffs to win and reducing the potential recovery for plaintiffs who did win. (Winning became easier for plaintiffs because plaintiffs could prevail if they proved the employer lacked good cause for their discharge rather than having to prove bad faith.) These changes could influence the outcome of cases, altering who won and who lost directly through the standard of proof change as well as indirectly by altering the characteristics of cases through changing the incentives for filing suit. Although most WDEA cases, like most cases in general, end up settling rather than being resolved on the merits, 12.3% of the cases in the data resulted in a determination on the merits for either the employee or the employer.

There was a significant change in the rate of merits determinations after *Meech* compared to the period between the WDEA and *Meech* but no significant change between the pre-WDEA and post-WDEA, pre-*Meech* periods. Although the censoring problem is particularly severe here, these results do suggest that, once upheld, the WDEA reduced the uncertainty over the outcome of a case, making disagreements over the value of a claim less likely and so trials less necessary. (In results not reported here, I found a similar pattern for trials, plaintiff trial victories, and defendant trial victories.)

The change in merits outcomes is largely due to a change in pretrial merits outcomes, which dropped significantly after the WDEA was upheld in *Meech*. Again, the censoring problem is particularly important because more recent cases have had less time for a pretrial merits motion to occur, but the similar results among the subset of uncensored cases suggests that more than censoring is happening here. A decline in pretrial merits motions after *Meech* is consistent with the substitution of WDEA claims for the multitude of tort claims presented by the typical pre-*Meech* suit. WDEA claims turn on fact questions—was there good cause for the discharge or not—while in many cases, the tort claims common before *Meech* also presented legal issues about whether the claim was available in a particular instance. Pretrial merits determinations are generally appropriate for the legal questions but not for the factual ones.

The final question that we can address using the difference in means tests is whether the WDEA has affected the likelihood that a case will settle. Again, censoring is a major concern, since the more recent cases will have less time to settle. The results suggest there has been no significant change in the probability of a settlement. This leaves open the question of whether there has been a change in how quickly a case might settle, conditional on it being a case that settles.

A difference in means test for case duration, comparing duration among the three periods found that mean case duration rose insignificantly after the WDEA and then fell significantly after *Meech* for both all cases and all uncensored cases, exactly the pattern one would predict but also a result that could be entirely due to censoring. To correct for censoring, however, requires more sophisticated statistical techniques.

Hazard models measure the influence of variables on the time it takes for an event to occur. They are a natural technique for examining the influence of case characteristics on the duration of a case. Here I use the Cox proportional hazard model.[78] One disadvantage of hazard models over more familiar forms of regression analysis lies in interpreting the coefficients. The relative magnitude of hazard model coefficients lacks the natural interpretation that ordinary least squares regression coefficients have, for example.[79] Here I limit my interpretation to two aspects of the coefficients: their significance level and whether they indicate that a particular variable speeds or slows the event. A negative coefficient, which produces an exponential term of less than one, slows the hazard rate and thus the event. A positive coefficient, which produces an exponential term of greater than one, speeds the hazard rate and thus the event.

The law and economics literature on resolution of legal disputes suggests several hypotheses about the WDEA's impact on wrongful discharge litigation. First, the WDEA's preemption of tort claims, cap on compensatory damages, and restriction of the availability of punitive damages should have made settlement of wrongful discharge claims easier. Consider, for example, a pre-WDEA wrongful discharge case that included both a claim for tort damages under the implied-covenant theory and a claim for intentional infliction of emotional distress. The potential value of such a case could range from zero to hundreds of thousands of dollars, with considerable uncertainty over both how a jury would evaluate the claim and whether the Montana Supreme Court would uphold an award. A post-*Meech* claim, however, would involve a much more limited range of potential damages and the potential disagreements among the parties over the valuation of the case would be correspondingly easier to bridge. Jarsulic's 1992 survey of concluded cases suggests that the WDEA did indeed reduce awards.[80]

---

[78] *See* D.R. Cox & D. Oakes, *Analysis of Survival Data* (1984). For more on hazard models *see also* Nicholas M. Kiefer, *Economic Duration Data and Hazard Functions*, 26 J. Econ. Lit. 646 (1988) and Tony Lancaster, *The Econometric Analysis of Transition Data* (1990).

[79] *See, e.g.*, Paul D. Allison, *Event History Analysis: Regression for Longitudinal Data* 19 (1984) (interpreting results by examining only t-statistics.)

[80] Jarsulic, at 115–116.

This is not, however, the only effect of the WDEA. The WDEA also changed the requirements for the plaintiff to succeed by substituting the "good cause" standard for the need to prove a violation of the implied covenant. Discharged employees who did not have a claim under the implied covenant theory could well thus have a claim under the WDEA. The strength of the marginal plaintiff's claim should therefore be lower after the WDEA than before it. This effect could increase the difficulty of settlement if plaintiffs and defendants disagreed over the evaluation of the facts.

The 1992 survey suggests that there is a third impact as well. The survey found that Montana plaintiffs' attorneys did not believe that the reduced damages available under the WDEA provided them with sufficient incentive to accept wrongful discharge cases or potential plaintiffs with sufficient incentive to bring wrongful discharge cases.

There are thus three potentially offsetting impacts of the WDEA on case duration. First, the reduced range of possible outcomes should make settlement easier and quicker. Second, the reduced legal standard for plaintiffs should result in weaker claims being brought, potentially making settlement more difficult and lengthier. Third, the reduced damages available should reduce the incentive for claims to reach the court system, potentially resulting only in stronger claims that are easier to settle. Jarsulic found that cases tried under the WDEA reached a final outcome faster than cases tried under the pre-WDEA legal regime,[81] which suggests that for those cases the dominant effect was the narrowing of the grounds for dispute. The hazard model provides an ideal means by which to examine whether the WDEA increased or decreased time to resolution for all outcomes.

The model of case duration used posits that duration is a function of four sets of influences. First, duration is affected by the type of defendant, classified as Montana corporation, out-of-state corporation, government, individual and partnership. Relative to a Montana corporate defendant, I hypothesized that governments and out-of-state corporations would take longer to make decisions about cases and so cause a case to last longer. Again, relative to a Montana corporation, I hypothesized that a partnership or individual defendant would be able to make decisions faster and so speed resolution of a case.

Second, the filing of motions, existence of discovery disputes and taking of depositions are all hypothesized to increase duration because they take time to be completed. Third, I hypothesized that attorneys who are engaged in repeat dealings would be able to resolve cases more quickly. I thus hypothesized that attorneys from the same county would be more likely to be engaged in repeat dealings and that the involvement

---

[81] Jarsulic at 111–112.

of an out-of-state attorney would be more likely to slow resolution of the case. Finally, there might be fixed effects associated with the county in which a case was filed (fewer cases, faster judges).

I tested two sets of hazard models: one for any outcome of the case and one for settlement (treating all other outcomes as censored observations.)[82] I also tested three hazard models for each group. First, I estimated a model that imposed an assumption of a uniform hazard rate on all three periods. Second, I estimated a model that allowed the hazard rate to vary across the pre-*Meech* and post-*Meech* periods. Third, I estimated a model that allowed the hazard rate to vary across all three periods. This enables examining whether or not the WDEA and *Meech* changed the underlying hazard rate. Table 4 gives the results of the hazard model analysis.

Table 4: Hazard Model Results

Variable	Uniform Hazard Rate		Pre/Post *Meech* Hazard Rates		Pre–WDEA/Interim /Post-*Meech* Hazard Rates	
	Any Outcome	Settled	Any Outcome	Settled	Any Outcome	Settled
Defendants						
Government	−.185	−.114	−.173	−.092	−.176	−.123
	(.235)	(.282)	(.235)	(.282)	(.237)	(.285)
Out of State Corp.	.119	.235	.133	.255	.139	.260
	(.124)	(.145)	(.124)	(.143)	(.125)	(.147)
Partnership	.757**	.866**	.775**	.870**	.775**	.859**
	(.238)	(.267)	(.238)	(.268)	(.239)	(.269)
Individual	−.133	−.130	−.143	−.135	−.166	−.140
	(.117)	(.139)	(.118)	(.140)	(.120)	(.142)
Pretrial Practice						
Discovery Disputes	−.234	−.205	−.218	−.201	−.224	−.194
	(.138)	(.158)	(.139)	(.158)	(.141)	(.161)
Depositions	.177	.332*	.136	.310*	.136	.300*
	(.122)	(.143)	(.122)	(.143)	(.123)	(.144)
Merits Motions	−.267*	−.414**	−.305*	−.459**	−.305*	−.442**
	(.126)	(.148)	(.130)	(.153)	(.122)	(.184)
Location						
Gallatin	1.01**	.735**	.983**	.694**	.978**	.676**
	(.164)	(.180)	(.166)	(.181)	(.168)	(.184)

[82] The "any outcome" results ignore the possible differences in the means of ending cases but allow examining the full set of potential outcomes.

Variable	Uniform Hazard Rate		Pre/Post *Meech* Hazard Rates		Pre–WDEA/Interim /Post-*Meech* Hazard Rates	
	Any Outcome	Settled	Any Outcome	Settled	Any Outcome	Settled
Lake	.682*	.495	.666*	.461	.667*	.458
	(.282)	(.321)	(.282)	(.321)	(.283)	(.322)
Missoula	.560**	.060	.536**	.030	.541**	.029
	(.144)	(.166)	(.145)	(.167)	(.146)	(.168)
Attorneys						
Out of State	.379	.377	.390	.380	.383	.363
	(.430)	(.524)	(.431)	(.524)	(.431)	(.525)
Same County	.213	.373**	.240*	.374**	.228	.370**
	(.118)	(.139)	(.119)	(.140)	(.119)	(.140)
Loglikelihood	−1743.10	−1260.06	−1546.59	−1118.30	−1484.60	−1072.64
N	489	489	486	468	478	460

*significant at the 5% level; **significant at the 1% level

The results show that partnerships are significantly faster in concluding cases than are Montana corporations, while governments, out-of-state corporations, and individuals are not. The partnership results are as predicted, while the insignificant results for the other classes of defendants are not. One reason for the lack of significance may lie in the many cases in which both individuals and other defendants were present. Ex-employees, for example, frequently name both the company they worked for and their supervisor as defendants, particularly in suits with tort claims concerning the supervisor's behavior (which are not preempted by the WDEA).

The filing of merits motions significantly delays resolution of a case, including resolution of a settlement. The taking of depositions significantly speeds settlements, while not significantly affecting the outcome of cases generally. The merits motions results were as hypothesized and suggest that, at least in wrongful discharge cases, seeking clarification from the court on legal issues does not sufficiently increase the speed of the resolution of the case by enough to offset the delay caused by waiting for the court to rule on the motions. The significant influence of depositions on settlements, but not on other resolutions, suggest that depositions do assist in settlements, presumably by clarifying the factual issues for the parties.

The presence of out of state attorneys does not significantly affect the resolution of cases generally or settlements. Cases involving only attorneys from the same county, on the other hand, are significantly faster to settle than cases involving attorneys from more than one county. The significant results for speeding settlements but not all outcomes of the involvement of same county attorneys suggest that settlement is influenced by the repeat player effect. There were also county effects, with cases filed in Gallatin County being resolved faster, reflecting differences among the courts and judiciary in the various counties. In addition, statistical tests that compared different assumptions about the uniformity of the hazard rate in the different periods suggested that the process by which cases proceed in general and by which cases settle are different in the three periods, further confirmation of the WDEA's impact.

What can we say about the WDEA in practice? It appears that the statute accomplished what may have been its primary purpose in limiting wrongful discharge actions in Montana. Its damages provisions have thus likely been its most important features. The innovative arbitration features, for example, did not produce an immediate rush to arbitrate employment cases. One reason, according to several Montana attorneys with whom I spoke, is that arbitration is simply too foreign to the Montana bar's practice. In short, attorneys are unfamiliar with it and so do not use it. This conclusion is also supported by the impact of the WDEA on employment statistics. An analysis of Montana employment found that the passage of the WDEA boosted employment in the state, reversing the impact of the appearance of the common law tort cause of action. [83]

Another Act? A National Tour?

Montana imported the at-will rule from New York with the Field Civil Code in 1895. Might it export the WDEA to other states? In the immediate aftermath of the *Meech* decision, Montana press accounts of the decision and the California amici speculated on the possibility that other states might follow Montana's lead. In fact, the only statute to similarly address the issues covered by the WDEA took the opposite approach. In 1996, Arizona adopted the Employment Protection Act,[84] which reaffirmed that state's at-will rule. It seems unlikely that other states will follow Montana's lead any time soon.

One reason other states are not likely to mimic Montana is that the wrongful discharge "crisis" has abated to some extent. State supreme courts are no longer expanding wrongful discharge theories. If anything, many state courts have retrenched on both liability and damages. Moreover, state common law wrongful discharge claims are less impor-

---

[83] Ewing, et al., *Employment Effects,* at 26–27.

[84] Ariz. Legis. Ch. 140 (1996) codified at Ariz. Rev. Stat. § 23–1501 et seq.

tant for many employers than are federal and state statutory anti-discrimination claims.

It is conceivable that the Montana Supreme Court may one day reconsider the constitutionality of WDEA. After *Meech* the court examined a number of other statutes under the same constitutional provision challenged in the WDEA litigation. In every other case, the statutes were struck down. Since then, however, the Montana Supreme Court's membership has shifted, and the court has become somewhat less inclined toward judicial activism. Should its membership shift again, it is not difficult to imagine that a future court could revisit *Meech* and reach a different result.

The story of the WDEA is a complicated one, starting with a nineteenth century law reform effort and ending (for now) with a legislative victory in a long-running battle between the court and legislature.

Contributors

Cynthia Estlund recently became the Catherine A. Rein Professor of Law at New York University School of Law. She is a leading scholar of labor and employment law, and has written extensively on the relationship between the workplace and democracy. She graduated *summa cum laude* from Lawrence University, in Appleton, Wisconsin, in 1978, and then studied government programs for working parents in Sweden as a Thomas J. Watson Fellow. She earned her J.D. at the Yale Law School in 1983, and was a Notes Editor for the Yale Law Journal. After clerking for Judge Patricia M. Wald on the U.S. Court of Appeals for the D.C. Circuit, Estlund reported on the prosecution of human rights abuses in Argentina as a J. Roderick MacArthur Fellow. She practiced law for several years, primarily with the labor law firm of Bredhoff & Kaiser. Estlund joined the University of Texas School of Law faculty in 1989, and then the Columbia Law School faculty in 1999, where she was the Isidore and Seville Sulzbacher Professor of Law until her move to NYU in 2006. Publications include "The Ossification of American Labor Law," *Columbia Law Review* 2002; "Rebuilding the Law of the Workplace in an Era of Self–Regulation," *Columbia Law Review* 2005, and her book *Working Together: How Workplace Bonds Strengthen a Diverse Democracy* (2003).

Samuel Estreicher is Dwight D. Opperman Professor of Law at New York University School of Law, director of its Center for Labor and Employment and co-director of its Opperman Institute of Judicial Administration. He has published several books including casebooks in labor law and employment discrimination and employment law; edited conference volumes on sexual harassment, employment ADR processes, and cross-global human resources; and authored over 100 articles in professional and academic journals. He received his A.B. from Columbia College, his M.S. (Industrial Relations) from Cornell University and his J.D. from Columbia Law School, where he was editor-in-chief of the Columbia Law Review. After clerking for the late Harold Leventhal of the U.S. Court of Appeals for the D.C. Circuit, practicing for a year with a union-side law firm, and then clerking for the late Lewis F. Powell, Jr. of the U.S. Supreme Court, Estreicher joined the NYU faculty in 1978. He is the former Secretary of the Labor and Employment Law Section of the American Bar Association, a former chair of the Committee on Labor and Employment Law of the Association of the Bar for the City of New York, and chief reporter of the new Restatement of Employment Law, sponsored by the American Law Institute. He has delivered named lectureships at UCLA, Chicago–Kent, Case Western and Cleveland State law schools, testified twice before Secretary of Labor Reich's and Secretary of Commerce Brown's Commission on the Future of U.S. Worker–Management Relations, and has run over 100 workshops for federal and state judges, U.S. Department of Labor lawyers, NLRB lawyers, EEOC lawyers, court law clerks, employment mediators and practitioners generally. He is of counsel to Jones Day in their labor and employment and appellate practice groups.

Joseph R. Grodin is a Distinguished Professor Emeritus at University of California, Hastings College of the Law, and a former justice of the California Court of Appeal and the California Supreme Court. He received his B.A. from the University of California at Berkeley, his J.D. from Yale Law School, and a Ph.D. in labor law and labor relations from the London School of Economics. He was an associate, then a partner, in a union-side labor law firm in San Francisco for 17 years, then became a member of the faculty at Hastings where he taught labor law and related subjects for seven years, with time out for visits to Stanford Law School and a year's service as a member of California's first Agricultural Labor Relations Board. In 1979 he was appointed to the California Court of Appeal, where he was the author of the opinion that is the subject of his essay in this volume. In 1982 he was appointed to the California Supreme Court, where he served for five years, then returned to his academic career at Hastings, interspersed with service as a mediator and arbitrator. He is the author of numerous articles and several books on the subjects of labor law and state constitutional law. Now partially retired, he continues to teach, write, and serve as an ADR neutral.

Catherine L. Fisk is Professor of Law at Duke University School of Law, where she teaches and writes in the area of labor and employment law, civil procedure, and intellectual property. Professor Fisk is the co-author of *Labor Law Stories* 2005; other publications include "Credit Where It's Due: The Law and Norms of Attribution," 95 *Georgetown Law Journal* (forthcoming 2006); "Privacy, Power, and Humiliation in the Workplace: The Problem of Appearance Regulation," 66 *Louisiana Law Review* 2006, and "Removing 'the Fuel of Interest' from 'the Fire of Genius': Law and the Employee Inventor, 1830–1930," 65 *University of Chicago Law Review* 1998. She has recently completed a book manuscript, *Working Knowledge: Employee Innovation and the Rise of Corporate Intellectual Property, 1800–1930*, and is co-authoring *Labor Law in the Contemporary Workplace* (forthcoming, 2007). She has also taught at the law schools of the University of Southern California, Loyola Marymount University in Los Angeles, UCLA, and the University of Wisconsin. She received an A.B. from Princeton University, a J.D. from the University of California, Berkeley, and an LL.M. with a focus on labor law history from the University of Wisconsin.

Alan Hyde is Professor and Sidney Reitman Scholar at the Rutgers Law School, Newark. He received his A.B. from Stanford and his J.D. from Yale Law School. He is the author of *Working in Silicon Valley: Economic and Legal Analysis of a High–Velocity Labor Market* (2003), *Bodies of Law* (1997); the co-author of *Legal Rights and Interests in the Workplace: Cases and Materials on Labor and Employment Law* (forthcoming 2006) and *Cases and Materials on Labor Law* (2d ed., 1982). Hyde has been a visiting professor at Yale, Cornell, Columbia, New York University, Cardozo, and the University of Michigan law schools. His current research projects include the game-theoretic analysis of transnational labor standards; analyzing labor markets using the economics of information; design of a North American Free Labor Market; work relations in labor markets with extremely short tenures and rapid turnover, such as Silicon Valley, California; new bargaining structures and representational organizations for low-wage service workers; and new global labor markets characterized by extensive transnational outsourcing of production and labor migration. He is a director of the Association for Union Democracy, Inc., and has represented the organization in litigation. He has also represented the American Civil Liberties Union and its projects in litigation concerning worker privacy and constitutional aspects of worker action.

Pauline Kim is Professor of Law at Washington University School of Law in St. Louis. Prior to joining the faculty in 1994, she was a staff attorney at the Employment Law Center/Legal Aid Society of San Francisco, where she litigated cases involving race, sex and disability discrimination, racial and sexual harassment, and unlawful working conditions. She is a graduate of Harvard Law School and Harvard College and served as a clerk to the Honorable Cecil F. Poole on the United States Court of Appeals for the Ninth Circuit. Professor Kim is the co-author of *Work Law: Cases and Materials* (2005). Her research focuses on employment law topics, including employee privacy, employer misuse of genetic information, and at-will employment, as well as courts and judicial decision-making and she has published articles in journals such as the Columbia Law Review, the Cornell Law Review, the Northwestern University Law Review, and the University of Illinois Law Review.

Gillian Lester is a Professor of Law at U.C. Berkeley School of Law (Boalt Hall). She obtained her Bachelor of Science from the University of British Columbia, and LL.B. from the University of Toronto Faculty of Law. While at the University of Toronto, she was Editor-in-Chief of the University of Toronto Faculty of Law Review. Following graduation, she clerked in the Court of Appeal for Ontario, and later obtained her J.S.M.

and J.S.D. degrees from Stanford Law School. Between 1994 and 2006, she was on the faculty of the UCLA School of Law. In 2000, she was Sloan Visiting Professor at Georgetown Law School. Publications include "A Defense of Paid Family Leave," 28 *Harvard Journal of Law & Gender* 2005; "Unemployment Insurance and Wealth Redistribution," 49 *UCLA Law Review* 2001; "Restrictive Covenants, Employee Training, and the Limits of Transaction Cost Analysis," 76 *Indiana Law Journal* 2001; "Careers and Contingency," 51 *Stanford Law Journal* 1998; and the book *Jumping the Queue: An Inquiry into the Legal Treatment of Students with Learning Disabilities* (Harvard University Press, 1997) (with Mark Kelman). She is also is co-author of *Employment Law: Cases and Materials* (forthcoming 2007).

Andrew P. Morriss is H. Ross and Helen Workman Professor of Law and Professor of Business at the University of Illinois College of Law and a Research Fellow of the NYU Center for Labor and Employment Law. He received his A.B. from Princeton, his J.D. and M.Pub.Aff. from the University of Texas at Austin and his Ph.D. (in economics) from M.I.T. He has written extensively on both employment at will and Montana's legal history and is a co-author of *Cross-Border Human Resources, Labor and Employment Issues* (2004) *Property Stories* (2004), and *Regulation by Litigation* (forthcoming, 2007).

Stewart J. Schwab is the Allan R. Tessler Dean of the Cornell Law School. After earning an M.A. (in labor economics and industrial organization) a J.D. (*magna cum laude*) and a Ph.D. (in economics) from the University of Michigan, he clerked for the Hon. J. Dickson Phillips of the U.S. Court of Appeals for the Fourth Circuit and for U.S. Supreme Court Associate Justice Sandra Day O'Connor before joining the Cornell faculty in 1983. He is reporter for the American Law Institute's Restatement of Employment Law project. He is the co-author of *Foundations of Labor and Employment Law* (forthcoming, 2007) and *Employment Law: Cases and Materials* (2002). He has written about employment discrimination, workplace accommodations to people with disabilities, sexual harassment in the workplace, constitutional tort litigation and labor law reform and has contributed numerous chapters to books on employment law. Dean Schwab has published articles in scholarly law journals at Yale University, the University of Chicago, New York University, William and Mary College, University of Michigan, and Cornell, and he is currently co-editor of the *Journal of Empirical Legal Studies*. He was a distinguished visiting professor at the University of Nebraska Law School in spring 2003 and a Fulbright senior scholar at the Australian National University's Centre for Law and Economics in January 1998. He has been a visiting fellow at Oxford University's Centre for Socio–Legal Studies, the Chapman Tripp Visiting Lecturer at Victoria University Faculty of Law, New Zealand, an Olin visiting research professor of law and economics at the University of Virginia Law School and a visiting professor at law schools at Duke University and the University of Michigan. Dean Schwab has also consulted for the World Bank on reform of labor and employment laws in parts of the former Yugoslavia and Soviet Union.

J.H. (Rip) Verkerke is Professor of Law and Director of the Program for Employment and Labor Law Studies at the University of Virginia School of Law. He received a B.A. from Loyola College, an M.Phil. (in economics) from Yale and his J.D. from Yale Law School, where he was articles editor and articles administrator for The Yale Law Journal. He then clerked for Judge Ralph K. Winter Jr. of the U.S. Court of Appeals for the Second Circuit. Verkerke has held a number of fellowships, including the John M. Olin Fellowship in Law, Economics, and Public Policy, and was the recipient of a three-year grant from the University of Virginia's Academic Enhancement Program to establish the Program for Employment and Labor Law Studies at the Law School. He has visited at the University of Texas School of Law, has participated in an ABA project to draft a new labor code for the transitional government of Afghanistan, and is the author of numerous articles the field of labor and employment law.

†